Leon Kellner

Historical Outlines of English Syntax

Leon Kellner
Historical Outlines of English Syntax
ISBN/EAN: 9783337311643

Printed in Europe, USA, Canada, Australia, Japan

Cover: Foto ©Andreas Hilbeck / pixelio.de

More available books at **www.hansebooks.com**

HISTORICAL OUTLINES

OF

ENGLISH SYNTAX

BY

LEON KELLNER Ph.Dr.

LECTURER ON ENGLISH PHILOLOGY IN THE UNIVERSITY OF VIENNA
EDITOR OF CAXTON'S "BLANCHARDYN AND EGLANTINE"

London

MACMILLAN AND CO.

AND NEW YORK

1892

The Right of Translation and Reproduction is Reserved

RICHARD CLAY AND SONS, LIMITED,
LONDON AND BUNGAY.

TO THE

REV. RICHARD MORRIS, M.A., LL.D.,

AUTHOR OF "HISTORICAL OUTLINES OF ENGLISH ACCIDENCE,"
EDITOR OF HAMPOLE'S "PRICKE OF CONSCIENCE,"
"EARLY ENGLISH ALLITERATIVE POEMS"
"THE STORY OF GENESIS AND EXODUS"
"THE AYENBITE OF INWYT" ETC., ETC.
SOMETIME PRESIDENT OF THE PHILOLOGICAL SOCIETY

This Book is Dedicated

PREFACE

THE present volume is intended to accompany the *Historical Outlines of English Accidence* by Dr. Morris. But for this, I should have preferred to call it *Lessons in English Syntax*, implying thereby that I do not pretend to (or aim at) completeness of detail, but have rather contented myself with giving principles of English Syntax, and with picking out from among the infinity of syntactical facts, those that seemed most interesting and worthy of note. I selected first those idioms which struck me as out of the common in old and modern texts, and from these I chose such as seemed noteworthy from the standpoints of psychology, historical development, and comparative grammar.

I did not think it advisable to swell the book by giving detailed accounts of every preposition and conjunction; both these parts of speech are fully dealt with in the Dictionaries, and in the well-known works of Mätzner, Koch, Dr. Abbott, Einenkel, and Mr. T. L. Kington Oliphant.

Altogether I am at one with Chaucer's *Man of Law*:—

> " Me lust not of the caf ne of the stree
> Make so long a tale, as of the corn."

I must say a few words with regard to the **arrangement of the** *Syntax*. Many English scholars and students might prefer what is known as " Becker's system " (strictly observed in Mätzner's grand work). It would have been very easy for me to adopt this arrangement, and follow in Mätzner's track. But it was precisely Mätzner's example which warned me against adopting Becker's system in all its consequences. If Mätzner had been less systematic his work would have been more generally appreciated, and English syntax better known. I thought it, therefore, best to sacrifice system to usefulness, and to deal with the " Syntax of the Parts of Speech " fully and separately, starting with the sentence, the creator of syntax, and then working through its component parts. In the " Syntax of the Sentence " I have adopted Mr. Mason's arrangement (*English Grammar, including Grammatical Analysis*, by C. P. Mason, B.A., F.C.P. Thirty-second edition. London, 1890), which has, apart from its internal merits, the advantage of being well known to English students. This book being, in the first place, intended for students, I had to avoid as much as possible the discussion of doubtful points, reference to other languages, and superfluity of instances. In the large edition which I am preparing I shall give full accounts of other people's opinions, make constant use of what Comparative Grammar offers to explain English Syntax, and show clearly the development of every idiom, by giving instances from all the periods of English, at intervals of fifty years.

I gratefully acknowledge my obligations to several eminent English scholars for repeated advice and valuable suggestions. Of these, Dr. Furnivall has the greatest claim on my gratitude. It was he who suggested to me the idea of working into their present English shape the materials which he knew I had been collecting for years, and it is through his help and untiring kindness that I have been able to overcome the many difficulties which naturally stood in my way. The quotations in my book will show what it owes to the Early English Text Society, a Society which has at last made possible a real study of the history of English, a Society which has earned the right to ten times the support it gets from English-speaking folk.

L. KELLNER.

BRITISH MUSEUM,
August 1892.

CONTENTS

INTRODUCTION

	PAGE

The Object of Syntax—
Division of Syntax (§ 1) 3
Syntax closely connected with and dependent on Phonetics
and Accidence (§ 2) 3
Syntax and Accidence dealt with separately (§ 3) 4
The Three Parts of Syntax (§ 4) 4
Specimen of Old English Syntax (§ 5) 4
Its Want of Proportion in general (§ 6) 7
And in particular (§ 7) 8
Absence of Proportion and Unity characteristic of Early
English (§ 8) 9
Psychology (§ 9) 9
Popular Talk (§ 10) 10
And History must be consulted in the Study of Syntax (§ 11) 11
Instances: *"These kind of knaves"* (§ 12) 11
"*Who is to prevent me marrying?*" (§ 13) 12

Some Principles of Syntax—
Difficulty of bringing Syntax under strict Laws (§ 14) . . . 14

Analogy—
Syntactical Groups (§ 15) 14
Common Use (§ 16) 14
'Irregular' Combinations in consequence of Analogy (§ 17) . 15
Mixed Construction (§ 18) 16

Decay of formal Endings (§ 19) 17

Concrete Combinations supplanted by Abstract ones (§ 20)—
Instances:
Plural of Abstract Substantives (§ 21) 18
Absolute Participle (§ 22) 18
"Pardon my doing so and so" (§ 23) 18
Redundant Object (§ 24) 18

Anacoluthic Expression (§ 25) 19

Economy (Ellipsis) (§ 26)—
Origin of Ellipsis (§ 27) 20

	PAGE
Continued (§ 28)	21
Instances (§ 29)	21
Tautology, the Reverse of Ellipsis (§ 30)—	
Tautology the natural vehicle of Emphatic Speech (§ 31)	21
Tautology frequent in Older Periods (§ 32)	21
Double Genitive (§ 33)	22

PART I

SYNTAX OF THE SENTEN

Relation of Words—
    Three Syntactic Relations (§ 34) 27
Predicative Relation (§ 35) 27
Attributive Relation—
    The Adjective (§ 36) 28
    The Noun in Apposition (§ 37) 28
    Its wanting an Article in former Periods (§ 38) 28
    Its tending to supplant the Partitive Genitive (§ 39) . . . 28
    Want of Concord between a Noun and its Apposition (§ 40) . 29
    Continued (§ 41) 30
    Place of the Apposition (§ 42) 30
    A Substantive in the Possessive Case (§ 43) 30
    A Substantive preceded by a Preposition (§ 44) 30
    An Adverb used as an Adjective, following the Noun (§ 45) . 30
    Preceding the Noun (§ 46) 31
    An Adjective Clause (§ 47) 31
The Adverbial Relation—
    The Object (§ 48) 31
    The Adverb (§ 49) 31
    The Noun in the Oblique Case (§ 50) 31
    Genitive Case (§ 51) 32
    Dative (Instrumental) Case (§ 52) 32
    Adverbial Adjuncts in the Genitive and Dative Case (needs,
        whilom) (§ 53) 32
    The Cognate Accusative (§ 54) 33
    A Substantive preceded by a Preposition (§ 55) 33
    A Substantive or Pronoun with the Participle Absolute (§ 56) 33
    Origin of the Absolute Participle (§ 57) 34
    An Adverbial Clause (§ 58) 35
Subject and Predicate—
The Subject—
    The Subject in an Oblique Case (§ 59) 35
Simple, Compound and Complex Subject (§ 60)
Simple Subject—
    A Single Substantive (§ 61) 35

	PAGE
A Pronoun Subject omitted (§ 62)	36
A Substantive Subject omitted (§ 63)	36
Adjectives used Substantively (§ 64)	37
An Infinitive Mood or Gerund (§ 65)	37
Any Word made the Subject of Discourse (§ 66)	37

Compound Subject (§ 67)—
Complex Subject (§ 68)—

A Substantive Clause as Subject (§ 69)	38
A Substantive or Pronoun with the Infinitive as Subject (§ 70)	38
"*for*" + Substantive (Pronoun) + Infinitive as Subject (§ 71)	39

Reduplication of the Subject—

Repetition of the Subject making special stress (§ 72)	40
Reduplication of the Subject by means of a Personal Pronoun (§ 73)	40
Repetition of the Subject after an extensive member of the Sentence (§ 74)	41

Omission of the Subject—

Personal Pronoun omitted (§ 75)	41

The Predicate—
Simple Predicate (§ 76)—
Complex Predicate (§ 77)—

Complement of the Predicate (§ 78)	42
"*It is me*" (§ 79)	42
Discrepancy between Grammatical and Psychological Predicate (§ 80)	43
Ellipsis of the Copula "*to be*" (§ 81)	44
Omission of the Predicate (§ 82)	45
Omission of the Infinitive after "*shall*" and "*will*" (§ 83)	45

Concord (§ 84)—

Collective Nouns with Predicates in the Plural (§ 85)	46
Plural Nouns with a Singular in the Predicate.—The Verb precedes the Noun (§ 86)	47
The Subject is determined by Numerals (§ 87)	47
The distance between the Subject and Predicate accounts for the inaccuracy of the expression (§ 88)	48
The Endings -*es* and -*eth*, *is* and *was* used both in the Singular and Plural (§ 89)	48
Concord of the Predicate with several Subjects (§ 90)	49
Concord of the Copula.—The Copula agrees in Number with the Subject (§ 91)	49
The Copula agrees in Number with the Predicate (§ 92)	50

Object—

The Substantive Clause as Object (§ 94)	50
The Substantive with Infinitive as Object (§ 95)	51

Complex Sentences—

Awkward Structure of Sentences in Old English (§ 96)	51
The Complex Sentence in shape of two Co-ordinate Sentences (§ 97)	51

	PAGE
Coordination or Parataxis (§ 98)	52
Subordination or Hypotaxis (§ 99)	52
Instances (§ 100)	53
The Independent Sentence introduced by a Particle (§ 101)	54
Independent and Dependent Sentence introduced by the same Particle (§ 102)	55
Dependent Sentence alone introduced by the Particle (§ 103)	56

The Substantive Clause—
Its four Stages (§ 104)	56
Stage II. still kept (§ 105)	57
Explanation and Instances (§ 106)	57
Direct and Indirect Speech (§ 107)	59
Change of Direct and Indirect Speech (§ 108)	60

The Adjective Clause—
Omission of the Relative (§ 109)	61
Explanation (§ 110)	62
Instances (§ 111)	63
Development of the Adjective Clause (§ 112)	65
The Older Construction consistent with psychical facts (§ 113)	65
The Relative is in the Nominative Case (§ 114)	66
The Relative is an Oblique Case (§ 115)	66
The Correlative always appears in the Nominative Case (§ 116)	67
The Correlative is the Subject (§ 117)	68
The Correlative is the Object of the Sentence (§ 118)	68
The Relative Sentence precedes its Correlative (§ 119)	69
Noun Clause and Adjective Clause intermixed (§ 120)	69
"*That*" introducing the Noun Clause is dropped (§ 121)	70
Relative Subordination instead of Demonstrative Co-ordination (§ 122)	71

The Adverbial Clauses (§ 123)—
Adverbial Clause relating to Place (§ 124)	72
To Time (§ 125)	72
Adverbial Clauses used to denote Causal, Conditional, and Adversative Relations (§ 126)	72
Adverbial Clauses relating to Manner and Degree (§ 127)	73
Adverbial Clauses used in a Concessive Sense (§ 128)	74
Adverbial Clauses relating to Cause (§ 129)	74
To Purpose and Consequence (§ 130)	75
To Condition (§ 131)	75
Imperative Sentences used in a Conditional Sense (§ 132)	76
The Relative Sentence used for the Conditional one (§ 133)	76

PART II

SYNTAX OF THE PARTS OF SPEECH

	PAGE
The Substantive—	
Substantives used as Adjectives (§§ 134—136)	79
Classes of Nouns interchanged—	
Abstracts and Concretes interchanged (§ 137)	81
Abstract Nouns used in a Concrete Sense (§ 138)	82
Concrete Nouns used in an Abstract Sense (§ 139)	84
Collective Nouns used as Class Nouns (§ 140)	84
Proper Names used as Common Names (§ 141)	85
Singular and Plural of Substantives—	
Subjective Character of the Number (§ 142)	86
Number of Abstracts (§ 143)	87
Pluralis Majestaticus (§ 144)	89
Plural of Proper Names (§ 145)	89
Plural of Material Names (§ 146)	90
Number of Common Nouns (§ 147)	90
Cases—	
"*Of*" and "*To*" in Middle and Modern English, make up for the Lost Endings (§ 148)	91
The Nominative Case—	
Functions of the Nominative (§ 149)	92
Nominative after "*hátan*" (§ 150)	92
Nominative instead of the Oblique Case in Old Impersonal Verbs (§ 151)	93
Nominative instead of the Dative in Passive Constructions (§ 152)	93
The Nominative Absolute (§ 153)	94
"*With*" in connection with the Participle (§ 154)	95
The Nominative with the Infinitive (§ 155)	95
Nominative in Apposition (§ 156)	96
The Nominative supplanted by the Oblique Case (§ 157)	96
The Genitive Case—	
Signification of the Genitive (§ 158)	96
The Genitive denotes Birth and Relation (§ 159)	97
The Genitive denotes Rule or Power (§ 160)	98
The Genitive denotes Possession (§ 161)	98
Abstract Substantive instead of an Adjective (§ 162)	98
The Genitive Superlative (§ 163)	99
The Objective Genitive (§ 164)	100
The Objective Genitive replaced by "*over*," "*towards*," "*against*" (§ 165)	101
The Qualifying Genitive (§ 166)	102
Some Peculiarities of the Qualitative Genitive—	
"*Worms of every kind*" = all sorts of worms" (§ 167)	103

	PAGE
"*Alles cunnes wurmes*" = all sorts of worms (§ 168)	104
"*Alle kinne sinne*" = all sorts of sins (§ 169)	105
"*Three manners of freedom*" (§ 170)	107
"*Ten manere zennes*" = ten sorts of sins (§ 171)	107
"*These sort of things*" (§ 172)	108
The Partitive Genitive (§ 173)	108
Juxtaposition instead of the Partitive Genitive (§ 174)	109
"*Three the noblest rivers*" (§ 175)	110
"*One the best knyghts*" (§ 176)	111
The Elliptic Genitive (§ 177)	112

The Pseudo-Partitive Genitive—
Development of the idiom "*a friend of mine*" (§§ 178–180)	113
Genitive instead of Apposition (§ 181)	116
Genitive governed by Verbs and Adjectives (§ 182)	117
The Genitive denoting Origin, Cause and Reference (§ 183)	118

The Genitive used adverbially—
Denoting Space (§ 184)	119
Time (§ 185)	119
Manner (§ 186)	120

The Dative Case—
General Remark (§ 187)	121
The Dative after Verbs and Adjectives (§ 188)	121
After "*weorðan*" (§ 189)	121
"Dativus Commodi et Incommodi" (§ 190)	121
The Ethic Dative (§§ 191–192)	122
The Dative represents the Instrumental Case (§§ 193-194)	123
The Dative instead of the Genitive (§ 195)	124
The Dative Absolute (§ 196)	125

The Accusative Case—
Signification of the Accusative Case (§ 197)	126
The Accusative as the Object of Transitive Verbs (§ 198)	126
The Accusative governed by Intransitive Verbs (§ 199)	127
The Cognate Accusative (§ 200)	127
Double Object (§§ 201–202)	128

Accusative as Adverb denoting—
Place (§ 203)	128
Time (§ 204)	129
Manner (§ 205)	129
The Objective Absolute (§ 206)	129

Interchange of the Cases—

I. *Nominative instead of the Oblique Case—*
The Nominative after "*but*" and "*save*" (§ 207)	130
Nominative after "*hátan*" (§ 208)	131
Anacoluthic Nominative (§ 209)	131
Nominative with Verbs once Impersonal, and in Passive Constructions (§ 210)	133
The Absolute Pronoun in the Oblique Case (§ 211)	133
"*You*" supplanted "*Ye*" (§§ 212–213)	133

	PAGE
"*Me*" for "*I*" (§ 214)	135
"*All them*" = all they (§ 215)	135

The Article—
General Remark (§ 216)	136

The Definite Article (§ 217)—
Names of Persons with the Definite Article (§§ 218–219)	136
Nouns preceded by Possessive Pronouns with the Definite Article (§§ 220-222)	138
Nouns in the Vocative Case with the Definite Article (§ 223)	139
The Definite Article before Numerals (§ 224)	139

The Indefinite Article (§ 225)—
"*A*" before Numerals (§ 226)	140
The Indefinite Article used pleonastically (§ 227)	141
Omission of the Article (§§ 228–235)	142

The Adjective—
Adjectives used as Substantives (§ 236)	144
Substantives named after Quality (§ 237)	144
Ellipsis of the Noun (§§ 238—241)	145
Present Participles used as Substantives (§ 242)	148
Adjectives denoting Nations and Tribes (§ 143)	149
Adjectives referring to Things (§ 244)	149
Abstract Neuters in Old English (§ 245)	150
Abstract Neuters in Middle English (§ 246)	151
Adjectives for Colours and Languages (§ 247)	152
Abstract Neuters in Modern English (§ 248)	152
"*Voice*" of the Adjectives (§ 249)	154
Adjectives with Active and Passive Meaning (§ 250)	154
Adjectives with Transitive and Causative Meaning (§ 251)	155
Adjectives instead of Substantives in the Genitive Case (§ 252)	157
"*Half the day*," "*Double the sum*" (§ 253)	159

Comparison of the Adjective—
Double Comparison (§ 254)	159
The Comparative and Superlative used absolutely (§ 255)	160
Adjectives followed by "*One*" (§ 256)	161

The Numerals—
Cardinals—
Cardinals used Substantively (§ 257)	162
"*A*" Hundred, "*A*" Thousand (§ 258)	162
"*A' five men*" (§ 259)	162

"*One*."
"*One*" = Alone (§ 260)	163
The Personal Pronoun with "*One*" (§ 261)	163
"*One*" following Substantives and Adjectives (§ 262)	165
"*One*" = A Certain (§ 263)	165
Cardinals instead of Ordinals (§ 264)	165
Cardinals instead of Multiplicatives (§ 265)	166

Ordinals—
Fractional Numerals (§ 266)	166

b

	PAGE
Ordinals followed by "*Some*" (§ 267)	167

The Pronouns—
Personal Pronouns 167
Omission of the Pronoun (§ 268)
    The Imperative (§ 269) 167
    The Pronoun must be supplied from the Context (§ 270) . . 168
    The Pronoun omitted in the Second of Two Co-ordinate Sentences (§ 271) 168
    The Pronoun omitted in the Subordinate Sentence (§ 272) . 170
    The Pronoun supplied from the Oblique Case (§ 273) . . . 171
    "*I pray to God me graunt this bone*" (§ 274) 172
    The Object Pronoun omitted (§ 275) 173
    Use of "*We*" instead of "*I*" (§ 276) 173
    "*Thou*" and "*You*" (§ 277—278) 174
    Use of "*It*" (§ 279) 176
    "*It*" is used as predicate of any Gender or Person with the Verb "*to be*" (§ 280) 176
    "*It*" instead of "*There*" (§ 281) 178
    "*It is*" emphasizing Nouns and Sentences (§ 282) 178
    "*It*" used redundantly (§ 283) 179
Pleonastic Use of the Personal Pronoun (§ 284)
    The Pronoun precedes the Noun (§ 285) 180
    The Pronoun follows the Noun (§ 286) 181
The Personal Pronoun used redundantly in Complex Sentences (§§ 287—289).
The Emphatic Pronoun—
    The Personal Pronoun strengthened by "*Self*" (§ 290) . . 183
    "*Self*" used appositively (§ 291) 183
    "*Self*" in Connection with the Dative (§ 292) 183
    "*Self*" as a Subject (§§ 293—294) 184
    "*Himself*" as Subject (§ 295) 185
    "*Myself*" (§ 296) 186
    "*Self*" in Connection with a Pronoun as Object (§§ 297—298) 187
The Reflexive Pronoun (§§ 299—300) 188
The Possessive Pronoun—
    "*The fall of 'Him'*" (§ 301) 189
    Relative referring to a Possessive Pronoun (§ 302) . . . 189
    "*Both their hope*)" (§ 303) 190
    The Possessive Pronoun before Substantival Adjectives (§ 304) 190
    The Possessive Pronoun preceded by a Demonstrative one (§ 305) 191
    "*My Lord*" (§ 306) 191
    The Possessive Pronoun used indefinitely (§ 307) 191
    "*His*" instead of the Genitive Case (§ 308) 192
    "*I did it in my defending*" (§ 309) 193
    The Possessive Pronoun emphasized (§ 310) 193
    "*Of Mine*" (§ 311) 194

	PAGE
The Possessive Pronoun used Substantively (§ 312)	194
The Dative of the Personal Pronoun instead of the Possessive Pronoun (§ 313)	196

The Demonstrative Pronoun—
General Remark (§ 314)	196
"*An*" (one) used as a Demonstrative (§ 315)	196
"*Sum*" used in a Demonstrative Sense (§ 316)	196
"*These Seven Years*" (§ 317)	197
"*Ere this*" (§ 318)	197
"*This*" and "*That*" (§ 319)	197
"*That*" = "*The*" (§ 320)	198
"*That*" in Connection with the Genitive (§ 321)	198
"*Such*" as a Demonstrative Pronoun (§ 322)	199
"*The Same*" instead of the Personal Pronoun (§ 323)	200

The Interrogative Pronoun—
"*What*" used Substantively (§ 324)	200
"*What*" Referring to Persons (§ 325)	201
"*What*" used Adjectively (§ 326)	202
"*What*" as an Exclamation (§ 327)	202
"*Who is Who*" (§ 328)	203

The Relative Pronoun—
Origin (§ 329)	203
The Demonstrative Pronoun (§§ 330–332)	204
"*Swá*" (§ 333)	205
"*Swile*" = Such (§ 334)	206
Interrogative Pronouns used as Relatives (§§ 335–336)	207

The Verb—
Impersonal Verbs (§§ 337–338)	208
Intransitive, Transitive and Reflexive Verbs (§ 339)	209
Transitive and Intransitive Verbs Interchanged (§§ 340–344)	211
Transitive Verbs used in a Reflexive and Passive Sense (§§ 345–346)	216

Auxiliary Verbs—
Functions of the Auxiliary Verbs (§ 347)	218
"*Be*" (§ 348)	218
"*Have*" (§ 349)	219
"*Will*" (§ 350)	220
"*Let*" (§ 351)	220
"*Do*" (§§ 352–354)	221
"*Stand*" (§ 355)	222
"*Shall*" and "*Will*" used Elliptically (§ 356)	222
"*Shall*" and "*Will*" forming the Future Tense (§ 357)	222
"*Should*" with Infinitive instead of the Subjunctive Preterite (§ 358)	223
"*May*" (§ 359)	223

Voice—
Relation between Reflexive and Passive (§§ 360–362)	224
Passive of Verbs with a Double Object (§ 363)	225

CONTENTS

		PAGE
Passive of the Infinitive (§§ 364-365)		226

Tense—
- The Present Tense (§§ 366-367) 228
- The Historical Present (§ 368) 229
- "*I have got*" = *I have* (§ 369) 229
- The Preterite and the Perfect Tenses (§ 370) 230
- Sequence of the Tenses ("consecutio temporum") (§ 371) . . 230
- The Present instead of the Preterite Tense (§ 372) 230
- The Preterite instead of the Past Perfect Tense (§ 373) . . . 231
- Past instead of the Present Tense (§§ 374-375) 232

Mood—
- Development of Mood (§ 376) 234
- The Preterite instead of the Present (§§ 377-379) 234
- Clauses implying Unreality (§ 377) 234
- Noun Clauses dependent on Impersonal Verbs (§ 378) . . . 235
- Noun Clauses after Verbs expressing Wish (§ 379) 235

The Decay of the Subjunctive Mood (§§ 380—391)—
- The Subjunctive in Principal Sentences (§ 381) 236
- The Subjunctive in Dependent Clauses (§§ 382—391) . . . 237
- The Subjunctive in Noun Clauses (especially Indirect Assertion, Oratio Obliqua) (§ 382) 237
- The Subjunctive in Clauses expressing Wish or Command (§ 383) 238
- The Subjunctive in (Indefinite) Adjective Clauses (§ 384) . . 239
- The Subjunctive in Adverbial Clauses (§§ 385—391) 240
- Clauses of Place (§ 385) 240
- Clauses of Time especially in a Future and Indefinite Sense (§ 386) 241
- Clauses of Manner (with a Sense of Reality) (§ 387) 242
- Clauses of Manner (with a Sense of Unreality) (§ 388) . . . 243
- Clauses of Condition (supposed as unreal) (§ 389) 244
- Concessive Clauses (supposed as real) (§ 390) 245
- Final Clauses (§ 391) 246

The Infinitive—
- The Simple and Gerundial Infinitive (§§ 392—393) 247
- "*To*" after Auxiliaries (§ 394) 248
- For to (§ 395) 248

Functions of the Infinitive—
- General Remark (§ 396) 249
- Infinitive instead of the (modern) Gerund (§ 397) 249
- Infinitive used instead of a whole Clause (§ 398) 250
- The Absolute Infinitive (§§ 399—400) 250
- The Accusative with the Infinitive (§§ 401—405) 253
- The Nominative with the Infinitive (§ 406) 255

The Participles—
- Voice of the Participles (§§ 407—408) 256
- The Absolute Participle (§§ 409—412) 257

The Verbal Noun—
- Functions of the Verbal Noun (§ 413) 259

	PAGE
The Verbal Noun used Substantively (§ 414)	260
The Verbal disguised as a Predicate (§ 415)	260
The Verbal Noun preceded by Prepositions (§§ 416—417)	261
Verbal Noun interchanged with the Present Participle (§§ 418—419)	262
The Verbal Noun in Compounds (§ 420)	264

The Adverb—
Relation between Adjective and Adverb (§ 421)	265
Adverbs used in the form of Adjectives (§§ 422—423)	266
Adverbs used as Adjectives (§ 424)	266

The Prepositions—
Close Relations between Prepositions and Conjunctions (§ 425)	268
Development from Local to Temporal and Modal Meaning (§ 426)	269
The Prepositions make up for the Case-endings (§§ 427-432)	270
"*Of*" replacing the Genitive (§ 428)	270
"*To*" replacing the Objective Genitive (§ 429)	271
"*To*" replacing the Dative (§ 430)	271
"*With*" replacing the Instrumental Case (§§ 431—432)	272
Prepositions introducing the Agent(in Passive Constructions) (§§ 433—435)	273
"*For*" + Accusative and Infinitive (§ 436)	275
"*With*" in Connection with Participles (§ 437)	276
Prepositions omitted ? (§§ 438—442)	276
Dependent Prepositions (§ 443)	278

The Conjunctions—
Development from the Concrete to the Abstract (§ 444)	279
Relation between Preposition and Conjunction (§ 445)	279
"*And*" used redundantly (§ 446)	280
"*That*" used redundantly (§ 447)	281
"*That*" used as a Substitute for other Conjunctions (§ 448)	281

PART III

ORDER OF WORDS

General Remarks (§ 449)	285
Subject and Predicate (§ 450)	286
Inversion (§ 451-458)	286
Place of the Verb in Clauses (§ 459)	290
Position of the Object (§ 460-461)	291

Place of the Attributive Determinant—
Place of the Article (§ 462)	293
Place of the Numerals (§ 463)	293

	PAGE
Place of the Adjective (§ 464-465)	294
Adjectives separated from their Adverbial Determinants (§ 466)	295
Place of the Possessive Pronoun (§ 467)	296
Place of the Preposition (§ 468)	296
Apposition (§ 469)	298
Place of the Adverbial Determinants (§ 470)	299
Arrangement of Words in Contracted Sentences—	
General Remark (§ 471)	300
Two Adjectives and one Noun (§ 472)	300
Two Subjects and one Predicate (§ 473)	301
One Verb and two Objects (§ 474)	301
One Object governed by two Verbs (§ 475)	302
Chiastic Arrangement of Words (§ 476)	302

SUMMARY AND CONCLUSION.

PERIODS OF ENGLISH SYNTAX.

Internal Development of Syntax (§ 477)	303
External Influence (§ 478)	304
Latin Influence (§ 479)	306
French Influence (§ 480)	307
Periods of English Syntax (§ 481)	310
Old English (§ 482)	311
Middle English (§ 483)	312
Modern English (§ 484)	315

HISTORICAL OUTLINES
OF
ENGLISH SYNTAX

INTRODUCTION

INTRODUCTION

THE OBJECT OF SYNTAX

§ 1. SYNTAX is divided into three parts: 1, Syntax of the sentence. 2, Syntax of the parts of speech. 3, Order of words.

§ 2. Phonetics deal for the most part with the physical and physiological side of human speech; they show how sounds, the primitive elements of every language, are from time to time modified by various causes. Accidence and syntax have but little to do with physical facts—only so far as changes of sounds exercise influence on them. The proper department of accidence and syntax is to study psychical processes as they reveal themselves in the structure of human speech. A strictly scientific treatment of grammar would not deal with accidence and syntax separately, but would treat them as one subject as a whole. All grammatical forms are the outcome of syntactic relations, and every syntactical fact is most closely connected and interwoven with the elements of inflexion. Thus, for instance, every case-ending expresses a certain syntactic relation, every finite verbal form represents syntactic constructions.

On the other hand, every loss in the department of accidence, that is, every falling away of inflexion, is followed by some new syntactical formation, as for instance, the decay of mood-endings brought in the use of auxiliaries as their substitute.

§ 3. At present, however, there is no hope of this model of a scientific grammar being realised. As it is, we must be satisfied with two separate divisions of grammar (accidence and syntax). In accidence we deal simply with grammatical forms, while in syntax we treat of the functions and relations of those forms, and show how, when these forms decay, new syntactical relations replace them. This is by far the most important part of syntax.

§ 4. But the parts of speech and their grammatical functions are always dependent on the place which they occupy in the sentence. Thus a substantive is often turned into an adjective, and *vice versâ*, e.g. *exercitus victor* (Livy), the traitour servant = the treacherous servant (*Gesta Romanorum*, p. 316); "and when the devil was cast out, the *dumb* spake" (*Matthew*, ix. 33). It is, therefore, from the sentence and its growth that we must start in studying the history of English syntax, and the subject will be treated accordingly in the following divisions :

I.—SYNTAX OF THE SENTENCE.

II.—SYNTAX OF THE PARTS OF SPEECH.

III.—ORDER OF WORDS.

THE STUDY OF SYNTAX

§ 5. The historical study of English syntax is of so recent a date, and so little has been done in this department of grammar, that we must give several pages to what would be considered superfluous in any other branch of philology, namely, to the explanation of the *method* followed in this book.

For this purpose, and as we shall have frequent occasion to refer to old English as opposed to modern English, we start from King Alfred's introduction to his translation of Gregory's *Pastoral Care.*

Ælfred kyning hateð gretan Wærferð biscep his wordum luflice & freondlice ;
& ðe kyðan hate þæt me com suiðe oft on gemynd,
hwelce wutan gio wæron geond Angelcynn, ægðer ge godcundra hada ge woruldcundra ;
& hu gesæliglica tida þa wæron geond Angelcynn ;
& hu þa kyningas þe ðone anwald hæfdon ðæs folces Gode & his ærendwrecum hirsumedon ;
& hu hi ægðer ge hiora sibbe ge hiora sido ge hiora anwald innanbordes gehioldon, & eac ut hiora oeðel rymdon ;
& hu him ða speow ægðer ge mid wige ge mid wisdome ;
& eac ða godcundan hadas hu georne hie wæron ægðer ge ymb lare ge ymb leornunga, & ymb calle þa ðeowutdomas þe hie Gode don sceoldon ;
& hu mon utanbordes wisdom & lare hider on lond sohte, & hu we hi nu sceoldon ute begietan gif we hie habban sceoldon.

Swa clæne hio wæs oðfeallenu on Angelkynne ðætte swiðe feawe wæron behionan Humbre þe hiora ðenunga cuðen understandan on Englisc, oððe furðum an ærendgewrit of Lædene on Englisc areccan ;
& ic wene ðætte nauht monige begeondan Humbre næren.
Swa feawe hiora wæron ðætte ic furðum anne anlepne ne mæg geðencean besuðan Temese ða ða ic to rice feng.

King Alfred bids greet bishop Wærferth with his words lovingly and with friendship ;
4 and I let it be known to thee that it has very often come into my mind,
what wise men there formerly were throughout England, both of sacred
8 and secular orders ;
and how happy times there were then throughout England ;
and how the kings who had the power
12 over the nation obeyed God and his ministers ;
and how they preserved peace, morality, and order at home,
16 and at the same time enlarged their territory abroad ;
and how they prospered both with war and with wisdom ;
20 and also the sacred orders how zealous they were both in teaching and learning, and in all the services they owed to God ;
24
and how foreigners came to this land in search of wisdom and instruction,
and how we should now have to get
28 them from abroad if we were to have them.
So general was its decay in England that there were very few on this side of the Humber who could understand
32 their rituals in English, or even translate a letter from Latin into English ;
36 and I believe that there were not many beyond the Humber.
There were so few of them that I cannot remember even a single one south
40 of the Thames when I came to the throne.

Gode ælmiehtegum si ðonc ðætte we nu ænigne onstal habbað lareowa. Forðam ic ðe bebeode ðæt ðu doo swa ic gelife ðæt ðu wille, ðæt ðu ðe þissa woruldðinga to þæm geæmettige swa ðu oftost mæge, ðæt ðu ðone wisdom þe ðe God sealde ðær ðær ðu hine befæstan mæge, befæste. Geðenc hwelc witu us þa becomon for ðisse worulde, þa þa we hit nohwæðer ne selfe ne lufedon ne eac oðrum monnum ne lifdon: ðone naman anne we hæfdon ðætte we Cristene wæron, & swiðe feawe þa ðeawas. ða ic þa ðis eall gemunde ða gemunde ic eac hu ic geseah, ærþæmþe hit eall forheregod wære & forbærned, hu þa cirican geond eall Angelkynn stodon maðma and boca gefylda & eac micel menigu Godes ðeowa & þa swiðe lytle feorme ðara boca wiston, for þæmþe hie heora nan wuht ongietan ne meahton, for þæmþe hie næron on hiora ægen geðeode awritene. Swelce hie cwæden: "Ure ieldran, ða þe ðas stowa ær hioldon, hie lufedon wisdom & ðurh ðone hi begeaton welan & us læfdon. Her mon mæg giet gesion hiora swæð, ac we him ne cunnon æfterspyrigan, forðæm we habbað nu ægðer forlæten ge þone welan ge þone wisdom, forðamþe we noldon to ðæm spore mid ure mode onlutan." ða ic þa ðis eall gemunde, þa wundrode ic swiðe swiðe þara godena witena þe giu wæron geond Angelcynn & þa bec befullan ealla geleornod hæfdon, þæt hi hiora þa nanne dæl noldon on hiora ægen geðiode wendan. Ac ic þa sona eft me selfum and-

Thanks be to God Almighty that we have any supply of teachers among us now. And therefore I command thee to do as I believe thou art willing, to disengage thyself from worldly matters as often as thou canst, that thou mayest apply the wisdom which God has given thee wherever thou canst. Consider what punishments came upon us on account of this world, when we neither loved it ourselves nor suffered other men to love it: we had the name only of Christians, and very few of the virtues. When I considered all this, I remembered also how I saw, before it had been all ravaged and burnt, how the churches throughout the whole of England stood filled with treasures and books, and there was also a great multitude of God's servants, but they had very little benefit from the books, for they could not understand anything of them, because they were not written in their own language. As if they had said: "Our forefathers, who formerly held these places, loved wisdom, and through it they obtained wealth and bequeathed it to us. In this we can still see their tracks, but we cannot follow them, therefore we have lost both the wealth and the wisdom, because we would not incline our hearts after their example." When I considered all this, I wondered extremely that the good and wise men who were formerly all over England, and had perfectly learnt all the books, did not wish to translate them into their own language. But again I soon answered myself and

INTRODUCTION

wyrde & cwæð: "Hie ne wendon þætte æfre men sceoldon swa reccelease weorðan & sio lar swa oðfeallan; for ðære wilnunga hi hit forleton, & woldon ðæt her þy mara wisdom on londe wære ðy we ma geðioda cuðon."
ða gemunde ic hu sio æ wæs ærest on Ebreisc geðiode funden, & eft, þa þa hie Crecas geleornodon, þa wendon hi hie on hiora ægen geðiode ealle, & eac ealle oðre bec.

And eft Lædenware swa same, siððan hi hie geleornodon, hi hie wendon ealla ðurh wise wealhstodas on hiora agen geðeode.
& eac ealla oðra Cristena ðioda sumne dæl hiora on hiora agen geðiode wendon,
Forðy me ðyncð betre, gif iow swa ðyncð, þæt we eac suma bec, ða þe nidbeðyrfesta sien eallum monnum to witanne, þæt we þa on ðæt geðeode wenden þe we ealle gecnawan mægen...

said: "They did not think that men would ever be so careless, and that learning would so decay; through that desire they abstained from it, and they wished that the wisdom in this land might increase with our knowledge of languages."
Then I remembered how the law was first known in Hebrew, and again, when the Greeks had learnt it, they translated the whole of it into their own language, and all other books besides.
And again the Romans when they had learnt it, they translated the whole of it through learned interpreters into their own language.
And also all other Christian nations translated a part of them into their own language.
Therefore it seems better to me, if ye think so, for us also to translate some books which are most needful for all men to know into the language which we can all understand...

King Alfred's West-Saxon Version of Gregory's "Pastoral Care" (ed. Sweet). E. E. Text Soc. 1871, pp. 1—6.

The general impression which this piece of original Old English prose produces on the modern reader is that of clumsiness, or even slipshod English. But which are the elements that make this impression?

§ 6. First of all it is the structure of the sentences, a certain disproportion between the phrases and the ideas which they serve to convey. The first thought which struck Alfred, and which he wants to express, is the contrast between what had been before and what was in his time. Now, Alfred makes it rather difficult for his reader to find out that this is the idea he wants to convey, for after describing *England's welfare and learning of former times* in seven subsequent clauses dependent on one principal sentence (*me com on gemynd*), all of a sudden the drift of the sentence is changed, and the eighth and last clause (*and hu we hi nu sceoldon ute begietan*), though syntactically running shoulder to shoulder with the preceding clauses, is intended abruptly to introduce the reader to the *decay of the later periods*.

§ 7. Looking at the whole of the introduction we are struck by a similar absence of proportion. Alfred wants to explain how he came to translate the *Pastoral Care*. First he remembered the glorious past (lines 1-26), and was sorry for the decay of his own times (lines 27-41); secondly, he was astonished that the scholars of the former ages had not cared to translate the works of learning from foreign languages into the vernacular (lines 83-88), but accounted for it by the fact that learning had been so common in England at that time that the scholars did not think of the possibility of such an utter decay (lines 89-97); lastly, he remembered that the Holy Bible itself is but a translation (lines 98-109); and thus he feels encouraged and authorised to venture the attempt at turning into English this work of Gregory's (lines 110-114). But the flow of these simple ideas is checked by interruptions without any outward marks (*conjunctions*), to show whether the connection between the phrases be that of cause, consequence, contrast, &c. Again, how easily one construction, even within the same sentence, is given up for another! Look at the very first lines: Alfred begins by speaking of himself as of a third person (*Alfred greteð*, &c.); but even in line 3 the construction is changed: *ic*, &c. (lines 3, 4); cf. also line 98: the construction begins as a clause (*hu sio æ*, &c., lines 98, 99), dependent on *ða gemunde ic*, then the ruling verb is forgotten, and the sentence *ða wendon hi hie*, &c., stands by itself as if it were a principal one instead of a clause.

§ 8. What, then, is the characteristic feature of this specimen of Old English prose as opposed to modern style? *It is the absence of proportion and unity in the structure of the sentence.*

This may be observed in every work of the older periods, and it is not before the sixteenth century, when the admirable models of Greek and Latin were eagerly studied throughout England, that *proportion and unity* became the first requirements of good prose.

Instances of the following type are scarcely to be met with in literary prose after the time of Queen Elizabeth:

Se se, þe ealne ðone wísdom ðæra uferrena gásta oferstígð & ǽr worlde ricsode on hefonum, hit is awriten on ðǽm godspelle, Judéas cómon & woldon hine dón nídenga to kyninge. (He who surpasses all the wisdom of the higher spirits, and reigned in heaven before the world was, it is written in the Gospel, the Jews came and wished to make him king by force).—Gregory's *Pastoral Care*, p. 32.

Þa cuǽdon hie þæt *hie* hie þæs ne onmunden þon má þe *eowre* geféran þe mid þam cyninge ofslægene wǽrun. (*They* said moreover that *they* should mind that [offer] "no more than did *your* mates who were slain with the king."—*Chronicle*, a. 755.

§ 9. Hitherto we have dealt merely with the philological facts. But how are we to account for them in a psychological way? The syntax of older periods is natural, *naïf*, that is, it follows much more closely the drift of the ideas, of mental images; the diction, therefore, looks as if it were extemporised, as if written on the spur of the moment, while modern syntax, fettered by logic, is artificial, the result of literary tradition, and therefore far from being a true mirror of what is going on in the mind.

Alfred changes his construction in consequence of every change going on in his mind, while in a modern author the flow of the ideas is checked by the ready pattern of the syntactical constructior

The same psychological law of development from natural to artificial expression is seen in the constant procession from the concrete to the abstract, or, as Mr. Earle has it, 'from the more to the less material, palpable, or sensible; towards that which is remoter from the senses and more representative of mental operations.'[1]

Striking instances of this change are offered by the development of the articles *a* (*an*), and *the*, from what was originally a numeral and a demonstrative pronoun. For other instances see below, p. 18. In the study of syntax psychology must be consulted throughout.

§ 10. Another help which the students of syntax cannot do without is *popular talk*.

It is obvious to every close observer of vulgar and colloquial talk that there is the greatest resemblance between the syntax of the older periods and that of the "people" of our own days. In old English as well as in modern rustic talk the syntax is natural, while the literary language of modern times is an artificial, and, to a certain extent, a foreign plant. From this point of view, in the study of English syntax, the vulgar talk cannot be overlooked, nay,—but for the difficulty of getting trustworthy materials,—we ought, in discussing the evolution of syntax, to start from the rustic talk, just as a botanist in dealing with the evolution of the strawberry, will not take the artificial fruit, but the wild strawberry of the wood as the starting point of his study.

What, therefore, is the only course open before us?

§ 11. In studying the evolution of English syntax, our first object must be to find out what was the original form of syntactical combination, when sentences came fresh from the mind as images of psychical operations, and then to

---

[1] *English Prose, its Elements, History, and Usage.* London, 1890.

learn by what circumstances they became what they are now. In solving these difficulties we must call in the aid of *psychology, history*, and *popular talk*.

§ 12. A few instances will show how these three aids may be used in explaining syntactical facts.

> "*These kind of knaves* I know, which in this plainness
> Harbour more craft and more corrupter ends
> Than twenty silly ducking observants
> That stretch their duties nicely."
> *Lear*, ii. 2, 107.

How is the plural *these* in the passage quoted to be explained? It admits of no *logical* explication. One feels tempted to consider "kind" as a collective noun so that it would rightly be connected with an attributive in the plural. There are, however, no other instances of such an irregularity; it is only the verb predicate which is constructed κατὰ σύνεσιν (according to the sense), *e.g.* the family *were* assembled; but "these family" would be absolutely incorrect. In fact, the phrase as it stands by itself can hardly be explained. Now, if we turn to Old and Middle English Literature, we find quite a different expression. The phrase "all kinds of man" went through the following stages:

1. *Alles cynnes men* (omnis generis homines), (Old and Middle English). But the genitive-endings of adjectives became disused—*es* in *alles* was dropped, or it was no longer understood. Hence we have:

2. *Alle kynnes men*, or *alle skynnes men*. Chaucer, *House of Fame*, 440. Then the English *cyn* was replaced by the Romance *maner*, and then the expression became:

3. *All maner men*, and lastly,

4. All maner *of* men.

So far history helps us. But how are we to account for the unexpected appearance of the preposition *of*? Here history fails us, and psychology comes to our assistance. The new expression is the result of a new psychical process. In Old English as well as in Old Norse, the conception with regard to this expression was quite different from what it is now. Whenever people were thinking about a certain class of things, it was the things which were prominent in their minds, while the class to which the things belonged came after as an accessory quality, as an attribute. If, therefore, they wanted to say "all sorts of worms," they put it in a different and more concrete way than we do; they said "worms of every kind," *alles cunnes wormes.*

The more abstract expression, however, came in as early as the thirteenth century, so that both conceptions were in use at the same time; but, later on, the modern one prevailed, but still without wholly supplanting the older use.

The concrete conception never wholly disappeared, and we are not at all astonished that it should re-occur in Shakspere, though in a somewhat modern and altered garb. It is only the plural of *these* which shows that Shakspere's conception was just as concrete as that of the Old English *alles cynnes men,* or the Latin *omnis generis homines.*

§ 13. We will take another example—

"I should like to know who is to prevent *me* marrying Lady Anne Newcome's daughter?"—THACKERAY, *The Newcomes,* ii. 249.

Orthodox grammarians, no doubt, will condemn this expression as vulgar, but there is the authority of Thackeray and other writers to recommend it, and the tyrant "Usage" seems to favour it more and more now.

Who is right, the grammarian who calls it vulgar, or the tyrant Usage?

If ancestors make nobility, the expression is certainly not vulgar, for there are several unmistakable instances of it in Caxton. But how do we account for the change of idiom from *me* to *my*? It is psychology again which supplies us with the explanation. In the older periods of English, writers and speakers looked upon the person or thing acting as a real subject of perception, feeling, or thought, and not upon the abstract action or state. We find in the *Old English Miscellanies* as well as in Wyclif, "against the rising sun" = at sunrise; "after the sunne goyng down" = after sunset, just as we have in Latin *Augusto regnante* = during Augustus' reign. This conception, in fact, kept on for a long time, and has not quite disappeared. Hence the following expressions:

"They set him free, without his ransom paid."
1 *Henry VI.* iii. 3, 72.

"Nor delay'd the wingèd Saint
After his charge received."
MILTON, *Paradise Lost*, v. 248.

But while this usage was the rule in the older periods, and is still a favourite among common people and poets, in literary language it soon began to decay, and the verbal noun took the place of the old present participle. Thus Purvey alters the instance quoted above, to "aftir the going down of the sunne." *Cf.* Exod. xxii. 26, Deuteronomy xi. 30.

From this point of view we can satisfactorily explain the syntactical doublets of *me* and *my* in connection with verbal forms in *-ing*. The former is certainly the older expression and more natural, the latter is abstract and, in fact, more consistent with logic.

Some Principles of Syntax.

§ 14. We have seen that psychical or mental processes are the chief causes of growth and change of all syntax. There are then the same difficulties in regard to syntax as to psychology, but great light has been thrown upon syntax by the admirable results of modern psychology.

Innumerable and recondite are the causes which are at work in creating and destroying syntactical formations, and it will scarcely ever be possible to bring syntax under strict laws. But from the many facts, which are furnished by historical and comparative grammar, we are able to deduce at least a few leading principles.

§ 15. *Analogy.* It is one of the fundamental laws of psychology that every word, as well as every ending, and every combination of words, is connected in our minds with other words. All the store of our linguistic acquirements is thus divided into groups. Hence, every word we learn associates itself with some group according to certain psychological laws of similarity, contrast, &c.

Thus the verbs *bind, find, wind,* are associated in our mind as one group, the link being the same gradation of vowels in the conjugation (*ablaut*); the words *young* and *old, poor* and *rich, good* and *bad* call up one another in the memory on account of the contrast existing between them. Now, there are not only groups of words, but also groups of combinations, syntactical groups.

Thus every transitive verb is associated with the idea of an object, e.g. *to write a letter,* so all transitive verbs form the group "verb + object." A genitive usually requires another substantive; every subject is followed by a predicate, &c. These are syntactical groups.

§ 16. The growth and decline of all syntax is influenced more or less by means of these groups. Every syntactic combination must belong to one or other of them, just as every word must associate itself with a formal and significant group.

Now there are certain groups fixed by ancient usage, as:

1. Subject + predicate.
2. Singular subject + singular predicate.
3. Plural subject + plural predicate.
4. Adjective + substantive.
5. Adverb + verb.
6. Transitive verb + object, &c.,

and if a new combination is in accordance with any one of them, we say that it agrees with the *common use*.

§ 17. But a combination may differ from one of the traditional syntactical groups, as for instance in the phrase 'I am friend*s* with him,' a strange deviation from the group "singular subject + singular predicate." How do we account for this irregularity?

In this case, as in many others, the irregular combination proved stronger than the regular and grammatical group, and the new and free combination took the place of the common phrase, "*I and he are friend*s," without which the ungrammatical expression "I am friend*s* with him" would not have arisen.

English syntax exhibits a great many instances of such deviations from the ordinary grammatical groups.

A *two-penny* loaf, a *two-foot* rule, a *three-shilling* novel, are gross sins against one of the first rules of concord, but the analogy of the unit, viz. "a penny-loaf, a shilling-novel," and the analogy of such expressions as "two foot six," "five fathom," "a thousand pound," proved of greater force than the general rule.

The phrase "*in his heart of hearts*" is from a logical point of view nonsensical, but it is the analogy of the superlative genitive which accounts for the expression. We say "the song of songs," "the heaven of heavens," "the king of kings," meaning to express by it the highest quality; hence "in his heart of hearts" = in his very heart.

There is only one opinion among grammarians with regard to *hisself* ("He may make hisself easy." Dickens, *Pickwick* ii. 55). They all condemn it as utterly vulgar. Here again the common talk is, psychologically, quite accurate. Analogy is no doubt in favour of *hisself* and *theirselves*. In fact several attempts were made in Middle English to follow the analogy of *my*self throughout, and Roger Ascham uses *theirselfe*. But the modern *themselves*, which is of later origin (sixteenth century), and is neither logically nor psychologically right, prevails. For a full account of this, see § 290-298.

§ 18. Another effect of *analogy* is mixed construction, that is, an expression vacillating between the analogies of two groups, and showing the influence of both. The following passages exhibit an instructive instance of such construction.

"But of all Fraunce I am one of the best and truest *knyght* that be in it."—CAXTON, *Aymon*, 272/23.

This odd expression is the result of two constructions:

> One the best knyght;
> One of the best knyghtes.

Result: One of the best knyght.

Thus we find also in the *Romance of Melusine* (about 1500): "*how* they had to name" (p. 120), made up of the two constructions:

> *How* they were called;
> *What* they had to name.

As a more modern instance we may take the phrase: "A child of three years old" (a child of three years + a child three years old).

The expression "*these* kind of knaves" (Lear), which was explained above, § 12, is in a manner also the result of two different combinations.

§ 19. A second factor, of great weight, is the *decay of formal endings;* apart from the well-known fact that the great importance of prepositions and auxiliaries in Modern English is due to the decay of case and verbal endings. The above-quoted text of King Alfred's exhibits several instances of this sort. "*His wordum,*" for instance, is an instrumental case; in Modern English we must say *with* his words. "*Freondlice*" is an adverb by virtue of the final -*e*, but this having disappeared in Modern English, we must render it by saying "in a friendly way," or (as Dr. Sweet does) "with friendship." In addition to this there are many other instances that illustrate the close relation between changes in the department of accidence and syntactical expression. A striking instance of this kind is the passive of intransitive verbs. An expression like "I was answered" would have been impossible in Old English, and it is unknown in Modern German. In English it was brought about by the decay of the case-ending. The -*e* of the dative being dropped, the dative was no longer distinguished from the accusative; and the object governed by verbs like *answer, command* was consequently looked upon as an accusative case, and treated as such, so that it became capable of the passive construction. Another outcome of the same decay was the decrease of impersonal verbs. We are so used to expressions like "as I please," that their grammatical irregularity escapes notice altogether. We are surprised at such a phrase as "I am woe," = woe is me (Chaucer, Shakspere), which arises out of the same construction as the expression "as I please" = it pleases me. Both originated with the decay of the dative-ending. In such instances as "Wo was this king" (Chaucer), an indirect object was mistaken for the nominative case. See Nominative, § 151.

C

§ 20. *Concrete combinations supplanted by abstract ones.*—The constant transition from the concrete to the abstract, accounts for many changes in the department of syntax.

§ 21. The plural of abstract substantives, even when no more than one person was referred to, which was very frequent in older periods, becomes rare in modern English. We cannot say might*s*, strength*s*, which were quite common in Old- and Middle-English. This change of usage is accounted for by the fact that abstract nouns were not quite the same thing in the older periods as they are now. In the Gothic instance "*mahtins* mikilos gatavidedum" (we did powerful things, Matth. vii. 22), *mahts* is not exactly *power*, but *something powerful*.

§ 22. The so-called absolute participle was by no means felt as such in Old Teutonic times, nor was it apprehended as an isolated expression by the early Romans; for then the concrete active subject was present in the mind of the speaker, not action itself as an abstract. Hence Latin *post urbem conditam* instead of *post urbis conditionem*, hence in Old English *him lifigendum* (he living) instead of "in his lifetime." *Cf.* below, § 409–412.

§ 23. The change of the older expression "pardon *me* doing so and so," into the modern "pardon *my* doing," is explained by the same principle. The use of the adjective instead of the adverb in such phrases as "slow and sure comes up the golden year" (Tennyson) is in all probability due to the same conception, language preferring to qualify the concrete substantive rather than the abstract verb. *Cf.* § 423.

§ 24. What was formerly called *prolepsis*, or redundant object, is simply an interesting remnant of the old concrete way of forming noun-clauses. We now say "he saw that the work was good," the noun-clause being apprehended as abstract; but the biblical expression "he saw the work that it was good," is psychologically the only correct one. *Cf.* § 94.

§ 25. *Anacoluthic expression*, i.e. a sentence begun in one way and finished in another not syntactically accordant (§ 9) is frequently met with in the older periods of English.—We have seen above (§ 9) that language cannot follow the swiftness of thought, or (to use Herbert Spencer's metaphor) that there are frictions which the vehicle of thought, that is, human speech, has to overcome. And out of these frictions come all anacoluthic or incoherent expressions. In good prose we avoid anacolutha by consciously stopping the swift flow of thought, but in a state of excitement, when reflection gives way to unconsciousness, or when we are overwhelmed by new ideas, we lose the control over our minds, and then we speak in an incoherent anacoluthic way, one thought following another before any of them is quite completed. In fact, the history of syntax shows that the anacoluthon is peculiar to the older periods of the language, to common unreflecting talk, and—last but not least—to poetry. The following instances will illustrate this use. The author of the *Ancren Riwle* (A.D. 1200–1220), telling her readers of the martyrdom of Christ, says:

"Auh þerof nimeð ȝeme, mine leoue sustren, þet ower deorewurðe spus, þe luuewurðe lauerd & helinde of heouene, Jesu, Godes sune, þe weldinde of the worlde, þeo he was þus ileten blod, understondeð hwuc was his diete þet dei." (But take heed of this, my dear sisters, that your dear spouse, the loveworthy lord and saviour of heaven, Jesus, the son of God, the ruler of the world, though he was thus let blood—understand what was his diet that day.) p. 112.

The *Gesta Romanorum* (A.D. 1440) has the following passage:—

"So aftirward whenne the knyght was on his bed, and grete labour þat he hadde on the day afore made him to slepe hard, and alle þe tyme þe tode had folowed him after. And whenne the knyght was aslepe, þe toode enteryd into his bed " (p. 5).

The older construction of the adjective clause is an instructive instance of anacoluthon in older periods. See § 112–119.

§ 26. *Economy* (*Ellipsis*).—Ellipsis is a kind of compensation for the slowness of speech, a kind of economy in the use of linguistic elements. The term ellipsis, which has played such an important part in old descriptive grammars, has led to so many absurdities and abuses, that a very strong feeling against it prevails among scholars who follow the modern historical study of speech, or have been trained in the modern science of language. They are inclined to deny elliptic expressions altogether. But in this they are certainly wrong. Not only psychology and daily speech, but also historical syntax proves the existence of ellipsis. When one is asking for a railway ticket at the booking-office and says " Brixton, second, single " —who would hesitate to call this an omission of several words, that is, an ellipsis? Of course the omission is not always so evident as in the example we have quoted, and there may be sometimes other psychological influences at work in elliptical expressions where we are tempted to use economy of speech, as for instance in the omission of the copula ("*omnia præclara rara*," " first come first served "); but the example cited above clearly proves the existence of ellipsis in the department of syntax, just as in the formation of words.

§ 27. Psychologically, ellipsis arises in two different ways; first, as the spoken words are too slow to follow thought, we often omit a word or phrase, when it can be done without injury to the meaning of what we want to say, and sometimes even when the word or phrase cannot well be spared, when we are too preoccupied by our ideas to have regard for the hearer. It is just the same as omitting or abbreviating words in writing, a fact which everybody will admit.

§ 28. Secondly, it often arises from anxiety to secure the hearer's or reader's attention. We know by experience that brevity is not only the soul of wit, but also one of the principal means of drawing attention to what we say or write, and we endeavour therefore to make the recipient follow us with the least possible expenditure of words.

§ 29. The syntax of English speech offers many examples of *ellipsis.* A few instances will suffice.

The so-called elliptic genitive, "he is at a friend's," (sc. house) is of a comparatively recent date. But there are parallel expressions in Latin and Old Norse. Cf. *ad Martis* (sc. *templum*), *ex Apollodori* (sc. *libro*). *At Heimis* (in the house of Heimir), *at Aegis*, &c. (Edda).

It is also ellipsis which causes adjectives to become substantives, *cf.* the rich and poor, the Almighty, &c.

Verbs which were usually transitive, may become intransitive through ellipsis. Thus *drive* may become intransitive by omitting the object horse, as, "he drives slowly." Cf. *appello* (sc. *navem*) = to land.

§ 30. *Tautology.*—Tautology, though the reverse of economy, is a principle of no less importance in the historical treatment of syntax. Of course, the same individual will never indulge in economy and tautology at one and the same time, but there are some occasions for omission, and there are others for tautology.

§ 31. The first condition of ellipsis is, as we have seen, a certain degree of mutual understanding between the speaker and hearer. Tautology, on the contrary, usually occurs when the speaker is not quite sure of his hearer's capacity or willingness to apprehend what he says; then he emphasizes his words by repeating them again and again. *Tautology is the natural vehicle of emphatic speech.*

§ 32. Old English poetry is full of tautology. Cf. "cyning wæs áfyrhted, egsan geaclad" (the king was afraid, terrified with fear). *Elene*, 56, 57. Tautology of this kind is, of course, familiar to all. But apart from this tautology which is naturally found in every language and at every period, English speech is very rich in tautological expressions which have a different origin. The fact of two languages existing along with each other in the same country at the same time—namely, of French and English, made tautology in Middle English a necessity. Often, when the author of the *Ayenbite of Inwyt* (A.D. 1340) used a French expression, and was not quite sure whether his readers would understand his meaning, he took care either to add an English word to the French, or to paraphrase the French word by several English terms when he could not find one that exactly conveyed the meaning of the French. The same method was followed by all the translators of Middle English, from Trevisa down to Caxton and Malory. During this period, authors as well as the reading public got so accustomed to periphrastic expressions, that *tautology* became a fashion. What had been a sheer necessity at first, now became an ornament of speech. This is best seen by the fact that Pecock in his *Repressor*, an original work, and Caxton in his own *Prologues* and *Epilogues*, indulge as much in unnecessary tautology as the translators who preceded them. *Cf.* Caxton's "as nyghe as I *can* or *may*," Blades, 139; "ended and fynished," *ibid.* 131; "new and late mad," 139; "*faithful trewe* servant," 133; "to *bylde* and *edifye* their *habitation* and *dwelling*," 184.

§ 33. This fashion exercised its influence upon the syntax as well as upon the vocabulary of English speech. The double comparative, for instance, is due to tautology. It occurs very early, and was in use after the Elizabethan period. *Cf.* § 254. The double use of the preposition, before and after the substantive, is due to the same principle. *Cf.* "*in* what array that I was *inne*" (Chaucer). In this instance we are inclined to see a preposition in the first (in), and an adverb in the second (inne); but many instances with *of* prove that it is simply a tautology. Seeing how common this usage is, we are not surprised to find *a double Genitive*, of which we have unmistakable proofs. We find in the *Story of Genesis and Exodus* the following passage : " If his breðere *of liues* ben," 2834. At a later period we find : " And the remnant for to kepe to the use *of* the *husbond*ES of the seyde Isabell," *Early English Wills*, p. 103. "The Church *of* St. ClementIS," *ibid.* 16.

PART I

SYNTAX OF THE SENTENCE

SYNTAX OF THE SENTENCE

I.

Relation of Words.

§ 34. All the relations that subsist between the words and groups of words of which a sentence is built up, namely :—

  I. Predicative Relation,

  II. Attributive Relation,

  III. Adverbial Relation,

have been in existence from the earliest period of English, *cf.*, *e.g.*, the first sentence of Alfred's introduction (p. 5, above), in which all the three relations occur.

But while, logically speaking, these relations have remained unaltered to the present day, the means of expressing them have from merely grammatical causes undergone many changes.

§ 35. I. *The Predicative Relation.*—This being to a great extent dependent on the subject will be dealt with further on, § 76–90.

II. *The Attributive Relation*, may be of the following kinds:

§ 36. 1. The adjective (including the articles, pronouns, numerals and participles) used attributively occurs in the early periods of English; substantives used attributively in an adjectival sense are of recent date. . . . . . "leaving out both the *quack* theory and the *allegory* one." Carlyle's *Heroes and Hero-worship*, 189, *cf.*, below, § 134-136.

§ 37. 2. The noun in apposition, as, "Ælfred *cyning* háteð grétan" (King Alfred bids greet), above, p. 5. The development of the apposition offers several noteworthy points.

§ 38. *a*. The absence of the article was much more frequent than now.

Old English.—"Ælfred cyning" (in the quoted instance); the same in *Chronicle* a. 871.—"ða sende se cyning æfter Anláfe cyninge Aelfeah biscop" (there the King sent bishop A. after King Anlaf). *Chronicle*, 994.

Middle English.—"Daviþþ Kingess burrh." Orm. 7262. "Of Cadwane Kinge." Layamon, iii. 203.

§ 39. *b*. From several facts we may conclude that *the apposition* in Middle English, tended towards supplanting to a great extent the partitive genitive (as was the case in German), but was stopped in this tendency by the influences of French and later on of Latin and Greek. Thus we find in Chaucer "a bushel venym" (*Troylus*, iii. 976); "no morsel bred" (*The Monkes Tale*, 444); "the beste galoun wyn" (*The Maunciples Tale*, Prologue, 24).

Trevisa has "Oute of þilke hilles springeþ þre þe noblest ryueres of al Europe." Trevisa, Higden's *Polychronicon*, i. 199.

Caxton: "Other her gentyllwomen." *Blanchardyn*, 76, 31.

In modern English apposition has yielded much of its domain to the genitive, as in Old English; but still it has held its ground in many cases when Old English required the genitive: "*máðma* fela" (many treasures). *Beowulf*, 36. *Cf.* below, § 173-176.

§ 40. *c.* In the following instances there is a striking want of concord between a noun and its apposition.

"In *his* capacity *as a justice.*"—FIELDING, *J. Andrews*, ii. 3.

According to the strict grammatical rule we should expect "as a justice's." But the want of concord which appears in this instance does not stand alone. In *Latin* we find such constructions as: "Sempronius causa ipse pro se dicta damnatur"; "flumen Albim transcendit, longius penetrata Germania quam quisquam priorum" (Tacitus). This want of concord is universal in similar cases:—

"The assemblies of the senate displayed the abilities of Julian as an orator, and *his* maxims as a republican."—GIBBON, *Decline and Fall*, xv.

"Owen, whose probity and skill...rendered *his* services invaluable *as a handclerk.*—SCOTT, *Rob Roy*, 1.

A still more striking inaccuracy is that exhibited in the following instances:

"His top was dockud lik a *preest* biforn."
CHAUCER, *Canterbury Tales, Prologue*, 590.

"Hys necke he made lyke no *man.*"
Guy of Warwick, 1, 8054.

Cf. Gower, *Confessio Amantis*, i. 261; Berners' *Huon*, 568, 22.

"Mine (*scil.* opinions) as an honest man."—MRS. WARD, *Robert Elsmere*, ii. 175.

"My work as a clergyman has suffered."—*Ibid.* ii. 222.

§ 41. The nominative instead of the dative occurs pretty often.

"To whom the lond was attendant
As *he* which heir was apparant."

GOWER, *Confessio Amantis*, i. 214.

Another striking want of concord in the personal pronoun used appositively is recorded below, § 156 and § 209.

"Sith that mine honour cowardly was stole by caitiff *he*."—GEORGE PEELE (?), *Sir Ciyomon and Sir Clamydes*, p. 497, a.

§ 42. *d.* The place of the apposition in Old and Middle English, is remarkable.

Old English.—"For Saxulfes luuen þes abbodes" (for the love of the abbots).—*Chronicle*, 656.

Middle English.—"Þurh daviðes muð þe prophete" (through the mouth of David the prophet).—*Old English Hom.* i. 139.

§ 43. 3. A substantive in the possessive case, as "Milton's works."

§ 44. 4. A substantive preceded by a preposition, as "the trees in the garden." This use is not frequent in the earlier periods.

Old English.—"Þæt synd þá leóhtan *steorran on þam heofonlican rodore*" (there are the bright stars in the sky).—BASIL, *Hexameron*, 7.

Middle English.—"Bi þære sæ stronde *biside Scottlonde*" (by the sea-strand near Scotland).—LAYAM. ii. 94.

§ 45. The use of an adverb instead of an adjective may be traced back to Middle English, but then the adverb always follows the noun.

"My saulle lufes my lord abuf."—*Townley Myst.* p. 82.

§ 46. But the adverb preceding the noun is of recent date and probably due to the influence of Greek.

> " The seed of *the then* world."
> BYRON, *Cain*, i. 1.

§ 47. 5. An adjective clause, as 'All things that offend.' Matth. xiii. 41. For the development of the adjective clause see § 112-119.

III. *The Adverbial Relation.*

A. *The Object.*

§ 48. The objective relation in modern English is perhaps the most striking instance of the influence exercised by the decay of inflexion on the department of syntax. There is in Modern English practically no barrier between the direct and indirect object, between the dative and the accusative case, and this is the result of the decay of the old endings -e and -um, which first became -e and then were dropped altogether. It is only in certain cases, where both the direct and indirect object occur in the same phrase, that the indirect object is preceded by *to.* The syntactical consequences of this amalgamation are dealt with in their proper place. Change of the cases, § 210. Impersonal verbs, § 338. Passive Construction, § 363.

B. *Other Adverbial Adjuncts.*

§ 49. 1. The Adverb.

§ 50. 2. The Noun in the oblique (objective) case is used to denote *space, time, manner.*

In Old English these adverbial qualifications were for the most part expressed by the genitive, dative, and instrumental cases.

§ 51. *Genitive Case.*

Old English.—"Ongan þá drihtnes & dæges and nyhtes georne cyðan" (began to preach the Lord's law by day and night).—*Elene*, 198.

"Wendon him þa oðres weges hám weard" (they returned homeward by another way).—*Chronicle*, 1006.

"þis wæs feórðes geáres" (this was in the fourth year).—*Ibid.* 47.

Middle English.—"Fure þe neuer ne apeostrede winteres ne sumeres" (fire that never became dark, neither in summer nor in winter).—LAYAM. i. 121.

"Gif þu agultest wið þine efennexta unðonkes, bet hit þin þonkes hu se þu miht" (if thou sinnest against thy neighbour unwillingly, make amends for it willingly whatsoever way thou canst).—*Old Engl. Hom.* i. 17.

Cf. Genitive, § 184–186.

§ 52. *Dative* (Instrumental) *Case.*

Old English.—"hie heora yfelum þurhwunedon" (they remained in their evils).—*Blickling Hom.* 79, 8.

"Hǽlend com syx dagum ǽr eastrum to Bethania" (the Saviour came six days before Easter to B.).—*Ibid.* 71, 24.

"forþan ic hine sweorde swebban nelle" (I will not kill him with sword).—*Beow.* 680.

§ 53. In Modern English there are only a few traces of adverbial adjuncts in the genitive and dative case as *needs, noways, whilom* (Old English *hwilum*); but on the whole the simple adverbial noun is restricted to what we may call the *objective case,* as in the following instances :

Space.—"Th' other way Satan went down."—MILTON, *Parad. Lost*, x. 414.

"The Duke will not draw back *a single inch.*"—COLERIDGE, *Piccolomini* 1, 1.

Time.—"Nine days they fell."—MILTON, *Paradise L.* vi. 871.

"Her fate is fixed this very hour."—BYRON, *Bride of Abydos.*

Manner.—"Their residence, both in reputation and profit, was better *both ways.*"—*Hamlet*, ii. 2, 345.

"He will *every way* be mocked."—*Merry Wives*, v. 3, 20.

"I am so *many ways* obliged to you."—DRYDEN (Globe ed.), p. 37.

§ 54. 3. The so-called *cognate accusative* may also be looked upon as an adverbial adjunct.

Old English.—"Gefeoht gefuhton" (they fought a fight).—*Chronicle*, 887.

Middle English.—"He þam sult sli *sceuing sceau*" (he should show them such a vision).—*Cursor Mundi*, 10707.

Modern English.—"Well hast thou fought the better fight."—MILTON, *Paradise L.* vi. 29.

§ 55. 4. A substantive preceded by a preposition, as "he hopes for success."

In the early periods of English this sort of adverbial adjunct was much rarer than nowadays; the case-endings expressed then what is now the function of the preposition. *Cf.* the following instances:

"þær mihten deaþlice men *gyrnan* þara uplicra burhwara & þæs écean geférscipes" (so that mortal men might there yearn for the citizens on high and for the everlasting fellowship).—*Blickling Hom.* 197.

"Ne þearf he þær næfre leohtes *wénan*" (there need be never hope for any light).—*Ibid.* i. 63.

"Ar wæs on ófoste eft-síðes georn" (the messenger was in haste yearning for the return).—*Beówulf*, 2784.

"gódes grǽdig" (greedy after wealth).—*Salomon and Saturn*, 344.

§ 56. 5. A substantive or pronoun (accompanied by some attributive adjunct) with the participle absolute; as, "This done, he retired."

In earlier periods, and even as late as Milton, the substantive appeared in the dative case.

D

Old English.—"þa sóþlice him swá wépendum, þa com þara sacerda caldorman þe Petrus him tósende" (and then, indeed, they thus weeping, came the ruler of the priests whom Peter had sent to them).—*Blickling Hom.* 153.

"& þá him swá sittendum þá com þær semninga úre Drihten mid myccle mengeo engla" (and suddenly while they were thus sitting, our Lord came there with a great company of angels).—*Ibid.* 155.

Middle English.—"And siþ petir was sathanas for he wolde haue lettid cristis deþ & saluacion of mannus soule, *him vnwyttynge;* moche more þes prelatis ben sathanas . . ." (and since Peter was Satan, because he wanted to prevent Christ's death and the salvation of man's soul, he not knowing [unconsciously]; the more are thes prelates Satans . . .).—*Unprinted English Works of Wyclif,* ed. Matthew, p. 56.

"And þer-fore in þe popis lawe decrees & decretals symony is generally clepid heresie, & orible peynes ordeyned aʒenst men þat don symonye on ony manere bi hem self or oþere mene persones, bi here wille & consent, & in sum cas *hem vnwyttynge.*"—*Ibid.* p. 68.

Modern English.

"At least our envious foe hath failed, who thought
All like himself rebellious; by whose aid
This inaccessible high strength, the seat
Of Deity supreme, *us dispossessed,*
He trusted to have seized . . ."

     MILTON, *Paradise Lost,* vii. 139.

"For only in destroying I find ease
To my relentless thoughts; and *him destroyed,*
Or won to what may work his utter loss,
For whom all this was made, all this will soon
Follow, as to him linked in weal or woe."

     Ibid. ix. 129.

§ 57. It is doubtful, whether the Absolute Participle in Old English and in the other Teutonic dialects is akin to the similar constructions in Latin and Greek and thus of Aryan origin, or whether it is only borrowed from Latin; but it is obvious that both Wyclif and Milton were under the influence of the *ablativus absolutus* when they tried to introduce again the old English construction. As a fact, this had dropped out of use as early as the fourteenth century. Cf. Nominative Absolute, § 153. Participle Absolute, § 409-412.

§ 58. 6. An adverbial clause, as

"The star stood over where the young child was."—*Matth.* ii. 9.

See Complex Sentences, § 124.

SUBJECT AND PREDICATE.

The Subject.

§ 59. The subject of a finite verb is put in the nominative case.

This elementary rule of syntax has never been trespassed upon;[1] only the area of the *subject* is, in Modern English, much wider than it was in earlier periods. *The objects of many impersonal and transitive verbs have been turned into subjects.* Instead of the Old English "*me lícað,*" we say "I like;" instead of "*me langað,*" "I long;" and as early as the time of the "Ancren Riwle" (thirteenth century) we meet with the construction "I am given gall to drink," instead of what would be in Old English, "*Me* is given gall to drink."

Cf. Interchange of Cases, § 210.

§ 60. The subject of a sentence may be

    1. Simple.   2. Compound.   3. Complex.

§ 61. 1. The subject of a sentence is simple when it is

---

[1] It is only in the vulgar talk that *me, him (her), us, them,* occur instead of *I, he, she, we, they.*

"What a sermon ! *Me* and Julia cried so up in the organ-loft."—THACKERAY, *The Newcomes,* ii. 73.

"We'll have a spree, my boy, you and *me* together."—BESANT, *When the Ship comes Home,* 307.

"He laughed, miss, not *me.*"—*Ibid.* 322.

"You" was originally objective, but has become "nom."

(*a*) A single substantive (noun or pronoun), as "Men are mortal;" "I love truth," or an adjective used substantively.

§ 62. In Early English (as nowadays in colloquial speech) the pronoun was often omitted.

Old English.—". . . . módsorge wæg Rómwara cyning, ríces ne wénde for werodléste : hæfde wigena tó lyt" (sorrowful thought the king of the Romans, [he] did not hope to reign for want of people, [he] had too few warriors).—*Elene*, 61-63.

Middle English.—"Swiche teres schedde ure drihten þa he isch Martham and Mariam Magdalena þe sustren wepe for hore broðer deð, and ure drihten þurh rouðe þet he efde of hom, schedde of his halie eʒene hate teres, and hore broðer arerde, and (scil. heo, they) weren stille of hore wope." (Such tears shed our Lord when he saw the sisters Martha and Mary Magdalene weep for their brother's death ; and our Lord, in compassion for them, shed hot tears from his holy eyes, and raised their brother, so that *they* ceased their weeping.)—*Old English Hom.* i. 157.

Tudor English.—"Thys sayde the false traitour, by cause he desyred no thyng elles, but one of the sonnes of duke Seuyn myght sley Charlot, wherby he thought shuld be dystroyed in acusynge them of murder, wherby he myght come to his dampnable intent."—BERNERS' *Huon*, 19, 11.

(i.e. *they* should be destroyed.)

Cf. Personal pronouns, § 268-274.

§ 63. A substantive subject omitted.

It is commonly the name of God which is dropped.

Middle English instances are scarcely to be met with.

Modern English.—"Save his majesty."—SHAKSP. *Tempest*, ii. 1, 168[1]).

"Bless you, sir."—*Merry Wives*, ii. 2, 160.

"Give you good night."—*Hamlet*, i. 1, 16. Cf. "*God give* you good morrow, sir."—PEELE, *The Old Wives' Tale*, p. 455, b.

NOTE.

"The guilt, say what I will, I cannot roll off from me."—COLERIDGE, *Piccolomini*, iv. 4.

"Do all we can, women will believe us."—GAY, *Beggars' Opera*, ii. 2.

---

[1] The Globe edition has : "*God* save his majesty."

Some grammarians find omission of the subject in these instances. "In the singular as well as in the plural, an omission of the subject occurs with all personal forms, whenever a concessive sentence is followed by a collateral sentence containing the subject belonging also to the preceding sentence." (Mätzner). I am inclined to look upon these expressions as formed in analogy of sentences of the second person, in which the personal pronoun was never the rule.

Try what you will is quite correct, and it was on this type that all the other sentences were modelled : "try what he will," "try what I will."

§ 64. Adjectives used substantively were much more frequent in *Old* and *Middle English.*

Old English.—" Se þe underféhð rihtwísne on rihtwíses naman, he onféhð rihtwíses méde " (he that receiveth a righteous [man] in the name of a righteous [man] shall receive a righteous [man]'s reward).—*Matthew* x. 41.

Middle English.—" Al þat seȝ þat *semly* syked in hert, & sayde soþly al same segges til oþer, Carande for þat *comly* . . ." (All that saw that fair one sighed in their heart, and said truly one man to the other, out of care for that comely one.)—*Sir Gawayne,* 672-4.

Cf. Adjectives, § 236-247.

§ 65. (*b*) An Infinitive Mood or Gerund, as

" To be, contents his natural desire."—POPE, *Essay on Man,* i. 109.

"Your being Sir Anthony's son, Captain, would itself be a sufficient accommodation."—SHERIDAN, *Rivals,* iii. 3.

§ 66. (*c*) Any word which is itself made the subject of discourse.

" A bitter and perplexed 'What shall I do?'
Is worse to man than worst necessity."

COLERIDGE, *Piccolomini,* i. 2.

§ 67. 2. The subject of a sentence is compound when it consists of two or more substantives coupled together by the conjunction *and*, as "Abraham and his wife Sarah went home." This is a contraction of two sentences : A. went home, and S. went home ; and, in fact, primitive tribes say "the father came, and the son came." In Early English, and here and there also in modern times, we find a construction which keeps the middle course between the primeval repetition and the modern contraction.

Old English.—"ond æfter þám Hengest féng to ríce and Aesc his sunu" (after that Hengest succeeded to the kingdom and Aesc his son) — *Chronicle*, 455.

Middle English —"*He* suanc and swet *and cue* his wif" (he worked and sweated and Eve his wife).—*Cursor Mundi*, 1047.

Cf. Order of words, § 473.

§ 68. 3. The subject of a sentence is complex when it consists of an infinitive or gerundive phrase, of *a substantive clause*, or of a quotation.

It is only the substantive clause which shows a noteworthy development.

§ 69. (*a*) In Early English substantive clauses with "that" are well known, only the predicate always precedes.

Old English.—"*Sélre is* þæt we hine syllon tó ceápe Ismahelitum" (it is better that we should sell him to the Ishmeelites).—*Gen.* xxxvii. 27.

Middle English.—"The first statute was that thei sholde beleeven and obeyen in God immortalle."—MAUNDEVILLE, p. 225.

But in Modern English the substantive clause with "that" often takes the usual place of the subject, namely at the head of the sentence.

"*That there should have been such a likeness* is not strange."—MACAULAY, *History*, i. 27.

§ 70. (*b*) Instead of the substantive clause as the subject of a verb, we find in Older English the *substantive* or pronoun *with the infinitive* after impersonal expressions.

"ðor was nogt wune on and on
ðat orf ðor to water gon."

(It was not the custom for the cattle to go to water one by one.)—
Story of Genesis and Exodus, 1640.

"No wondur is, *a lewid man to ruste*."—CHAUCER, *Cant. Tales, Prol.* 502.

"(This folke) putte hem self vpon their enmyes, so that it was force *the polonyens to recule* abak."—BLANCHARDYN, 107, 18.

"*Thow to lye* by our moder, is to muche shame for vs to suffre."— *Morte d'Arthur*, 453, 4.

Elisabethan English.—"A heavier task could not have ben imposed, than *I to speak* my griefs unspeakable."—SHAKSP. *Comedy of Errors*, i. 1, 33.

§ 71. As early as 1474 the preposition "*for*" preceding the substantive came into use, and in this shape the old construction has come down to our days.

"It is an evil thing *for* a man to have suspecion."—CAXTON, *Game of the Chesse*, p. 90.

"It is better *for* a synner to suffre trybulacyon."—*English Works of John Fisher*, ed. Mayor (E. E. T. S.), p. 41, l. 9.

"*For* Coriolanus neither to care whether they love or hate him manifests the true knowledge he has."—SHAKSP. *Coriol.* ii. 2, 13.

"The Lilliputians think nothing can be more unjust than *for* people . . . to bring children into the world, and leave the burden of supporting them upon the public."—SWIFT, *Gulliver's Travels*, vi.

"There is nothing so rare as *for* a man to ride his hobby without molestation."—W. IRVING, *Bracebridge Hall*, ii. 22.

Reduplication of the Subject.

"And *peace*, O Virtue! *peace* is all thy own."
                                                                POPE.

"*She* early left her sleepless bed,
   The fairest maid of Teviotdale."
                                                                SCOTT.

"*Your husband he* is gone to save far off,
   Whilst others come to make him lose at home."
                                                                SHAKSPERE.

§ 72. 1. The repetition of the subject by one and the same word as marking special stress, is very common in elliptic phrases, *e.g.*, a thief! a thief! but as a conscious rhetorical means it is of modern date, and restricted to literary language.

§ 73. 2. Another sort of reduplication of the subject is that of repeating the subject by means of a personal pronoun (as exhibited in the above instances). These instances illustrate two different psychological processes, and accordingly two different constructions.

In the first case the subject is foremost in the consciousness of the speaker, and the other idea connected with it, viz., the predicate, is dimmed for a moment, so that it takes the speaker some time to catch hold of it again.

In the second case the speaker is so much under the impression of what he is going *to predicate*, that he forgets for a moment to tell the person addressed what he is predicating about, and it takes some time until he finds out his mistake.

In both cases there is a distinct pause between the two expressions for the same subject, in both cases the hearer has the impression that there is some emotion at work in the mind of the speaker. Both these circumstances make the expression a favourite figure of speech.

For instances see personal pronoun, § 284–289.

NOTE.—It is the same psychological process which brings forth sentences like the following, the so-called anacoluthic sentences.

Old English.—"Swá se læce, þonne he on untíman lácnað wunde, hie wyrmseð ond rotað" (so the physician, when he doctors a wound at the wrong time, it corrupts and putrifies).—*Cura Pastoralis*, 152, 2.

Middle English.—"He that saieth a pater noster, and thinkith of worldly thinges, his prayers profiteth not."—*Knight of la Tour Landry*, p. 7.

The principle is the same, the only difference consisting in the case.

§ 74. Another sort of repetition is that of the subject after an extensive member of a sentence or collateral sentence, where the only aim is to recall the more remote subject to recollection.

"Manetho also, who lived about the time of Nebuchadon-Asser, Asser being a Syriac word usually applied as a surname to the kings of that country, as Teglat-Phael-Asser, Nabon-Asser, *he*, I say, formed a conjecture equally absurd."—GOLDSMITH, *Vicar of Wakefield*, 14.

The same principle probably accounts for the pleonastic use of the personal noun following *relative sentences*.

"*The only begotten Son*, which is in the bosom of the Father, *he* has declared him."—*John* i. 18.

Cf. Relative Sentences below, § 217.

Omission of the Subject.
Personal Pronoun omitted.
"*Thank you, Sir.*"

§ 75. What is wanted in this instance is not the psychological, but the grammatical subject, the former being implied in the verbal form. *Cf.* Pronouns, § 268, and above, § 62.

A Substantive Subject omitted. *Cf.* § 63.
The Predicate.

The predicate of a sentence may be
  1. Simple.   2. Complex.

Simple Predicate.

§ 76. The predicate of a sentence is simple when the notion to be conveyed is expressed by a single finite verb, as "The moon shines," "We come."

Complex Predicate.

§ 77. Many verbs do not make complete sense by themselves, but require some other word to be used with them to make the sense complete. Of this kind are the intransitive verbs "*be, become, seem, can, do, shall, will,*" &c., and such transitive verbs as "*make, call.*" Besides these there are other verbs which are only *occasionally* incomplete, as in the instances:

"I will *live* a bachelor."—*Much Ado,* i. 1, 248.

"How *stand* you affected to his wish?"—*The Two Gentlemen of Verona,* i. iii. 60.

"I *stood* engaged."—*All's Well that Ends Well,* v. iii. 96.

"Wouldst thou *remain* a beast with the beasts?"—*Timon of Athens,* iv. iii. 326.

In these cases it is not the verb which is prominent in the mind of the speaker, but the adjective or noun, and accordingly these are the predicates, and the verbs must be looked upon as mere *auxiliary* ones, like *be*.

It is, therefore, quite correct to say, "Slow and sure comes up the golden year" (Tennyson), "we live happy," *slow* and *happy* being adjectives used predicatively, not adverbs qualifying the verbs.

§ 78. In Early English the complement of the predicate, when a noun, was often used in the dative preceded by "to."

Old English.—"Cweð, þæt þás stánas tó hláfe geweorðon" (command that these stones be made bread).—*Matthew,* iv. 3.

Middle English.—"He warrþ till atell defell off shene enngell" (of a bright angel he became a dreadful devil).—*Orm.* 13679.

§ 79. The expression "*it is me*" which is constantly gaining ground, is of comparatively recent date. The historical development of this construction is shown in the following instances.

Old English.—"Habbað geleáfan, ic hyt eom" (have belief, I it am).—*Matthew*, xiv. 27.

"Gyf þú hyt eart" (if thou it be).—*Ibid*. 28.

Middle English.—"Jhesus heom to seyde, 'lo ich hit em'" (Jesus said to them, 'Lo! it is I').—*Old English Miscell.* 42, 184.

Later on, a slight change takes place.

"Forsothe it am nat I."—CHAUCER, *The Knightes Tale*, 602.

"It is not he that slewe the man, hit is I."—*Gesta Romanorum*, 201.

Modern English.—"She would not speak of the occasion of those words, which was *me*."—RICHARDSON, *Pamela*, 43, *b*.

Discrepancy between grammatical and psychological Predicate.

§ 80. The psychological predicate is far from being the same as the grammatical one. In the sentence "I did it, not you," there can be no doubt from the grammarian's point of view, that *I* is the subject of the sentence; but psychologically speaking, he is certainly wrong, the psychological construction being "the person who did it was *I*, not you."

To avoid this discrepancy between grammatical and psychological predicate, the periphrastic expression with "it is" was introduced.

Old English.—"þæt wæs on þone mónandæg æfter Marianmæsse þæt Godwine becom" (it was on Monday after M. that G. came).—*Chronicle*, 1052.

Cf. Use of *It*, § 280.

Middle English.—"*It is I* that dede him kylle."—*Coventry Mysteries*, p. 291.

"*It is þe spirit* þat quykeneþ."—WYCLIFF, *John*, vi. 36.

Modern English instances abound.

Ellipsis of the Copula "to be."

"No one so deaf as he that will not hear."—LONGFELLOW.

§ 81. It is quite consistent with the psychological facts, as well as with the science of language, that the simple juxtaposition of subject and predicate is anterior to the connection by means of a copula. The original state is still kept in proverbs and similar expressions : "first come, first served," &c. *Cf.* Latin, *Quot homines, tot sententiæ. Omnia præclara rara. Summum jus, summa injuria.*

The absence of this omission in Old English is probably due to the fact that there are no sufficient remains of popular literature for such expressions to turn up. We meet, however, with a few examples in Middle English.

" Wexen boden ysaac sunes,
And ðhogen, and adden sundri wunes ;
Esau wilde man huntere,
And Jacob tame man tiliere."

(Isaac's sons grew up and throve and had different occupations. Esau [was] a hunter, and Jacob a husbandman.)—*Story of Genesis and Exodus*, 1481. = Esau *was* wilde man huntere.

" ðan coren wantede in oðer lond,
ðo ynug [was] vnder his hond."

(There was want of corn in other lands, while there was enough under his hand.).—*Ibid.* 2156.

"ȝif mennus soulis gon to helle bi brekynge of goddis commandementis, *no warde*, so þat þe peny come faste to fille here hondis & coffris" (no warde = no matter).—WYCLIF, *Unprinted Works*, ed. Matthew, p. 72.

" *Goddis forbode* y schulde be so lewde for to so seie."—PECOCK, *The Repressor*, p. 25 ; *ibid.* 98, 99, 228, 253, 537.

Cf. Goddis forbode *be* it. *Ibid.* 537.

Omission of the Predicate.

" Lights there ! "

§ 82. The absence of the predicative verb in such expressions is common in all periods of the language. Then, as in the above instances, the predicate has to be gathered by the person addressed from what he sees, if he follows the direction to which the attention is called, or can read the meaning of gestures.

Middle English.—" nu ut quoð strenðe farlac ne schaltu na lengere leuen in ure ende" ("Now, Fear, [go] out," quoth Strength, "thou shalt no longer remain in our quarters ").—SAWLES WARDE in *Old English Homilies*, i. 265.

"Now to schyp, on and othir !"—*Richard Cœur de Lion*, 6649.

Modern English.—"To horse ! to horse ! urge doubts to them that fear."—*Richard II.* ii. 1, 299.

§ 83. NOTE.— It is in the same way that we account for verbs of movement being omitted in the infinitive mood after auxiliary verbs, especially after "shall" and "will."

Old English.—"Ic him æfter sceal" (I shall [go] after him).—*Beówulf*, 2817.

"ða he him from wolde ða geféng he hine" (when he would [depart] from him, he seized him).—*Cura Pastoralis*, 35, 19.

Middle English.—"Bot I wyl to þe chapel, for chaunce þat may falle."—*Sir Gawayne*, 2132.

Modern English.—"I must to the Jew."—MARLOWE, *Jew of Malta*, ed. Wagner, l. 1459.

"Let him to our sister."—*Lear*, i. 3, 14.

"She will not from my memory."—BEAUMONT AND FLETCHER, *The Scornful Lady*, 98, a.

"Like will to like."

Concord.

§ 84. The first rule of every syntax, namely, that a finite verb agrees with its subject *in number*, is very often sinned against in all periods of English.

Collective Nouns with Predicates in the plural.

"All the world *are* good in your eyes."—JANE AUSTEN, *Pride and Prejudice*, 15.

§ 85. Of this concession made by grammar to psychology, there are instances from Old English down to our own day.

Old English.—" þæt *folc sæt* . . . and *arison*" (people sat down and arose).—*Exodus* xxxii. 6.

"se here swór þæt hie woldon" (the army swore that they would...). —*Chronicle*, 921.

" þín ofspring sceal ágan *hebra* feónda gata" (thy offspring shall own their enemies' gates).—*Genesis* xxii. 17.

Middle English.—" þat israelisshe folc was walkende toward ierusalem on swinche, and on drede, and on wanrede, and þo wile was hersum godes hese. Ac efter þan þe *hie weren* wuniende in ierusalem . . . þo *hie forleten* godes lore." (The Israelitish folk were walking towards Jerusalem, in toil, in dread, and in affliction, and were at that time obedient to God's behests. But after that they were dwelling in Jerusalem . . . then they forsook God's love.)—*Old English Homilies*, ii. 51.

" ðis wird of engeles metten him" (this host of angels met him).— *Story of Gen. and Exodus*, 1790.

In Modern English this irregularity has become the rule.

Plural Nouns with a Singular Predicate.

"There *is* no more such Cæsars."—SHAKSPERE.

"Here *is* twenty angels."—GREENE.

§ 86. Plural nouns often take a singular predicate. Of this striking irregularity which is found very early, and is very frequent in the fifteenth century and in the time of Shakspere, three different sorts can be distinguished :—

1. The verb precedes the noun, and the sentence is introduced by *here* (*there*). This answers accurately to the French expression : *il arrive des revolutions, il est (il y a) des gens;* German : *es gibt noch ehrliche Leute.*

Old English.—" On þæm selfan hrægle *wæs* eac awriten þa naman ðara twelf heahfædra " (on the same robe were also written the names of the 12 patriarchs).—*Cura Pastoralis*, 6, 15.

Middle English.—" Here *is* grete merveylles."—CAXTON, *Aymon*, 444, 31.

Tudor English.—" There *is* more nobler portes in England."— ANDREW BOORDE, *Introduction and Dyetary*, p. 120.

" There *is* at Bath certain waters."—*Ibid.*

" There *was* many Dukes, Erles, and barons."—LORD BERNERS' *Huon*, 2, 22.

" What shooting is, how many kindes there *is* of it is tolde."— ASCHAM, *Toxophilus*, 31.

§ 87. 2. The subject of the sentence is determined by numerals. In this case the singular of the predicate is explained by the old substantival collective nature of numerals. *Cf.* a thousand, a hundred. See Numerals, § 257.

Old English instances are rare.

Middle English.—" Seue maistres *is* her come."—*Seuyn Sages*, 2397.

" The 80 mark þe which *is* in Thomas Harwodes hand."—*Early English Wills*, 44, 12.

Tudor English.—"XVIII Scottish pens *is* worth an Englysshe grote."—ANDREW BOORDE, *Introduction and Dyetary*, p. 137.

"There *is* five trumps besides the queen."—*Gammer Gurton*, 193.

"Here *is* four angels for you."—GREENE, *Looking Glass*, 125, a.

§ 88. 3. In the third group it is the distance between the subject and predicate which accounts for the inaccuracy of the expression.

"Our neighbours, that were woont to quake
And tremble at the Persean Monarkes name,
Now *sits* and *laughs* our regiment to skorne."
MARLOWE, *Tamburlaine*, 115.

"Fortune's blows,
When most struck home, being gently wounded, *craves*
A noble cunning."
Coriolanus, iv. 1, 7.

§ 89. NOTE.—Most of the irregularities turning up in Middle English, and even in the sixteenth century, may be simply accounted for by the fact that not only the endings *-es* and *-eth*, but also *is* and *was* were used both in the singular and in the plural. Instances of unmistakable character abound.

"Alle his wundres þat he doþ, *is* þurch þene vend (fiend)."—*The Passion of our Lord*, 60 (*Old E. Miscellany*, 49).

"Alle his wunders þat he doþ, *is* þurch þene quede (evil one)."—*Ibid*. 250.

"out tak the forsayd matyns bokys that *is* bequethe to Thomas my sone."—*Early E. Wills*, v. 14.

"þis *es* the dettis þat *es* [h]owynge to me."—*Ibid*. xxxix. 34.

"ðor *was* sundri speches risen."—*Story of Genesis and Exodus*, 668.

"On the finger *was* wretyn wordis: 'percute hic.'"—*Gesta Romanorum*, p. 7.

Cf. Zupitza, note to *Guy of Warwick*, *l*. 298.

Concord of the Predicate with several Subjects.

" Her joye and life *is* gone."—*Gammer Gurton.*

" My purse, my coffer, and myself *is* thine."
MARLOWE.

"The grape, the rose, *renew*
The juice nectareous, and the balmy dew."
POPE.

§ 90. As a rule, several subjects which stand to one another in a copulative relation, require a predicate in the plural ; but in this, more than in any other department of concord, the subjective point of view decides as to the number. Thus synonymous nouns are easily conceived as one notion and one subject, *e.g.*,

"I applaud the sound, right sense, and love of virtue, which *appears* through your whole letter."—CHATHAM, Letters, 3 ;

or one of the subject-nouns is prominent in the mind of the speaker at the moment when he is going to utter the predicate, *e.g.*

" Lo ! Burns and Blomfield, nay, a greater far,
Gifford *was* born beneath an adverse star."
BYRON, *English Bards and Scotch Reviewers.*

Concord of the Copula.

" Our fraught *is* Grecians, Turks, and Africk Moors."
MARLOWE.

" But now, two paces of the vilest earth
Is room enough."
SHAKSPERE.

§ 91. As a rule, the copula agrees in number with the subject. Accordingly, we say :

"The rugged mountain's scanty cloak
Was dwarfish shrubs of birch and oak."
SCOTT, *Lady of the Lake*, v. 3.

"His pay *is* just ten sterling pounds per sheet."—BYRON, *English Bards and Scotch Reviewers*.

§ 92. But the predicate is very frequently of greater weight than the subject, especially when it is in the plural, and accordingly intrudes its number on the copula. Hence the following expressions. German: *das sind zwei verschiedene Dinge;* French: *ce sont là des vertus de roi.*

Old English.—"Gyf þæt leóht þe on þe ys, *synt* þȳstru, hû mycle beoð þa þystru" (if therefore the light that is in thee be darkness, how great is the darkness!).—*Matthew*, vi. 23.

Middle English.—"Bretons *was* þe verste folc þat to engelonde com."—*Rob. of Gloucester*, 57.

"The schon that sal be your feet upon,
Is not ellys but exawnpyl of vertuis levyng."
Coventry Mysteries, p. 273.

Object.

§ 93. While there has scarcely been any change in the construction of the simple object, that of the complex object, consisting 1. of a substantive clause, 2. of a substantive accompanied by an indefinite mood, is different now from what it was in earlier periods.

§ 94. 1. The substantive clause when used as an object was formerly more concrete. Expressions like "The Egyptians beheld the woman that she was beautiful" (Gen. xii. 14) are now restricted to the Bible; but in the early periods of English this construction was quite common.

Middle English.—"Gif þu *hine* iseȝe þet *he* wulle asottie to þes deofles hond and to his werkes, þet þu hine lettest." (If when thou sawest him about to fall foolishly into the devil's hand, and to his works, thou checkest him . . .)—*Old English Homilies*, i. 17.

"And þis man wat we wel þat he es al wit-uten plight" (and we know well this man that he is without sin).—*Cursor Mundi*, 16729.

Tudor English.—"Whan Huon herd *the kyng, how he toke* his wordes, he stept forthe and said."—BERNERS' *Huon*, 27/21.

§ 95. 2. The substantive accompanied by an infinitive (*accusativus cum infinitivo*) as an object is recorded in the earliest periods of English, but is of limited range. See Infinitive, § 401–404. But it becomes quite common in the Elizabethan time.

II.

COMPLEX SENTENCES.

§ 96. After examining Alfred's Introduction to his Translation of the *Pastoral Care*, we noticed as the most striking feature of Old English syntax, the awkward structure of the sentence, and the combination of sentences. See Introduction, p. 8. In fact, Old English, as well as the other Teutonic languages, was far behind the wonderful elasticity of Greek and Latin prose-diction. If we may keep the old metaphor which calls language the garb of thought, we should be inclined to say that the Teutonic dialects were, from a syntactical point of view, heavy steel armour, permitting the mind to move, but very awkwardly, while the Latin was, at a very early date, like a supple soft dress, splendidly adapted to follow every brisk movement of thought.

The Complex Sentence in shape of two Co-ordinate Sentences.

"Sow well, reap well."

§ 97. The complex sentence of Greek and Latin, with its admirable expressiveness was, in the time of Alfred the Great, just beginning to grow on English and German soil. While in Latin and Greek the complex sentence, as a combination of independent and dependent sentences, expressed precisely the inward connection existing between the principal and accessory thought, the simple sentences in the Teutonic dialects showed a mere heap of phrases running parallel with each other, the reader being free to make out what was the intended connection. Compare the following instances :

"unte ni galeiþiþ imma in hairto, ak in vamba, jah in urrunsa usgaggiþ, gahraineiþ allans matins." (Because it entereth not into his heart, but into the belly, and goeth out into the draught, purgeth all meats.)—*Mark*, vii. 19.

"Hit wæs after Moyses forðsiðe, Drihten spræc tó Josue" (it was after the death of Moses [that] the Lord spake to Joshua).—*Joshua*, i. 1.

This is the oldest way of syntactic combination, and in this respect Old Teutonic very much resembles the Hebrew, which never attained to a higher stage of development.

"And there came two angels to Sodom at even ; and Lot sat in the gate of Sodom ; and Lot saw them and rose up to meet them ; and he bowed himself with his face toward the ground."—*Genesis*, xix. 1.

Thus the original text ; the authorised version alters into "and Lot *seeing* them rose up to meet them."

§ 98. We call this sort of combination which indiscriminately places sentences of different syntactic value one by the side of the other, paratactic ($\pi\alpha\rho\alpha\tau\acute{\alpha}\tau\tau\omega$) combination, parataxis or *coordination*. The absence of connecting particles is a characteristic feature of this combination, and thus the sentences look as if there were no connection whatever between them, as if they were *independent* of each other.

§ 99. But what seems to be *parataxis*, mere coordination in this connection, is only apparent ; in fact we find that a parataxis with complete independence of the sentences nowhere occurs ; that it is scarcely possible to connect sentences together without a certain kind of *hypotaxis* or subordination.

The mere fact that two sentences are put paratactically to each other proves that there is a logical connection between them, that is, that one sentence in some way modifies the other. In short, what was formally a paratactic connection, is logically hypotaxis or subordination. Thus, in the sentences "sow well, reap well," there is parataxis formally only, each sentence being independent of the other; but logically the first serves to determine the meaning of the second, and the construction, therefore, is hypotactic κατὰ σύνεσιν (according to the sense) "if you sow well, you will reap well."

§ 100. This first stage of development, which is very common in all the Aryan languages, is found in Old English poetry, and has not yet disappeared. Considering the importance of the subject, some examples are necessary.

Latin.—"et *sensi,* hic sonitum fecerunt fores."—PLAUTUS, *Mil.* 1377.

"*audivi,* Archilis, Lesbiam adduci jubes."—TER. *Andr.* 228.

"non potest sine malo fateri, *video.*"—*Eun.* 714.

"magis jam *faxo* mira *dices.*"—PLAUTUS, *Amph.* 1107.

Gothic.—"in urrunsa usgaggith, gahraineith allans matins" (it goeth out into the draught, purgeth all meats).—*Mark,* vii. 19.

"galaith than in ain thize skipe, thatei vas Seimonis, haihait ina aftiuhan fairra statha leitil" (and he entered into one of the boats, which was Simon's, asked him to put out a little from the land).—*Luke,* v. 3.

Old High German translations prove that asyndetic co-ordination was consciously felt as equivalent to Latin subordination. The following instances will serve to prove this fact :—

"(scalhes) farawa infenc, wortan wardh kahoric untaz za tode" (he took the shape of a servant, remained obedient until death) = "formam servi accipiens effectus est obediens usque ad mortem."

"sine jungirun ouh warun hungrage, bigunnun raufan diu ahar" (his disciples were hungry, began to pluck ears) = "discipuli autem ejus esurientes cœperant vellere spicas."

"argengun do uz pharisara, worahtun garati" (there the Pharisees went, they held council) = "exeuntes pharisei consilium faciebant."

"er antwurta, quat im" (he answered, said to them) = et respondens ad eos dixit."[1]

Old English.—"þis carme wíf me gesóhte, *séde* þæt ic mihte hyre to þé geþingian" (this poor woman sought me, *said* that I could intercede for her to thee).—ÆLFRIC, *Lives of Saints*, 60, 174. Cf. *Cura Pastoralis*, 118, 21 ; 218, 23.

"Ic wát, inc waldend god ábolgen wyrð" (I know with you two the Almighty God will be wroth).—CÆDMON, *Genesis*, 551.

"Simon . . . sægde hy drýas wæron" (Simon said they were sorcerers).—*Juliana*, 301.

Middle English.—"al ich am well ipaied euerichon sigge þet hire best bereð on heorte" (I am very well pleased (*that*) everyone (should) say . . .), &c.—*Ancren Riwle*, 44.

"ðe olde lage we ogen tu sunen
ðe newe we hauen moten."

(The old law we ought to shun, [since] we have the new.)—*Old English Miscellanies*, 10.

"Hit bifel þer afturward swythe longe ynoȝ
Out of þe lond of Scitie other folk þider droȝ.
Rob. of Gloucester, 953.

"Ebrauk his sone was of age,
Had þis lond in heritage."
ROBERT DE BRUNNE, *Story of England*, 2149.

Modern English.—Fast bind, fast find.—*Merchant of Venice*, ii. 5, 54.
Live thou, live I.—*Ibid.* iii. 2, 61.

The Independent Sentence is introduced by a Particle (originally a Demonstrative).

"I heard a voice whisper him ; I knew the voice, and then they both went out by the back way ; *so* I stole down, and went out and listened."—BULWER.

§ 101. The first step towards the development of grammatical subordination was the use of a pronoun or a demonstrative adverb connecting the two sentences, *e.g.*, He

---

[1] *Germania*, vol. xxiv. p. 168.

always talks of himself; *that* makes me despise him; or, it is going to rain, *so* we had better go.

The use of *though* in Modern English offers an interesting illustration of the second stage of development. While commonly used to introduce the dependent sentence, it has at the same time kept its old place in the principal sentence, as in the following instance: "A foolish coxcomb," "Ay! let him alone *though*," Coleridge, *Piccolomini*, i. 6 = Though he is a foolish coxcomb, let him alone. *German* : er ist ein thörichter Geck, *doch* lasst ihn gehen.

This function of "though" answers to that of many other particles in Old Teutonic dialects.

Both the Independent and the Dependent Sentence are introduced by the same Particle (Correlation).

"*Then* Gerames saw how the shipp was commynge to that porte, *then* he sayd to his company, syrs, lett vs go."—BERNERS' *Huon*.

§ 102. The next step was to introduce both sentences by the same particle, this sort of parallelism serving to express the correlation existing between the two sentences. Many instances in Old High German, Old English and Middle English bear witness of this third stage of development.

Old High German.—"*nû* thû thaz arunti so harto bist formonânti *nu* wirdû (wird thû) stummêr sâr" (now thou art despising the message so strongly, thou wilt be dumb).—*Otfrid*, i. 4, 65.

"*nu* er then tôd suachit.... *nu* sîmês garawe alle mit imo zi themo falle" (now he seeks death, let us be all prepared with him for the fall). —*Ibid*. iii. 23, 59.

Old English.—"þær þæt gemynd bið, þær bið þæt andgyt and se wylla" (where the mind is, there is the understanding and the will).— THORPE, *Anal.* p. 65.

"þær þin goldhord ys, þær ys þin heorte" (where thy treasure is, there is thy heart).—*Matthew*, vi. 21.

"þonne hit dagian wolde, þonne tóglád hit" (when it was going to dawn, then it glided away).—*Chronicle*, 979.

Middle English.

" And *there* he loggith anon,
    Ther Darie hadde beon erst apon."
                        Alisaundre, 4098.

" ffor *ther* he is, *ther* wold I be."—*Coventry Mysteries,* p. 323.

This use is found as late as the sixteenth century. See the instance quoted at the head of this section.

The Dependent Sentence alone is introduced by the Particle.

" Though thou liv'st and breath'st,
    Yet art thou slain in him."
                        SHAKSPERE.

§ 103. The last stage was that of dropping the particle in the principal sentence, so that the subordinate clause remained outwardly perceptible by means of the particle.[1] The history of the evolution of the complex sentence throws a new light on many hitherto unexplained points in the subordinate sentences. Thus the so-called "*omission of the relative,*" and many peculiarities in the noun sentences are easily explained, if we bear in mind the four stages of development through which the complex sentence passed, before it got its present shape; for convenience' sake we follow the traditional order.

The Substantive Clause.

" You see that I am composed."—DICKENS.

" And God saw the light that it was good."—*Genesis.*

§ 104. The substantive clause (object clause) offers instances of all the four stages of its development.

---

[1] For the arrangement of words in the dependent sentence, see below, § 459.

I. He is a clever man, you know (no particle whatever).

II. He is a clever man, you know *that* = the fact (pronoun in the principal sentence).

III. Of stage III. there are instances in Old, Middle, and even here and there in Modern English.

Old English.—" And eác we magon oncnáwan ðæt, ðæt þa earman and þa untruman sint to retanne" (and we can also understand that the poor and weak are to be cheered).—*Cura Pastoralis*, 180, 20.

Middle English.—" Thei seyn ȝit, *that* and he had ben crucyfied, *that* God had don aȝen his rihtewisnesse."—MAUNDEVILLE, p. 134.

In all the instances quoted, editors put the comma before the first *that;* but originally *that* belongs to the principal sentence.

IV. You know *that* he is a clever man (particle in the dependent sentence).

§ 105. But though the last stage of development was reached even in Old English, the psychological principle which brought about stages II. and III., was long after at work (as, in fact, it is still), so that the expression II. or a very similar one, was kept even in modern times.

§ 106. A sentence, as a whole, is always an abstract. Now, the imagination is not very fond of abstracts; hence the modern way of expressing noun clauses, as in the following instance, is grammatically quite correct, but psychologically hard to conceive. In the phrase "You see that I am composed," the object clause is understood to be the object of the verb see; but psychologically speaking you cannot very well apprehend an abstract clause as the object of *see*. In fact, the old expression of stage II. is psychologically much easier to understand.

The verb in the principal sentence gets as its object the pronoun *that*, which is the indefinite expression, as it were, a dim image, of the clause following.

The same principle accounts for the similar, but still more concrete construction of noun clauses, which is not unfrequent in Greek.

Compare the two following sentences: "And God saw the light, [and saw] that it was good," "And God saw that the light was good."[1]

Logically speaking, the two constructions are equivalent; but psychologically, how different is the idea which they represent! In the first case the sentence expresses an abstract result; in the second, the verb "see" has a concrete object, in which a certain attribute is perceived.

Old English.—"Wénð, gif he hit him iewe, ðæt he *him* nylle geðafian ðæt he hiene sniðe" (he thinks that if he show it him, he will not allow him to cut him.—*Cura Pastoralis*, 184, 26.

Middle English.—"Gif þu *hine* iseȝe þet *he* wulle asottie to þes deofles hond, end to his werkes, þet þu hine lettest." (If, when thou sawest him about to fall foolishly into the devil's hand, and to his works, thou checkest him...).—*O. E. Homilies*, i. 17.

"he scal soðfeste men setten him to irefen, and for godes eie libban his lif rihtliche, and beon on erfeðnesse anred an edmod on stilnesse, *and his ofspringe ne iþauie þet hi beon unrightwise.*" (He shall appoint him trustworthy men for sheriffs, and for the fear of God lead a good life, and be unmoved in tribulation and meek in peace [prosperity], and shall not suffer his offspring to be unrighteous.)—*Ibid.* i. 115.

" ful wel þu *me* iseie, þauh þu stille were,
   Hwar ich was and *hwat i dude*, þauh þu me ouerbere."

(Thou sawst me full well, though thou wert still, where I was and what I did...).—*On God Ureisun of ure Lefdi* (*Old Engl. Miscellany*), 105, 106.

"(They) louen more here folye avowis to fulfille *hem* þan to fulfille goddis hestis."—WYCLIF, *Unpr. Works*, ed. Matthew, p. 103.

   " When the emperowre harde telle
      All þat case, how hyt felle,
      That Saddok was so slayne,
      Therof was he nothyng fayne.
              Guy of Warwick, ed. Zupitza, 1498.

---

[1] *Cf.* also: "The Egyptians beheld *the woman that* she was very fair."—*Gen.* xii. 14. "And Lot...beheld all the plain of Jordan that it was well watered everywhere."—*Ibid.* xiii. 10.

Tudor English.—"Whan Huon herd *the kyng how he toke* his wordes, he stept forthe and said."—BERNERS' *Huon*, 27, 21.

"Whan Gerame vnderstode þe *companye how they thought* they were skapyd fro the dwarfe, he began too smyle."—*Ibid.* 69, 15.

"Let me (my Lord) disclose unto your grace
This hainous tale, what mischief it contains."
                                                Gorboduc, 627.

"To see fair *Bettris how bright she is* of blee."—GREENE, *George-A-Greene*, p. 264, b.

"I know you what you are."—*Lear*, i. 1, 272.

For the construction of the object noun clauses, which are at the same time adjectival ones, see below, § 120.

Direct and Indirect Speech.

§ 107. Both the direct and the indirect speech (oratio recta, oratio obliqua) may be apprehended as substantive sentences. The former is anterior to the latter, and there is a construction which may perhaps be looked upon as a remnant of the stage of transition from direct to indirect speech by means of *that* added to the principal sentence.

"He sayd full angerly to the styward, *that* to an euyll owre hath your lady ben so madde as to mary her self to a ladde, a straunger."—CAXTON, *Blanchardyn*, 184, 9.

"Merlyn late wryte balyns name on the tombe with letters of gold, *that* here lyeth balyn le Saueage."—*Morte d'Arthur*, 98, 35.

"*I said* THAT '*all the years* invent;
. . . . .
Were this not well to bide mine hour
Tho' watching from a ruined tower
How grows the day of human power?'"
                              TENNYSON, *The Two Voices.*

There are other instances in the Bible, but these are probably faithfully copied from the Greek original.

Gothic.—"Quiþandans þatei praufetus mikils urrais in unsis" (saying, A great prophet is arisen among us).—*Luke,* vii. 16.

Old English.—" And cwǽdon, þæt mære witega on ús árás." (Same verse.)

Cf. *Old French.*
"Quant Joseph ha ce entendu,
Mout liez et mout joianz en fu
Et dist *que* 'ce n'est pas a moi
Meis au seigneur en cui je croi.'"

(When Joseph has heard that, he was very glad and joyful therefore and said *that* "it is not to me but to the Lord in whom I believe ").—*Saint Graal,* 2321.

Change of Direct and Indirect Speech.

"(Huon) embrassyd *hym* and sayde how often tymes *he* had sene Guyer, *his* brother the prouost, wepe for *you,* and whan *I* departyd fro Burdeux I delyveryd to him all my londes to gouerne."—LORD BERNERS' *Huon,* 62, 31, 32.

"They told him that *they* were poor pilgrims going to Zion, but were led out of their way by a black man, clothed in white, who bid *us,* they said, follow him."—BUNYAN, *Pilgrim's Progress,* 133.

§ 108. The indirect speech, though it may be traced back to the oldest periods, is something artificial, and was always felt as such. In poetry and popular writings we notice a certain struggle against the constraint; hence the many examples of sudden transition from the indirect to the more natural direct speech.

Latin.—"Diogenes censet, si voluptas aut si bona valetudo sit in bonis, divitias quoque in bonis esse ponendas ; at si sapientia bonum sit, non sequi, ut etiam divitias bonum esse dicamus. Neque ab ulla re, quæ non sit in bonis, id, quod sit in bonis, nulla ars divitiis contineri potest."—C. *Fin.* iii. 15, 49.

"Videmusne nullum ab iis, qui in certamen descendant, devitari dolorem ? Apud quos autem venandi et equitandi laus viget, qui hanc petessunt, nullum fugiunt dolorem."—*Tusc.* ii. 26, 62.

Old Saxon.—"quað, that im neriandas ginist ginâhid wâri ; 'nu is the hêlago Krist kuman'" (quoth, that the Saviour's salvation was near ; "now is Holy Christ come ").—HELIAND, 521.

Old English.—" þa cuædon *hie* þæt hie *hie* þæs ne onmunden þon má þe *eowre* geféran þe mid þam cyninge ofslægene wǽrun " (*they* said moreover that they should mind that [offer] "no more than did *your* mates who were slain with the king."—*Chronicle,* 755.

"ða cwæð se cyng. ðæt mihte beon geboden him wið clænum legere. ac ic hæbbe ealle ða spæce to Aelfhege læten" (then said the king, that that might be offered him, in consideration of a grave in consecrated ground: "but I have given over the whole discussion to Aeltheah").—EARLE, *Handbook to Land Charters*, p. 201. (EARLE, *English Prose*, p. 379.)

Middle English.
"Wex derke, ðis coren is gon,
Jacob eft bit hem faren agon,
Oc he ne duren ðe weie cumen in,
'but go wið us senden beniamin.'"

(It became dark [dearth?], the corn is gone,
Jacob bade them go again,
But they durst not go the way,
"but *ye* send with us Benjamin.")
Story of Genesis and Exodus, 2240.

"The dewke depyed Gye there
And bad, yf hys wylle were,
That Harrawde schulde haue wyth hym eche dell
Fyve hundurde knyghtys armed well
And wende forthe, wythowte fayle,
Boldely them for to assayle,
'And ye, syr Gye, a thousande
Bolde men and wele bydande'".
Guy of Warwick, ed. Zupitza, 1785.

THE ADJECTIVE CLAUSE.

The Oldest Stage of the Adjective Clause (Omission of the Relative Pronoun).

"I know a charm shall make thee meek and tame."—SHELLEY.

§ 109. The oldest shape of the adjective clause was also that of two sentences put together without any outward mark of connection (conjunction).

"Hér on þis geáre gefór Aelfred wæs æt Baðum geréfa." (In this year went hence Alfred [who] was count in Bath.)—*Chronicle*, 906 (Parker MS.).

But while the other clauses, *e.g.*, those determining time, look in appearance like independent co-ordinate sentences, and may be apprehended as such, it is quite different with the adjective clause. In the following instance, "*Se fæder hire sealde áne þeówene Bala hátte*" (the father gave her a servant [who] was called Bala), *Genesis*, xxix. 29, the clause *Bala hátte* may perhaps be looked upon as an independent sentence, but the following passage cannot be interpreted in the same way.

"Þis is ánlícnes engelcynna þæs bremestan, mid þam burgwarum in þære ceastre is" (this is a true image of the most famous of the hosts of angels [who] is in the hall with the inhabitants of the castle).— ANDREAS, 717.

§ 110. In fact, the adjective clauses are felt from the very outset as subordinate to the principal sentence, and the whole construction may be apprehended as a sentence *with one subject and two predicates.* This is the so-called construction ἀπὸ κοινοῦ. The starting point was afforded by sentences of the type exhibited in the following instances :

"In war was never lion [that] raged more fierce."—*Richard II.* ii. 1, 173.

"There be some sports are painful."—*Tempest*, iii. 1, 1.

"There is a devil haunts thee."—1 *Henry IV.* ii. 4, 492.

where the common subject of the two sentences stands in the middle. The next step was to use the same construction also with an object in the middle, as in the following examples :

"I have a brother [who] is condemned to die."—*Measure for Measure*, ii. 2, 33.

"I have a mind [which] presages."—*Merchant*, i. 1, 175.

"And sue a friend [who] 'came debtor for my sake."—*Sonnets*, 139.

Later on, there came in also constructions, in which the common clause takes precedence, or is inserted between the first predicate and its qualification. In this use it may serve as subject, or as object, or as any other kind of adverbial qualification; and further, it need not necessarily bear the same relation to both predicates.

Cf. the following passages:

"What wreck discern you in me [that]
Deserves your pity?"
Cymbeline, i. 6, 84.

"You are one of those [who]
Would have him wed again."
Winter's Tale, v. 1, 23.

"Declare the cause [for which]
My father, Earl of Cambridge, lost his head."
1 *Henry VI.* ii. 6, 86.

§ 111. The construction ἀπὸ κοινοῦ is not a construction peculiar to the Teutonic or Indo-European languages; it is founded on a common psychological principle, and we may safely say that it has sprung spontaneously into existence at several epochs and in different languages independent of and without connection with one another.

Old High German.—"thaz selba sie imo sagêtun, sie hiar bifora zelitun" (they said the same thing to him that they had said before).—OTFRID, iv. 16, 46.

"wer ist, thes hiar thenke?" (who is here that could think such a thing?).—*Ibid.* iii. 16, 30.

"nist man nihein in worolti, thaz saman al irsagêti" (there is no one in the world who could tell all that together).—*Ibid.* i. 17, 1.

Old English.—"Mid heora cyningum, Rædgota and Eallerica wǽron hátene, Románe burig ábrǽcon" (with their kings [who] were called Radagisus and Alaric they stormed the city).—BOETH. I.

Similar instances with the verb *hátan* are frequent.

"Hér on þys geáre gefór Aelfred wæs æt Baðum geréfa." (In this year died Alfred [who] was gerefa in Bath.)—*Chronicle*, 907.

"Ac forðon monige seondon on Ongolðeode, [þa þe] þissum maanfullum gesinscipum wǽron gemengde sægde—ac heo beon to monienne, þæt heo ahebban heo from swylcum unrihtum" (but as there are many in England [who] were said to have been united in this sinful wedlock, so they are to be warned to abstain from such unrighteousness).—*Beda*, i. 27.

Middle English.—" þa he com to þere dune oliveti is ihaten " (when he came to the hill which is called Olivetus).—*Old English Homilies*, i. 3 A.D. 1200.

" ðowgte ðis quead, 'hu ma it ben,
Adam ben king and eue quuen
Of alle ðe ðinge in werlde ben.'"

(The wicked one [Satan] thought: how may it be that Adam is king and Eve queen of all things [which] are in the world.)—*Story of Genesis and Exodus*, 297, A.D. 1250.

" Abram, ðu fare ut of lond and kin
To a lond ic ðe sal bringen hin."

(Abraham, go thou from this land and thy kin, to a land [that] I shall bring thee to.)—*Ibid.* 738.

" Nov ist a water of loðlic ble,
Men callið it ðe dede se;
Ilc ðing deieð ðor-inne is driuen."

(There is a water of lothly colour, men call it the Dead Sea; everything dies [that] is driven therein.)—*Ibid.* 751.

Cf. also *ibid.* 3672.

" He spoken þer-offe, and chosen sone
A riche man was under mone."

(They spoke thereof and soon chose a rich man [that] was under the moon.)—HAVELOK, 373, A.D. 1280.

"Vor þou art mon of strange londe, and Cristine non non, and eke þei icholde myne barons hit wolde wiþsege echon" (for thou art a stranger, and no Christian, and also they [whom] I hold my barons will gainsay everyone).—*Robert of Gloucester*, 2490.

At the end of the thirteenth century the omission of the relative pronoun is quite common, as may be seen from the following figures. The relative pronoun is wanting in the *Cursor Mundi*, A.D. ab. 1300, lines 82, 240, 2392, 2504, 3186, 3359, 3993, 4892, 5202, 5264, 5302, 5916, 6976, 7096, 7112, 7188, 7192, 7868, 7873, 8056, 8212, 8561, 8635, 9062, 10071, 10285, 10395, 10552, 10677, 10741, 10848, 10899, 11187, 11472, 11603, 11666, &c.

Development of the Adjective Clause.

§ 112. Though the hypotactic (subordinate) adjective clause turns up in the oldest periods of English, a thousand years of development elapsed before it appeared in its modern shape. Only at the end of the fifteenth century do we see the relative clause in its modern garb. There is an essential psychological and grammatical difference between the old construction, which is still met with in colloquial and vulgar speech, and the concise expression which is the rule in good conversation and literary works. The adjective clause of the older periods is deficient in point of consistency and unity—it is pleonastic and anacoluthic—the modern one is grammatically correct.

"for *he* that smytes, *he* shal be smyten."—*Townley Mysteries*, p. 188.

"Now tourne we unto sire Lamorak *that* upon a daye *he* took a lytel Barget and his wyf . . ."—*Morte d'Arthur*, 330, 24.

"The londe *that* they hold, gyue *it* to Charlot your sone."—BERNERS, *Huon*, 5, 13.

§ 113. As in many other cases, the construction of the older periods is more appropriate to the psychical facts, while the modern one is ruled by logical considerations. In the following instances—"*they* that were about hym rebell, he dompted and subdewed *them*" (Caxton, *Charles the Grete*); "*he* that berethe the diamond upon him, it geueth *hym* hardynesse and manhode" (Maundeville, p. 159)—"they" and "he" are, no doubt, the psychological subjects—that is, they are prominent in the mind of the speaker, and it is to them that the predicate is applied. The modern speaker would also think in this case of *they* and *he* as subjects, but he is trained to think in whole sentences, therefore he sees before that there are other subjects following which require "them" and "him" as their logical objects, and he would begin accordingly with "them" and "him."

F

There are three principal types of relative constructions :—

1. *The Antecedent or Correlative is a Noun in a Complete Sentence, which is followed by a many-worded Adjective or Relative Clause.*

"He tires betimes, *that* spurs too fast betimes."—SHAKSPERE.

§ 114. If the relative pronoun is in the nominative case, the construction, as a rule, is as regular as that of the quoted instance. But the older periods exhibit a pleonastic personal pronoun.

"Ine þise zenȝeþ moche uolk : ine uele maneres, ase þise fole wyfmen, þet uor a lite wynnynge, hy yueþ ham to zenne." (In this, many people sin in many ways, as these foolish women, *that* for a little winning *they* give themselves to sin.)—*Ayenbite*, 45.

"A knight there was, and that a worthy man,
That, from the tyme that he first began
To ryden out, *he* lovede chyvalrye."
CHAUCER, *Cant. Tales, Prol.* 43—45.

"here is a worshipfull knyght sir Lamorak, *that* for me *he* shal be lord of this countreye."—*Morte d'Arthur*, 334, 2.

"sir Trystram, *that* by aduenture *he* cam . . ."—*Ibid.* 407, 21.

The Relative is an Oblique Case.

"Mrs. Boffin, which her father's name was Henry."—DICKENS.

§ 115. Then, as a rule, the relatives are used in connection with the corresponding preposition, "Of whom, to whom, whom or which," &c. But there are exceptions in this case too. Instead of the simple relatives we find—

In the genitive : relative + his (her), their.

In the dative and accusative : relative + him (her, it), them.

Old English.—"Hwæt se god wære, þe þis *his* beácen was" (who that god was, whose sign this was).—*Elene*, 162.

Middle English.—"þe pope Gregorie þþat ȝe fende *him* hadde wel neiȝ icauȝt" (the pope Gregory whom the fiend had nearly caught).—*Gregorius*, 16, *a*.

"a doughter þþat wiþ *hire* was hire moder ded" (a daughter with whom her dead mother was).—*Ibid.* 32, *a*.

"*the whiche* thenne, by old age and lyuynge many yeres, *his* blood was wexen colde."—CAXTON, *Eneydos*, 14, 21.

"of *whom* may not well be recounted the valyaunce *of hym*."—CAXTON, *Charles the Grete*, 38, 20.

This use continued in the sixteenth century.

Tudor English.—"I know no man lyuyng *that* I or my brother haue done *to hym* any dyspleasure."—BERNERS, *Huon*, 19, 24.

"*the whiche treasure* I gaaf *part thereof* to the kynge."—*Ibid.* 263, 9.

"I pray thee, show me what be yonder two prynces, that goth up the stayres, and *that* so moch honour is done *to them*."—*Ibid.* 286, 9.

II. *The Correlative Sentence is divided into two parts by the Relative Clause.*

"No man hath seen God at any time; *the only begotten Son*, which is in the bosom of the Father, *he* hath declared him."—*John*.

§ 116. In Old and Middle English this type is nearly always a sort of anacoluthon to our modern eyes and ears, and perhaps it was such indeed. The essential point in which this construction differs from the modern use is, that *the correlative always appears in the nominative case*, without regard to its place in the sentence; it is only the redundant pronoun, personal or possessive in the second part, which marks the subjective or objective case of the correlative; *e.g.*, "and *she* that was not lerned to receyue suche geestes, sore harde was his acquaintance *to her*" (Caxton's *Blanch.*,

67, 29, 30). Accordingly we may distinguish two groups of type II.

§ 117. (*a*) The correlative is the subject of the sentence. Then the redundant *personal* pronoun appears in the nominative case.

This pronoun is very frequent in Old English and Middle English. Perhaps we might say that this is the rule; at least the *Old English Homilies* seem to suggest such a supposition. There are in the second series 23 instances of the redundant pronoun, while only six passages omit it. Later Middle English tends to restrict the use of the personal pronoun.

§ 118. (*b*) The correlative is, logically, the object (direct or indirect) of the sentence; then, as a rule, it is in the nominative case, and the redundant personal pronoun is either in the genitive (his, her, their) or dative (accusative) case.

Old English.—"þi þe God séceað ne áspringeð *him* nán gód" (they that seek God, no good shall ever fail them).—*Ps.* xxxiii. 10.

Middle English.—"Alle synfulle men þe heued-synnes don habbeð, and nelleð þerof no shrift nimen he bihat *hem* eche fur on helle." (*All sinful men* who have done capital sins, and will not take shrift thereof, he threateneth *them* with eternal fire in hell.)—*Old E. Hom.* ii. 41.

"þey þat etys me ȝitt hungres *thaym*, and þey þat drinkes me, ȝitt þristes *thaym*" (they that eat me, yet they are hungry, and they that drink me, yet they are thirsty).—HAMPOLE, *Prose Treat.* p. 3.

"he perceyued a right mighty nauey, wherof *they* that were come upon lande, he sawe *hem* in grete nombre."—CAXTON, *Blanch.* 162, 3.

Tudor English.—"With my sworde I so defendyd me, that *he that* thought to haue slayne me, I haue slayne *hym*."—BERNERS, *Huon*, 27, 5, 6.

"*He that* lieth there deed before you, I slew *him* in my defence."—*Ibid.* 34, 11.

"*all the mete that* he could get in the towne, he shuld by *it*."—*Ibid.* 84, 33.

III. *The Relative Sentence precedes its Correlative.*

"*Who alone suffers*, suffers most i' the mind."—SHAKSPERE.

§ 119. The use of the personal pronoun in the correlative is the same as in type II. In Old and Middle English the pronoun is almost the rule, its omission is quite exceptional. The pleonastic personal pronoun occurs in the sixteenth century as well, and here and there in modern times.

"Whosoever that hath not seene the noble citie of Venis, *he* hath not seene the bewyte and ryches of thys worlde."—ANDREW BOORDE, *Introduction and Dyetary*, p. 181.

"whosoeuer wil buylde a mancyon place or a house, *he* must cytuate it . . ."—*Ibid.* p. 233.

Cf. ibid. pp. 236, 238, 242.

Shakspere has often *what—it:*

"*What* our contempt doth often hurl from us,
We wish *it* ours again."
Antony, i. 2, 127.

"*What* you have spoke, *it* may be so perchance."
Macbeth, iv. 3, 11.

Noun-Clause and Adjective-Clause intermixed.

"I bring you something, my dear, *that* (*I believe*) *will make you smile*."—GOLDSMITH.

"And in these fits I leave them, while I visit
Young Ferdinand *whom* they suppose is drowned."
SHAKSPERE, *Tempest*, iii. 3, 92.

§ 120. Whenever the object noun-clause is at the same time an adjectival one, we now use a sort of parenthesis in order to avoid the clumsiness and confusion arising out of two clauses interlaced with each other. Thus we say, "The origin of his own practice, *which* he says *was a tendency* he never could deviate from" (Lewes); or, with a more accurate punctuation, "The origin of his own practice, which,

he says, was a tendency he never could deviate from." In this instance the noun-clause is replaced by the interpolated principal sentence. But this is not the oldest stage of the construction. In Old and Middle English (and here and there in modern times) the noun-clause was treated as if it were dependent on the preceding adjectival clause. Thus the following instance, " I am he *that thou knowe that dyd doo destroye* [whom thou knowest did cause to be destroyed] Rome your cyte, and slewe the Pope and many other, and bare awaye the relyques that I there founde" (*Charles the Grete*, 52, 30), may be decomposed into three parts:—
I am he + that thou knowe (adjective-clause) + that dyd doo destroye (noun-clause).

Old English.—" Eác wæs gesewen on þæm wage atifred ealle þa heargas Israhela folces, & eac sio gitsung þe *Sanctus Paulus cwæð ðæt wære hearga & idelnesse geféra* " (there were also seen painted on the wall all the idols of the people of Israel, and also the cupidity *which St. Paul said was* the companion of idols and vanity).—*Cura Pastoralis*, 156, 5.

Tudor English.—" The fayr pucelle and proude in amours myght not seasse nor leue her sorowe therfore that she contynually made for her right dere frende blanchardyn; that for the loue of her *she trowed that he had other be lost or ded.*"—CAXTON, *Blanchardyn*, 120, 11.

"And so shull ye haue wel rewarded me of all *that ye say that* my brother and I haue don for you and for your realme."—*Melusine*, 153, 1.

§ 121. The construction becomes less clear when *that* introducing the noun-clause is dropped (*cf.* I know he is good).

"and thanne all they that were there bygan to sorowe and wepe for the pyte they had of the kyng, And also of the sorow that they sawe [that] the virgyne, his daughter, made so pitously."—*Melusine*, 154, 22.

Hence the following expressions:

"Of Arthur *whom* they say *is killed* to-night."
King John, iv. 2, 165.

"The nobility . . . *whom* we see *have sided.*"
Coriolanus, iv. 2, 2.

Relative Subordination instead of Demonstrative Co-ordination.

"Caius Ligarius doth bear Cæsar hard,
 Who [since he] rated him for speaking well of Pompey."
                                            SHAKSPERE.

§ 122. This function of the relative pronoun is due to the influence of the Latin, which favours the subordination in every respect. There are faint beginnings of this imitation in the last centuries of the Middle English period, but they develop into full bloom in Elizabethan times.

Middle English.—" Sithen the storiyng which Girald makith of this voice is this, It is rad that such voice was in the eir, et cætera, Girald ʒildith him silfin so storiyng that he is not the fundamental storier ther of, but that ther of is an other storie bifore him, fro which he takith his storiyng of the same voice : *wherfore* if noon other storie be founde eeldir than the storie of Girald, in which eeldir storie mensioun is maad of this same voice . . . it folcwith that at the leest vnto thilk eelder storiyng be founde, the storiyng of Girald in mater of this voice is not to be bileeued."—PECOCK, *Repressor*, p. 356.

Cf. ibid. p. 496.

Modern English.
"*Archbishop.* It was young Hotspur's case at Shrewsbury.
 Lord Bardolph. It was, my lord : *who* [for he] lined himself with hope."—2 *Hen. IV.* i. 3, 27.

" A large glass of claret was offered to Mannering, *who* [= and he] drank it to the health of the reigning prince." — SCOTT, *Guy Mannering*, 36.

The Adverbial Clauses.

§ 123. Though the original state of coordination is still kept in Old and Middle English, the modern shape of these clauses, their complete subordination, is found in the oldest stages of English. The development of these clauses consists in the change which the particles, the mood, and the order of words have undergone.

Adverbial Clauses relating to Place.

" *Where a great regular army exists,* limited monarchy, such as it was in the middle ages, can exist no longer."—MACAULAY, *History of England,* i. 41.

§ 124. The state of parataxis is marked in Old and Middle English by the correlative use of the same particles; in Modern English there is sometimes correlation, but the particle in the dependent clause is always different from that in the principal sentence, so that the subordination is made perceptible.

Old English.—" þær þin goldhord ys, þær ys þin heorte " (where thy treasure is, there is thy heart).—*Matthew,* vi. 21.

Middle English.— " ffor *ther* he is, *ther* wold he be."—*Coventry Myst.* p. 323.

Adverbial Clauses relating to Time.

"*When Columbus arrived at Cordova,* the court was like a military camp."—IRVING, *Columbus,* 2, 3.

§ 125. These keep the correlation of the particles even longer than the clauses relating to place.

Old English.—" And þá þá he slép þá genam he án ribb of his sídan " (and when he slept, he took a rib out of his side).—*Genesis,* ii. 21.

Middle English.—" þa þis folc isomed wes . . . þa sette þe kaisere arimen al þæne here " (when this folk was assembled, the emperor caused all the army to be counted).—*Laȝam.* iii. 6.

"And *thenne* Beaumayns sawe hym soo well horsed and armed, *thenne* he alyghte doune and armed hym."—*Morte d'Arthur,* 222, 26.

Tudor English.—" *Then* Gerames saw how the shipp was commynge to that porte, *then* he sayd to hys company . . ."—LORD BERNERS, *Huon,* 129, 11.

§ 126. The transition of local into temporal and modal meaning which we shall notice with regard to prepositions and conjunctions, takes place in adverbial clauses. Hence local and temporal clauses are sometimes used to denote causal, conditional, and adversative relations. *Cf.* the following instances.

Causal.   " Yet not to Earth's contracted span
            Thy goodness let me bound,
            Or think thee Lord alone of Man,
            When thousand worlds are round."
                            POPE, *Universal Prayer.*

Conditional.—" It is never well to put ungenerous constructions, *when others, equally plausible and more honorable are ready.*"—LEWES, *Goethe's Life,* i. 8.

Adversative.—"*When they will not give a doit to relieve a lame beggar,* they will lay out ten to see a dead Indian."—SHAKSPERE, *Tempest,* ii. 2, 33.

Adverbial Clauses relating to Manner and Degree.

" He is just as good as he is wise."

§ 127. In this kind of clause too the correlation is more frequent in Old and Middle English than in modern times.

The modal clauses often become causal ones.

Old English.
            " Þu scealt greót etan
            þine lífdagas, swá þu láðlíce
            wróhte onstealdest."

(Thou shalt eat dust all the days of thy life, as thou committedest a loathly crime.)—CÆDMON, *Genesis,* 910.

Middle English.
            " Lete me fro this deth fle,
            As I dede nevyr no trespace."
                            Coventry Myst. p. 281.

Modern English.—" My eldest son George was bred at Oxford, as I intended him for one of the learned professions."—GOLDSMITH, *Vicar.*

§ 128. They are also used in a concessive sense.

Old English.
" Swá he us ne mæg ǽnige synne gestǽlan,
  þæt we him on þam lande láð gefremedon, he hæfð us þeáh þæs leóhtes
  bescyrede."

(Though he cannot accuse us of any sin . . . he has robbed us of the light.)—CÆDMON, *Genesis*, 391.

Middle English.—"heo makede him sunegen (sin) on hire, *so holi king ase he was.*"—*Ancren Riwle*, p. 56.

" for Longeus that olde kny[gh]t, blynd *as* he was,
  A ry[gh]t sharpe spere to Crystes herte shall pythe."
                                              Coventry Mysteries, 14.

Modern English.
" *Fond as we are, and justly fond of faith,*
  Reason, we grant, demands our first regard."
                                              YOUNG.

Adverbial Clauses relating to Cause.

" I thank my God *that I believe you not.*"—SHELLEY.

" Freely we serve *because we freely love.*"—MILTON.

§ 129. The former instance illustrates the close relation between the noun clauses and the causal ones. In fact, every causal clause may be expressed also by an abbreviated subject or object noun clause, *e.g.* It makes me angry to think of his behaviour = I get angry when I think of his behaviour.

For modal clauses turning into causal ones see above, § 127.

Adverbial Clauses relating to Purpose and Consequence.

" Satan has desired to have you, *that he may sift you as wheat.*"—*Luke*, xxii. 31.

" The roads were so bad that few travellers had ever visited it."—MACAULAY.

§ 130. There are two noteworthy points in the development of these clauses.

1. While in Old English the subjunctive is the rule in final clauses, it begins to give way to the indicative in Middle English, and tends to disappear altogether in modern times. See Mood, § 380–391.

2. Instead of a consecutive clause with *that*, the gerundial infinitive comes in in a double function.

(*a*) When the subject is the same in the principal sentence and clause, *as* is now used after *so, as, such,* while in older periods there was no particle at all. *As* comes in as early as 1429 A.D.

"Do me this ease *as to* len (lend) me yor chariott."—Letter written by Salisbury, the Kingmaker's father, quoted by Mr. Oliphant :—*The New English,* i. 241.

"(I was) at such a distance *as* never to hear from any part of the world that had the least knowledge of me."—DEFOE, *Robinson Crusoe,* p. 60.

(*b*) When the subject is not the same, we sometimes find the *infinitive with for.*

"No drinking to find the King's cursed shilling at the bottom of the glass, *for thy mother to come* crying and pestering."—CRAIK, *John Halifax,* i. 26.

"She (the boat) was too low in the water *for it to be* possible for us to blow her up."—LADY BRASSEY, *Voyage in the* "*Sunbeam,*" i. 20.

Adverbial Clauses relating to Condition.

"*If you have tears,* prepare to shed them now."—SHAKSPERE.

§ 131. The distinction between conditional clauses implying reality, and those expressing a mere conception of the mind, steps more and more to the background in Modern English, as may be seen from the fact, that the subjunctive mood which is characteristic of the latter kind of conditional clauses, tends to be more and more replaced by the indicative. See Mood, § 381-391.

This clause may also be replaced by the infinitive with *for*.

"I should be glad *for you to hear* what we are saying."—M. EDGEWORTH, *Popular Tales*, i. 301.

Imperative Sentences are often used in a Conditional Sense.

§ 132. "*Suppose he should relent* . . . with what eyes could we stand in his presence?"—MILTON, *Paradise Lost*, ii. 237.

"Tell me a liar, and I'll tell you a thief."

"Live thou, live I."—*Merchant of Venice*, iii. 2, 61.

Cf. Latin: *cras petito: dabitur* (Plautus); *sint Maecenates, non desunt, Flacce, Marones* (Martial).

§ 133. *Note.* In Middle English the relative clause is often used for the conditional one (*Cf.* who touches pitch, will be defiled = if somebody, &c.).

"Qua has to wenden ani wai
God es to go bi light o dai."

(Who has to go some way, it is good to go at daylight).—*Cursor Mundi*, 14194.

"He, that seyth, hyt ys any odur,
I wyll hyt preue, þogh he were my brodur."
Guy of Warwick, 669.

Tudor English.—"And I promyse you, that who shall hange Richarde, I shall goo to Reynawde, and shall put myself in hys pryson."—CAXTON, *Aymon*, 326, 23.

"for who that might take them fro the sarasyns, none of them shuld neuer retourne foot, in sury nor in thursy."—*Melusine*, 169, 32.

This usage is common in Old and Modern French. Qui prendrait garde de si près, jamais il ne sèmerait.—Qui se fait brebis, le loup le mange.

PART II

SYNTAX OF THE PARTS OF SPEECH

SYNTAX OF THE PARTS OF SPEECH

THE SUBSTANTIVE

Substantives used as Adjectives.

"The *chiefest* captain of Mycetes' host."
MARLOWE, *Tamburlaine*, 58.

"I have found thee *proof* against all temptation."
MILTON.

§ 134. WELL known as are the faults of the customary division of the parts of speech, there is a good foundation in general for the distinction between the substantive and the adjective, the former denoting substance, the latter quality. Occasionally, however, an adjective is converted into a substantive, *e.g., the righteous, the poor.*

Less familiar and more interesting is the converse process, the transformation of a substantive into an adjective. This comes about through the elimination of some part of its meaning—including at least the notion of substance—so that only the qualities attaching to the substance remain. This transformation virtually occurs as an occasional use, whenever a substantive is employed as a predicate, or attribute.[1] *Cfr.* Greek: ἀνὴρ πολίτης, ῥήτωρ, γυνὴ δέσποινα,

---

[1] *Cf.* F. Max Müller, *The Science of Thought*, p. 427.

παρθένος χείρ. Latin : "*exercitus victor*" (Livy); "*tirones milites*" (Cicero).

§ 135. In Middle and Modern English several Old English substantives became adjectives. First, they were parts of compounds, later on they got separated, and were used independently in an attributive sense.

Mán in Old English means sin, wickedness; but when forming the first part of a compound, it means "wicked," *e.g. mánað* (wicked oath, perjury. German : *meineid*), *mándǽd* (wicked deed). In the *Cursor Mundi* "man" occurs as an independent adjective.

"Bi fals godds suer ye nan,
Athes noiþer sothfast ne *man*."

(Swear not by false gods, neither true oaths nor false.)—6848.

On the same principle the following passages may be explained.

"For to make Gye to do message
To the sowdan, that ys so *rage*."
Guy of Warwick, 3474.

In old English *yrre* means both *anger* and *angry*.

French—il est colère.

"A broche *gold* and *asure*."
CHAUCER, *Troylus and Cryseyde*, iii. 321.

"The necke and hed that weren *golde*
He said how that betoken sholde."
GOWER, *Confessio Amantis*, i. 25.

"Men of levyng ben so *outrage*,
That . . . God wyl be vengyd on us sum way."
Coventry Mysteries, p. 41.

§ 136. In Modern English there are several instances of this double function of the substantive, viz., the words *cheap, chief, choice, dainty, earnest, proof*.

Cheap, originally sb. = barter, price (Old E. *ceáp*, Middle E. *chep*). The older idiom was 'to buy *good cheap*'; cf. French : bon marché. See below, § 194.

SYNTAX OF THE PARTS OF SPEECH

As late as the sixteenth century it is used in the same way.

"Aquitaine is the most plentifullest country for good bred and wine, consideryng the good *chep*, that I was ever in."—ANDREW BOORDE, *Introduction and Dyetary*, p. 194.

Chief was already an independent adjective in Elizabethan times, as may be seen by its being used in the comparative and superlative degrees.[1]

Choice, too, is found in the superlative degree.

"And heaven consum'd his *choicest* living fire."
MARLOWE, *Tamburlaine*, 4642.

For *dainty, earnest, proof*, see the Dictionaries.

Occasionally substantives are used as adjectives metaphorically.

"She was not thought sufficient fortune for him."—RICHARDSON, *Pamela*, 136, *b*.

In other instances this use is perhaps due to the omission of a particle.

"I had never furnished the people with bread that was not weight."—EDGEWORTH, *Popular Tales*, ii. 15.

"She was his own age."—W. BESANT, *Such a Good Man*, p. 20.

"Dear me, what a colour you are."—J. PAYN, *Found Dead*, p. 67.

CLASSES OF NOUNS INTERCHANGED.

Abstracts and Concretes interchanged.

§ 137. Grammarians, following the old system of logic, used to classify nouns—with reference to the mode in which they existed—into concrete and abstract, collective, proper and individual names. But this classification, though it may

---

[1] There is, however, one instance as early as 1400. See *The New Engl. Dict.* s. vv.

perhaps be applied to the advanced stages of human speech, when the creative imagination is no longer at work, will not hold good when tested by historical research. The science of language teaches us that all names were orginally both abstract and general. Every name was formed from one root, every root expressed originally a conception; if, therefore, anything had to be named, its name, as derived from a root, could predicate one attribute only. Hence, even though the name was meant for an individual object, it was, by necessity, the name of other objects likewise, of all things, in fact, which shared in the same attribute, or, of a class of things, until by the necessities of language, as a means of communication, it was more and more restricted, more and more defined, so that at last it meant one concrete object only.

This abstract and general character was innate in every word, and though it became hidden when words were applied to singular and concrete things, it breaks out again at once, as soon as the singular and concrete things vanish more and more from our mental focus, while the name remains what it was from the beginning, abstract and general.[1]

Hence the transition of abstracts into concretes, and *vice versâ* is to be met with in the earliest period of English as well as in the poetry and prose of our own day.

A few instances will do for our purpose.

§ 138. *Abstract Nouns used in a Concrete Sense.*

"Tormént, sweet friend, that base and crooked *age*,
That durst disswade me from thy Lucifer."
MARLOWE, *Faustus*, A, 1348.

Old English.—*Duguð*. (1) virtue, valour.

"Syððan ic for *dugeðum* Dæghrefne wearð to hand-bonan, Huga cempan" (since I, out of valour, became the murderer of D. the warrior of the Hugs). —*Beowulf*, 2502.

[1] *Cf.* M. Müller, *l.c.* 457 ff

(2) valiant men, warriors.

"Duguð unlytel Dena and Wedera" (many men of the Danes and W.).—*Ibid.* 498.

Geoguð. (1) youth, state of youth.

"hæbbe ic mærða fela ongunnen on geoguðe" (I began many famous exploits in my *youth*).—*Ibid.* 409.

(2) *òð þæt seó geoguð geweóx* (until the *youthful men* grew) *ibid.* 66.

Fultum. (1) help.

(2) army, very often so in the *Chronicle* and in quotation below.

Mægen. (1) power.

(2) army.

Cf. also *riht* (right, and property), *wuldor* (glory, and the glorious one), *þrym* (power, the powerful one).

Middle English.—*Lyf*, life = man.

"Some had lyf-lode of here lynage and of no *lyf* elles."—*Piers Plowman*, C. Passus, x. l. 197.

Several times in *Piers Plowman*. *Cf.* Skeat's *Notes* (*Early English Text Society*), pp. 193, 248, 391.

Retynaunce = a suit of retainers.

"And al þe riche retynaunce . . . were bede to þat brudale" (all the retainers were invited to the bridal).—*Ibid.* C. Passus, iii. 55.

Message = messenger, Chaucer, *Man of Lawes Tale*, 333.

Modern English.—Very frequent in Elizabethan times.

Adversity = loathsome fellow. *Troilus*, v. 1, 14; *admiration* = admirable person. *All's Well*, v. 1, 91; *affliction* = afflicted woman. *King John*, iii. 4, 36; *age* = old man. See above. *Ambition* = that which is coveted by the ambitious; *ancientry* = old people. *Winter's Tale*, iii. 3, 63; *baseness* = base fellow. *Merry Wives*, ii. 2, 21; *cure* = patient, person to be cured. Lyly, *Euphues*, p. 42; *favour* = a token of love. Marlowe, *Edw*. ii. 977; *thrift* = savings. Andrew Boorde, *Introduction and Dyetary*, 117, 32 (as now); of a more recent date are: *business* (Middle English, only the quality of being busy, active); *fare* = passenger; *farm* (Middle English = lease); *refuse*.

§ 139. *Concrete Nouns used in an Abstract Sense.*

"The *top* of my ambition is to contribute to that work."—POPE.

Old English.—*Hleó.* (1) Shelter, roof. *Swegles hleó*, the shelter of the sky. *Elene*, 507.

(2) protection. þæt he þone stán nime wið hungres hleó (that he take the stone as protection from hunger), *ibid*. 616. It occurs very often as an attribute of princes in Old English epic poetry.

Ord. (1) point, sword. (2) beginning. See Grein.
Ríce. (1) kingdom. (2) power. See Grein.

Middle English.—*Blood* = relationship. Skeat's *Notes to Piers Plowman*, p. 425.

Chief = beginning. CAXTON, *Blanchardyn*, 17, 4.

Hede in the same sense. *Morte d'Arthur*, 144, 8.

Modern English.—Instances abound, *e.g. field* = battle, *source* = origin, *top* = height, etc.

§ 140. *Collective Nouns used as Class Nouns.*

Real collective terms like *humanitas* (mankind), very easily become what are called secondary abstract terms. M. Müller, *l.c.* p. 449. Then, through the medium of abstraction, they become class nouns.

In this way several Modern English words can be easily explained.

Fairy in Middle English means (1) enchantment, (2) fairyland, (3) the people of fairyland. It was not until the sixteenth century that fairy became, from a collective, a common noun = one of the fairy.

> "The feasts that underground the *Faërie* did him make,
> And there how he enjoy'd the Lady of the Lake."
> DRAYTON, *Polyolbion*, iv. 307.

Paynim, Old French : *paienisme ;* Latin : *paganismus.* See Skeat, s. v.

County is often used = count, in the sixteenth century.

> "Gismund, who loves the *county* Palurin
> Guiscard, who quites her likings with his love."
> *Tancred and Gismunda*, p. 23.

Cfr. Greene, *Orlando Furioso*, p. 90, 91, 92, 94, 95.

§ 141. *Proper Names used as Common Names.*

> "You look like a *guy*."

Middle English.—*A Christofre*—

> "(He bar) on his brest of silver schene."

Chaucer, *Prologue*, 115 = a figure of St. Christopher, a brooch.

A Donet = a grammar, originally Aelius Donatus, the Latin grammarian, often in Middle English literature. See Skeat, *Notes to Piers Plowman*, p. 119.

A Lazar = a leper, from Lazarus.

> "He knew the taverns wel in every toun,
> And everych hostiler and tappestere,
> Bet then a *lazar*, or a beggestere."
> CHAUCER, *Prol.* 242; *ibid.* 245.

A *maumet* = idol, from Mahomet. As early as Layamon. See Madden's *Glossary*, and Stratmann. So still in Caxton, *Blanchardyn*, 137, 27.

Modern English.—Abigail, nickname given to a female servant.

Dunce, a stupid person. A proper name, originally in the phrase "a Dun's man." So Tyndall, *Works*, p. 88; Barnes, *Works*, p. 232, 272. The word was introduced by the Thomists, or disciples of Thomas Aquinas, in ridicule of the Scotists, or disciples of John Duns Scotus, the schoolman, died A.D. 1308.

Guy, a dowdy, from the puppets carried about on the fifth of November in memory of Guy Fawkes's conspiracy.

Cf. hansom (cab), from the name of the inventor; *pander*, a pimp, from Pandarus. For ethnographical and geographical names having become common terms, *cf. lombard* = a broker; *arras* = tapestry; *bantam, bedlam, bilbo, china, spa.*

SINGULAR AND PLURAL OF SUBSTANTIVES.

Subjective Character of the Number.

§ 142. Number passes into a grammatical category solely by the development of concord. Even in inflexional languages the plural is not in all cases indispensable where a plurality has to be designated. Every plurality may be conceived by the speaker as a unity. And thus there are designations for a definite number which are singular, such as *score, dozen*, just as originally *hundred, thousand*.

On the other hand, we often find the plural form where we see no notion of plurality, such as Old English *breóst* (breast), *heofonas* (sky, heaven); and again there are plurals in Modern English which were singular in older periods, such as *gallows* (Old English, *galga*), &c. It is this subjective character of the conception of number which accounts for the striking difference not only between different languages, but also between different periods of the same language.

Number of Abstracts.

"I tell thee, Peggy, I will have thy *loves*."—GREENE, *Friar Bacon and Fr. B.*

§ 143. The older stages of English, as well as the other Teutonic dialects, exhibit many instances of abstracts used in the plural.

Gothic.—"Frauja, frauja . . niu þeinamma namin *mahtins* mikilos gatavidedum?" (Lord, Lord! did we not many powerful things [literally, *powers*] in thy name?). *Matthew*, vii. 22.

Old Saxon.—*méron mahti* (more powers), Héliand, 2338.

Old High German.—*thino guati* (thy goodnesses), Otfrid, v. 23, 13.

Cf. Grimm, *Deutsche Grammatik*, iv. 285.

Old English.—"hwær áhangen wæs . . . rodora waldend *æfstum* þurh inwit" (where was hanged the lord of the heavens through *hates*).—*Elene*, 207. *eallum eáðmédum* (in all humilities), *ibid.* 1088; *in ermðum* (in miseries), *ibid.* 768; *mærðum and mihtum* (in fame and might), *ibid.* 15.

Cf. Grein, *s. vv. ófost, þeóstru, þrym.*

Middle English.—Here the plural of abstracts denotes either (*a*) singular repeated actions, (*b*) different kinds of the same conception, or (*c*) the unusual force of the conception.

(*a*) "ac þe ilke is to grat ; huanne eche daye onderuangeþ þe *guodnesses.*"—*Ayenbite of Inwyt,* p. 18.

Cf. Orm, *Dedication,* 252, 276, &c.

(*b*) "Twa *sarinesse* beoð, an is þeos uuele, oðer is halwende."—*Old E. Hom.* i. 103. "þa sarinessen þissere sterke worlde."—*Ibid.* 105. "þu dore stede ifullet of alle *dreorinesses.*"—*Ibid.* 253.

(*c*) "þe guodes of hap byeþ *heznesses, richesses,* delices, and *prosperites.*"—*Ayenbite,* p. 24.

Cf. mihtes, Gower i. 140 ; *hevinessis, Gesta Romanorum,* 174 ; *habundances, ibid.* 287 ; *anguysshes,* diseases, CAXTON *Blanchardyn,* 2, 3, 4.

In many instances the plural is due to French influence. Thus, in Dan Michel's *Ayenbite of Inwyt* (1340 A.D.), and in Caxton's translations of French romances, the plural of abstracts is most frequent.

"uor þet is þe manne þet alle þise þinges makeþ zuete, zuynch, zorzes, tyeaers and wepinges, *ssames*" (original, *hontes*).—*Ayenbite,* p. 83. (For that is the manna that makes all these things sweet : swink, sorrows, tears and weepings, shames, &c.)

"But their *corages* were neuer the lesse therfore" (original, *couraiges*). —CAXTON, *Aymon,* 262, 29.

"all *rewthis* layde aparte" (French, *regretz*).—*Ibid.* 17, 8 ; 20, 6.

In Modern English this use is continued in poetry, and is sometimes to be met with in prose.

"In so moche he thought in hymselfe for the grete labours in his *wepynges* almoost for to haue ben ouercomen."—JOHN FISHER, 17, 19.

"All these *wretchednesses* be rehersed of the prophete Dauyd."— *Ibid.* 53, 3.

Cf. ibid. 59, 16 ; 64, 21.

"Dismay thee not for the great *povertys* that thou hast sufferyd."—LORD BERNERS' *Huon,* 172, 17.

Cf. ibid. 59, 16; 64, 21.

"There ariseth in his soul many fears, and doubts, and discouraging *apprehensions.*"—BUNYAN, *Pilgrim's Progress.*

"Other weak men, who, meddling . . . do suddenly fall into thy *distractions.*"—*Ibid.*

"Your brother's *distresses.*"—SHERIDAN, *School for Scandal,* i. 1.

§ 144. Besides, we find in the second half of the sixteenth century, when the English renaissance was at its highest, a direct imitation of the Latin *pluralis majestaticus.*

"Rid me, and keep a friend worth many *loves.*"—GREENE, *Friar B. and Friar B.,* 166, *a.*

Cf. ibid. 165, *b*, 166, *a*, 166, *b*; Spenser, *Faerie Queene,* i. 1, 47, i. 2, 3.

"To tremble with the *terrors* of our looks."
LODGE, *Wounds of Civil War,* 128.

Cf. fears, *Mids. N. Dream,* v. 97; *Meas. for Meas.* iv. 2, 207. Love*s* and terror*s* are modelled on the Latin "amore*s* =amor," Verg. *Aen.* iv. 28; v. 334, &c.; "metūs," Verg. *Aen.* i. 463; Ovid. *Met.* v. 363; x. 466; "timores," Stat. *Silv.* iii. 2, 80.

Plural of Proper Names.

§ 145. *Proper names* form a plural—

(*a*) When they denote a plurality of individuals of the same name.

"As I hate hell, all *Montagues* and thee."—SHAKSPERE.

(*b*) If they become names of sorts in a figurative meaning.

"I demanded who were the present theatrical writers in vogue, who the *Drydens* and *Otways* of the day?"—GOLDSMITH.

Plural of Material Names.

§ 146. *Material names* appear in the plural, denoting—

(*a*) Several kinds of the same materials : oils, silks.

(*b*) Things made out of that material : coppers, irons.

(*c*) Poetical licence : "White as the snows of heaven." Instances are very frequent in modern poetry, and are probably due to Latin influence.

Number of Common Nouns.

§ 147. With regard to the *number of common nouns*, the use has, on the whole, undergone no change; but the so-called *pluralia tantum*—that is, substantives occurring only in the plural, as "bellows," "gallows"—are extremely rare in the older periods of the language.

In *Old English* there are words used both in the singular and the plural without any difference of meaning.

NOTE.—Analogy accounts for the plural in the phrase "I am friends with him," the frequent expression "we are friends," intruding itself, as it were, on the mind of the speaker.

"I am friends with thee."—MASSINGER, *A New Way to Pay Old Debts*, 292, *b*.

The following expression is perhaps to be explained in the same way :

"My ladyship's woman is much thy better*s*."—RICHARDSON, *Pamela*, 181, *a*.

"Master Godefrey, what do you want with me ? You're my elder*s* and better*s*, you know."—G. ELIOT, *Silas Marner*, 20.

Breóst both singular and plural means breast, though the

plural prevails. This use was common to all the Teutonic languages.

Gothic. "sa motareis . . . sloh in *brusts* seinos" (the publican beat his breast). (*Greek*, τὸ στῆθος; *Latin*, "pectus".) *Old Norse.* "er maðr eiga skal annars *briostum* í" (which man shall own in another's breast).—EDDA, *Hávamál*, 8, 6.

But the singular is more frequent than the plural. *Old Saxon.* Heliand has only the plural. *Old High German.* Both. See Grimm, p. 287. *Old English.* Beówulf has the singular, 2177 and 2332; but the plural, 453, 552, 2551. Thus still in Orm. *Ded.*, 220, 226, &c. *Heofon* too is used in the plural = heaven (like Gothic "himins"). Beówulf has the singular, 3157, 1572, &c.; the plural, 52, 182, 505. *Cf.* "rodor," singular, 1573; plural, 310, 1377, 1556.

The modern plurals like *tongs, scissors*, are of recent date.

CASES.

§ 148. From the point of view of Accidence only, it would be wrong to speak of cases in Modern English, there being practically no outward mark in the noun to distinguish either nominative, or accusative, or dative. There is, however, good ground to keep the old terms in syntax.

First, we have in the possessive case a valuable remnant of the old genitive, and the personal pronouns with their *I* and *me, he* and *him*, still keep alive the difference between the nominative and the accusative case.

Secondly, the prepositions *of* and *to* which became important as soon as the case-endings began to decay, were from the eleventh or twelfth century down to our times always felt as substitutes for the lost inflexions of the genitive and dative, just the same as *de* and *à* in French.

In dealing, therefore, with the cases, I shall consider it as understood that the terms of genitive and dative, when used with regard to Middle and Modern English apply only in so far as the prepositions *of* and *to* serve to express those functions which were formerly implied in the inflexions of the genitive and dative respectively.

THE NOMINATIVE CASE.

Functions of the Nominative.

§ 149. In Old English the functions of the nominative case are those of the subject and predicate, and these only.

"Ic com weg and sóðfæstnys and lif" (I am way, and truth, and life).—*John*, xiv. 6.

§ 150. In one case, however, the nominative is used in Old English, where we expect the accusative case. The verb *hátan* (to call) often governs the nominative.

"Hine mon scyle on bismer hátan *se anscoda*" (men shall call him in ignominy the one-shoed).—*Cura Pastoralis*, 45.

"Ðone beorhtan steorran ðe we hátað morgensteorra" (the bright star which we call the morning-star).—BOETHIUS, p. 114.

The same use occurs in Middle High German.

"der nennet sich der riter rôt" (he calls himself the red knight).—*Parzival*, 276, 21.

"man sol mich ein zage nennen" (men shall call me a coward).—*Willehalm*, 181, 7.

For other instances, both in Old English and Middle High German, see Grein, *s. v. hátan, nemnan*, and Grimm, *Deutsche Grammatik*, iv. p. 592.

This seeming anomaly may be explained as a sort of sudden transition from indirect to direct speech: "hine mon sceal hátan: 'se anscoda!'" (men shall call him: "the one-shoed!").

So far as the *logical* subject is concerned, there has been no change from Old English down to Modern English times. But the grammatical subject became much more frequent and important than ever it was before.

Nominative instead of the Oblique Case in old Impersonal Verbs.

§ 151. While Old English is very rich in impersonal verbs, there is a tendency in the later periods of Middle English towards the personal expression, that is to say (as Koch puts it), what once appeared as a dark sensation is made to appear as the conscious action of the free mind. Instead of "*hit hreóweð, hit sceameð, hit lícað, hit langað,*" there appear, "I repent, I am ashamed, I like, I long." This natural development was favoured by two external causes. In such instances as—

"Wo wes Brutus þer fore."—LAYAMON, i. 14;

"Wo was this Kyng."—CHAUCER, *Man of Lawes Tale,* 659;

what is an indirect object was mistaken for the nominative case, and secondly, the French model was of great importance. Hence the following expressions :

"I am ful wo."—*Coventry Mysteries,* p. 396.

"I am leuer ete,
What is drynk withoute mete?"
Townley Mysteries, p. 89.

"he were better his deth to take."—*Ibid.* p. 187.

See *Impersonal Verbs,* § 337.

Nominative instead of the Dative in Passive Constructions.

§ 152. The second encroachment of the nominative on the dative case took place in the passive constructions of transitive verbs governing an indirect, or both a direct and an indirect object, or in intransitive verbs followed by prepositions. This innovation was brought about first by the dative and accusative cases being confounded. Objects governed by verbs like "command, answer," &c., were consequently looked upon as accusative cases, and were treated as such, so that they became capable of the passive construction.

"þat we beon iquemed."—LAYAMON, 1, 40.

"Nes among al moncun oni holi dole ifunden þet muhte beon ileten blod."—*Ancren Riwle*, 112.

þ*et* is scarcely the dative ; nor is " Ure Lauerd " in " Ure Lauerd beo iðonked," *ibid.* 8, where MS. C has, " beo *hit* þonked " ; for another passage on p. 112 is indisputable : " þe *he* was þus ileten blood."

See the *Passive*, § 363.

The Nominative Absolute.

" *They* failing, I must die much your debtor."
Cymbeline, ii. 4, 8.

§ 153. *The nominative absolute* wholly supplanted the Old English dative, and became much more popular than the apparently learned Old English construction had ever been.

Old English.—" hys cnihtas cómon on nyht, and *eów* slǽpendum, þone lychaman forstlǽon " (his disciples came at night, and, you sleeping, stole his body).—*Evang. Nicod.* 17.

" þa sona eft *Gode* fultumiendum he mahte gesion and sprecan " (there soon, God helping, he could see and speak).—*Chronicle*, 797.

" Gif he *sunnan* scinendre þæt déð " (if he does it, the sun shining). —*Exodus*, xxii. 3.

In *Middle English* the dative is to be met with as late as the time of the *Townley Mysteries ;* but the nominative is quite common in Chaucer and his contemporaries.

" *Sche this in blake, lykynge to Troilus,*
  Over alle thinge he stode for to beholde."
CHAUCER, *Troylus and Cryseyde*, i. 309.

> "What couthe a stourdy housebonde more devyse,
> To prove hir wyfhode and her stedfastnesse,
> *And he* contynuyng ever in stourdynesse."
> 　　　　　　CHAUCER, *Clerkes Tale*, iv. 91.

> "And whan this Walter saugh hir patience,
> Hir glade cheer, and no malice at al,
> And he so oft hadde doon to hir offence,
> *And sche ay sad and constant as a wal,
> Continuyng ever hir innocence overal,*
> This sturdy marquys gan his herte dresse."
> 　　　　　　*Ibid.* vi. 109.

Tudor English.—"Thus when the Kynge and the prynces and barons hade dynyd, the noble Emperour called hys lordys before hym, *he syttyng* on a benche rychely aperelyd."—LORD BERNERS' *Huon*, 3, 7.

Cf. ibid. 29, 23 ; 39, 5.

Modern English.—"She failing in her promise, I have been diverting my chagrin."—SHERIDAN, *Trip to Scarborough*, i. 1.

§ 154. Along with the absolute construction runs another, which has a certain resemblance to that used in Gothic and Old Norse.

"Besides, *with* the enemy invading our country, it was my duty as the head of our family to go on the campaign."—THACKERAY, *The Virginians*, i. 165.

"*With* its warm breath gushing forth in a light cloud which merrily and gracefully ascended a few feet, then hung about the chimney-corner as its own domestic heaven, it trolled its song with that strong energy of cheerfulness, that its iron body hummed and stirred upon the fire."—DICKENS, *The Cricket on the Hearth*.

"There was nothing they wouldn't have cleared away, *with* old Fezziwig looking on."—DICKENS, *A Christmas Carol*.

"How could it (ever happen), with everybody against it but poor little me?"—CH. READE, *A Terrible Temptation*, ii. 255.

The Nominative with the Infinitive.

§ 155. Another function of the nominative case was that in connection with the infinitive, *e.g.* :

"The caul was put up in a raffle down in our part of the country, to fifty members at half-a-crown a head, the winner to spend five shillings."—DICKENS, *David Copperfield*, i. 2.

For a full account see *Infinitive*, § 399–400.

Nominative in Apposition.

§ 156. Quite exceptionally a pronoun referring as apposition to a noun or pronoun in an oblique case appears in the nominative, *e.g.*:

> "To whom the lond was attendant
> As *he*, which heir was apparant."
> GOWER, *Confessio Amantis*, i. 214.

See *Interchange of Cases*, § 209.

The Nominative supplanted by the Oblique Case.

§ 157. There are, however, two cases in which the nominative has been encroached upon by the oblique case.

(*a*) *You* instead of *ye;* see *Interchange of Cases*, § 212.

(*b*) It is *me;* see *Interchange of Cases*, § 214.

The Genitive Case.

Signification of the Genitive.

§ 158. First of all, we must distinguish between the genitive governed by verbs, and that connected with substantives. While the first category is rather limited even in older periods of the language, the genitive governed by substantives ranges in Old English (as well as in the other Teutonic languages) over a far wider area than in later and modern times, and its applicability was nearly unlimited. We may almost say of the Old English genitive what Professor Sayce states with regard to Accadian, viz. that the genitive was nothing more than an apposition implying some vague idea of a relation between two substantives.[1]

---

[1] "Here, then (*scil.* in Accadian), the relation would seem to be nothing more than what we term 'apposition,' that is, where two

SYNTAX OF THE PARTS OF SPEECH

But numerous though the functions of the Old English genitive were, there is one especially prominent, the *attributive* one. There is a very close relation between the genitive and the adjective (attribute), as may best be seen by the fact that the possessive pronouns my, thy, his (O.E. *mín, ðín, his*) are nothing else but genitives of the personal pronouns I, thou, he, &c.[1] And still in Middle English nouns in the genitive case are used even predicatively as adjectives: "Right as a *liues creature* she semeth," *i.e.* a live, a living creature. Gower, *Confessio Amantis*, ii. 14. See below, § 166.[2]

In Modern English there are but a few remnants of what once was the most important of all the cases.

The Genitive denotes Birth and Relation.

§ 159. This signification which gave the case its name (*genitivus* from *gigno*), and is most frequent in all periods of the language, is encroached upon by the dative.

"My lady Margarete . . . . Moder *unto* our naturel and souerayn lorde."—CAXTON, *Blanchardyn*, 1, 3.

"Blanchardyn, sone *vnto* the kynge of Fryse."—*Ibid.* 1, 27.

"Blanchardyn answerd that he was of the lande of Grece, and sone *to* a kynge."—*Ibid.* 100, 1.

"She is daughter *to* this duke."—SHAKSP. *Tempest*, v. 192.

"The fair sister *to* her unhappy brother Claudio."—*Measure for Measure*, i. 4, 20.

---

individual notions are placed side by side without any further effort being made by the mind to determine their exact relations beyond the mere fact that one precedes the other, and is therefore thought of first."
—SAYCE.

[1] Cf. Greek ὁ πατήρ μου instead of ὁ ἐμὸς πατήρ.
[2] In the Tibetan languages adjectives are formed from substantives by the addition of the sign of the genitive.—M. MÜLLER, *Lectures*, First Series, p. 106.

§ 160. *The Genitive denotes Rule or Power.*

Gothic.—"Quaþ þan sa frauja þis veinagardis" (quoth then the lord of this vinyard).—*Luke*, xx. 13.

Old Norse.—"þrymr sat á haugi, þursa dróttinn" (Th. sat on a hill, the lord of the giants).—*Edda, þrymskviða*, 5.

Old English.—"Aldor Dena" (prince of the Danes).—*Beówulf*, 668.

"Freá Scyldinga" (lord of the Scyldings).—*Ibid.* 291, 351, etc.

§ 161. *The Genitive denotes Possession.*

Gothic.—"In garda Paitraus" (in the house of Peter).—*Matthew*, viii. 14.

Old Norse.—"Aesirnir tóku lík Baldrs" (the A. took the body of B.).—SNORRA, *Edda*, 37.

Old Saxon.—"fagar folk godes" (the fair people of god).—*Heliand*, 412.

Old English.—"þryðærn Dena" (the palace of the Danes).—*Beówulf*, 658.

"Finnes hám" (F.'s house).—*Ibid.* 1157.

Abstract Substantive instead of an Adjective.

§ 162. In Old English poetry a concrete noun is often governed by an abstract one, where we should expect noun and adjective.

> "hie in beór-sele bidan woldon
> Grendles gúðe mid gryrum ecga."

(They would await in the beer-hall G.'s fight with the dreadful sword: literally, with the horrors of the swords.)—*Beówulf*, 483.

Cf. "billes bite" (the biting sword)—*Ibid.* 2061; "gáres fliht" (the flying spear)—*Ibid.* 1766.

The Genitive Superlative.

"The *curse of curses* is, our curse to love."—
YOUNG, *Night Thoughts*, 2, 42.

§ 163. We may, perhaps not improperly, give this name to that genitive, which elevates the noun governing it to the highest degree. Though this use may be traced back to the old Teutonic dialects, it is not improbable that its survival in Modern English is partly due to the fact that the same use is frequent in the Bible. Cf. *The Song of Songs*, "canticum canticorum": *servant of servants* = the lowest menial. Genesis, ix. 25. The phrase, "in his heart of hearts," is accounted for by the analogy of the other instances.

Old Norse.—"Hvat er þat hlym hlymja?" (What is that sound of sounds? = that most loud sound.)—*Edda, Skirnismál,* 14.

"Hverr er sá sveinn sveina, er stendr fyr sundit handan?" (who is the lad of lads that stands on the other side of the strait?)—*Edda, Harbarðslioð,* 1.

"Hverr er sá karl karla er kallar um váginn?" (who is the churl of churls that calls over the strait?)—*Ibid.* 2.

"nú er rœkkr rœkkra" (now is dark of darks, deepest darkness).—*Edda, Hyndlulioð,* 1.

Old High German.—"Kero 45ᵇ translates scurrilitas by skernes skern."—GRIMM, *Deutsche Grammatik,* iv. 726.

Old English.—"þá syððan wæs
   of róde áhæfen waldend,
   eallra þrymma þrym."

(Since was taken from the rood the ruler of heavens, the power of all powers.)—*Elene,* 483.

"þá . . .
  ealles leóhtes leóht, lifigende árás,
  þeóden engla."

(There . . . the light of all light arose living, the lord of the angels.)—*Ibid.* 486.

The expressions, "cyninga cyning" (king of kings), "þurh ealra worulda worold" (in secula seculorum = for ever and ever), which are very frequent in Old English, are borrowed from the Bible.

Middle English.—"Qui est verus samaritanus scilicet custos hominum. þat is alre herdene herde and alre lechene leche" (who is the herdsman of all herdsmen, and the physician of all physicians).—*Old English Homilies*, ii. 41.

"And alre bitere biterest" (the bitterest of all bitters).—*Ibid.* 99.

"Une drihten þe is alre louerde louerd beih of heuene to mannen" (Our Lord, who is the lord of all lords, stooped from heaven to men). —*Ibid.* 121.

"Hie is þe heuenliches kinges dohter and ec his moder, and alre maiden maide" (she is the daughter of the heavenly kyng and also his mother, and maiden of all maidens).—*Ibid.* 161.

"Lauedi (lady) scho es of leuedis (ladies) all."—*Cursor Mundi*, 101.

"He is kyng of kynges."—*Townley Mysteries*, p. 141.

See also Skeats's *Notes to Piers Plowman* (Early English Text Society), p. 33.

Modern English.—"That sprightly Scot of Scots, Douglas."
SHAKSP. 1 *Henry IV.* ii. 4, 377.

"But now to come to your face of faces, or courtier's face."—BEN JONSON, *Cynthia's Revels*, 2, 1.

§ 164. *The Objective Genitive.*

"Their tempered youth with *aged fathers awe.*"
—*Gorboduc.*

Gothic.—"Jah gaf im valdufni ahmanê unhrainjazê" (and gave him the power over impure spirits).—*Mark*, vi. 7.

Old Norse.—"Sólar sýn" (the sight of the sun).
—*Edda, Hávamál,* 68.

"þess bót" (improvement of this, amends for it).—*Edda, Volundar Kviða*, 19.

Old Saxon.—"than skalt thu eft word sprekan, hebbean thînaro stemna giwald" (then thou shalt speak words, have power over thy voice).—*Heliand*, 169: *cf.* 238, 1904, 1909.

Old English.—"for þæra Judéa ege" (for fear of the Jews).—*John*, vii. 13.

"fram synna lufan" (from love to sin).—BEDA, 4, 24.

"Habbað Godes trúwan" (have faith in God).—*Mark*, xi. 22.

"Wacigende on Godes gebede" (watching in prayer to God).—*Luke*, vi. 12.

Middle English.—"þet he nefre ne ete mennisses metes for drihtenes luue" (and never ate human food for God's love).—*Old English Homilies*, i. 11.

"Of hym that is oure soulis leche."—*Townley Mysteries*, p. 10.

"She bereth in her herte care ynough and dyspleysure for the loue of him."—CAXTON's *Blanchardyn*, 73, 33.

Ibid. 76, 5; 77, 25.

"For right moche he desyred to shewe hymself, for his ladyes loue."—*Ibid.* 83, 8.

§ 165. This genitive becomes more and more rare the more we approach modern times, when it is represented by *over, towards, against,* and other prepositions.

Modern English.
"Whiche perill shal be past, if in your life,
Their tempred youthe with aged fathers awe,
Be brought in vre of skilfull stayednesse."
                                        Gorboduc, 200.

Cf. ibid. 485, 571, 602, 613, 985, 1321.

"Hath not the only love of her made us raise up our thoughts?"—SIDNEY, *Arcadia*, p. 2.

"Hope of life."—*Ibid.* p. 8.

"Love of his people."—*Ibid.* p. 9.

"Retourning to his bed in torment great,
And bitter anguish of his guilty sight,
He could not rest."
                    SPENSER, *Faerie Queene*, I, 2, 6.

Cf. *ibid.* 1, 2, 16; 1, 2, 6; 1, 3, 13; 1, 6, 17.

Instances with "to" instead of "of".

"Nor have respect to age, nor yet to kinde."—GASCOIGNE, 64.

"Because they had respect to equitie."—*Ibid.* 70.

"His unfaynted love to his father."—SIDNEY, *Arcadia*, p. 12.

"Hate to me."—*Ibid.* p. 29.

§ 166. *The Qualifying Genitive* ("genitivus qualitatis")

"I am not of many words."—SHAKSPERE.

Gothic.—"Daúhtar vintrive tvalibe" (a daughter of twelve years).—*Luke*, viii. 42.

Cf. Grimm, *Deutsche Grammatik*, iv. p. 652.

Old Norse.—"Byskup gofugs máttar" (a bishop of power).—*Snorra Edda*, 185.

"hvers þeir 'ru kyns er koma" (of what kin are these who come)?—*Edda, Hávamál*, 132.

Old Saxon.—"Giu wârun thar aðalies man" (already there were men of nobility).—*Héliand*, 566.

Cf. "en aðales man," 2542 (Cotton Ms.).

Old English.—"Sinc gestreónum fættan goldes" (with treasures of beaten gold).—*Beówulf*, 1093, 4.

"wæs micelre sóðfæstnysse wer" (he was a man of great truthfulness).—BEDA, 3, 15.

"seo den wæs micelre brædo" (the den was of great breadth).—*Ibid.* 5, 13.

Middle English.—"Acle mon nom ane scale of rede golde" (everybody took a scale of red gold).—LAYAMON, I. 229.

"þe merminnen beoð deor of muchele ginnen" (mermaids are beasts of great deceit).—*Ibid.* i. 26.

"(he) was a yung mon of þriti yeren."—*Ibid.* i. 17.

"Herode let himm brinngenn to bisshopess off dep lare" (Herod had brought to him two bishops of deep learning).—*Orm.* 7205.

"Horrs off fir itt (karrte) droghenn" (horses of fire drew it).—*Ibid.* 8707.

"A dogter ich haue of gret prys noble and god also."—ROB. OF GLOUCES. 281.

In a few cases this genitive is looked upon and, accordingly, used as a pure adjective.

"Right as a *liues creature*
She semeth."
GOWER, *Confessio Amantis*, ii. 14.
CHAUCER, *The Knightes Tale*, 1537.

Cf. *Owl and Nightingale*, 1632; *cf.* Skeat, *P. P. Notes*, p. 220; R. OF GLOUCESTER, 1144, 3829; Morris, *Story of Gen. and Exodus*, note to l. 250; "worldes thinge" = worldly things, Gower, i. 323. The same in Old Norse.

"þeir er *lifs* eru" (these that are alive).—*Droplaugarsona Saga*, 26.

"hann stóð *lifs* þá enn í lyftinginni" (he was still standing, alive, on the quarter-deck.)—*Fornmanna Sögur*, x., 394.

Cf. Lund, *Ordföinings-lære* (Syntax of Old Norse), p. 163.

Malory in his *Morte d'Arthur* treats the genitive denoting quality just as if it were an adjective: "She is the fairest lady and most of beautie in the world," 357, 23; "More of beautie," 358, 13; 358, 18; 360, 33; 450, 13, and frequently.

Modern English.—"His very hair is of the dissembling colour."
SHAKSP. *As You Like It*, III. iv. 7.

"A prince of power."—*Temp.* i. 2. 55.

Instances abound.

Some peculiarities of the Qualitative Genitive.

"Right hard it was for wight which did it heare,
To read *what maner musicke* that mote be."
SPENSER, *F. Q.* 2, 12, 70.

"With the name of Whitefield or Wesley, or some other such great man as a bishop, or *those sort* of people."—FIELDING, *Joseph Andrews*, i. 17.

§ 167. To the grammarian who tries to explain every expression from the point of view of logic, these constructions must be a great puzzle. It is history, and history alone, which enables us to solve the riddle. In Old English as well as in Old Norse, the conception with regard to this expression was quite different from what it is now. Whenever people were thinking about a certain class of things, it was the things which were prominent in their mind, which they saw with their internal eyes, while the class to which the things belonged came next as an accessory quality, as an attribute. If, therefore, they wanted to say "All sorts of worms," they put it in a different and more concrete way than we do; they said "Worms of every kind," *alles cunnes wurmes.*

The more abstract expression, however, came in as early as the 13th century, so that both conceptions existed at the same time, until, later on, the modern one prevailed, but still without wholly supplanting the old use.

In Latin a parallel development may be seen. Livy nearly always has the same construction that is prevalent in Middle English: "omnis generis tormenta," *Liv.* xxxii. 16, 10; "ager copia omnis generis frugum abundans," xxii. 9, 3; "praeda ingens omnis generis," xxvi. 46, 10; "cum alia omnis generis praeda," xxvii. 5, 9; "omnis generis injurias in se commemoravit," xxvii. 17, 12; "navibus omnis generis contractis," xxxiv. 8, 5; "telorum omnis generis vis," xxxviii. 26, 4; "pecora omnis generis," xlii. 56, 10; "eloquentia sacrata scriptis omnis generis," xxxix. 40, 7; "concursus omnis generis hominum," xxi. 12, 8. Cæsar afterwards exhibits the same use, but Cicero usually has the later construction *omne genus alicuius rei.* See Forcellini, *s.v.*

§ 168. The genitive of *cun*, Old English *cynn*, was very early used as an adjective, perhaps not without being influenced by the same construction in Old Norse.

"*þesskonar* tolum" (with tales of this sort).—*Alexanders Saga*, 11.

"*nokkurskonar* list" (some sort of art).—SNORRA, *Edda*, 31.

"*margskonar* þjóð" (people of many kinds).—SNORRA, *Edda*, 31.

Cf. Lund, p. 161.

Old English.—" Se árleasa wolde þagyt cunnian ánes cynnes wite" (the impious one desired to try one kind of torment).—ÆLFRIC, *Lives of Saints,* 112, 400.

" Her beoþ oft numene missenlicra cynna weolcscylle " (here are often caught various kinds of shellfish).—BEDA, i. 1.

Middle English.—" Ne nanes kinness shaffte " (no sort of creatures). —ORM. *Ded.* 277.

"alles cunnes wilde dor" (all sorts of wild beasts).—*Old English Homilies,* i. 79.

"alles cunnes wurmes" (all sorts of worms).—*Ibid.*

"alles cunnes pinen" (all sorts of torments).—*Ibid.* 251.

"alles cunnes estes" (all kinds of pleasures).—*Ibid.* 257.

"*of* alles cunnes þing."—*Old English Miscellany,* 46, 229.

" nones cunnes dol" (no sort of division).—*Ibid.* 50, 446.

" ones kunnes treou" (a sort of tree).—*Ancren Riwle,* 150.

" ilk kinnes erf" (all sorts of cattle).—*Story of Gen. and Exod.* 183 [1]

" ilk kinnes beste."—*Ibid.* 220.

The original meaning of this genitive was, in all probability, misunderstood, as may be seen by the following instances :

" any *s*kynnes countenaunce."—*Sir Gawayne and the Greene Knight,* 1539.

" no *s*kynnes labour."—CHAUCER, *House of Fame,* 704.

"alle *s*kynnes condiciouns."—*Ibid.* 440.

§ 169. Moreover, the modern expression, viz., "all kind of condiciouns," and not "condiciouns of all kind," came in very early, so that the old construction soon drew towards its decay. In " fower kinne men," *Old English Homilies,* ii. 151, we may still see the old genitive plural, *kinne = cynna ;* but instances like the following evidently prove that the modern construction was used as early as the end of the twelfth or the first half of the thirteenth century.

[1] *Cf.* "gehwelces cynnes yrfe."—*Chronicle,* 910 (Parker MS.).

"monic kunnes men."—*Old English Homilies*, i. 151.

"alle kunnes sunnen" (sins of all kinds).—*Ibid*. 205.

"fure kunnes teres" (four kinds of tears)—*Ibid*. 159.

"fuwer kinnes men" (quatuor sunt genera hominum).—*Ibid*. ii. 123.

"Crabbe is an manere *of* fisce in þere sea."—*Ibid*. i. 51.

"feole cunne beoð of weldede" (there are many sorts of good deeds. —*Ibid*. i. 135.

"oþer manere of diadliche sinnes" (other sorts of deadly sins).—*Old English Miscellany*, 33.

The result was first the indifferent use of *kinnes* and kin*ne*, and later on *manere*, both singular and plural not followed by *of*, *e.g.* "ten manere zennes." *Ayenbite*, 70.

Instances abound; only a few can be quoted in this place.

"Inn alle kinne sinne."—ORM. 2250.

"On alle kinne wise."—*Ibid*. 2260, 2574, 2602, 2666.

"Onn aniȝ kinne wise."—*Ibid*. 2380.

"An fower cunne wise mon sulleð his elmesse" (in four ways man sells his alms).—*Old English Homilies*, i. 137.

"A þre cunne wise he vondi hine begon" (in three ways he began to tempt him).—*Old English Miscellany*, 38, 31.

"a fele cunne wise."—*Ibid*. 39, 53; 44, 241.

"fele kyn fisches."—*Sir Gawayne and the Greene Knight*, 890.

In the *Cursor Mundi* "kin" (without *s*) prevails, though the different MSS. differ in this point.

"sumkyn dedis," 165. "sumkyn gest," 207. "in quat kin curs," 230. "alkin things," 385. "over al oþerkin þing," 404. "tuinkyn scaft," 512. "nankin creature," 574.

"Kin*s*," in *MS. Cotton*, occurs 115, 195, 1790, 5208, 5575, 9080, 9486. The proportion of the instances exhibiting *kin* to those with *kins*, in the first 10,000 verses, is 49 : 7 = 7 : 1.

§ 170. *Instances with Maner.*

"For mensked wit tuin maner o scaft" (worshipped by two sorts of creatures).—*Cursor Mundi*, 425.

"Wit al maner o suet spices."—*Ibid.* 1028.

"Ne na maner gin of were" (no sort of war-engine).—*Ibid.* 9889.

In Dan Michel's *Ayenbite* only *maner* occurs; the instances with *maner + of* prevail.

"þri maneres of yefþes" (three manners of gifts).—42.

"oþre manyeres of zennes" (sins).—*Ibid.* 57.

"vif manere of yelpinges" (five manners of boasting).—*Ibid.* 59.

"ech manere of zenne."—*Ibid.* 70.

"þri maneres of guode."—*Ibid.* 80.

"þri maneres of vridom."—*Ibid.* 86.

"oþre manere of speches."—*Ibid.* 103.

"eche manere of hare kende" (each manner of their kind).—*Ibid.* 104.

§ 171. *Instances of "Maner" not followed by "of."*

"ten manere zennes."—*Ibid.* 70.

"þri manere guodes" (French original: "de biens").—80.

"tuo manere guodes."—91.

There are many instances of *kyn* as well as *kynnes* in the second half of the fourteenth century. See Skeat, *Notes to Piers Plowman*, pp. 53—69, and a full report on the construction on p. 216.

The trace of *kin* ends about the middle of the fifteenth century. There are instances of it in the *Gesta Romanorum:*

"he shall telle you what kynne tydinges that he has brought."—254.

"ye wote in what kynne state I am."—258.

"what kynnes treson is þis?"—316.

Caxton no longer uses *kin*, he always has *maner*, either with *of* or without, the former prevailing. Against eighteen instances with *of*, in *Blanchardyn and Eglantyne*, there are but three without. See Introduction to *Blanchardyn*, p. xvii.

Modern English.—In Elizabethan authors *maner* and *mister* without *of* still occur; instances, however, are rare.

> "The Redcrosse Knight toward him crossed fast
> To weet what *mister* wight was so dismayd."
> SPENSER, *Faerie Queene*, i. ix. 26, 2.

> "Right hard it was for wight which did it heare,
> To read what *manner* musicke that mote be."
> *Ibid.* ii. xii. 70, 6.

§ 172. NOTE.—Even in quite Modern English, *kind*, *sort*, sometimes are found as adjectives, though followed by *of*, as may be seen by the plural *these*, *those* in the following examples:

"*These kind* of knaves."—*Lear*, ii. 2, 107.

"With the name of Whitefield or Wesley, or some other such great man as a bishop, or *those sort* of people."—FIELDING, *Joseph Andrews*, i. 17.

"All *these sort* of things"—SHERIDAN, *School for Scandal*, i. 1.

"I hoped we had done with *these sort* of things."—*John Halifax*, ii. 243.

The Partitive Genitive.

§ 173. This genitive is governed by nouns, adjectives in the comparative and superlative degree, numerals, interrogative and indefinite pronouns.

Gothic.—"atta, gif mis, sei undrinnai mik *dail aiginis*" (father, give me that part of property which belongs to me).—*Luke*, xv. 12.

Old Norse.—"í þriðja part veraldar" (in the third part of the world). —*Stjörn* 68.

Old Saxon.—"Himilrîkeas gidêl" (part of kingdom of heaven).— *Héliand*, 2488.

Old High German.—"faz wînes" (a barrel of wine), "leip prôtes" (a loaf of bread).—See GRIMM, *Deutsche Grammatik*, 722.

Old English.—" Weorðmynda dǽl " (a good deal of adornments).—*Beówulf*, 1753.

" máðma menigeo " (many treasures).—*Ibid.* 2144.
" folca gedryht " (plenty of people).—*Elene*, 27.
" árleásra sceolu " (the band of the impious).—*Ibid.* 836.

Hund and *þúsend* always, the other numerals sometimes govern the genitive.

" An œðelinga " (one of the noblemen).—*Beówulf*, 1294.
" up ahóf rihtes réniend þara róda twá " (the ruler of right raised two rods).—*Elene*, 880.
" þara sint IIII " (of these are four). –*Ibid.* 744.

For the construction *ânra gehwylc*, see *Numerals*, § 260.

" Aénig ymbsittendra " (one of the inhabitants of the neighbourhood).—*Beówulf*, 2735.
" nán gúðbilla " (none of the fighting swords).—*Ibid.* 804.

Juxtaposition instead of the Partitive Genitive.

§ 174. In *Middle English*, especially in the thirteenth and fourteenth centuries, when *of* had not yet limited the possessive case, there are many instances of inflexionless substantives governed by nouns denoting quantity. These substantives seem to be nominatives, but they may have been felt still as genitives. On the other hand, from the same decay of the partitive genitive in Old Norse and German we may perhaps conclude that the idea of partition attached to so many words in Old English was about to be supplanted by that of simple apposition.

" þe þrydde del my kynedom y geue þe."—ROBERT OF GLOUCESTER, 283.
" þe þrydde del ys londe."—*Ibid.* 709.
" From þe on ende Cornewayle."—*Ibid.* 177.
" A busshel venym."—CHAUCER, *Troylus and Cryseyde*, iii. 976.
" No morsel bred."—*Ibid. The Monkes Tale*, 440.
" The beste galoun wyn."—*Ibid. Prologue of the Maunciples Tale*, 24.

"A peyre schetys."—*Early English Wills* (ed. Furnivall), 4, 16; 5, 8; 41, 24; 76, 16; 101, 18.

"A peyre bedes."—*Ibid.* 5, 3.

"A pece medowe."—*Bury Wills* (Camden Society), 47.

"A peyre spectaclys."—*Ibid.* 15.

"A quart wyne."—*Ibid.* 16.

"A galon wine."—*Ibid.* 30.

§ 175. But there was a sudden stop in the development towards apposition instead of the genitive, and at the end of the fifteenth century there was a sort of reaction in favour of the Old English use. Expressions like those quoted are not to be met with in Caxton.

From the Old English down to the Elizabethan age, indefinites and numerals, followed by adjectives in the superlative degree, appear as attributes, instead of governing a partitive genitive as in Modern English.

Old English.—"Healfdene for mid sumum þam here on Norþhymbre" (H. went with part of his army towards Northumberland.)—*Chronicle*, 875.

"þá fór Eadweard cyning mid sumum his fultume on East-Seaxe to Maldune."—(King E. marched with part of his army to M.) *Ibid. Parker MS.* 913.

"sum his fultum worhte þa burg" (part of his army made the castle). —*Ibid.* Cf. OROSIUS 18, 1; 140, 2; 162, 14, &c.

"Mid feáwum þám getrýwestum mannum" (with a few of his most faithful men).—*Apollonius of Tyre*, p. 6.

"þær wæron þreó þa betstan ele" (there were three of the best ointments, or rather, the very best of all).—*Blickling Homilies*, 73, 21.

"hit hæfð geworht áne þá mǽstan synne and gode þá láðustan" (it has done a sin, the greatest and most hateful to God).—AELFRIC, *Exodus*, xxxii. 21.

Middle English.—"This beoth threo the hexte lymes."—WRIGHT, *Popular Treatise on Science*, p. 138.

"Oute of þilke hilles springeþ þre þe noblest ryueres of al Europe." —TREVISA, i. 199.

"of two þe firste mathew spekeþ in his gospel."—WYCLIF, *English Works* (ed. Matthew), p. 2.

"I deuyse to Johane my daughter... III. the best pilives after choys of the forseyde Thomas my sone."—*Early English Wills*, 5, 9.

"A maide on of this worlde the beste preysed."
CHAUCER, *Troylus and Cryseyde*, v. 1474.

"Of hire delite or joies oon the leeste,
Were impossibile to my wit to seye."—*Ibid*. iii. 1261.

§ 176. The following passages offer a curious instance of a mixed construction :

"Oon of the grettest auctour that men rede" (Five MSS., one has "auctours").—CHAUCER, *The Nonne Prest his Tale*, 164.

"On of the best farynge man on lyue."—*Id. The Frankeleynes Tale*, 204.

"One of the best enteched creature."—*Ibid. Troylus and Cryseyde*, v. 832.

"But of all france I am one of the best and truest knyght that be in it."—CAXTON, *Aymon*, 272, 23.

This odd expression is made up of two constructions :

One the best knyght.
One of the best knyghtes.
Result : One of the best knyght.

Instances with indefinite pronouns :

"Other her gentyll women."—CAXTON, *Blanchardyn and Eglantine*, 76, 31.

"Other his prysoners."—*Ibid*. 121, 25.

"Affermyng that I ought rather tenprynte his actes and noble feates than of Godefray of Boloyne or *any the eight*."—CAXTON'S *Preface to Morte d'Arthur*, 2, 1.

Elizabethan English.

"Enough is, that thy foe doth vanquisht stand
Now at thy mercy : Mercy not withstand :
For he is one the truest knight aliue."
SPENSER, *Faerie Queene*, i. 3, 37.

"Or who shall not great Nightes children scorne,
When two of three her Nephewes are so foule forlorne?"
Ibid. i. 5, 23.

"His living like sawe never living eye,
Ne durst behold ; his stature did exceed
The high three the tallest sonnes of mortall seed."
Ibid. i. 7, 8.

"Was reckoned one the wisest prince that there had reigned."
SHAKSP. *Henry VIII.* ii. 4, 48.

Cf. the same use in *Old Norse.*

"féllu þeir men flestir er þar váru" (there fell most of the men who were there).—*Egils Saga*, 44.

Cf. Lund, p. 158.

Latin.—"Reperti sunt complures nostri milites, qui in phalangas insilirent."—CÆS. *B. G.* 1, 52, 5.

"Tres suos nactus manipulares."—*Ibid.* 7, 77, 7.

"Nostræ naves duæ in ancoris constiterunt."—*Ibid.* 3, 28, 1.

The Elliptic Genitive.

§ 177. Another partitive genitive is that which may be called the elliptic one, the governing word being omitted.

Old English.—"Hý clypodon and næs þara þe hig gehælde" (they called and there was none to heal them).—*Ps.* xvii. 39.

But commonly we find *of* followed by the dative, *e.g.* "Syllað ús of eowrum ele" (gif us of your oil). *Matthew*, xxv. 8.

Middle English.—"hwa se euer wule habbe lot wið þe of þi blisse: he mot deale wið þe of þine pine on eorþe" (whoever wants to partake of thy bliss, must partake of thy pain on earth).—*Old English Homilies*, i. 187.

"man eggeð his negebure to done oðer to speken him harm, oðer s(c)ame, and haueð nið elch wið oðer, and makeð him to forlese his aihte, oðer *of* his righte" (some one eggs his neighbour to harm him in word or deed, or to do him shame, and they envy each other, and one makes the other lose his property or his rights).—*Ibid.* ii. 13.

"Of smale houndes hadde sche, that sche fedde."
CHAUCER, *Canterbury Tales, The Prologue*, 146.

Modern English. —" I wyll ye take of your best frendys."—LORD BERNERS, *Huon*, 5, 25.

" this that I haue shewid you is of truth."—*Ibid.* 61, 26.

" I requyre you, shewe me of your newes and adventures that ye haue had."—*Ibid.* 566, 12.

" Englysh marchauntes do fetch of the erth of Irlonde to caste in their gardens."—ANDREW BOORDE, p. 133.

" I told him we must not presume to eat of our patron's bread."— *Robinson Crusoe*, 47.

Cf. *ibid.*, p. 170.

This use is still continued in the Bible, perhaps also in obedience to the original text :

" Bring of the fruit of the land."—*Num.* xiii. 21.

" She took of the fruit thereof."—*Gen.* iii. 6.

The Pseudo-Partitive Genitive.

§ 178. There is another sort of genitive, which we may, perhaps, not improperly term pseudo-partitive, viz., that which appears in phrases like "a castle of hers, a knight of Arthur's." It is true, that in many cases we might translate these phrases by "one of her castles, one of Arthur's knights"; but there are many examples in Middle English which do not admit of such an explanation, and the Modern English use ("that beautiful face of hers!") proves that no idea of partition is included in such expressions. After a close examination of the oldest instances met with in the fourteenth century (second half?), we see that they are brought into existence by another necessity.

In Old English the possessive pronoun, or, as the French say, "pronominal adjective," expresses only the conception of belonging and possession ; it is a real adjective, and does not convey, as at present, the idea of determination. If,

I

therefore, Old English authors want to make such nouns determinative, they add the definite article:

"hæleð mín se leofa" (my dear warrior).—*Elene,* 511.

"þú eart dóhtor mín séo dýreste" (thou art my dearest daughter).—*Juliana,* 193.

§ 179. In Middle English the possessive pronoun apparently has a determinative meaning (as in Modern English, Modern German, and Modern French); therefore its connection with the definite article is made superfluous, while the indefinite article is quite impossible. Hence arises a certain embarrassment with regard to one case which the language cannot do without. Suppose we want to say "she is in a castle belonging to her," where it is of no importance whatever, either to the speaker or hearer, to know whether "she" has got more than one castle—how could the English of the Middle period put it? The French of the same age said still "un sien castel," but that was no longer possible in English.

§ 180. We should expect the genitive of the personal pronoun ("of me," &c., as in Modern German)—and there may have been a time when this use prevailed—but, so far as I know, the language decided in favour of the more complicated construction "of mine, of thine," &c.

This was, in all probability, brought about by the analogy of the very numerous cases in which the indeterminative noun connected with *mine,* &c., had a really partitive sense (*cf.* the examples below), and, further, by the remembrance of the old construction with the possessive pronoun.

I. First, we find the indefinite article (or the equally indefinite words, *any, every, no*) in connection with *of mine, of thine,* &c.

II. Next, analogy introduces the indefinite article in connection with the double genitive of a noun (a knyght of King Arthur's).

III. Last, we come across definite pronouns (this, that) in connection with *of mine;*[1] and exceptionally the definite article occurs there also in connection with the double genitive of a noun (the knight of King Arthur's).

"A friend of his."—CHAUCER, *Troylus and Cryseyde*, i. 548; *ibid.* iii. 747; *ibid.* iv. 1355.

"an hors of his."—*Ibid. The Sompnoures Tale*, 381.

"an old felaw of youres."—*Ibid. The Pardoneres Tale*, 210.

"eny neghebour of myne."—*Ibid. The Prologue of the Monkes Tale*, 13.

"every knight of his."—*Ibid. The Wyf of Bathes Tale*, 234.

"I will that William . . . be paied of their billes for making off a liuery of myn."—*Early English Wills*, 53, 20.

"ȝif any servaunt of myn haue labord for me . . . "—*Ibid.* 53, 23.

(Both instances about 1420 A.D.)

"I will that Chace haue a habirion of myne."—*Ibid.* 54, 7.

"And more stuff I haue not occupied of hers."—*Bury Wills* (A.D. 1415), p. 23.

Gesta Romanorum (about 1440 A.D.) offers instances of II. but not of III.: "I am forrester of the Emperours," 206; "a noþere knyȝt of the Emperours," 241.

In Caxton group I. is represented by numerous instances.

"And for this cause departeth now my sayd lady from a castell of hers."—*Blanch. and Egl.* 38, 6.

(Original: "dun sien chastel.")

"He toke also a grete spere from the hande of a knyght of his."—*Ibid.* 107, 32.

Group II. is often met with in the *Morte d'Arthur*.

"A knyghte of the dukes."—37, 7; 37, 9.

"Syre gawayne, knyghte of kynge Arthurs."—*Ibid.* 146, 30.

---

[1] It is surprising to find the definite article in connection with 'of yours' as early as Ipomadon (about the middle of the 14th century):

"I wille werke after þe *wille of yours*," 2130 (ed. Kölbing).

"I am a knyghte of kynge Arthurs."—*Ibid.* 153, 32 ; 263, 31 ; 263, 34 ; 330, 22 ; 331, 19.

"a trusty frende of Sir Tristrams."—*Ibid.* 363, 8.

Of group III. there are *two* instances in *Blanchardyn and Eglantine* with *that*, and a few with the definite article in *Morte d'Arthur*.

"As for to wene to haue her, thou haste *that berde of thyne* ouer whyte therto ; thy face is so mykel wanne, and *that olde skynne of thyne* ys ouer mykel shronken togyder."— *Blanch. and Egl.* 186, 22—25.

Original : "vous auez la barbe trop grise, la face trop usce, et le cuir trop retrait."

Genitive instead of Apposition.

§ 181. A genitive of comparatively modern date is that *denoting apposition*, in expressions like "vice of a king," "riddle of a lady," "jewel of a man," &c., probably formed in analogy to the well-known connections, "the Isle of Man," "the land of Canaan," and others. I do not know of older instances than the fifteenth century :

"And he was a ryght good knyght of a yonge man."—MALORY, *Morte d'Arthur*, 117, 34.

"(Arthur) helde a Ryal feeste and table rounde with his alyes of kynges, prynces, and noble knyghtes."—*Ibid.* 160, 3.

Sixteenth Century:

"There was in þe castell a vii. score prisoners of Frenchmen."— BERNERS, *Huon*, 90, 30.

"The jewel of life."—SHAKSP. *King John*, v. 1. 40.

"This frail sepulchre of our flesh."—*Richard II.* i. 3. 196.

"A very little thief of occasion."—*Coriolanus*, ii. 1, 32.

For this use *cf.* French : "diable d'homme, diable de femme, fripon de valet." *Littré*, s.v. *de*, 13.

Genitive governed by Verbs and Adjectives.

§ 182. *The genitive governed by verbs and adjectives* is very common in Old English and the other Teutonic languages, and its range is much the same as in Greek and Latin. The substantive in the genitive is *the object exciting mental emotion, the thing remembered* (or forgotten), *the thing lacking or supplied,* &c.

VERBS.

Hrefn *weorces gefeah* (the raven rejoiced at the work).—*Elene*, 110.

þa welwillendan sint to manianne ðæt hie swæ *fægenien* óðerra monna gódra *weorca* ðæt hie eác selfe ðæs *ilcan lyste* (the benevolent are to be admonished so to rejoice in the good works of others as themselves to desire the same).—*Cura Pastoralis*, 228.

þa sint to manianne . . . ðæt hie ðara *yfela* þisse worulde *hiofen* (they are to be admonished to lament the evils of this world).—*Cura Pastoralis*, 393.

We þæs *hereweorces* . . . *myndgiað* (we remember the struggle). —*Elene*, 656, 7.

þa lǽrde he hie eác hú hie hie *gæmetigian* sceoldon óðerra *weorca* (he taught them also how they were to keep themselves free from other occupations). — *Cura Pastoralis*, 130.

Ond eác cwæð Salomon ðæt fremde ne sceoldon bion *gefylde úres mægenes* (Solomon also said that strangers should not be filled with our resources).—*Ibid.* 250.

ADJECTIVES.

Fægen wǽron *síðes* (they were glad of the journey).—*Andreas*, 1040.

He weard eft swǽ ungemetlice *grǽdig* þæs godan *deáðes* (he became so immoderately eager for the death of the good one).—*Cura Pastoralis*, 36.

Tohwon syndon ȝe þyses *weorces* swa *hefige*? (why are ye so grieved [on account] of this work?)— *Blickling Homilies*, 69.

He bið ðára swiðe *gemyndig* (he is very mindful of them).—*Cura Pastoralis*, 36.

On ús ne sý gemeted nǽnigu stów *ǽmetig gástlicra mægena* (let there be found in us no place devoid of spiritual power).—*Blickling Hom.* 36.

Hie wǽron ymb ealle útan mid eágum besett, and eác innane *eágena full* (they were covered outside with eyes, and also inside full of eyes).—*Cura Pastoralis*, 194.

§ 183. In Middle and Modern English the number of verbs governing the genitive becomes very small, that of adjectives remains nearly the same as in Old English. Instead of an object in the genitive, we find either the accusative (as after desire, want), or the object preceded by other prepositions than *of*, as rejoice *over*, long *for*, &c.

In Middle English it is especially the functions of origin, cause and reference which are still expressed by the genitive.

Origin :—

"Ye get no more of (= from) me."—CHAUCER, *Squyeres Tale*, ii. 335.

"Of many a pilgrym hastow Cristes curs."—*Ibid.*, *The Cokes Prologue*, 24.

"For enything that I have had of the."—*Ibid.*, *Freres Tale*, 334.

Of in the passive construction has the same meaning = Modern English *by*.

"I have ben schriven this day of my curate."—*Ibid.*, *Sompnoures Tale*, 395.

"But if he wolde be slayn of Symekyn."—*Ibid.*, *Reeves Tale*, 39.

In Caxton *of* still prevails, though *by* occurs frequently.

Cause :—

"þatt tu dreoriȝ nohht ne beo off nan earþlike unnseollþe" (that thou be not sorry *of* no earthly misfortune).—*Orm.* 4838.

"Off hiss dæþ swiþe bliþe" (very glad of his death).—*Ibid.* 8092.

"Weoren fæin of his scome" (glad of his shame).—LAYAMON, i. 327.

"Fful hevy here hertys wern of this dede." -*Coventry Mysteries*, p. 91.

"(They) judged hemself right happy of a successoure legytyme."—CAXTON, *Blanch. and Egl.* 12, 17.

Reference = as to, in respect of :—

"myȝty of goynge" (orig. ambulandi potentissimum).—CHAUCER, *Boethius*, 3280.

"myȝty of þe herbes" (orig. herbipotens).—*Ibid.* 3484.

"he was wys,
And of his port as meke as is a mayde."
CHAUCER, *Canterbury Tales, Prologue*, 69.

"Hire keverchefs weren ful fyne of grounde."—*Ibid.* 453.

"Bold was hir face, and fair, and reed of hewe."—*Ibid.*

"sore troubled of wyttis."—CAXTON, *Blanchardyn*, 45, 8.

"nought dommaged of nothing."—*Ibid.* 48, 31.

The Genitive used adverbially.

§ 184. The genitive denotes *space* ("genitivus loci").

Gothic.—"insandida ina haiþjôs seinaizôs" (he sent him on his estate.—*Luke*, xv. 15.

"gaggida landis" (he went into a country).—*Ibid.* xix. 12.

Old Norse.—"settisk hann miðra fletja" (he sat down in the middle of the floor).—*Rígsmál.* 3.

"gekk han miðrar brautar" (he went in the middle of the way.—*Ibid.* 2.

Old High German.—"gang ouh thînes sinthes" (go on thy journey, thy way).—OTFRID, iii. 4, 28.

Old English (not frequent).—"wendon him þa óðres weges hámweard" (they returned homeward by another way).—*Chronicle*, 1006.

§ 185. It denotes *time.*

Gothic.—"gistradagis" (yesterday).

"nahts" (at night).

Old Norse.—"ens hindra dags" (on the next day).—*Hávam.* 109.

"annars dags."—*Volundarkv.* 20.

"eins dags."—*Fornm.* i. 67.

Old Saxon.—"dages endi nahtes" (by day and night).—*Héliand*, 515, 2481.

Old English (very frequent).—"dæges and nihtes" (by day and night).—*Beówulf*, 2269.

"þis wæs feórðes geáres" (this was on the fourth year).—*Chronicle*, 47.

"þá þæs ylcan geáres fór Eádweard tó Coluceástre" (in the same year Eadweard marched to Colchester).—*Ibid.* 921.

Middle English.—"fure, þe neuer ne aþeostrede, winteres ne sumeres" (fire that never darkened, neither in summer nor winter).—LAYAMON, i. 121.

"Heo wolden feden þone king dæies and nihtes" (they would feed the king by day and night).—*Ibid.* i. 138.

Later on the old genitive is represented by *of*.

"For al such witte us yeuen is of birthe."—CHAUCER, *Prologue of the Wyf of Bathe*, 400.

"This Pandare that of al the day byforne
Ne myght han comen Troilus to see."—
Ibid., *Troylus and Cryseyde*, v. 282.

"I was warished of al my sorwe
Of al day after."—*Ibid.*, *Boke of the Duchesse*, 1103.

Modern English.—"'Tis but early days."—SHAK. *Troilus*, iv. 5, 12.

"There sleeps Titania sometimes *of* the night."—*Ibid.*, *Midsummer*, ii. 1, 253.

"Gerald and I are so hungry *of a morning*."—A. TROLLOPE, *The Duke's Children*, i. 267.

"Not a soul in the Grave House, *nights*, but Liston."—MRS. EDWARDS, *Pearl Powder*, 57.

§ 186. The genitive denoting *manner* is very frequent in all the periods of the language.

"Hi rícsodon, næs ðeáh *mínes ðonces*." (They reigned, but not by my will.)—*Cura Pastoralis*, 26, 15.

Middle English.—"Gif þu agultest wið þine efen-nexta unðonkes; bet hit þin þonkes hu se þu miht." (If thou sinnest against thy neighbour unwillingly, make amends for it willingly by whatsoever way thou canst.)—*Old English Homilies*, 1, 17. Cf. *ibid.* i. 31; ii. 63; LAYAMON, 4501, 7195.

"al swa ic ear cweð we ne maʒen alre coste halden crist bibode" (as I have before said, we are unable in any wise to observe Christ's behests). *Old English Homilies*, 1, 21.

"þu most al gan þrin, ant al beon bigotten þrin, for in þe ne mei hit nanesweis neomen in." (Thou must go therein altogether and be altogether possessed therein, for in thee may it in nowise enter.)—*Ibid.* 263.

"Willes and woldes" (with will and might).—*Ancren Riwle*, p. 6.

"Newes" (anew) —*Story of Genesis and Exodus*, 252.

In *Modern English* this genitive is very frequent. The old *s* is kept in nee*ds*, but in other cases *of*, sometimes *a* has taken the place of the old inflexion: "of course," "of a truth," "of necessity," "anew."

THE DATIVE CASE.

Functions of the Dative.

§ 187. The general function of the dative in Old English and the Teutonic languages is *influence or interest* (March). But two other cases, viz., the instrumental and locative, having become identical in their endings with the dative, this case represents the functions of three originally different cases.

§ 188. It is the indirect object of many verbs and adjectives like *gifan* (give), *lǽnan* (lend), *unnan* (grant), *secgan* (say), *cýðan* (announce), *þancian* (thank), *helpan* (help); of impersonals: *sceamian* (shame), *langian*, (long), &c.; of adjectives: *gehýrsum* (obedient), *leóf* (dear), &c.

In Middle and Modern English this function has undergone no change; only what was originally a dative is often mistaken for an accusative, so that the dative frequently becomes the subject of a passive construction. See above, § 152 and *Passive*, § 363.

§ 189. A substantive predicate, after the verb *weorðan*, is generally put in the dative.

"Cweð, þæt þás stánas tó hláfe geweorðon" (command that the stones shall turn into bread).—*Matthew*, iv. 3.

§ 190. The person to whose advantage or disadvantage something is done, is put in the dative ("dativus commodi et incommodi").

Gothic.—"ni maúrnaiþ saivalai izvarai, nih leika izvaramma" (do not mourn for your soul, nor for your body).—*Matthew*, vi. 25.

Old Saxon.--"hwô sie lof skoldin wirkean mid irô wordan them the thesa werold giskôp" (how they should work praise with their words for him who created this world).—*Héliand*, 810.

Old English.—"bæd him hláfas wyrcan" (bade make loaves for him).—*Crist and Satan*, 673.

In Middle English, as well as in Modern English, this use often occurs, though *for* is preferred.

"I'll pluck thee berries."—SHAKSP. *Tempest*, ii. 2, 164.

The Ethic Dative.

The ethic dative comes under this heading. We may distinguish two groups of it.

§ 191. (*a*) The dative is a reflexive pronoun, or, rather, looks like it, but it is always connected with intransitive verbs (go, move, &c.).

For instances in other Teutonic languages, see Grimm, *Deutsche Grammatik*, iv. 27*ff.*

Old English.—"wǽron *him* on Cent" (they were for themselves in Kent).—*Chronicle*, 1009.

"beóð *eów* stille" (be still for yourselves).—*Exod.* xiv. 14.

"*Him* Beówulf þanon . . . græsmoldan træd (B. walked hence)" . . . —*Beów.* 1880.

"Gá þe sylfa tó!" (go thou to it).—*Andreas*, 1350.

Cf. *Chronicle*, 1006, 1016.

Middle English.—"Leopen *heom* to horsen."—LAYAMON, ii. 467.

"Octa *him* ut ræd."—*Ibid.* ii. 395.

"He . . . swiðe gon *him* riden."—*Ibid.* ii. 216.

"Colgrim . . . flæh *him*."—*Ibid.* ii. 423.

Modern English.—"Sir, step *you* forth."—SHAKSP. *Cymbeline*, v 5, 130.

"Come thee on."—*Ibid. Ant. and Cleop.* iv. 7, 16.

§ 192. (*b*) The dative does not refer to the subject of the verb and this is a transitive one.

Middle English.—"Hure sinne ðu *him* forgiue" (our sins forgive us for his sake).—*Story of Genesis and Exodus*, 2495.

"Ile prince *me* take hise wond,
And do we us here in godes hond."—*Ibid.* 3821.

"Theise two þou most norissh *me* with thy melke."—*Gesta Romanorum*, 277.

Modern English.—"I am not yet of Percy's mind, the Hotspur of the north, he that kills *me* six or seven dozen of Scots at a breakfast."—SHAK. 1 *Henry* iv. 2, 4, 115.

"He presently . . . Steps *me* a little higher than his vow made to my father . . . Proceeded further; cut *me* off the heads of all the favourites." *Ibid.* 4, 3, 75, 85.

"One Colonna cuts *me* the throat of Orsini's baker—it is for our good."—BULWER, *Rienzi*, 1, 3.

§ 193. *The Dative represents the Instrumental Case.*

Gothic.—"niu tvai sparvans *assarjau* bugjandau" (are not two sparrows bought for a penny?).—*Matthew*, x. 29.

"jah andbahtos lofam slohun ina" (and the servants beat him with their palms).—*Mark*, xiv. 65.

Old Norse.—"þar var Olvir *höndum* tekinn" (there was O. taken with hands).—LUND, p. 127.

Old Saxon.—"ik hebbiu it sô griolîko, quað he, mînes drohtines drôru gikôpôt" (I have it [the silver], said he, dreadfully bought with my lord's blood).—*Héliand*, 5155.

"ak it firihô barn fôtun spurnat" (men tread it, viz. the salt, under foot).—*Ibid.* 1372.

Old High German.—"Nôti nimît" (he takes with force).—GRIMM, *Deutsche Grammatik*, iv. 707.

"giwâtitun inan sînen giwâtin" (they clothed him with his clothes). —*Ibid.*

Old English.—"forþan ic hine sweorde swebban nelle" (I will not kill him with sword).—*Beówulf*, 680.

"Stephanus wæs stánum worpod" (Stephen was killed with stones). -*Elene*, 492.

"wǽron Rómware sóna . . . gegearwod wǽpnum tó wígge" (there were the Romans soon armed with weapons for the fight).—*Ibid.* 48.

For other instances see Grimm, *Deutsche Grammatik*, iv. 708*ff.*

§ 194. *In Middle and Modern English* the instrumental case is represented by prepositions (*by*, *with*); there are, however, here and there a few remnants of the old case.

"(buggen) deore cheape" = to buy dear.—*Wohunge of ure Lauerd*, 281.

"(buggen) lihtlice cheape" = to buy cheap.—*Ibid.* 273.

Besides, what is now looked upon as an accusative in the following instances, was probably long felt as the old dative case:

"*His owne honde* than made he laddres thre."—CHAUCER, *The Milleres Tale*, 438.

"He hath with a dedly wounde,
Fightend his owne handes, slain
Branchus." GOWER, 90.

"My brother Reynawd has hanged hym, his owne handes."—CAXTON, *Aymon*, 343, 31.

"Whatt gate summ he ganngeþþ" (whatever way he goes).—*Orm.* 8216.

"Whatt gate maȝȝ icc berenn child" (what way may I bear child.—*Ibid.* 2437.

"And wiche wise he was more þenne ani oðer man of wifes bosme boren."—*Old English Homilies*, ii. 141.

"And hwiche wise to heuene stie."—*Ibid.* 145.

But in the same work instances with the preposition *a = on* are as frequent; *cf.* pp. 141, 143, 199 and often.

"ðis ebris waxen michil sped" (these Hebrews grow [with] much speed).—*Ibid.* 2548.

"þei sclaundren here parischenys many weies."—WYCLIFE, *Unprinted Works*, 145.

Cf. *ibid.* 171, 233.

"To lyue þe beste manere."—*Ibid.* 252.

§ 195. NOTE 1.—Here and there the dative appears where we expect the genitive.

"Nefde he nane neode *to us* ac we hefden to muchele neode *to him*" (he had no need of us, but we had of him).—*Old English Homilies*, i. 121.

"to speken him harm."—*Ibid.* ii. 11.

"Ac þe ilke þet zuereþ hidousliche be god . . . and zayþ him sclondres" (but he that swears hideously by God and speaks slanders of him).—*Ayenbite*, 6.

"To him he had envie."—*Guy of Warwick*, 600.

The Dative Absolute.

§ 196. A substantive and participle in the dative may make an adverbial clause of time, cause or coexistence. This too seems to have been a common Teutonic use.

Gothic.—"fairra imma visandin" (αὐτοῦ πόρρω) (he being far).—*Luke*, xiv. 32.

"usgaggandin imma" (he going out).—*Mark*, x. 17.

Very frequent.

Old Norse.—Only with *at.* See *Participles* below, § 409-412.

Old Saxon.—"helpandemo usemo drohtine" (our Lord helping).— GRIMM, *Deutsche Grammatik*, p. 905.

Old High German.—"sunnûn danne ûf stîganteru" (sole autem orto); "im ûz farantêm" (egredientibus illis).—GRIMM, *Ibid.*, 901.

Very frequent.

Old English.—"Him sprecendum, hig cómon" (they came while he was speaking).—*Mark*, v. 35.

"þinre dura belocenre, bide" (thy door having been locked, pray).— *Matthew*, vi. 6.

For other instances see Grimm, p. 905.

For an explanation of this so-called absolute construction, see *Participles* below, § 409-412.

The inflexion having decayed, the dative was mistaken for the nominative, hence such constructions as those quoted above, § 153. There are, however, instances of the dative as late as the fourteenth century.

"Hym spekynge þis þingis, manye bileueden into him."—WYCLIFFE, *John* viii. 30.

"And siþ petir was sathanas, for he wolde haue lettid cristis deþ and saluacion of mannus soule, him unwytyngge."—WYCLIF, *Unprinted Works*, p. 56.

"And þer-fore in þe popis lawe decrees & decretals, symony is generaly elepid heresie, & orible peynes ordeyned aȝengst men þat don symonye on ony manere bi hem self or oþere mene persones, bi here wille & consent, & in some cas hem vnwyttynge."—*Ibid.* p. 68.

"The son wax marke, *alle me* seand, when he died on the tree."— *Townley Mysteries*, p. 287.

Cf. *Syntax of the Sentence*, § 56.

The Accusative Case.

Signification of the Accusative Case.

§ 197. The relation of the accusative to its governing verb is analogous to that of the genitive to its governing substantive. With regard to its use in the older stages of the language, we may almost say that it denotes generally every conceivable kind of relation which a substantive can bear to a verb, except that of a subject to its predicate.

Besides the functions of this case when governed by verbs, it is used from the earliest times down to our days for the designation of what extends over space and time.

The Accusative as the object of Transitive Verbs.

§ 198. On the whole, the dominion of this accusative has, in Middle and Modern English, very considerably increased. Most of the verbs which, in Old English, governed the genitive, are now, and were even in Middle English, followed by the accusative, e.g., *ondrǽdan* (fear), *gyrnan* (desire), *wyscan* (wish), *missan* (miss), *costian* (try), &c. But there are a few verbs which, in Middle English, were still followed by the accusative, while now they are used only in connection with prepositions.

> "I pray to god so gif my body care
> Yif ever . . . .
> Herd I a miller better set a werke."
> CHAUCER, *The Cokes Prologue*, 12.

> "Hastow nought herd . . .
> The sorwe of Noe with his felaschipe?"
> *Ibid.*, *Millers Tale*, 353.

§ 199. Sometimes the accusative seems to be governed by *intransitive verbs*.

Old English.—"Hæfden sumne dǽl weges gefaren" (they had walked part of the way)—*Genesis*, xliv. 4.

Middle English.
> "They gone the downes and the dales
> With weping and with wofull tales."
> GOWER, ii. p. 54.

> "Gode sir, quod Gawayn, woldeȝ þou go myn ernde,
> To þe heȝ lorde of þis hous, herber to craue?"
> *Sir Gawayne*, 811.

But in such instances the accusative comes perhaps under the following heading.

The Cognate Accusative,

§ 200. Which repeats more specifically the notion of the verb (March), is frequent in all the periods of the language.

Old English.—"þá leofodon heora líf æfter scs Benedictus regule" (they lived their life after St. Benet's rule).—*Chronicle*, 1087.

"þæt gewin þe he won wið Harold eorl" (the battle that he won against Harold).—*Ibid.* 1063.

Middle English.—"Aelc his saȝe sæide" (each said his saw).— LAYAMON, iii. 47.

"Sonde he sende sone."—*Ibid.* ii. 562 : cf. iii. 4.

"þa bed he his bod."—*Ibid.* ii. 561.

"He had bled so mychel blood."—*Alisaundre*, 5863; cf. *Octavian*, 515 ; *Coventry Myst.* p. 163.

Modern English.—"I would fain die a dry death."—SHAKSPERE, *Tempest*, i. 1, 72.

"We have dreamt a dream."—*Genesis*, xl. 8.

"Well hast thou fought the better fight."—MILTON, *Par. L.* vi. 29.

For the accusative in such constructions as "I am banished the court," see *Passive*, § 363.

Double Object.

§ 201. 1. Some verbs of *asking* and *teaching* may have two accusatives, one of a *person* and the other of a *thing*.

"Ne meahton we geláeran leófne þeóden ríces hyrde ræd ǽnigne" (we could not teach the dear lord, the shepheard of the realm, any counsel).—*Beówulf*, 3080.

"hwæt heó hine bǽde" (whatever she might ask him).—*Matthew*, xiv. 17.

This construction, however, is rare in Old English; we find the accusative of person + the genitive of thing, or the accusative of thing + the dative of person.

§ 202. 2. Some verbs of *making, naming, regarding*, may have two accusatives of the same person or thing.

"Hé his englas déð æðele gástas" (he makes noble souls his angels). *Psalms*, ciii. 5.

"seó eá, þá weras Eufraten nemnað" (the river, which men name Euphrates).—CÆDMON, *Genesis*, 234.

For the nominative governed by *hátan*, see above, § 150.

There is no considerable change of this construction in Middle and Modern English.

Accusative with Infinitive. See *Infinitive*, § 401-404.

Accusative as Adverb denoting:

§ 203. 1. Place.

Old English.—"Hæfdon sumne dæl weges gefaren" (they had gone home part of the way).—*Genesis* xliv. 4.

Middle English.—"Saladyn was ten myle thenne."—*Rich. Cœur de Lion*, 2974.

"Apon a crosse, noght hens a wyle, To ded he yede."—*Townley Mysteries*, p. 273.

Modern English.—Quite common.

§ 204. 2. Time.

Old English.—"High fuhton fif dagas fight at finnesb."-*Chronicle*, 82.

"He rícsade xvii. gér."—*Ibid.* 189.

Middle English.—"þe bataile of Troie, þat laste fele ȝer."—Robert of Glouc. 208.

"This seven daies I n'el newt speke."—*Seuyn Sages*, 377.

Especially noteworthy are the expressions "never his life," "term of his life," and "tyme enough" = in time.

"Imeneus, that god of weddyng is,
Seigh neuer his life so mery a weddid man."
            Chaucer, *Marchaundes Tale*, 487.

"Many a wighte hath loued thynge he neuer saugh his lyue."—*Id. Troylus and Cryseyde*, v. 165.

"Neuer the days of her lyff she sholde wedde paynem nor no man infidele."—Caxton, *Blanchardyn and Eglantine*, 65, 15.

"(He) wend neuer to haue come tyme enough" (French: a tans [temps],—*Ibid.* 158, 4.

Cf. *ibid.* 170, 5; Caxton, *Aymon*, 265, 19; 343, 5.

"Neuer his lif."—Malory, *Morte d'Arthur*, 127, 23.

Cf. *ibid.* 228, 24; Berners, *Huon*, 332, 8; 334, 10.

§ 205. 3. Manner.

Cf. above, *Instrumental*, § 193-194.

§ 206. *The Objective Absolute.*

"All loose her negligent attire,
All loose her golden hair,
Hung Margaret o'er her slaughter'd sire."
                    W. Scott.

K

This use is scarcely to be traced back to the prehistoric Teutonic times, though it occurs in Old Norse, and is common in Modern German.

It occurs too in Old French, and this probably influenced the Middle English, where it becomes frequent in the fourteenth century.

"Hii . . . To him come . . . vnhosed and barevot, & vngurt al so, Hor armes to the elbowe naked, hor heued bar perto."—ROBERT OF GLOUC. 10827.

"Thei ben aboute the Souldan with swerdes drawen and gysarmez and axes, her armes lift up in highe with the wepenes."—MAUNDEVILLE, p. 40.

"Upon an amblere esely sche sat,
Wymplid ful wel, and on hire head an hat
As brood as is a bocler or a targe,
A footmantel aboute hire hupés large,
And on hire feet a paire of spores scharpe."
CHAUCER, *Canterbury Tales, Prol.*, 470.

"High on hors he sat,
Uppon his heed a flaundrish bever hat."
Ibid. 272.

Modern English.

"Thence more at ease their minds, and somewhat raised
By false presumptuous hope, the ranged Powers
Disband."
MILTON, *Par. Lost*, ii. 521.

"She started up: the thought of Liston in her heart, and Dr. Blair on the carpet."—MRS. EDWARDS, *Pearl Powder*, p. 279.

Interchange of the Cases.

I. Nominative instead of the Oblique Case.

The Nominative after "but" and "save."

§ 207. 1. The prepositions *"but"* and *"save"* are sometimes followed by the nominative; but then they must rather be looked upon as conjunctions, and the whole expression as an elliptic one.

Old English.—"Næfð he nán þing þe ne sí on minum anwealde búton þú" = *but it, be thou.*"—*Genesis*, xxxix. 9.

Middle English.—" Alle shalle be slain *but oonely we.*"—*Townley Mysteries*, p. 281.

" Noon *but I* have seen it."—CAXTON, *Blanchardyn and Eglantine*, 43, 32.

" Al be ded *sauf I.*"—CAXTON, *Charles the Grete*, 102, 31.

In Old French, *fors* too is often followed by the nominative.

" Un celier fit faire soutil Sous terre, u nus n'aloit *fors* il" (a cellar he caused to be made underground where nobody went but *he.*—*Le Roman de Mahomet*, 51.

Modern English.—" Earth up has swallowed all my hopes *but she.*" SHAK. *Romeo*, i. 2, 14.

> "What made thee, when they all were gone
> And none *but thou and I alone,*
> To act the devil?"
> BUTLER, *Hudibras*, 3, 3, 149.

A similar sort of ellipsis probably appears in the following instances :

> "Nor hope (I) to be myself less miserable
> By what I seek, but others to make such
> As I."
> MILTON, *Par. Lost*, ix. 126.

" She [superstition] taught the weak to bend, the proud to pray,
To power unseen, and mightier far *than they.*
POPE, *Essay on Man*, 3, 252.

" Believe that Rome has no firmer friend *than he* who, ordained to preserve order, finds himself impotent against aggression."—BULWER, *Rienzi*, i. 5.

§ 208. 2. Instead of the second object, the nominative appears after *hátan*. See above, § 150.

Anacoluthic Nominative.

§ 209. 3. In all these cases it is a sort of *anacoluthon* which produces the irregular construction, and it is especially striking in the following instances, in which a pronoun referring to a noun in an oblique case appears in the nominative.

"Unthank come on his heed that band him so,
And *he* that bettir schuld han knyt the reyne."
CHAUCER, *The Reeves Tale*, 163.

"Demetrius men saiden tho
The better knight was of the two,
To whom the lond was attendant
As he, which heir was apparent."
GOWER, i. pp. 213, 214.

"Goo agen to Tormaday to see the noble lande of that lady, *she* of whom thou arte amorouse soo moche."—CAXTON, *Blanch. and Egl.* 186, 19.

"To go and come, of custom free or any other task,
I mean *by Juliana, she,* that blaze of beautie's breeding."
Clyomon and Clamydes, p. 491, *b.*

"Do never view *thy father, I*, in presence any more."—*Ibid.* 497, a.

"Sith that mine honour cowardly was stole *by caitiffe he.*"—*Ibid.*

"But shall I frame, then, mine excuse, *by serving Venus, she.*"—*Ibid.* 501, *b.*

"Than thus to see *fell fortune, she,* to hold her state in spite."—*Ibid.* 505, *b.*

"Clamydes, ah, *by fortune, she,* what froward luck and fate
Most cruelly assigned is unto thy noble state."—*Ibid.* 507, *b.*

"Fie *on fell fortune, she.*"—*Ibid.* 508, *a.*

"Although that *with Clamydes, he,* I have not kept my day."—*Ibid.* 511, *a.*

"Yet though *unto Neronis, she,* I may not show my mind."—*Ibid.*

"Neronis, daughter to the kyng, by the kyng *of Norway, he,*
Within a ship of merchandise convey'd away is she."—*Ibid.* 514, *a.*

"So do I fly from *tyrant, he,* whose heart were hard than flint."—*Ibid.* 515, *a.*

There is a similar instance in Shakspere, but it is apparently a quotation from some romantic poem.

"For we that take purses go by the moon and the seven stars, and not by *Phœbus, he,* 'that wandering knight so fair.'"—SHAK. 1 *Henry IV.* i. 2, 16.

Cf. also the following instances:

"Through the encouraging words of *he* that led in front."—BUNYAN, *Pilgrim's Progress*, 299.

"Between you and I."—DICKENS, *Pickw.* i. x.

Nominative with Verbs once Impersonal, and in Passive Constructions.

§ 210. 4. Another interchange of the nominative and the oblique case was brought about by the decay of the inflexion in the :

(*a*) Impersonal and

(*b*) Passive constructions.

In instances like : "Wo was this king," "God be thanked," what was originally the dative was mistaken for the nominative, and hence arose the constructions : "I am woe," "I am thanked."

See *Impersonal Verbs*, § 337, and *Passive*, § 363.

The Absolute Pronoun in the Oblique Case.

§ 211. II. The oblique case instead of the nominative.

There is a decided tendency in Middle and Modern English to use absolute personal pronouns in the dative (or accusative) case. This tendency, which in French was strong enough to divide the pronouns into two different classes (*conjoints* and *absolus*) produced, in English, the following changes.

"*You*" supplanted "*ye*."

§ 212. The oldest instances that have come to my notice are those in *Sir Tristrem* (ed. Kölbing), about 1320 A.D.

"Send ȝou ȝare."—1150.

"ȝou miȝt haue slain me ynouȝ, þo þat y Tramtris hiȝt."—*Ibid.* 1598.

But in both cases we have probably to read þou.

There are, however, certain instances as early as the middle of the fourteenth century :

"Ye show your lady lytille love
That *you* so herttly preyse."
Ipomadon, 1807.

"Fynde *you* him, yff that ye may."
Ibid. 5298.

Other instances occur in *Guy of Warwick*, ed. Zupitza, 15th century version (ll. 4192, 6352, 7053, 7217, 7218, 9847), and they are frequent in Caxton; but even there it is mostly in the inverted position (imperative, less frequent in interrogative sentences) that *you* is introduced; but the number of *ye's*, even in that position, prevails.

In *Blanchardyn and Eglantine* there are two *you's* in the imperative:

"Come *you* with me."—60, 28.

"Be *you* sure."—185, 17.

"But knowe *you*, that Hernyer dyde mysse of his enterpryse."—*Aymon*, 90, 15.

"Fayr chyldren, now be *you* sure."—*Ibid.* 129, 1.

"Defye *you* hym on my behalfe."—*Ibid.* 157, 32.

"Now gyue *you* me good counseyll."—*Ibid.* 203, 14; 361, 9; 412, 26.

§ 213. *Interrogative Sentences.*

"What be *you*, fayre knyghte?"—CAXTON, *Aymon*, 91, 25.

"Telle me, how thynke *you*?"—*Ibid.* 170, 1.

"What thynge aske *you* of me?"—*Ibid.* 246, 20; 184, 31; 343, 17; 373, 29.

There are, however, several instances of *you* in another position.

"*You* holde."—CAXTON, *Aymon*, 26, 18.

"Cosin, seyd Reynawde, *you* speke well and wisely."—*Ibid.* 132, 33.

"No up, Ogyer, and *you* duke Naymes."—*Ibid.* 157, 23.

"Yf *you* wyl yelde yourselfe to his merci."—*Ibid.* 189, 22.

Cf. *ibid.* 432, 14; 438, 10.

"*Me*" for "*I*."

§ 214. "It is me" instead of "it is I," or the Middle English "it am I." I do not find any instance of this now widely spread use before the eighteenth century. In Steele's comedy, *The Funeral*, even common people, using colloquial English, say "it is I."

"Nay, good madam, *'tis I*, *'tis I*, your ladyship's own woman : *'Tis I. . . .*"—172, *b*.

But Richardson offers several instances of "it is me."

"She would not speak of the occasion of those words which was me." —*Pamela*, 43, *b*.

"If ever there was a rogue in the world, it is *me*."—*Ibid.* 64, *a*.

Him = *he* and *them* = *they* occur in Elizabethan writers:

"Here be *them* can perceive it."—BEN JONSON, *Every Man in his Humour* (1598 A.D.), I. 1.

"Lay on, Macduff,
And damned be *him* that first cries 'Hold, enough!'"
Macbeth, v. 8, 34.

§ 215. In connection with *all* and numerals, and after *than* and *as*, the oblique case instead of the nominative is pretty frequent.

"Whan thise wordes were fynysshed, all the foure brethren, and all *theym* of theyr companye arayed themselfe" . . . CAXTON, *Aymon*, 78, 22.

"The base courte began to be sore moved, and the crye was so great, for al *them* of the dongeon defended themselfe valyantlye."— *Ibid.* 94, 12.

"But I telle you, upon your feythe that none other shal knowe the same, but only we, *us* three, unto the tyme that the dede be accomplysshed."—*Ibid.* 212, 30.

"He thought himself as worthy as *hym* that hym created."—*Townley Myst.* p. 20.

"For ther is nothyng more suspecte to euyl peple than *them* whom they knowe to be wyse and trewe."—CAXTON, *The Curial*, 4, 18.

Modern English.—"Is she as tall as *me?*"—SHAKSP. *Antony,* iii. 3, 14.

"No mightier than thyself or *me.*"—*Jul. Cæs.* i. 3, 76.

See Abbott, §§ 206—216.
In modern prose, instances abound.
For the oblique case in connection with *self,* see § 292.

THE ARTICLE.

§ 216. In Old English, especially in poetry, the language can do without the article, just as in Latin, though both the definite and indefinite articles are found in the oldest monuments. The former is pretty frequent both in poetry and prose, the latter is rare even in the tenth century.

The Definite Article.

§ 217. On the whole, the functions of the definite article, from Old English down to our times, have undergone no essential change. But there are several points worth noting.

Names of Persons with the Definite Article.

§ 218. Names of persons which, logically speaking, exclude every determination, admit of the definite article, not only when preceded by attributes, but also when alone.

Old English.—*Se* preceding names of persons is frequent, but then it does not mean *the,* but *this, that.*

"Eart þu se Beówulf, se þe wið Brecan wunne" (art thou that Beówulf who foughtst with Brecan ?)—*Beówulf,* 506.

"se Columba" = this Columba.—*Chronicle,* 565.

"se Cuþa."—*Ibid.* 571.

"se Birinus."—*Ibid.* 634.

Middle English.
"How þe magdalen wit grete
Com for to was our lorde fete."
Cursor Mundi, 159.

So the Cotton and Fairfax MSS., the Göttingen and Trinity MSS., have "mari magdalain" (maudeleyn).

"He made als, goon ys a grete while, Origenes upon *the* Maudeleyne."
—CHAUCER, *Legend of Goode Women*, 428.

"Ascayn biget Silui, of whom þe Brut com."—ROBERT OF GLOUC. 220; cf. 288, 299.

"The Waleis wes to drawe."—WRIGHT, *Polit. Songs*, p. 213.

"Sire Robert *the* Bruytz."—*Ibid.* p. 215.

"*The* Longespay was a noble knyght."—*Rich. Cœur de Lion*, 6983.

"Thei take Jhesu and lede hym in gret hast to *the* Herowde."—*Coventry Myst.* p. 303.

"I saw *the* Daphene closed under rinde."—*Complaint of the Black Knight*, 64.

Cf. Mätzner, iii. 165.

Modern English.

"*The* Douglas and *the* Hotspur both together
Are confident against the world in arms."
SHAK. 1 *Henry IV.* v. 1, 116.

"Laws were the most sure
When like *the* Draco's they were writ in blood."
MARLOWE, *Jew of Malta*, Prol.

"Stout Choiseul would discern in *the* Dubarry nothing but a wonderfully dizened Scarlet woman."—CARLYLE, *French Revol.* i. 1.

§ 219. *Names of Persons preceded by Attributes* take the article in Old English, but drop it as early as the time of Layamon and Orm, and in the Elizabethan authors the omission of it prevails.

I have examined three sixteenth century plays of three different authors with regard to this point, and the result is invariably the same. Greene's *Orlando Furioso*, Peele's *Arraignment of Paris*, Lodge's *Wounds of Civil War*, gave the following proportions:

1. Without article : with article = 47 : 6.
2.   Ditto   :   ditto   = 16 : 3.
3.   Ditto   :   ditto   = 42 : 4.

Personifications are dealt with in the same way:

"Cruell Revenge, and rancorous Despight."
SPENSER, *Faerie Queene*, 2, 7, 22.

As for the other proper names (seas, rivers, mountains, countries), the use is not bound by fixed rules.

Nouns preceded by Possessive Pronouns.

§ 220. In Old English as in Gothic, Old Norse and Old High German, nouns with possessive pronouns may take the definite article.

"hæleð mín *se* leófa" (my dear youth).—*Elene*, 511.

"þú eart dóhtor mín *séo* dýreste" (thou art my dearest daughter.—*Juliana*, 193.

"þæt tácnode Leoniða¹ on his *þæm* nihstan gefeohte" (that Leonidas showed in his next battle).—OROSIUS, 84, 31.

"Mammea his *sio* góde modor" (his the good mother Mammea).—*Ibid.* 270, 26.

"mid hire *þære* yfelan sceónnesse" (with her evil temptation).—*Blickling Homilies*, 5, 1.

§ 221. The article preceding the possessive pronoun:

"Se heóra cyning" (their king).—OROSIUS, 56, 31.
"seo heora iugoð" (their youth).—*Blickling Homilies*, 163, 3.
"seo hire gebyrd" (her birth).—*Ibid.* 163, 9.

For Gothic, see Grimm, *Deutsche Grammatik*, iv. 392; for Old Norse, *ibid.* 433; for Old High German, 403.

§ 222. In Caxton, possessive pronouns used substantively are sometimes preceded by the article:

"Thenne toke the prouost his spere, and so dyde Blanchardyn *the his*."—*Blanch. and Eglant.* 48, 20 (French original: la sienne).

"I praye you that euery man force hymself to do worthily hys deuoyr, that your worship and *the oures* be kepte."—*Aymon*, 72, 21.

"In whiche he hath not rendred the reason or made any decision, to approve better *the his*, than that other."—*Eneydos*, 23, 19.

This use (or rather abuse) seems due to French influence.

Nouns in the Vocative Case.

§ 223. In the older periods of the language, nouns in the vocative case are preceded by the definite article instead of " *Oh!* "

Old English.—Frequent in *homilies:*

"Men þa leófestan" (dearest brethren).—*Blickling Homilies*, p. 61; Wulfstan, 134 (elsewhere he prefers 'leófan men').

"Geþenc nú, *se* mǽra maga Healfdenes" (remember, now, the famous son of Halfdene).—*Beówulf*, 1475.

"Herra se góda" (good lord).—CÆDMON, *Genesis*, 676.

Middle English.—"O Aurilie þe king, þu fræinest me a sellic þing" (O king A., thou askest me a strange thing).—*Ibid.* ii. 293.

"Farwelle, *the* semelyst that ever was seyn."—*Townley Mysteries*, p. 171.

"Farwelle, *the* luflyst that ever was bred."—*Ibid.*

"Sith that we haue lost thee, farewell *the* joye of this world."—CAXTON, *Aymon*, 574, 30.

"Then syr Launcelot cryed: *the* knyght wyth the blak shelde, make the redy to Juste with me!"—MALORY, *Morte d'Arthur*, 392, 16.

Modern English.
"*The* restful place! renewer of my smart,
The labour's salve! increasing my sorrow,
The body's ease, and troubler of my heart,
Quieter of mind, mine unquiet foe."
WYATT, *Poems*, p. 33.

"My lord, *the* king, *the* king!"—SHAK. *Wint. T.* iii. 2, 143.

"Brother, my lord the duke,
Stand to and do as we."
Tempest, iii. 3, 52.

The Definite Article before Numerals.

§ 224. *Numerals denoting* part of a whole, are sometimes preceded by the definite article.

"And sins he ran . . . .
And borwed him large boteles thre;
And in *the* two his poysoun poured he;
The thrid he keped clene for his drynke."
CHAUCER, *The Pardoneres Tale*, 410.

"And if thou maist so fer forth wynne,
That thou resound erst byginne,
And woldest seyn thre thingis or mo,
Thou shalt fulle scarsly seyn *the* two."
Romaunt of the Rose, v. 77.

The Indefinite Article.

§ 225. Though the Teutonic languages agree in the later development of the indefinite article *a, an*, out of the numeral, that use was probably not common Teutonic. In Gothic and Old Norse *ains* or *einn* is always a numeral, in Old High German it does not appear before the tenth century, and in Old English poetry there are but faint traces of it. There are no instances in Cynewulf; Cædmon offers *án* = *sum, some one ;* but there are two examples of it in Beówulf and many in prose.

"Swá þá driht-guman dreámum lifdon eádiglíce, óð þæt án ongan fyrene fremman, feónd on helle" (thus the valiant men lived in joy happily, until a fiend of hell began to work evil).—*Beówulf*, 100.

"he geheóld tela fiftig wintru (wæs þa fróð cyning, eald éðel-weard), óð þat *án* ongan deorcum nihtum draca rícsian" (until a dragon began to lord it in dark nights).—*Ibid.* 2211.

"An man hæfde twegen suna" (a man had two sons).—*Matthew*, xxi. 8.

"þa com án man þæs nama wæs Jairus" (there came a man whose name was Jairus).—*Luke*, viii. 41.

"Cerdic and Cynric of slógon ánne Bryttiscne cyning" (C. and C. slew a British king).—*Chronicle*, 508.

The function of the indefinite article being nearly the same in Middle English as in modern times, I need only draw attention to a few points.

"A" before Numerals.

§ 226. *A* is often used before numerals, sometimes with the meaning of "*about*"; the numeral, then, is looked upon as a sort of collective noun, in analogy to *hundred* and *thous-*

and. In Old English this use is very rarely met with. Mätzner quotes the following instance:

"Man singe ylce frigdæge æt ylcum mynstre *án* fiftig sealmas for þone cyng" (men shall sing each Friday in each cloister about fifty psalms for the king).—*Legg.* ix. 3.

Middle English.—"Alle bute *a* fyue men one."—ROB. OF GLOUC. 770.
"That is *a* 5 myle on this half Damasce."—MAUNDEVILLE, p. 124.
"Thens *a* 4 myle."—*Ibid.* p. 110.

Modern English.—This *a* is very frequent in Berners's *Huon.*

"And they were in all *a* iiii score horsses."—18, 12.
"(The knyght) sayd how that a vii yere passyd that duke Seuyn our father had taken iii castels."—29, 16.
"So it fell that after the deth of his father *about a* vii yere, kinge Charlemayn sent for him."—210, 3.
"She dyed thereof *a* v yere past" (ed. 1601: *about*).—210, 19.

Cf. *ibid.* 61, 3; 62, 18; 63, 16; 63, 18; 66, 23, &c.

"I have not past *a* two shillings or so."—BEN JONSON, *Every Man in his Humour*, 1, 4.

The Indefinite Article used Pleonastically.

§ 227. Here and there *a* puts in an unexpected appearance in analogy to *so* + adjective + *a*:

"It nedeth not to be doubted that he is come to his extremyte of prowes and valyantes, wythout that amours hathe be the cause in the persone of *some hyghe a* pryncesse."—CAXTON, *Blanchardyn and Egl.* 72, 20.
"he gaf to hym-self grete merueylle, and was wel abashed of *that soudayne a* wylle that was come to hym."—*Ibid.* 126, 9.
"which is the most fayr, and the most noble, and the moste complete *a* lady, and most pleasaunt of all the remnaunt of the world."—*Ibid.* 156, 13.
"This so pleasant a path."—BUNYAN, *Pilgr. Progr.* p. 2.

Omission of the Article.

§ 228. As late as the fourteenth century the article was omitted in passages where we should expect it. *Cf.* the following instances in Trevisa, Higden's *Polychronicon*:

"After solempne and wise writers of arte."—TREVISA, i. 3.

(Harleian MS. add *the*).

"But besines of writers to oure unkunnynge hadde i-holde and i-stregned mynde of olde dedes."—*Ibid.* i. 4.

(Harleian MS.: *the* solicitude of writers, *the* memorie of thynges.)

"þe brennynge of the temple of Jewes."—*Ibid.* i. 29.

"þe comynge of Saxons."—*Ibid.*

"þe processe of Holy Writt."—*Ibid.* 31.

"In þat lond beeþ noble citees and famous Neopolis and Puteoli."—*Ibid.* i. 203.

"For saltnesse of þe erþe."—*Ibid.* 265.

"melteþ wiþ hete of fiʒtynge as snow droop wiþ hete of þe sonne."—*Ibid.* 269.

§ 229. From the sixteenth century the use or omission of the article was, on the whole, ruled by the same principles as now-a-days; but poets retained for themselves great liberty in that respect. Thus, Spenser in his poems, especially in the *Faerie Queene*, quite resembles Chaucer in this point, and even goes beyond him.

Most cases of omission occurring in poetry may be brought under the following headings:

§ 230. 1. Before the second object.

"The wretched woman, whom vnhappy howre
Hath now made thrall to your commandement."
SPENSER, *Faerie Queene*, 1, 2, 22.

§ 231. 2. Before a substantive used predicatively.

"You know that I am legate to the pope."—MARLOWE, *Edw.* ii. 342.

"Oh, must this day be period of my life?"—*Ibid.* 1277.

"Faire harbour that them seems, so in they entred ar."—SPENSER, *F. Q.* 1, 1, 7, 9.

§ 232. 3. Before a substantive in apposition.

"Conduct these warlike men
To Rome, unhappy mistress of our harms."
LODGE, *Wounds of Civil War*, 119.

"Not Euripus (unquiet flood) so oft
Ebbs in a day."
Tancred and Gismunda, 37.

"Prince of Suavia, noble soil."—*Sir Clyomon and Sir Clamydes*, 491, *a*

§ 233. 4. After *never* and *ever*.

"Where *never* blow was dealt with enemy."—GASCOIGNE, 58.

"I *never* saw bear go a-milking in all my life."—*Mucedorus*, 212.

"As *ever* you had man in all your life."—*Ibid.* 224.

"Will euer wight beleue that such hard hart
Could rest within the cruell mothers breast?"
Gorboduc, 1280.

Instances abound.

§ 234. 5. After *as* in comparisons.

"As hound that hath his keeper lost,
Seek I your presence to obtain."
WYATT, *Poems*, p. 44.

"Think not . . . . I'll
Keep the house as owlet does her tower."
SHERIDAN KNOWLES, *Hunchback*, 2, 2.

§ 235. 6. Before nouns beginning with *s* or *th*, the definite article is shunned.

"Whose cheerful voice doth comfort *saddest* wights."—GASCOIGNE, 49.

"To glad their heart *with sight* of pleasant sparks."
To fill their ear *with sound* of instruments."—*Ibid.* 58.

"Who was unmoved *with sight* of the most horrible continuances of death."—SIDNEY, *Arcadia*, p. 26.

"In *sight* of God and us your guilt is great."
SHAK. 2 *Henry VI.* II. iii. 2.

"The dismallest object that ever eye *with sight* made hard lament."—TITUS, ii. 3, 205.

"He, leaving *throne* alone."—GREENE, *Alphonsus*, 240, *a*.

"I will have all *things* my lord doth want."—GREENE, *George a-Greene*, 254, *a*.

"He, making speedy way through *spersed* ayre."—SPENSER, *F. Q.* I. i. 39^1.

"The false Duessa, leaving noyous Night,
Returnd to *stately* pallace of Dame Pryde."
Ibid. I. v. 45^2.

THE ADJECTIVE

Adjectives used as Substantives.

§ 236. The adjectives (answering to the Aristotelian category of ποίον, *quale*) were formed, at first, like substantives, and many of them could be used in both characters. There are languages in which adjectives are not distinguished from substantives.[1]

The English adjectives may become substantives in three different ways.

Substantives named after quality.

§ 237. The quality of a thing is so striking, that the name of the adjective is adopted for the substantive itself. In this manner many nouns were formed in prehistoric times, *e.g. wheat*, A.-S. *hwǽte*, Goth. *hwaiteis*, from the root *hwit* = white, so named from the whiteness of the meal; *gold*, from the root *ghar*, to be yellow.

---

[1] M. Müller, *l.c.* 442. In Arabic and often in Hebrew substantives are used where we expect adjectives. Instead of saying "every man," "some men," the Arabs say "the totality of men," "a portion of men."—SILVESTRE DE SACY, *Grammaire Générale: Adjectif. Cf.* the old English instances above.

Ellipsis of the Noun.

§ 238. An adjective may, according to the nature of the quality denoted by it, refer to one noun only, or it may be very often found as an attribute of one particular noun; in both cases the result is the same, viz. the adjective by itself conveying at once the idea of the noun to which it belongs, the latter is dropped. This ellipsis, which chiefly applies to adjectives referring to God and man, seldom to animals and things, was common to all the Teutonic languages.

Gothic.—"Jah biþe usdribans varþ unhulþo, rodida *sa dumba*" (and when the devil was cast out, the dumb spake).—*Matthew,* ix. 33.

"Laistidedum afar imma *tvai blindans*" (two blind men followed him).—*Ibid.* ix. 27.

"Urreisand dauþans" (the dead rise).—*Luke,* xx. 37.

Old Saxon.—"Warð thâr lêf sô manag, halt géhêlid, endi hâf sô sama, blindun gibôtid" (there were cured many sick [people], halting, palsied, blind).—*Héliand,* 3754—56.

Cf. 2096, 2304, and *passim.*

Old High German.—"Ther dôto" (the dead man).—OTFRID, iii. 24, 60.

"Ther blinto" (the blind man).—*Ibid.* iii. 23, 8.

Cf. *ibid.* iii. 20, 73; v. 21, 9.

§ 239. While the Germans preserve this usage to the present day, the English language did not favour it in the same degree through all the periods of its development.

Old English.—

1. Adjectives referring to God. Examples are very frequent.

"cwæð þæt se ælmihtiga eorðan worhte" (he said that the Almighty created the earth).—*Beówulf,* 92.

Cf. Blickling Hom. 29, 2, 31, 25.

"hie unscyldigne, synna leásne feore beræddon" (they robbed of life the innocent, him who was free of sins, *sc.* Christ).—*Elene,* 496.

L

2. Adjectives referring to man, and describing qualities of body and mind, may be used as well in the singular as in the plural, in the positive as well as in the comparative and superlative degree.

"Se blinda, gyf he blindne lǽt" (the blind, if he lead a blind [man]).—*Matthew*, xv. 14.

"Se þe underféhð rihtwisne on rihtwises naman, he onféhð rihtwises méde" (he that receiveth a righteous [man] in the name of a righteous [man] shall receive a righteous [man's] reward).—*Ibid.* x. 41.

"Hie for feos lufan earmne fordemaþ buton scylde" (for the sake of bribes, they condemn the innocent poor [man]).—*Blick. Hom.* 63, 11.

"Se blinda him ondswerode" (the blind [man] answered him).—*Ibid.* 15, 23.

"twegen landes men and án ælþeódig" (two natives and one stranger).—ÆLFRIC, *Hom.* ii. 26, 20.

Some adjectives which appear in the comparative degree alter their meaning with their grammatical function. These are: *gingra*, originally younger, but substantively = disciple; *yldran*, elders, parents.

Cf. German: *der Jünger, die Eltern.*

"se biscop biþ Godes gingra" (the bishop is God's vassal).—*Blick. Hom.* 45, 17.

"Crist sylfa his geongrum sægde" (Christ himself said to his disciples). —*Ibid.* 109, 7.

"forþon ure yldran swultan" (for our parents died).—*Ibid.* 195, 24.

Very frequent.

§ 240. *Middle English.*—The singular of these adjectives becomes very rare in prose; perhaps we may say that it is limited to poetry only.

"Al þat seȝ þat *semly* syked in hert,
Sayde soþly al same segges til oþer,
Carande for þat *comly.*"

(All that saw that fair one, sighed in their heart, and said truly one man to the other, out of care for that comely one).—*Sir Gawayne*, 672.

"Hit were a fole fele-folde, *my fre,* by my trawþe" (it would be a many-fold fool, my noble one, by my faith).—*Ibid.* 1545.

Cf. 1549, 1783.

"þis haþel heldeȝ him in, & þe halle entres" (this noble one moves in, and enters the hall).—*Ibid.* 221.

Cf. 234, 256, 655, 844.

Other adjectives used substantively in *Sir Gawayne* are :

auncien (ancient), 948 ; dere (dear, noble), 678, 928 ; felle (cruel, of a boar), 1585 ; gay, 970, 1215, 1822, 2035 ; hende (fair), 827, 946, 1252, 1813, 2330 ; swete, 1108, 1222 ; wyly, 1905.

"For he nought helpeth the needful in his neede."
CHAUCER, *Man of Lawes Tale*, 14.

"As saith the wise."—*Id. Sompnoures Tale*, 307.

"Com doun, my leef" (my darling).
Id. Marchaundes Tale, 1145.

Adjectives substantively used in the plural occur pretty often in Middle English prose. Apparently the English language, like later Latin, is against the usage (adopted by the Slavonic and Germanic idioms) which makes an individual represent a whole class.

"And botnede blinde, þe dumbe ant te deaue, ant te deade arerde to lif" (he cured the blind, the dumb and the deaf, and raised the dead to life).—*Marharete*, 1.

"And bitacneð þis tur þe hehschipe of meidenhad, þat bihald as of heh, alle widewen under hire and *weddede* baðe" (and this tower typifies the elevated state of virginity, that beholds as from high, all widows under it and *wedded women*).—*Hali Maidenhad*, 5.

"He nalde mid his tocume þa sunfullen fordemen" (he would condemn the sinful at his coming).—*O. E. Hom.* i. 95.

"iselic beoð efre þa mildheortan" (blessed are ever the meek-hearted).—*Ibid.* 109.

"þe lauerd seal beon liðe þan godan, and eisful þan dusian" (the Lord shall be gentle to the good, and awful to the wicked).—*Ibid.* 111.

In poetry examples are very numerous.

§ 241. *Modern English.*—The licence of using adjectives referring *to persons* as substantives may be said to have disappeared as early as the time of the Tudors ; but the traces left by it are visible even in the present stage of the language.

Some adjectives have become exclusively substantives, as : a saint, a sage.

Some old formulas still survive, as : the rich and the poor, old and young, high and low, the just and the unjust, the good, the wicked ; but only in the plural.

The old comparatives of *old and young* not only survived, but gave rise to analogous formations : in analogy of "my elders, my youngers," were introduced "my inferiors, my superiors," &c.

Present Participles used as Substantives.

§ 242. They are very frequent in poetry, less numerous in prose. Some are real substantives.

Feónd (fiend), present participle of *feón*, to hate ; Goth. *fijands*, German *feind.—Beówulf*, 164, 726, &c.

Freónd (friend), present participle of *freón*, to love ; Goth. *frijonds*, German *freund.—Beów.* 1386, 1865, &c.

Hetend (enemy), pres. part. of *hetan* (*hatian*), to hate.

"Syððan wæpen ahóf wið *hetendum*" (since he took up arms against his enemies).—*Elene*, 17, 8. *Cf.* 119 ; *Beów.* 1829, &c.

Wigend (warrior) and its compounds *burgwigend, byrnwigend, lindwigend.—Beów.* 3100, 1126 ; *Elene* 106, 984, &c.

The adjectives referring to God are :

Hélend (the Saviour), Old Saxon : *Héliand, O. H. G. heilant ; Elene*, 726 &c. ; *Blick. Hom.* 11, 21, 15, 15 &c.

Nerigend (Saviour), Goth. *nasjands, Luke* i. 47, ii. 11 ; Old Sax. *neriend.—Héliand*, 3718 &c. ; *O. H. G. nerrendeo ; Elene*, 461, 465 &c.

Wealdend (Ruler) (Old Sax. *waldand ; Héliand passim ;*) *Beów.* 17, 183 &c.; *Elene*, 4, 80 &c.; CÆDMON, *Exodus*, 16, 432.

Alýsend (Redeemer), *Blick. Hom.* 65, 30, 87, 9.

Fréfrend (Comforter), *Ibid.* 105, 17, 131, 23.

Sceppend, Scyppend (Creator), *Ibid.* 5, 35, 9, 23, &c.

Scyldend (Protector), *Ibid.* 141, 14.

This group soon disappears without leaving any trace in the later periods of the language. Only *hǽlend* occurs in the literature of the twelfth and the first half of the thirteenth century. Layamon, 9144; Orm, 2216; *Old English Hom.* i. 83; *Ancren Riwle*, 912; *Marh.* 1.

§ 243. *Adjectives denoting Nations and Tribes.*

"Da ætsǽtton ða Centiscan" (there settled the people of Kent).— *Chronicle* (Parker MS. a.) 905.

"And on ðara Deniscena healfe wearð ofslægen Eohric hira cyng" (and on the part of the Danes was killed E. their king).—*Ibid.*

"And him cierde eall þæt folc to þe on Merena lande geseten wæs, ægþer ge Denisc ge Englisce" (and there turned to him all the people that lived in the Mercian country, the English as well as the Danes).— *Ibid. a.* 922.

"þa Judeiscan" (the Jews).—ÆLFRIC, *Hom.* 56, 31.

This group is not very frequent in Middle English.

"The Flemmysshe yherden telle the cas."—WRIGHT, *Political Songs*, p. 189.

"To liuer þam has drihtin mint,
And give egypcian a dint"

(the Lord has in mind to deliver them, &c.).—*Cursor Mundi*, 6018 (Cotton MS.).

Three other versions read: "Egypcians," as substantive.

"And thoru þe grece ouercomen," (and overcome by the Greeks), *ibid.* 7060. Cotton MS. The others again have *-es*.

Modern English.—The adjectives referring to nations partly survived (the English, the Scotch, the Chinese), and they were followed by adjectives describing religious sects, political parties, &c., as: Christians, Presbyterians, Lutherans, Stoics, Cynics, Jacobites, &c.

Adjectives referring to Things.

§ 244. The same ellipsis which accounts for the substantival use of adjectives referring to man sometimes applies to things: cf. Latin *ferina, sc. caro* (venison), *altum, sc. mare* (high sea).

Old English.—*Blanca* = a white or grey horse.

Middle English.—þe broun = deer.—*Gawayne*, 1162.
þe sylucner = sylueren = plate.—*Ibid.* 124.
þe wylde = the wild beasts (cf. German *Wild*).

"At þe fyrst quethe of the quest quaked þe *wylde*" (at the first cry of the hounds the beasts quaked).—*Ibid.* 1150.   Cf. *Destruction of Troy*, 2347.

"Now keep you from the *white* and from the *rede*,
Namely from the white wyn of Leepe."
CHAUCER, *Pardoneres Tale*, 100: cf. *ibid.* 64.

Certeyn = *quantity*, from the French.

"And she to soper come when it was eve,
With a *certeyn* of hire own men."
CHAUCER, *Troylus and Cryseyde*, iii. 547.

Modern English.—The number of these adjectives has considerably increased, only most of them are no longer looked upon as adjectives: they form the plural with -s. Such are: common, cordial, fluid, green, initial, liquid, particular, solid, vegetable; many of them are plurals only: bitters, canonicals, combustibles = a combustible, credentials, delicates, &c.

It is obvious that most of these substantives are simply taken from the Latin of the Middle Ages. For the etymology see the dictionary of Skeat.

Abstract Neuters.

§ 245. The third sort of adjectives which may be used as substantives are those denoting abstract ideas, as *good, evil*. This usage, too, is common to all the Teutonic languages.

Gothic.—*ubil* (evil).—*John* xviii. 23.   Cf. *Matth.* v. 37.

Old Saxon.—*gôd, Héliand*, 1348, 3409; *reht* (that which is right), *ibid.* 3014, 3814; *unreht* (wrong), 1957, 3478; *ubil*, 1356, 3409.

Old High German.—*guat*, OTFRID iii. 18, 10; *ubil*, ii. 12, 91; *reht*, v. 23, 126.

Old English.—In poetry and prose very frequent.

"Ne geald he yfel yfele" (he did not pay evil with evil).—*Elene*, 493.

"þæt hio þære cwéne oncweðan meahton, swá *tiles*, swá *tráges*" (that they might answer to the queen, were it something good, were it something bad).—*Ibid.* 325.

"and ge þám *ryhte* wiðroten hæfdon" (and you had rebelled against right).—*Ibid.* 369.

"sóð and riht" (truth and justice).—*Beów.* 1701.

Cf. *Ibid.* 532; 1050; 2865.

"gemyne he ðæs yfles þe he worhte" (he may bear in mind the evil that he did).—ÆLFRED, *Cura Past.* 24.

"Gemyne þe sylfne hu mycel yfel þe gelamp" (bethink thee how great an evil befell thee).—*Blick. Hom.* 31, 12.

"dyde mare yfel þonne god" (he did more evil than good).—*Ibid.* 43, 34.

"gyf þu godes folce riht bodast" (if thou preachest justice to God's people).—*Ibid.* 7, 7 : cf. *ibid.* 27, 16; 29, 5; 156, 13.

§ 246. *Middle English.*—This usage keeps on until the second half of the fifteenth century, when we perceive that the neuter of the adjective is supplanted by the corresponding substantive.

"ȝif we þonkien ure drihten alles þinges þe he us sent, þet gode and þet ufele" (if we thank our Lord for all things that he sends us, the good and the evil).—*Old Eng. Hom.* i. 7.

"hu scolde oþer monnes god dede comen him *to gode*, þe nefre on þisse liue *nanes godes* ne rohte?" (how should another man's good deeds profit him, who never in this life took thought of any good thing)?—*Ibid.* 9.

  "Whannse he seþ þatt Godess *rihht*
  Godess laȝhe riseþþ"

(whenever he, *sc.* the wicked, sees that God's right and law rises.)—*Orm.* 203, 4.

Cf. 16 141.

"soþ & rihht to reȝȝsen" (to raise truth and justice).

  "ðe sunes *bright*
  Is more ðanne ðe mones bright"

(the sun's brightness is greater than the moon's light).—*Story of Genesis and Exodus*, 143.

"þou ne sselt nime godes name in ydel" (thou shalt not take God's name in vain.—*Ayenbite*, 6.

"huo þet onworþeþ his uader and his moder . . . oþer hem missayþ mid kueade, zeneʒeþ dyadliche" (whosoever offends his father and mother, or slanders them through *wickedness*, commits a deadly sin).—*Ibid.* 8.

Cf. 11, 14.

Chaucer makes very frequent use of this licence.

"whan that the *soth* is wist."—*Man of Lawes Tale*, 974.

"as in a tombe is al the *fair* above."—*Squyeres Tale*, 172.

§ 247. It is doubtful whether the adjectives for *colours and languages* are to be understood as abstract neuters; there may be an ellipsis as well: the red, *sc.* colour, is too bright; German, *sc.* language, is hard. The adjectives for colours occur several times in Chaucer, but the definite article is always omitted; this circumstance makes it probable that they were felt as abstract neuters.

Cf. "he was clad in coote and hood of grene," *Cant. Tales Prologue*, 103; *ibid.* 116; *ibid.* 665. There are, however, instances of the use of the definite article.

"Have here a light and look on alle the blake."—CHAUCER, *Troylus and Cryseyde*, ii. 1320.

"Whan this knyght in the red beheld Balyn."—*Morte d'Arthur*, 97, 3.

§ 248. *Modern English.*—While the writers of the second half of the fifteenth and the first half of the sixteenth century shun the use of adjectives as abstract substantives, there is a sudden revival of the old licence in the time of Queen Elizabeth, probably due to the influence of the classic languages so zealously and universally studied at that period.

"To make them prove more feelingly the grief
That *bitter* brings."

Tancred, 51.

"And fold me in the riches of thy *fair* (beauty)."—GREENE, *Looking Glass*, 1189.

Cf. Shaks. *Sonn.* 68.

"And sucked up their dying mother's blood,
Making her death their life, and eke her hurt their *good*."
Faerie Queene, i. 1, 25[8].

"The Lyon, Lord of every beast in field,
Quoth she, his princely puissance doth abate,
And mightie proud to humble *weak* (= weakness) does yield."
Ibid. i. 3, 7[1].

"I learne that little *sweet*
Oft tempred is with muchell smart."
Ibid. i. 4, 46[3].

Cf. i. 12, 39.

"His ruddy lips did smyle, and rosy *red*
Did paint his chearefull cheekes, yet being ded."
Ibid. ii. 1, 41.

"Nor can coy fortune *contrary* allow."—*Mucedorus*, 206.

"If any spark of *human* rest in thee,
Forbear, begone."
Ibid. 204.

"Tut, Sylla's sparkling eyes should dim with *clear*
The burning brands of their consuming light."
LODGE, *Wounds of Civil War*, 118.[1]

"And sudden *pale* usurps her cheek."—*Venus and Adonis*, 589.

Cf. *Winter's Tale*, iv. 3, 4.

"Till Fortune, tired with doing *bad*,
Threw him ashore to give him *glad*."
Pericles, ii. Prol. 38.

"Say what you can, my *false* o'erweighs your *true*."—*Measure*, ii. 4, 170.

The same use occurs here and there even in prose.

"For the hurt that cometh therby is greater then the *good*."—SPENSER, *View of the Present State of Ireland*, 624.

---

[1] Here the editor remarks: "Lodge and other writers not unfrequently use the adjective for the substantive; thus in *The Discontented Satyre*:—

'Blush, daies eternal lamp, to see thy lot,
Since that thy *cleare* with cloudy *darks* is scared.'"

"He may command them as well to *ill* as to *good*."—*Ibid.* 624.

"Because he can express the *true and lively* of every thing."—PUTTENHAM, 21.

"But peradventure moe by a *peculiar*, which our speech hath in many things differing from theirs."—*Ibid.* 21.

"My *earthly*, by his *heavenly* overpowered..."
MILTON, *Paradise Lost*, viii. 453.

This licence seems to have died out with the Elizabethan authors; only a few adjectives in the positive degree, as *good*, *ill*, and many in the superlative most used in adverbial phrases have survived: "I'll do my best."—"He got the worst of it."—"At least," &c.

"*Voice*" of the Adjectives.

§ 249. Like the verb, the adjective, in daily prose, is either transitive or intransitive, active or passive. *Fearful* is said of one who fears, but *frightful* of one who frightens, *hateful* of one who hates, *hated* of one who is hated.

In Elizabethan English (and most probably also in earlier times, though I have looked in vain for instances older than the fourteenth century) the adjective is nearly indifferent with regard to voice.

Wherof the *dredful* hertes tremblen (dredful = timid).—GOWER, *Confessio Amantis*, I. p. 247.

Adjectives with Active and Passive Meaning.

§ 250. Some adjectives, especially those ending in *-ful*, *-less*, had in Tudor times both an active and a passive meaning.

Careless, pass. = not cared for.

"To throw away the dearest thing he owed
As 't were a *careless* trifle."
SHAK. *Macbeth*, i. 4, 11.

Disdainful, pass. = despicable.

"*Disdainful* Turkesse and vnreuerend Bosse."—MARLOWE, *Tamb.* 1261.

> "In vaine I striue and raile against those powers
> That meane t' inuest me in a higher throane,
> As much too high for this *disdainfull* earth."
> *Ibid.* 4513.

Greedy, pass. = greedily desired.

> "I do not meane, alonely husbandmen,
> Which till the ground, which dig, delve, mow and fowe,
> Which swinke and sweate, while we do sleepe and snort
> And serch the guts of earth, for *greedy* gain."
> GASCOIGNE, 67.

> "Thereat the fiend his gnashing teeth did grate,
> And griev'd so long to lacke his *greedie* pray."
> SPENSER, *Faerie Queene,* 2, 7, 34^2.

Hateful, act. = full of hate.

"Little office the *hateful* commons will perform for us."—*Rich. II.* ii. 2, 138.

Cf. *Troilus,* iv. 1, 33; MARLOWE'S *Jew,* 1336, 2266; *Lucrece,* 486; S. Schmidt, *s.v.* 1.

Helpless, pass. = irremediable, incurable.

"What *helpless* shame I feel."—*Lucrece,* 756.

"Such *helplesse* harmes yts better hidden keep."—SPENSER, *Faerie Queene,* II. 8, 34.

Ruthful, pass. = piteous.

> "Sweet Almeda, pity the *ruthfull* plight
> Of Callapine, the sonne of Baiazeth."
> MARLOWE, *Tamb.* 2484.

> "Trojan, thy *ruthful* tale hath made me sad."
> MARLOWE, *Dido,* 595.

Terrible, pass. = awe-struck, affrighted.

"What paper are you reading? Nothing, my lord. No? what needeth, then, that *terrible* despatch of it unto your pocket?"—*Lear,* I. 2, 32.

§ 251. *Adjectives with Transitive and Causative meaning.*

Cold = chilling.

> "And, that more wondrous was, in either jaw
> Three ranckes of yron teeth enraunged were,
> In which yett trickling blood, and gobbets raw,
> Of late devoured bodies did appeare,
> That sight thereof bredd *cold* congealed feare."
> SPENSER, *Faerie Queene,* I. 11, 13.

Lively = enlivening.

"Oh! that my sights could turn to *lively* breath."—MARLOWE, *Jew*, 1196.

Luckless = fatal.

"What! will you thus oppose me, luckless stars?"—*Ibid.* 494.

"*Luckless* woods."—*Muced.* 210; *ibid.* 225.

Mortal = deadly.

"Whose direfull hand gaue him the *mortall* wound."—*Gorboduc*, 1266.

"Her huge long taile her den all overspred,
Yet was in knots and many boughtes upwound,
Pointed with *mortall* sting."
SPENSER, *Faerie Queene*, 1, 1, 15.

"And in his bosome secretely there lay
An hatefull snake, the which his taile up tyes
In many folds, and *mortall* sting imployes."—*Ibid.* 1, 4, 31; 3, 1, 28; 3, 1, 65; 3, 4, 14; 3, 7, 4; 4, 7, 37.

Joyous = joy-producing.

Cf. *glad.* *2 Henry VI.*, iv. 9, 7.

"For since mine eie your *joyous* sight did mis,
My chearefull day is turnd to chearelesse night."
SPENSER, *Faerie Queene*, 1, 3, 27[6].

Weary = wearying, becoming weary.

"The silent night, that bringes the quiet pawse,
From painefull trauailes of the *wearie* day,
Prolonges my carefull thoughtes."
Gorboduc, 2.

"There auncient Night arriving did alight
From her nigh *weary* wayne."
SPENSER, *Faerie Queene*, 1, 5, 41[2].

Merry = producing merriment.

"Or Bacchus *merry* fruit they did invent,
Or Cybeles franticke rites have made them mad."
Ibid. 1, 6, 15[2].

"Thou Saint George shalt called be
Saint George of *merry* England, the signe of victoree."
Ibid. 1, 10, 61[9].

Kitchin observes: "Church says that in this phrase 'merry' signifies pleasant, delightful; attributing it to the pleasantness of the country, not to the cheerfulness of the inhabitants." "Merry" in Early English writers bears the sense of lively, joyous. So Chaucer, *Tr. and Cr.* iii. 1514, has "this murye morwe." He also speaks of "merry weather." *Cf.* Latin *laeta arva*.

Piteous = pity-producing.
"But most was moved at the *piteous* vew
 Of Amoret, so neare unto decay."
  SPENSER, *Faerie Queene*, 4, 8, 20³.

Stony = benumbing.
"And *stony* horrour all her senses fild."—SPENSER, *ibid.* 1, 6, 37, 3.

Unhappy = mischievous, fatal.
"Know that this Medor, whose *unhappy* name
 Is mixed with the fair Angelica's,
 Is even that Medor who enjoys her love."
  GREENE, *Orlando Furioso*, 97, *b*.
"Uncle to this *unhappy* traitor, king."—PEELE, *Battle of Alcazar*, 422, *a*.
"This *unhappy* sight."—*Tancred*, Argument.
"Comparing him to that *unhappy* guest."—SHAK. *Lucr.* 1565
"O most *unhappy* strumpet."—*Err.* IV. iv. 127.

Cf. Schmidt, *s.v.* 3.

Adjectives instead of Substantives in the Genitive Case.

§ 252. The adjective being, in its functions, akin to the genitive, is often interchanged with it. The genitive denoting quality is dealt with above, § 166; but sometimes the adjective is used very freely where we expect the genitive, e.g. *hungri ʒere* = years of famine. *Story of Gen. and Exod.* 2136.

Elizabethan literature is very rich in such instances; perhaps Latin had some influence. *Cf.* "æquitate deum erga bona malaque documenta" (= "bonitatæ malitiæque"), Tacitus, *Ann.* 16, 33; "honestum exemplum Cassii" (= "honestatis"), *ibid.*

"While slumbring on his *carefull* bed he restes."—*Gorboduc*, 1272.

Cf. *careless* day, Spenser, *Faerie Qu.* iii. 5, 1, 7 :

"It stirreth up to sensuall desire,
And in lewd slouth to wast his careless day."

= day spent in carelessness.

"Your grace should now in these graue yeres of yours,
Haue found ere this the price of *mortall* ioys.
Yet the grasshopper with all his summer-piping,
Starveth in winter with *hungry* griping."
Ralph Royster Doyster, v. 4.

"Mine eyes no more on vanitie shall feed,
But seeled up with death shall have their *deadly meed.*"
Faerie Queene, 1, 7, 23.

= reward of death.

"Well hoped I, and faire beginnings had,
That he my *captive languor* should redeeme."
Ibid. 1, 7, 49.

= my evil condition of languor or faintness; "captive" being used like Ital. *cattivo*, or Eng. "caitiff"; or perhaps "captive languor" refers to the dull captivity of her parent in the brazen tower (Kitchin).

"And on his arme a bounch of keyes he bore,
The which *unused rust* did overgrow."
Ibid. 1, 8, 30.

a Latinism : = the rust arising from disuse (Kitchin).

"Lovers' *absent hours.*"—SHAKSP. *Othello*, iii. 4, 174 = absence hours, hours of absence or separation.

"A *fruitful prognostication.*"—*Antony*, i. 2, 53 = a prognostication of fruitfulness.

"Their *sterile curse.*"—*Jul. Cæs.* i. 2, 9 = curse of sterility.

"With mirth and laughter let *old wrinkles* come."—*Merchant of Venice*, i. 1, 80 (the wrinkles of age).

"Who in rage forgets *aged contusions* and all brush of time."—2 *Henry VI.* v. 3, 3 (the contusions of age).

"When *old time* shall lead him to his end."—*Henry VIII.* ii. 1, 95.

"The *aged wrinkles* in my cheeks."—*Titus Andronicus,* iii. 1, 7

"Too early I attended a *youthful suit*" (the suit of a youth).—*A Lover's Compl.* 79.

"My *youthful travel* therein made me happy" (travels made in youth).—*Two Gentlemen of V.,* iv. 1, 34.

§ 253. *Note.*—In older English some adjectives are used attributively, while nowadays they are represented by nouns. "*Nigon nihtum ǽr middum sumere*" (nine nights before midsummer). *Chronicle,* 897, "*to middum sumere,*" *ibid.* 920. This use, which is well known from Latin ("in media urbe, in summa arbore"), prevails also in the other Teutonic languages.

Gothic.—"Jah nimands barn gasatida ita in midjaim im" (and taking the child he set it down in the middle of them.)—*Mark,* ix. 36.

Old Norse.—"nær miðri nótt" (near midnight); "til miðsdags" (till the middle of the day).—LUND, p. 230.

This becomes rare in *Middle English.*

"buton ane treowe þe stent on midden paradise" (except one tree that stands in the middle of the paradise).—*Old English Hom.* i. 221.

"in middes þe land."—*Cursor Mundi,* 1314.

Cf. *ibid.* 655, 1032, 5967, 7184; *Ipomadon,* 5478.

Constructions like "half the day," "double the sum," are survivals of this old use.

Comparison of the Adjective.

Double Comparison.

§ 254. This may be accounted for as a sort of mixed construction; the language, hesitating between the Old English and the French way of comparison, often uses both.

Middle English.—"þu eær (t) muchele ahtere and ec mare hærdere" (= much braver and eke more hardier).—LAYAM. 4349.

"That lond is meche more hottere."—MAUNDEVILLE, 4.

"More greter than is a destrere" (equus dextrarius).—*Ibid.* 28.
"more zuyþere" (more sooner).—*Ayenbite*, 61.
"more feller."—*Ibid.*
"more worse."—*Ibid.* 64.
"more swifter."—*Ibid.* 66.
"more gratter."—*Ibid.* 66, 79, 100.
"more stranger."—*Ibid.* 75.
"more werse."—CAXTON, *Blanch. and Egl.* 23, 33.
"more better."—*Ibid.* 91, 35.
"the most valyauntest."—*Charles the Grete*, 41, 27.
"more sonner."—*Ibid.* 44, 18.
"most next."—*Ibid.* 44, 17.
"more gretter."—*Curial*, 5, 13.

Cf. Malory, *Morte d'Arthur*, 74, 37; 142, 8; 144, 29; 144, 35; 148, 5; 215, 29; 218, 3, &c.

Modern English.—Very frequent in Elizabethan times. See Abbott, § 11.

The Comparative and Superlative used absolutely.

"Helpe then, O holy virgin! chiefe of nyne,
Thy *weaker* Novice to perform thy will."
SPENSER (Globe ed.) p. 11.

§ 255. Naturally the use of an adjective in the comparative degree requires two objects, one of which is superior to the other in a certain respect: "Senectus natura loquacior quam iuventus." But the second (inferior) object being sometimes too obvious to be mentioned, it is dropped altogether, and the comparative is used *absolutely*. Thus in the instance quoted "quam iuventus" was omitted, and the Latin saying got its well-known shape, "Senectus natura loquacior." This Latinism was imitated by Elizabethan writers, but seems to have been a stranger to English both before and after that period.

> "And in the midst thereof one pretious stone
> Of wondrous worth, and eke of wondrous mights,
> Shapt like a Ladies head, exceeding shone,
> Like Hesperus an,ongst the lesser lights,
> And strove for to amaze the *weaker* sights."
> SPENSER, *Faerie Queene*, 1, 7, 30⁵.

= the eyesight of men *too weak* to endure it (Kitchin).

> "But nether darkenesse fowle, nor filthy bands,
> Nor noyous smell, his purpose could withhold,
> (Entire affection hateth *nicer* [= *too nice*] hands."
> *Ibid.* 1, 8, 40³

> "None but that saw (quoth he) would weene for troth,
> How shamefully that Mayd he did torment:
> Her *looser* golden lockes he rudely rent,
> And drew her on the ground."
> *Ibid.* 2, 1, 11⁵.

= *too loose*, dishevelled by her tormentor (Kitchin).

Cf. 1, 1, 3; 1, 2, 23; 1, 3, 2; 1, 5, 2; 1, 6, 4; 1, 7, 9.

Adjectives followed by "*one*".

§ 256. The modern *one* after adjectives which refer to preceding nouns, is of recent date. I notice the first instance of *one* after an adjective in the positive degree in the fourteenth century (A.D. 1380).

> "Wan he was armed on horsesbak, a fair knyȝt a was to see,
> A *iolif on* wyþ oute lak, boþe strong & fers was hee."
> *Sir Ferumbras*, 251.

> "And after whan thou shalt haue employed thy body, thy tyme and thy goodes for to deffende the, another *new one* cometh to the courte, and shall supplante thy benediction."—*Curial*, 12, 13.

In Middle English it frequently occurs after nouns.

> "Robert þat hosebond was *on*."—ROB. OF GL. 11302.
> "a servaunt was I on."—CHAUCER, *Knightes T.* 956.
> "Apostel was he siþen an."—*Cursor Mundi*, 19733.

Cf. ROBT. OF GL. 405, 5535, 7096; *Cursor Mundi*, 13363, 13972, 17994, 18209; *Ipomadon*, 4602, 5700.

M

The Numerals
Cardinals.
Cardinals used substantively.

§ 257. With the exception of *hundred* and *thousand*, which are always substantives, the numerals were in Old English used both as

(*a*) Substantives (governing the genitive case) and

(*b*) Adjectives.

(*a*) "úp áhóf rihtes réniend þára róda twá" (the minister of right raised two roods).—*Elene*, 880.

"feówer tida syndon on þæm geáre, on þæm we oft ágyltað" (there are four times in the year in which we oft sin).—*Blick. Hom.* 35.

(*b*) "Cómon twegen englas" (there came two angels).—*Genesis* xix. 1.

"þa nam he fíf stánas" (he took five stones).—*Blick. Hom.* 31.

§ 258. In Middle and Modern English the substantival nature of *hundred* and *thousand* is kept, hence *a* hundred, *a* thousand; but as early as the thirteenth century they are no longer followed by the genitive case.

§ 259. It is probably owing to the analogy of *hundred* and *thousand* that, later on, other numerals too were preceded by *a* (*an*).

"A fyue men."—Rob. of Glouc. 770.
"Aboute ane four hondred ȝer."—*Ibid.* 1017.
"After oure loɪdes deþ a seue hundred ger."—*Ibid.* 1428.

There are very numerous instances of this use in Berners's *Huon*.

"And they were in all a iiii score horsses."—18, 12.
"And (the knyght) sayd how that a vii yere passyd."—29, 16
"A xxx yere passyd I cam hether."—61, 3.

Cf. 68, 18; 63, 16; 66, 23; 69, 4; 70, 14; 73, 7, &c.

One.

Of all the numerals *one* plays the most prominent part. There are several noteworthy points about its use.

§ 260. *One = alone.*

Old English—"(He) gecóde eall Britene búton Contware ánre" (he conquered all Britain, except Kent only).—*Chronicle*, 617.

Very frequent.

The expression *ánra gehwylc = each one*, is hard to explain.

"Hi þá se déma onbryrde, swá he déð ánra gehwylcne" (them the judge inspired, as he does each one).—*Judith*, 95.

"ic eów bidde and halsige þæt ánra manna gehwylc sceawige hine sylfne on his heortan" (I pray and beseech each of you to contemplate himself in his heart).—*Blick. Hom.* 57.

Perhaps the following instances may be regarded as a remnant of the Old English construction.

"He was archer with best of an." (of any)—*Cursor Mundi*, 3078, C.

"þen was he archer best of ane."—*Ibid. F.*

"An archer was he best of an."—*Ibid. G.*

Middle English.
"And we ðe ben fro heuene driuen,
Sulen ðusse *one* in sorwe liuen"

(and we that are driven from heaven shall thus *alone* live in sorrow).—*Story of Gen. and Exod.* 308.

"ðo fleg agar fro sarray
Wimman wið childe, *one* and sori,
In the diserd, wil and weri"

(then Hagar fled far away, woman with child, *lonely* and sorry, into the desert, homeless and weary).—*Ibid.* 974.

Cf. *ibid.* 2015, 3489.

"ðe dragunes *one* ne stiren nout" (the dragons *alone* stir not).—*Old Eng. Miscell.* p. 24, l. 759.

§ 261. The personal pronoun with *one* in this sense appears first in the dative, afterwards in the genitive case.

"bi his eadi beoden in hulles *him one*" (by his blessed prayers in the hills alone).—*Old Eng. Hom.* p. 207.

"for þu þe *ane* dreddes nawt wið þin anre deore bodi to fihte aȝaines alle þe ahefulle deueles of helle" (for thou alone dreadest not with thine own dear body to fight against all the awful devils of hell).—*Ibid.* 271.

"all him ane."—*Orm* 1025.

Cf. *ibid.* 11747, 11754.

"þe gome vpon Gryngolet glydez hem vnder,
   þurȝ mony misy and myre, mon al *hym one*."
      Sir Gawayne and the Gr. Knight, 749.

"þat apel Arthure þe hende haldez *hym one*."—*Ibid.* 904.

"he made his mone
Within a gardin all *him one*."
      GOWER, i. 148.

The last quoted work contains two passages with the genitive case, 1048, 1230.

In the *Cursor Mundi* all the three expressions, viz. *him ane, his ane, alane*, are found in the several manuscripts' rendering of the same passage.

"His heuen he sal haue allan."—*C.* 809.
"His heyuen salle he haue him ane."—*F.*
"His heuen sal he haue bi his on."—*G.*
"His heuen shal he haue his one."—*T.*
"Drunken on slepe lai bi him an."—*C.* 2021.
"Dronkin on slepe lay bi his ane."—*F.*
"Drunken on slepe lai bi him ane."—*G.*
"Drunke he lay and slept his one."—*T.*
"Wandran in wildernes hir an."—*C.* 3052.
"Wandrande in wildernes allane."—*F.*
"Wandrand in wildernes alane."—*G.*
"In wildernes wandrynge allone."—*T.*
"And iacob lai him an þat naght."—*C.* 3931.

"Jacob lay him stille atte naȝt."—*F.*
"Jacob lay bi him-selue þat night."—*G.*
"Jacob lay bi him self þat nyȝt."—*T.*
"He wald ete seuen scep him an."—*C.* 7454.
"He walde ete vii shepe him allane."—*F.*
"He wild ete seuen schep his an."—*G.*
"Seuen sheep he wolde ete his one."—*T.*
"Þe sorful wark him ane he wroght."—*C.* 8983.
"Þe sorouful werk him ane he wroȝt."—*F.*
"Þat soruful werk þaim self þai soght."—*G.*
"Þat sorweful werke hem self hit souȝt."—*T.*

"*One*" *following Substantives and Adjectives.*

§ 262. In Middle English *one* follows substantives redundantly as early as Orm, and later on also adjectives referring to preceding nouns.

Cf. *Adjectives*, § 256.

One = a certain.

§ 263. *One* preceding proper nouns = *a certain* is scarcely to be found in *Old English*.

"*Oon* Grecus þat reigned there sometyme."—TREVISA, HIGDEN's *Polychronicon*, i. 175.

"Therfor he spak to *on* his frende, a cryten man."
          CAXTON, *Godfrey of Bol.* 219.

Later instances are frequent.

Cardinals instead of Ordinals.

§ 264. There are several instances in *Middle English* of cardinals being used instead of ordinals.

"Ebrius seigen, wune hem wex her
  To algen ilk *fiftene* ger."

the Hebrews say that then began the custom of keeping each *fifteenth* ear holy).—*Story of Gen. and Exod.* 918.

"ðe seuene and forwerti dai" (the forty-seventh day).—*Ibid.* 3439.

"He sailed þe seuen day
On rade."—*Sir Tristrem*, 800.

"Coppe and claper he bare
Til þe fiften day."—*Ibid.* 3174.

"Of seynt Hyllary the churche ys,
The twenty day of yowle ywys,
As ye may understande."
            Le bone Florence, 1897.

"The threttene artycul, the fowrtene artycul, the fyftene artycul— articulus xiiius xiiiius articulus quindecimus."—HALLIWELL, *Early History of Freemasonry*, 21.

"The ten parte = tenth."—*Townley Mysteries*, p. 7.

'The lynage succeded from heyre to heyres vnto the foure and twenty kyng."—CAXTON, *Charles the Grete*, 21, 18.

§ 265. *Cardinals instead of Multiplicatives.*

Old English.—"Dá hét Alfred cyng timbran lang scipu ongen þá æscas, þá wǽron fulneah *tú swá lange* swá þá óþru" (then King Alfred gave orders to build long ships against the 'aescas' [Danish ships]; those were well nigh *twice* as long as the others).—*Chronicle*, a. 897.

Professor Zupitza quotes several *Middle English* instances exhibiting this use.

"We sall garre feste þam *foure so* fast" (we shall cause them to be bound four times as fast).—*York Plays*, 86, 308.

"Yette was y *ten so glad.*"—*Sir Amadas*, 746.

"*Fowre so* gud thoffe hit were" (though it were four times as good). —*Ibid.* 350.

Elizabethan English.—"He would kiss you *twenty* with a breath" (twenty times).—SHAKSPERE, *Henry VIII.* I. iv. 30.

Ordinals.

Fractional Numerals.

§ 266. The fractional numerals were formed by the ordinal and *dǽl*, later on *part*.

The Old and Middle English use of *half* in connection with ordinals is remarkable.

Oðer healf means one + half of the second, i.e. 1 + ½.

Ðridda healf means two + half of the third, i.e. 2 + ½, &c.

Cf. *German*, "anderthalb," "dritthalb," "vierthalb," &c.

Old English.—"Nán rén com ofer eorðan feorðan healfan geáre" (no rain came over the earth for three years and a half).—WRIGHT, *Popular Treatises*, p. 18.

"He rícsode nigonteoðe healf geár" (he reigned eighteen years and a half).—*Chronicle*, 855.

Middle English.—"þa wass wel hallf feorrþe ger, þatt comm na reggn."—*Orm.* 8621.

"þa scipen wenden to wundre oðer half hundred" (the ships went to destruction a hundred and fifty).—LAYAMON, i. 335.

"þritti wynter and þridde half yer havy woned in londe her."—*Harrowing of Hell*, p. 15.

§ 267. NOTE.—The use of numerals in connection with *sum* (some) is worth noting.

Old English.—"And Hannibal óþfleáh *feówera sum* tó Aþrametum" (and Hannibal fled with four [others] to Adrumetum).—*Orosius*, 202, 16.

"Húru se snotra sunu Wihstánes
ácígde of corðre cyninges þegnas
syfone tósomne þá sélestan,
eóde *eahta sum* under inwit-hróf"

(the wise son of Wihstan called the seven best thanes of the king from out the host, he [himself] went the eighth into the den).—*Beowulf*, 3124.

As may be seen from these two examples, *sum* is either comprised in the preceding cardinal number (as in *eahta sum*, he with seven others), or it means one more (as in *feówera sum* (with four others).

In *Middle English* it is probably the French influence which accounts for the ordinal number in the following examples. French: *lui quinzième*, he with 14 others.

> "Tristrem dede as he hiȝt,
> He busked and made him ȝare;
> His fiftend some of kniȝt
> Wiþ him ȝede na mare"

(*i.e.* he with fifteen others).—KÖLBING, Notes to *Sir Tristrem*, p. 133

> "Finde me min askeing,
> Mine fiftend som of kniȝt."—*Ibid.* 1375.

THE PRONOUNS.

Personal Pronouns.

Omission of the Pronoun.

§ 268. In the prehistoric times of the Teutonic languages the inflexions of the verbal forms were sufficient to express the three persons, as in Greek, Latin, Lithuanian, and Slavonic. But we have only the Gothic to confirm this supposition, the literary remains of the other Teutonic languages having kept but a few remnants of that old, undoubtedly Indo-European use.

As the omission of the pronoun is the rule in Gothic, instances abound on every page. For exceptions, *cf.* Grimm, *Deutsche Grammatik*, iv. p. 202. For Old High German see *ibid.* p. 210.

In Old and Middle English, less frequently after the fifteenth century, the pronoun is often omitted, when it may be supplied from the context or has been mentioned in a previous sentence, principal or subordinate.

§ 269. *The Imperative,*

as a rule, has no pronoun. But there are very numerous exceptions, especially in poetry In Cynewulf's *Elene*, for instance it is just as many times used as omitted. In-

SYNTAX OF THE PARTS OF SPEECH

stances are very frequent. The common arrangement of words, then, is imperative + pronoun; for exceptions, viz. "thou give" instead of "give thou", see *Order of Words*, § 452.

The other cases of omission may be divided into the following groups:

The Pronoun must be supplied from the Context.

§ 270. *A.* This is the case in the 3rd person plural.

> "þær æt hýðe stód hringed-stefna,
> isig and út-fús, æðelinges fær;
> á-lédon þa leófne þeóden,
> beága bryttan on bearm scipes,
> mærne be mæste"

(there in the harbour stood the [ship] ringed at the stem, shining and ready, the warrior's vessel; they laid the dear lord, the giver of rings, in the bosom of the ship, the famous close by the mast).—*Beówulf*, 34.

álédon, viz., his warriors.

"Gewiton him þá féran" (they set out on their journey).—*Ibid.* 301.

Viz., Beówulf and his men.

The Pronoun omitted in the Second of two Co-ordinate Sentences.

§ 271. *B.* When the subject is the same in two co-ordinate sentences, it is omitted in the second. The omission is striking whenever there is a clause inserted between the two principal sentences.

Old English.
> "Wiht unhǽlo
> grim and grǽdig gearo sóna wæs,
> reóc and réðe, and on ræste genam
> þritig þegna: þanon eft gewát
> húðe hrémig tó hám faran"

(the disastrous wight, grim and greedy, was soon ready, fierce and cruel, and in [their] rest took thirty thanes; then went thence to turn homeward, rejoicing in his prey).—*Beówulf*, 123.

"módsorge wæg
Romwara cyning, ríces ne wénde
for werodléste : hæfde wigena tó lýt"

(sorrowful thought the king of the Romans, [he] thought that his kingdom would fail for want of people, [he] had too few warriors).—*Elene*, 61—63.

Cf. *ibid.* 92, 401, 469, &c.

"sum wæs æhtwelig ríce ȝeréfa, rondburȝum wéold, eard weardade oftast symle in þære ceastre Commodia, heóld hordȝestreón" (there was a wealthy count, reigned over fortified towns, [he] defended his home very oft in the town Commodia, held the treasure).—*Juliana*, 18—22.

Cf. *ibid.* 28, 48, 52, 73, &c.

"Her cóm Eomer from Cwichelme West-Seaxna cininge. þóhte þæt he wolde ofstingan Eadwine cininge" (then came E. from C. the king of the West-Saxons ; thought to slay Eadwine).—*Chronicle*, 626.

Cf. *ibid.* 656. Cf. *Blick. Hom.* 177, 22 ; 189, 17 ; 223, 7.

Middle English.—"þa he iseh Martham and Mariam Magdalena þe sustren wepe for hore broðer deð, and ure drihten ðurh rouðe þet he. hefde of hom, schedde of his halie eȝene hate teres, and hore broðers arerde, and [scil. *heo*, they] weren stille of hore wope."—*Old Eng. Hom.* i. 157.

Cf. *ibid.* ii. 93 ; iii. 119, &c.

"Al it was for abraham—is wif,
ðat he hire held ðor wið strif ;
ðo bi-ðhogte him ful wel"

(it was all for Abraham's wife, that he kept her to her grief ; then [he] bethought him full well).—*Story of Gen. and Exod.* 1183.

Cf. *ibid.* 1729 ; *Old Eng. Miscellany*, p. 4, 5, 19.

"Geten and born was so
þe child, was fair and white."
Sir Tristrem, xxiii. 244.

"So ranne the vasselles to gyder, and roughte eche other by suche a force upon the sheldes, that they were brusen and broken all to peces ; theire speres (that sore bygge and stronge were) broke also all to peces. And thenne toke theire swerdes [*scil.* they]."—CAXTON, *Blanchardyn*, 28, 11.

Cf. *ibid.* 43, 5 ; 49, 29 ; 64, 16, &c.

The Pronoun omitted in the Subordinate Sentence.

§ 272. *C.* When the subject is the same in a principal and a subordinate sentence, the pronoun is omitted in one of them.

Old English.—"hé manegum wearð mannum tó hróðer, syððan wǽpen áhóf wið hetendum" (he became the protection of many men, since he raised arms against enemies).—*Elene*, 15 ff.

"hér sægþ...hú se Alýsend þysses menniscan cynnes hine sylfne geeaþmedde þæt of heáþe þæs fæderlican þrymmes to eorþan astág" (here is related... how that the merciful Lord and the Redeemer of mankind so humbled himself that [he] descended from the exaltation of the paternal glory into this earth).—*Blick. Hom.* 65, 28.

Middle English.—"and ȝif he hit naueð, aȝefe (*scil.* he) swa muchel swa he mai" (and if he hath it not, let him restore as much as he is able).—*Old Eng. Hom.* i. 29.

"þu seist þat on gode bileuest (*scil.* thou)."—*Ibid.* ii. 25.

Cf. *ibid.* ii. 71.

"auh hwon heo so haueð idon, do (*scil.* heo) ase deð þe pellican."—*Ancren Riwle*, p. 118.

Cf. Introduction to Caxton's *Blanch. and Egl.* xxxiv.

Modern English.—"If any man will applye these thinges together, shall not se the one farre differ from the other."—ASCHAM, *Toxophilus*, p. 19.

"which dayly we may beholde & perceyue in many, that yf they had wanted these pleasures sholde more dylygently haue holden themselfe in the path that bryngeth & ledeth vs vnto the blyssed lyfe."—JOHN FISHER, 23, 24 ff.

"Thys sayd ye false traitour, by cause he desyred no thyng elles, but one of the sonnes of duke Seuyn myght sley Charlot, wherby he thought shuld be dystroyed in acusynge them of murder, wherby he myght come to his dampnable intent."—BERNERS's *Huon*, i. 19, 11 ff.

Viz., "the sonnes of duke Seuyn" (not Charlot, as Lee suggests).

"Whan Huon had thus made his othe erle Amaury stept forthe all afrayde and sware how Huons othe was false, and that [he] surely knew that it was Charlot when he slewe him."—*Ibid.* 40, 3.

The Pronoun supplied from the Oblique Case.

§ 273. *D.* When the subject of a subordinate sentence is not the same as that of the principal one, and is yet omitted, it must be supplied from the context, generally from a preceding oblique case.

Old English.—" ic þé biddan wille, þæt [þu] me þæt goldhord, gásta scyppend, geopenie" (I will ask thee that thou, Creator of spirits, mayest open to me the treasure).—*Elene*, 789.

"wæs him noma cenned Heliséus, hæfde ealdordóm micelne and mǽrne" (he was called Heliseus, [he] had great and famous authority). —*Juliana*, 25.

Cf. *ibid.* 265, 382, 447. Cf. *Blick. Hom.* 25, 22; 53, 27; 233, 2.

Middle English.—"and þeh us ure sinnes rewe. and [we] imint hauen þat we hem wile forleten, naðeles we sitteð forð þat we hem forleten" (and though we be sorry for our sins, and have purposed to forsake them, nevertheless we sit until we forsake them).—*Old English Hom.* ii. 101.

"Fil me a cuppe of ful god ale,
And wile drinken, her y spelle."
HAVELOK, 14, 15.

Where Skeat reads "And y wile."

"þu me to kniȝt houe,
And kniȝthod haue proued."
KING HORN, 1267, 68.

Where Mätzner (*Sprachproben*, i. 227) reads "haue y proued."

"Tristremes schip was ȝare,
And asked his benisoun."
Sir Tristrem, cvi. 1157.

"But he, which alle thinges may childe,
Thre yere til that she cam to londe
Her ship to stere hath take on honde,
And in Northumberlond arriveth."
GOWER, i. 183.

"And with that worde his hewe fadeth,
And saide." *Ibid.* 251.

Cf. Caxton, *Blanch.* 39, 15; 44, 12; 45, 16.

In *Modern English* the omission of the pronoun is only to be met with in colloquial language.

First Person.

"'Cannot sing.' 'Prithee, Hermogenes.'
'Cannot sing.'"
BEN JONSON, *Poetaster*, 2, 1.

"Pray thee, Roman."—*Ibid.* 1, 1.

"Pr'ythee what art, what rhetoric didst thou use,
To gain this mighty boon?"
ADDISON, *Cato*, 3, 3.

"Would to God we had died."—*Exodus* xvi. 3.

"O would that she loved me!"—SHERIDAN KNOWLES, *Hunchback*, 4, 1.

"Thank ye, George! I ask no more."—GOLDSMITH, *She Stoops to Conquer*, 4.

The *second person* is often omitted in questions.

"Dost hear?"—SHAKS. *Tempest*, 1, 2.

"Dost court abundance for the sake of peace?"—YOUNG, *Night Thoughts*, 6, 494.

"How dost? And where hast been these eighteen months?"—LEIGH HUNT, *Legend of Florence*, 1, 1.

"Why, where hast been?"—COLERIDGE, *Piccolomini*, 2, 8.

"Hast honestly confess'd it to thyself?"—*Ibid.* 4, 4.

§ 274. The peculiar sort of omission which appears in the following instances is accounted for in the same way as the omission of the relative pronoun. The same word belongs to two different sentences (construction ἀπὸ κοινοῦ).

"I pray to *God* so gyf my body care,
Yif ever, sith I highte Hogge of Ware,
Herd I a miller better set a-werke."
CHAUCER, *The Cokes Prologue*, 11.

"I pray to *God* me graunt this bone."
Coventry Mysteries, p. 42.

Cf. also *ibid.* 50, 102, 139. There are, however, instances of the same phrase with the pronoun.

"I praye to God *he* spede your way."
Coventry Mysteries, p. 104.

The Object Pronoun omitted.

§ 275. The pronoun as object is scarcely ever omitted. There are, it is true, two cases, which one would be inclined to look upon as examples of omission, but both may be explained in another way.

First, an object when governed by two verbs was put only once in older periods, while we repeat it now; in the second case there is a sudden change of construction.

A.—"But the knyght that was right courteys, guyded hym and conduyted a whyle."—CAXTON, *Blanch.* 39, 30.

Cf. for other instances *Order of Words*, § 474.

B.— " As for the good he taketh none hede,
He saith, but only of the love,
Of which he wend have been above."
GOWER, i. 251.

' For as to his fadir, he wolde not touche."—CAXTON, *Aymon*, 85, 29.

Cf. Starkey, *England in the Reign of Henry VIII.*, 71, 66 :

" As for thys matter, we shal ryght wel *avoyd.*"

Use of "we" instead of "I".

§ 276. The *pluralis majestatis* as used by sovereigns, is not known in Old English. The Anglo-Saxon kings in introducing their laws always have "ic." "Ic Ine mid godes gyfe Westseaxna cyning. Ic Aelfréd, ic Aeðelstán." It is only when speaking for themselves and council that they use "we"[1]. But the "we" of authors appears very early, probably in imitation of the Latin.

[1] March is wrong in his statement with regard to *we* = *ic* in Beówulf 958 and 1652; the context shows that the plurai refers to Beówulf and his men.

"þá láre þe we nu willað on Engliscum gereorde secʒean" (the lore that we will now say in English).—*S. Basilius*, Prologue, ed. Norman.

"We willað furðor ymbe þás emnihte swiðor sprecan" (we will speak farther about the equinox).—WRIGHT, *Popular Treatises*, p. 4.

Cf. Ælfric, *Hom.* i. 580, 26.

"*Thou*" and "*You*."

§ 277. It is not before the thirteenth century that the plural of courtesy is to be met with.

"Jacob eft bit hem faren agon,
Oc he ne duren ðe weie cumen in,
'But *ge* wið us senden beniamin'"

(Jacob bids them go again [to Egypt], but they dare not come that way, "unless *ye* send with us Benjamin").—*Story of Genesis and Exodus* (about 1250 A.D.) 2240.

"'Louerd,' he seiden everilc on,
'ʒur siluer is ʒu brogt agon'"

("Lord," they said every one, "*your* silver is brought *you* back again").—*Ibid.* 2260.

"þe emperour was stille þo, and ne ʒaf him non ansuere.
'Sire emperour,' quaþ þe erle þo, 'ne be ʒe no so bolde.'"
        ROBERT OF GLOUCESTER, 1341.

"Sire king, w[h]i lete ʒe mi moder and me binore þe lede?"
        Ibid. 2757.

Four MSS. have "*thou.*"

Robert de Brunne, in his translation of PETER LANG-TOFT'S *French Chronicle* (A.D. 1307) offers several instances.

King Richard is addressed by Isaac's messengers:

"Your wille wille he alle do and be at ʒour mercy."—PETER LANGTOFT'S *Chronicle*, p. 163.

By subjects, as by Robert of Thornham:

"þat ʒe wille þer lie, it is to ʒour honoure."—p. 165.

By the bishop:

"ʒe ere so trew a kyng."—p. 175.

§ 278. From this time downward the two pronouns are seen struggling for existence, the polite, courtly *ye* more and more displacing the honest old *thou*, the latter being only used from superiors to inferiors, or from equals to equals as a sign of contempt or defiance. Very often both are used by the same person in the same speech, as in the instance quoted from Robert of Gloucester, the change in the address denoting also a change in the speaker's mind. There is a very instructive example of this change in *Sir Gawayne and the Greene Knight*. The lady of the castle constantly addresses Gawayne with "ye", but being offended with his resistance, she, getting into a kind of temper, continues :

"þou hatȝ for-ȝeten ȝederly þat ȝisterday I taȝtte alder-truest token of talk þat I cowþe" (*thou* hast soon forgotten that yesterday I taught token of talk, truest of all that I knew).—1485, 86.

But in most of the other instances both *thou* and *ye* seem to be used indiscriminately.

"For sothe, fadur, y yow telle,
Noo lengur wyll y here dwelle,
Fadur, yf thy wylle bee,
Y wyll wende ouyr the see."
Guy of Warwick, 461—65.

"'Thou art a curtes man,' quod Gye,
'Syr dewke,' he seyde, 'gramercy.
Y schall yow helpe wyth all my myght."
Ibid. 1699—1702.

Numerous instances are quoted in my Introduction to Caxton's *Blanchardyn*, pp. xxix., xxx. *Cf.* also Skeat, *William of Palerne*, xlii., Zupitza, *Guy of Warwick*, p. 351. A similar change takes place in the use of *thy* and *your*.

"I moot do with *thy* daughter for the beste . . .
But natheles withoute *youre* witynge
Wol I not doon."
CHAUCER, *The Clerkes Tale*, iii., 41—44.

"Kate, Kate, art *thou* not ashamed to deceive *your* father so?"— GOLDSMITH, *She Stoops to Conquer*, 3.

"A willing pupil kneels to *thee*, and lays
His title and his fortune at *your* feet."
SHERIDAN KNOWLES, *Hunchb.* 1, 3.

For *you* supplanting *ye*, see above, § 212.

Use of "it."

§ 279. With impersonal verbs: it snows. Omitted in Old and Middle English whenever the verb is followed by an object.

Old English.—"hú him gelamp" (how it happened to him).—*Juliana*, 662.

Middle English.—Me thynketh, me semeth, me wondreth, &c.

Instances abound.

But sometimes *it* is also omitted when there is no object governed by the impersonal verb.

"But [it] seemed that she sholde slee herself to be more hastely venged."—CAXTON, *Blanchardyn*, 43, 26.

"So [it] taryed not long after thys was doon that the tempeste ceased."—*Ibid.* 137, 29.

Cf. Introduction to Caxton's *Blanchardyn*, xxxiv.

Modern English.—Sentences like the following become quite rare: "Boots not man, to tell," *Gammer Gurton's Needle.* Cf. *Serves him right.* In subordinate clauses, however, the omission is often to be met with.

"In part I thinke *as has ben saide* before."—*Gorboduc*, 1, 2.

"*If as beseems* a person of thy state,
Thou hast with honour us'd Zenocrate."
MARLOWE, 1 *Tamb.* 5, 2.

"Such news, my lord, as *grieves* me to report."—SHAKS. *Richard III.* 2.

§ 280. "*It*" *is used as Predicate of any Gender or Person with the Verb* "*to be*".

"Etað þisne hláf, *hit* is mín líchoma" (eat this loaf, it is my body).—*Blick. Hom.* 15, 16.

"hit is Hælend se Nazarenisca" (it is the Saviour of Nazareth).—*Ibid.*

Under this heading comes the expression "it is I," which develops itself in the following way.

Old English.—"Habbað geleáfan, ic hyt eom" (have believe, I it am).—*Matthew*, 14, 27.

"Gyf þu hyt eart" (if thou it be).—*Ibid.* 28.

"Ic hyt eom" (I it am).—*Luke*, 24, 36.

"Geseoð mine handa and mine fét, þæt ic sylf hit eom" (see my hands and my feet, that I self it am).—*Ibid.* 39.

Middle English.—Precisely the same expression may have been continued for a while.

"Thesue heom to seyde, lo ich hit em."—*Old Eng. Miscellany*, 42, 184.

But later on, a slight change takes place. Instead of "ic it am" we find "it am I".

"For sothe it am nat I."—CHAUCER, *The Knightes Tale*, 602.

"I am thy mortal foo, and it am I
That loveth so hoote Emelye the brighte."
Ibid. 878.

The modern expression may perhaps be traced back to as early as the beginning of the fourteenth century.

"'Es þat,' he said, 'mi sun daui?'   'Ya, soth,' he said, 'it es i."—*Cursor Mundi* (Cotton, Fairfax, and Gottingen MSS.).

This is, however, doubtful, as *es*, in the *Cursor Mundi*, is equal to *am;* but there are instances in writers of the fifteenth century.

"It is not he that slewe the man, hit is I."—*Gesta Romanorum*, 201.

"It was I my self that cam in the lykenesse."—*Morte d'Arthur*, 38, 22.

"It was I said balyn that slewe this knyght."—*Ibid.* 83, 25.

For "it is *me*," see above, § 214.

"*It*" *instead of* "*there*".

§ 281. *It* is sometimes used in Middle English, and still in the sixteenth century, where we say "*there*".

> "God him bad, bi ðe tail he it nam,
> And *it* a-non a wond it bi-came."
> *Story of Gen. and Exod.* 2807, 8.

> "He wenden to wisse
> Of here lif to misse,
> Al þe day and al þe niȝt,
> Till *hit* sprang day liȝt."
> *King Horn*, 121—24.

"Of þe erth *it* groues tres and gress."—*Cursor Mundi*, 545 (Cotton MS.).

"Bot now *it* es þis appell etten."—*Ibid.* 873.

"Sua lang *it* lathed seth liue."—*Ibid.* 1456.

Cf. *ibid.* 1644, 1850, 2131, &c.

"Bot hit ar ladyes in-noȝe."—*Sir Gawayne and the Gr. Kn.* 1251.

"Saynt Austyn sayth *it* semeth to be a noble kynred bytwene this blyssed vyrgin & sinners."—JOHN FISHER, 50, 9.

"If thou synne ones *it* is nedefull to the one mercy."—*Ibid.* 97, 22.

"*It is*" *emphasizing Nouns and Sentences.*

§ 282. The origin of this use is traceable to Old English, though the French "*c'est*" may have favoured its development in the Middle English period.

Old English.—"þæt wæs on þone mónandæg æfter Marianmæsse, þæt Godwine becom" (it was on Monday after Mary mess that Godwine came).—*Chronicle*, 1052.

"Is þæt for mycel gecynd þæt úrum lichoman cymð call his mægen of þam mete þe we þicgað" (it is through mighty nature that to our body comes all its strength from the food which we eat).—BOETH. 34, 11.

"For þam þingum wæs gio þæt se wisa Catulus hine gebealg" (it was on account that formerly the wise Catulus was angry).—*Ibid.* 27, 1.

Middle English.—"In þe tyme bitwene Abraham & Moyses, it was, þat men come verst to Engelond."—ROB. OF GLOUC. 204.

"Hyt is in the deyd name that I spyke."—WEBER, *Amadas*, iii. v. 284.

"How is it that the modyr of God me xulde come to?"—*Coventry Mysteries*, p. 226.

Later on, *it is* is used without much force or meaning, as may be seen by the suppression of the relative pronoun.

"*It*" used redundantly.

"Dangerous peer,
That smooth'st *it* so with king and commonweal."
2 *Henry VI.* ii. 1. 22.

§ 283. The same conception which accounts for the cognate accusative, viz., the idea of any activity as its own object, brought about the use of *it* as exhibited in the quoted instance. When, for instance, we see somebody fighting, and we want to say that he fights well, we may say either (as we commonly do), "he fights well," or with a cognate accusative, "he fights the fight well." Now, the modern languages are not very fond of the latter expression, it being probably felt as a badly sounding tautology; hence the object, which, in fact, is but a dim idea of the activity, was not improperly expressed by *it*.

The use, which is quite familiar in Middle and Modern German ("er treibt es nicht schlecht; er gibt es gut; cf. *French*, "il *le* lui donne bien"), may be traced back to the older periods of the language, though we are not able as yet to see all the stages of the development, the links between Old, Middle and Modern English being but imperfectly known.

Old English.—"Min Drihten Hǽlende Crist, hú mæg ic *hit* on þrim dag um gefaran? ac má wén is þæt þu onsende þinne engel, se *hit* mæg hrædlicor geferan; forðon, min Drihten, þu wást þæt ic eom flæxlic man, & ic *hit* ne mæg hrædlicor þider geferan, forðon þe, min Drihten, se síþfæt is þyder to lang, & þone weg ic ne con." (My Lord Jesus Christ, how can I go thither in three days? It were better, I think, that thou

shouldst send thine angel, who may perform the journey more speedily;
for thou knowest, my Lord, that I am but a man of flesh, and I cannot
perform this journey very quickly, for the way thither is too long, and I
know not the road.) — *Blick. Hom.* 231. *Cf.* 235.

"swá swá hé *hit* macode on his life" (as he made it in his life, *i.e.*
as he lived in his life). — ÆLFRIC's *Hom.* ii. 354, 24.

"gif hi *hit* æfter ðære godspellícan gesetnysse carfullíce healdað" (if
they carefully hold it after the evangelic rules). — *Ibid.* i. 370, 12.

Middle English.
>"(He) straunge made *it* of hir mariage,
>His purpos was for to bystowe hir hye
>Into som worthy blood of ancetrye."
>CHAUCER, *Reeves Tale*, 60.

"He made *it* straunge, and swore, so God him save,
Lasse than a thousand pound he wolde nought have."
Id. Frankeleynes Tale, 487.

"Whi makest þow *hit* nowe so straunge to me?" — *Gesta Rom.* 220.

Modern English. — "To revel *it* with him and his new bride." —
3 *Hen. VI.* iii. 3, 225.

"I cannot daub *it* further" (= continue my former dissembling). —
Lear iv. 1, 54.

"Lord Angelo dukes *it* well." — *Measure for M.* iii. 2, 100.

"He wanted to rough *it* like the commonest labourer in Paris." —
BRADDON, *Ishmael*, i. 88.

Pleonastic use of the Personal Pronoun.

"The nobles, *they* are fled, the commons cold." — SHAKSPERE.

§ 284. In order to emphasize a noun as subject, its personal pronoun is made to precede or to follow it.[1]

The Pronoun precedes the Noun.

§ 285. *Old English.* — *He* þá se eádiga wer Gúthlác heora worda ne
gímde" (he there the blessed man G. did not care for their words). —
Gúthlac, 5.

"And *he* sanctus Georgius him to Dryhtne gebad" (and he St.
George prayed to the Lord). — SWEET, *Oldest English Texts*, p. 178.

---

[1] For the psychological origin of this use see Double Subject, § 73.

Middle English—"And *he* swa dude sone, þe king of Denmarke" (and he did so, the king of Denmark).—LAYAMON, ii. 558.

"*Thai* ar so long taryyng, the fowles, that we cast out."—*Townley Myst.* p. 33.

"And thus she spake, this mayden ying."—*Lay Le Freine*, 121.

"But sche ne told no man her sore
The emperesse."
Octovian, 653.

"The way he shalle you lede,
The kyng of alle man-kyn."
Townley Myst. p. 136.

Instances with the pronoun in the oblique case.

"Who gaf Iudith corage or hardinesse
To sleen *him* Olofernus in his tente?"
CHAUCER, *Man of Laws Tale*, 939.

"For jelousie and fere of him Arcite."
Id. Knights Tale, 475.

In *Modern English* this use is restricted to poetry.

"She early left her sleepless bed,
The fairest maid of Teviotdale."
SCOTT, *Last Minstrel*, 2, 25.

"What may it be, the heavy sound,
That moans old Branksome's turrets round?"
Ibid. 1, 12.

The Pronoun follows the Noun.

§ 286. *Old English.*—"Se ofersprǽca wer ne wierð *he* nǽfre geryht ne geldred on þiss worlde" (the loquacious man will never be corrected or taught in this world).—*Cura Pastoralis*, 278, 22.

Middle English.—"þe knigtes þai were hende."—*Sir Tristrem*, 62; A.D. 1320.

Modern English.
"The mother *she* has dyed her cruell handes
In blood of her owne sonne."
Gorboduc, 1350.

Very frequent in Elizabethan writers.

"For God *he* knows."—SHAKSP. *Richard III.* iii. 7, 236.

Cf. Abbott, § 243.

"My wife *she* was to go to her father's."—*Pepys' Diary*, a. 1559.

The Personal Pronoun used redundantly in Complex Sentences.

§ 287. If the predicate is separated from the subject by any adverbial, participial or adjectival clause, a personal pronoun is often pleonastically inserted to mark the subject.

§ 288. (*a*) After adverbial or participial clauses the pronoun occurs very often in the fifteenth century.

"So the knyght, whenne he sawe the scheter drawe his bowe, *he* swapte his hed undir þe watir."—*Gesta Rom.* 3.

"The which knyȝt as he rode or ȝede in a certeyne day in erndis of þe emperour, *he* sawe afer a serpent."—*Ibid.* 5.

"Every knyght aftir þat he myght no more use armys, *he* should be put oute of the empire."—*Ibid.* 45.

"The kyng thenne, after the knyght had thus spoken to hym, *he* gaff commaundement."—CAXTON, *Blanch.* 102, 16.

"How Gryffon of Haultefelle and Guenelon, after that they hadde slayne the Duke Beues of Aygremonte, *they* retorned to Paris."—CAXTON, *Aymon*, 58, 13.

"þe messager heringe these wordes *he* turned home agene."—*Gesta Rom.* 171.

"Butt thenne on of them, beholdyng the gracious fase of the childe, *he* was mevid by mercy."—*Ibid.* 209.

"The emperour, trowing that it were the herte of the childe, *he* caste hit into the fire."—*Ibid.* 210.

§ 289. (*b*) After adjectival or relative clauses this use may be traced back to the earliest periods of the English language. A few instances will suffice for the present occasion.

"Ac þa lond on eást healfe Danais þe þær nihst sindon, Albani hi sind genemnede" (but the countries on the east of the Danaïs which are next, *they* are called Albani).—*Orosius*, 14, 23.

"And he Ninus Soroastrem Bactriana cyning, se cúðe manna ǽrest drýcraftas, *he hine* oferwann and ofslóh" (and he Ninus overcame and slew S. the king of Bactriana, who of all men was the first to know magic art).—*Ibid.* 30, 10.

Cf. *ibid.* 12, 16; 26, 20; 72, 13; 98, 2; 124, 16; 188, 26; 204, 6.

"Ure ældren, þa þe þas stówa ær hioldon, hie lufedon wisdom" (our ancestors, who held these places before, they loved wisdom).—*Cura Pastoralis*, p. 4. *Cf.* 22.

Old Eng. Hom. i. pp. 3, 7, 9, 25; ii. pp. 19, 41, &c.
Old English Miscellany, pp. 17, 18, 40.
Story of Gen. and Exod., ll. 1003-4, 1065, 3839.
Cursor Mundi, ll. 283, 285, 7184, 8940, 9014, &c., &c.
Cf. below, *Adjectival Clauses.*

The Emphatic Pronoun.

§ 290. The personal pronoun is strengthened by *self*.

"*Self*" used appositively.

§ 291. As in Gothic and Old High German, *self* is in Old English first an adjective, and if added appositively to the personal pronoun, it agrees with it in number, gender and case.

"Swa þu self talast" (as thou sayest thyself).—*Beówulf*, 595.

"Nú we seolfe geseóð sigores tácen" (now we ourselves see the token of victory).—*Elene*, 1121.

Instances abound.

"*Self*" in connection with the Dative.

"He did it *himself.*"

§ 292. As early as the ninth century *self*, as subject, is found preceded by *him*.

The fact that the first instances of *self* preceded by *him* are met with mostly in connection with intransitive verbs, gives us the key to this curious expression. We have seen above (cf. *Ethic Dative*, § 191) that such verbs, especially those denoting movement, were often followed by the dative of the personal pronoun in Old English as well as in the other Teutonic languages, *e.g.* "gewát *him* þá se æðeling" (there went *him* the nobleman). Now the subject of this sentence may be occasionally emphasized by the pronoun *self;* then we have "*gewát him self* se æðeling." This is indeed very often the case in Old English.

"And him *self* siþþan to þæm ríce féng" (and he himself succeeded since to the kingdom).—*Orosius,* 66, 6.

"Marius and Sylla gefóran him *self*" (Thorpe: died voluntarily.)—*Ibid.* 236, 24.

"And gestód him *self* on þæm hiehstan torre" (and stood himself on the highest tower).—*Ibid.* 260, 33.

"(he) bær him sylf his lác" (he bore himself his offering).—ÆLFRIC, *Lives of Saints,* vi. 236.

"Ic cóm me *sylf* tó eów" (I came to you myself).—ÆLFRIC, *De Nov. Test.* 18, 7.

Other instances:

Cura Pastoralis, 90, 11; 425, 10.
Ælfric, *Homilies,* ii. 62, 23; 410, 12; 514, 12.
Wulfstan, 218, 28; 241, 13.

"*Self*" as Subject.

§ 293. The Old English expression, viz., personal pronoun in the nominative case and *self* agreeing with it as an apposition (*ic self, we selfe,* &c.) soon gets out of use. It occurs in Layamon, and is still in the Cotton MS. of the *Cursor Mundi;* but Orm seems to have discarded it altogether.

"þu seolf (þu þi seolf) wurð al isund."—LAYAM. i. 135.
"He seolf (he B.) him wolde specken wið."—*Ibid.* ii. 32.
"As godds suld þee seluen be."—*Cursor Mundi,* Cotton MS. 780.

But the other MSS. have:

"As goddis sulde ȝe þen be."—Fairfax MS.
"Als goddes suld ȝur seluen be."—Gött. MS.
"As Goddes shulde ȝe boþe be."—Trinity MS.

"And wroght he self in þat labore."—*Ibid.* Cotton MS. 1726.
"And wroȝt his-self in þat labour."—*Ibid.* Fairfax MS.
"And wroght himself in þat labur."—*Ibid.* Göttingen MS.
"And him self dude his cure."—*Ibid.* Trinity MS.
"He self þe dore þan has he stoken."—*Ibid.* Cotton MS. 1758.
"Him-self þe doer he has stokyn."—*Ibid.* Fairfax MS.
"Him-self þe dur suith had stokin."—*Ibid.* Göttingen MS.
"Him self þe dore soone had stoken."—*Ibid.* Trinity MS.

Cf. *ibid.* 2010, 2559, 2713, &c.

§ 294. Next we find the personal pronoun in the nominative case + dative of the personal pronoun + "self" (*ic me self, þu þe self*, &c.).

From the fact that, in Orm, *self* appears without any inflexion in the singular, we may safely infer that, in the twelfth century, this expression is exactly the same as in Old English, i.e. *self* has not yet been attracted by the (ethical?) dative of the pronoun.

"I me sellf sahh godess gast."—*Orm.* 12592.
"ȝif þu arrt te sellf millde."—*Ibid.* 1252.
"þurrh þatt he wollde ben himmsellf i wæterr fullhtnedd."—*Ibid.* 195.
"ȝho wass hire sellf god widdwe."—*Ibid.* 8685.

It must be observed, however, that the *Old English Homilies* exhibit several instances of inflected *self*. See ii. pp. 21, 111, 137, 139, 147, 153, 155, 183, 189.

"*Himself*" as subject.

§ 295. The pronoun in the nominative is dropped, and only the dative is used.

"Him seolf mid wæne ferde into ane watere" (he himself went with difficulty into a water).—LAYAM. i. 93.

"Swa himsulf wolde."—*Ibid. A.* ii. 130.

"Heom seolf nomen hire lond."—*Ibid.* B. i. 255.
"Alls himmself itt wollde."—*Orm*, 4227.
"Cumm þe sellf."—*Ibid.* 12798.

Cf. *Old Eng. Hom.* i. 9; ii. 45, 51, 61, 87, &c., and so very often.

Myself.

§ 296. *The personal pronoun + myself* is scarcely to be met with before the thirteenth century. I do not find it in the *Old English Homilies*, but there are instances in Layamon, and *Ancren Riwle*.

"Ich mi seolf neore" (if I had not been there myself).—LAYAM. i. 376.
"Bute ȝif þi sulf it makie."—*Ancren Riwle*, p. 124.

Cf. ROBERT OF GLOUCESTER, 4009 (mi sulf), 8361 (mi sulf), 1082 (þi sulf).

In the fourteenth century it becomes frequent.

There are two facts which seem to suggest that this construction was brought into existence by some change in the pronunciation of the *e* in m*e* self, th*e* self, so that it was confounded with the *i* in m*y* self, th*y* self. First, all the instances of this construction found in the thirteenth century exhibit only *miself* and *þiself*, never *ourself* or *yourself*, which do not occur before the fourteenth century.

"Þaȝȝe ȝour-self be talenttyf to take hit to your-seluen" (though you yourself are willing to undertake it).—*Sir Gawayne and the Gr. K.* 350.

Cf. *ibid.* 1964.

Secondly, the use of the inflected form of self ("myselue*n*") shows that self in this connection was at first not looked upon as a substantive. It was not until the use of *myself* had become the rule, that the other persons were formed after the same fashion. Only the third person with its three distinct genders resisted the analogy of *myself;* there are, however, not unfrequent instances of even the third person used in the same way.

> "Alle thaa that blisses the
> Sal *tham* self blessed be."
> *Cursor Mundi*, 5378 (Cotton MS.).

The Fairfax and Trinity MSS. have *thai* (*thei*).

"Had thair ouerman *ham* selfe."—*Ibid.* 6968 (Cotton MS.).

Fairfax : be *thaire* selue.

"Thof *he* self was clene o sin."—*Ibid.* 7263 (Cotton MS.).

The Göttingen and Trinity MSS. have *him*self; Fairfax has *his* self. *Cf.* 3408.

"The stif kyng *his* seluen."—*Sir Gaw. and the Green Kn.* 107.

Cf. "al *his* one," *ibid.* 1048 ; "*oure* one," *ibid.* 1230.

"*Self*" in connection with a Pronoun as Object.

§ 297. *A.* Personal pronoun in the oblique case + *self* agreeing with it in number, gender and case. Until the fourteenth century I generally find *self* in the oblique case, *e.g.* :

"and sone sum he cuþe ben Himm ane bi himm sell*fenn*" (not *self!*). —*Orm.* 822.

But in the *Cursor Mundi* "self" becomes very common.

§ 298. *B.* The possessive pronoun + *self* appears as early as the first half of the 13th century :—

> "For þine luue ich worsocal þat me leof was,
> And ȝef ðe al *mi suluen*"

(for thy love I forsook all that was dear to me, and gave thee all myself).—*On God Ureisun of Ure Lefdi* (Old Engl. Hom.), i. 197.

"þu dest me god, and hermest þi *sulf.*"—*Ancren Riwle,* p. 124.

Modern English.—Both in the direct and oblique case the possessive pronoun in the first and second person is the rule, while the personal pronoun, with a few exceptions, is kept in the third.[1]

Note.—"Own" is sometimes inserted.

"For your cursidnes I shall hange you my *owne* self at this gibet."—*Aymon*, 339, 13.

The Reflexive Pronoun.

§ 299. There is no special pronoun in Old English to denote an action reflected upon the agent, the personal pronoun being used in its stead. There are, however, numerous instances of personal pronouns emphasized by *self*, as in Modern English.

"Gemyne þe sylfne."—*Blick. Hom.* 31, 12.

In Middle English the compound forms are steadily increasing, but as early as Caxton's time they seem to be the rule. Of thirty instances occurring on the first forty-two pages of *Blanchardyn*, only three are simple, namely, 1, 22; 2, 10; 41, 21.

§ 300. As for the inflection of *self* it is not used as a substantive with *s* in the plural before the middle of the sixteenth century. John Fisher has still only *selfe;* Starkey vacillates between "selfe" and "selves" (20 "themselfe," 23 "themselfys"); Ascham has already only "themselves."

---

[1] "Almighty god in *his* selfe."—FISHER, 8, 6.
"*His* self wittnesseth."—*Ibid.* 72, 10.
"To saue *his* self.—BERNERS'S *Huon*, i. 108.
"The nine muses *their* selfe."—ASCHAM, *Toxophilus*, (ed. Arber), p. 44.
"He may make *hisself* easy."—DICKENS, *Pickwick*, ii. 55.

The Possessive Pronoun.

§ 301. The possessive pronoun having its origin in the genitive of the personal pronoun, is often replaced by "of" + pronoun.

Middle English.—" (ðe) strengðe *of* ðe helpe mi muchele wacnesse" (may the strength of thee help my great weakness).— *Old English Homilies*, i. 273, A.D. 1200.

"I byseke you, knightes, for the love of me.
Goth and dresseth my lond among my sones three."
Tale of Gamelyn, 35.

"We haue seen þe glorie of hym."—WYCL. *Joh.* i. 14.

"That I may feylle the smelle of the."—*Town Mys.* p. 43.

Modern English.—"The native myghtiness and fall of him."— SHAK. *Henry V.* 2, 4.

"The lamentable fall of me."—*Rich. II.* 5, 1.

"I never met with the fellow *of her.*"—RICHARDSON, *Pamela*, 29.

Cf. Mätzner, iii., p. 230; Introduction to Caxton's *Blanchardyn*, § 5.

Relative referring to a Possessive Pronoun.

§ 302. Owing to the original meaning of "my" = of me, a possessive pronoun is often antecedent to a relative one.

Middle English.—
"Prest we ben for the to deye,
And for *his* love *that deyd* on rood."
Richard Cœur de Lion, 4468.

"Unthank com on *his* heed *that* band him so."—CHAUCER, *The Reeves Tale*, 162.

Modern English.—
"They shall strike
Your children yet unborn and unbegot,
That lift your vassal hands against my head."
SHAK. *Rich. II.* 3, 3, 89.

"Let grief and sorrow still embrace *his* heart,
That doth not wish thee joy."
SHAK. *Tempest*, 5, 214.

> The tents
> Of wickedness, wherein shall dwell *his* race
> *Who* slew his brother."
> MILTON, *Paradise Lost*, 11, 607.

§ 303. *Note.*—In the following instances the possessive pronoun is equivalent to a personal pronoun, the preceding *both* having lost its genitival inflexion :

> "But I have sworn to frustrate *both their* hopes."—MARLOWE, *Jew*, 2, 2.

> " But clay and clay differs in dignity
> *Whose* dust is *both* alike."
> SHAK. *Cymbeline*, iv. 2, 4.

> " Have I not *all their* letters to meet me in arms?"—SHAK. 1 *Henry IV.* ii. 3, 28.

> " Tell her 'tis *all our* ways—it runs in the family."—SHERIDAN, *Rivals*, 4, 2.

Compare the Middle English instances :

> " þurrh þeȝȝre baþre bisne" (through the example of them both).—*Orm.* 2794.

Cf. *ibid.* 3301, 9762, &c.

> " And after, by *her bother* rede,
> A ladder they set the hall to."
> ELLIS, *Metric Rom.* iii. 65.

The Possessive Pronoun before Substantival Adjectives.

§ 304. The possessive pronoun is followed by the adjective used substantively, denoting equality, superiority, and inferiority, and others in the comparative degree.

Old English.—" Drihten hwá is þín gelíca?" (O Lord, who is thy equal?).—*Ps.* xxxiv. 11.

" þæt nán man nis *his gelíca* on corðan" (that no man is his like on earth).—*Job* iii. 16.

" þá *his betera* læg" (now that his lord lay dead).—BYRHTNOTH, 276 (Grein).

" þá me *yldra mín* ágeaf andsware" (then my elder, *i.e.* father, gave me answer).—*Elene*, 462.

"Secgað swylc wundru *eówrum gingrum*" (say such wonders to your youngers).—*Ps.* xlviii. 13.

Middle English.—"Ne nat ich a wærulde riche cniht *his iliche*" (I know not in the world a rich knight his like).—LAYAMON, ii. 109.

"His per in the world ne was" (his like was not in the world).— ROBERT OF GLOUCESTER, 255.

Cf. *ibid.* 399.

Modern English instances are very frequent.

§ 305. In Old and Middle English the possessive pronoun is often preceded by a demonstrative pronoun. See above, § 221.

§ 306. *My* is used as a term of courtesy. This is probably borrowed from the French.

"Maria sought þan til him son
And said, '*mi lauerd*, quat has it don
þis bodi, ded worþei to be?'"

(Mary went to him soon and said, "my lord what has it done, this child, to deserve death?")—*Cursor Mundi*, 11966, A.D. 1300.

Mr. Kington Oliphant quotes "mi lord the Douke," from Weber, *Metrical Romances*, A.D. 1330. *The New English*, i. 14.

Cf. Introduction to Caxton's *Blanchardyn*, § 12 (*b*).

But I find an instance of this use in Aelfred :—

"Mid þy þæt fýr him nealecte, þa wæs he him ondrædende and forht geworden, cwæð tó þam engle: *Mín domne*, hwæt is þis fýr?" (When the fire came near him, he was frightened and alarmed, said to the angel: "*My lord*, what is this fire?")—BEDA, iii. 19.

Cf. also *ibid.* iii. 14 :

"Hwæt woldest þú, *mín domne biscop*, þæt cynelice hors þæm þearfan syllan"? (why wouldst thou, my lord bishop, give that royal horse to the poor?)

The Possessive Pronoun used Indefinitely.

§ 307. In Modern English the possessive pronoun is used indefinitely, with a slight shade of contempt.

"*Your fat king* and *your lean beggar*, is but variable service; two dishes, but to one table."—SHAK. *Hamlet*, iv. 3, 24.

"I would teach these nineteen the special rules, as *your punto, your reverso, your stoccata, your imbroccato, your passada, your montanto.*"—BEN JONSON, *Every Man in his Humour*, 4, 5.

"Tell me how to put a young friend of mine in the way of seeing something of Paris life, more than *your* fool of a tourist generally sees."—MRS. WARD, *David Grieve*, ii. 99.

"*His*" *instead of the Genitive Case.*

§ 308. This use may be traced back to Old English, where not only *his*, but also other possessive pronouns, are found after proper nouns, in order to make up for the want of the genitival inflection.

"þær Asia and Europa *hiera* landgemircu togædre licgað" (where the boundaries of Europe and Asia lie).—*Orosius*, 8¹⁰.

"Africa and Asia *hiera* landgemircu onginnað of Alexandria" (the boundary between Africa and Asia begins at Alexandria).—*Ibid.* 8²⁸.

"þær we gesáwon Enac his cynryn" (we saw the children of Anac there).—*Num.* xiii. 29.

In the first period of Middle English the same use is to be found mostly in proper nouns.

"Argal his broðer."—LAYAMON, i. 279.

"To Cornwale his eærde."—*Ibid.* i. 175.

"Al it was for Abraham—is wif."—*Story of Gen. and Exod.* 1181.

"And al ðo briðere, of frigti mod, fellen bi-forn ðat louerd—is fot" (and all the brothers of fearful mood fell to that Lord's feet).—*Ibid.* 2272.

"Decius Cesar his tyme."—TREVISA, i. 39.

But the second version of Layamon's *Brut* exhibits a few instances of *his* replacing inflectional *s*.

"Min hem his mochele mod" (= mine uncle's).—i. 375.

"Urne þe teares uppe þe king his leores" (the tears ran down the king's cheeks).—iii. 214.

"þe bissop his broþer."—ii. 276.

Cf. Introduction to Caxton's *Blanch. and Egl.*, p. 36, *d.*

O

Modern English.—The sixteenth century makes a very large use of *his* = *s*, it occurs in the seventeenth and the eighteenth centuries, and has not died out even in our own time.

§ 309. *The Possessive Pronoun occurs sometimes in connection with the Gerund, where we should expect the Oblique Case of the Personal Pronoun.*

"Another homicidy is doon for necessite, as whan a man sleth another in *his defendant*."—CHAUCER, *Persones Tale*, p. 312.

"Thou knowest well, that I dyde was in *my deffendynge*."—CAXTON, *Aymon*, 82, 26.

"It was I that slewe this knyght in *my deffendaunt*."—MALORY, *Morte d'Arthur*, 83, 25.

The Possessive Pronoun emphasized.

§ 310. The possessive pronoun was in Old English emphasized by *own* ("ágen"), *one* ("án"), and *self*, the latter being invariably used in the genitive case.

(a) "se ege his ágenra unðeawa" (the fear of his own vices).—*Cura Pastoralis*, 24, 1.

"his ágen wif" (his own wife).—*Ibid.* 397, 17.

"þin ágen geleáfa þe hæfþ geháledne" (thy own belief has cured thee).—*Blick. Hom.* 15, 14.

(b) *Án* in connection with the possessive pronoun is rare.

"witigan witigodan . . . þæt se wolde cuman . . . & him ealle þás cynericu on his *ánes* æht geagnian" (prophets foretold . . . that he would come . . . and possess for himself all these kingdoms as his own possession).—*Blick. Hom.* 105, 7 *ff.*

(c) "hiera selfra gilp" (their own boast).—*Cura Pastoralis*, 108, 20.

"hiere selfre suna sende gife unscynde" (she sent to her own son a blameless gift).—*Elene*, 1200.

"ðæs willgifan, hiere sylfre suna" (of the joyous giver, her own son).—*Ibid.* 222.

"Crist cwæþ þurh his sylfes múþ" (Christ said through his own mouth).—*Blick. Hom.* 59, 1.

"he mid his sylfes willan to eorþan ástág" (he, by his own will, descended to the earth).—*Ibid.* 83, 30.

Of these expressions only the first, that with *own*, has come down to Modern English times.

The expression "of mine."

§ 311. In Old English the possessive pronoun, or, as the French say, "pronominal adjective," expresses only the conception of belonging and possession; it is a real adjective, and does not convey, as at present, the idea of determination. If, therefore, Old English authors want to make nouns preceded by possessive pronouns determinative, they add the definite article.

"hæleð mín se leófa" (my dear youth)—*Elene*, 511.

"þú eart dóhtor mín séo dýreste" (thou art my dearest daughter).—*Juliana*, 93.

For other instances see above, § 220–22.

Later on, the possessive pronoun apparently implies a determinative meaning (as in Modern German and Modern French); therefore its connection with the definite article is made superfluous, while the indefinite article is quite impossible. Instead of the old construction we find henceforth what may be termed the genitive pseudo-partitive. See above, § 178–180.

The Possessive Pronoun used Substantively.

§ 312. The possessive pronoun is also used substantively in Old English without any difference of inflexion, in the later periods with an *s* added to our, your, her, their. Besides, this use, in Modern English, is much more restricted than in Old English.

(*a*) Of persons.

Old English.—"Hig wǽron þine" (they were thine).—*John*, xvii. 6.

"Þa férdon sume of úrum tó þǽre bergenne" (and some of ours went to the tomb).—*Luke*, xxiv. 24.

"Eác sume wíf of úrum ús brégdon" (some women of ours amazed us).—*Ibid.* 22.

Middle English.—"Fare we bihalues, alse we of *heoren* weoren" (go we aside, as if we were of their party).—LAYAMON, i. 178.

"ȝif þu and þine þer wurðeð dæd."—*Ibid.* i. 419.

"To þe & to alle þyne."—ROBERT OF GLOUCESTER, 335.

"I haue herde that ye haue called me and my broder the sones of a traytour, and that the kyng knoweth well that our fader slewe yours by trayson, wherof I wylle ye wyte that ye lie falsely, but your fader dyde assaylle *our* by trayson."—CAXTON, *Aymon*, 545, 10.

"Ye wolle enforce yourselfe to rescue oute of daunger of deth, my lorde and *youre*, my good husband Sadoyne."—CAXTON, *Blanchardyn*, 189, 25.

(*b*) Of things.

Old English.—"Nis hit ná mín inc tó syllene."—*Mark*, x. 40.

"He nimeð of mínum."—*John*, xvi. 14.

The following example, in the plural, is a literal translation of the Greek original:

"Ealle mine synd þýne, and þýne synd mine."—*John*, xvii. 10.

Original: "τὰ ἐμὰ πάντα σά ἐστιν καὶ τὰ σὰ ἐμά." Vulgata: "mea omnia tua sunt, et tua mea sunt."

Cf. *Cura Pastoralis*, 318, 16; 326, 12.

Middle English.—"Ane lete hem gon, eche lord to *his owne*."—MAUNDEVILLE, p. 89.

Modern English.—"He shall receive of *mine*."—*John*, xvi. 14.

"He shall take of *mine*."—*Ibid.* xvi. 15.

"He speaketh of *his own*."—*Ibid.* viii. 44.

"Let no man seek *his own*."—1 *Cor.* x. 24.

"Charity . . . seeketh not *her own*."—*Ibid.* xiii. 5.

The Dative of the Personal Pronoun instead of the Possessive Pronoun.

§ 313. When speaking of the parts of the human body, we use the possessive pronoun in Modern English; the older periods omit it altogether as superfluous, or make up for it by the dative of the personal pronoun.

"Abraham hæfde him on handa fýr and swurd" (A. had in his hand fire and sword).—ÆLFRIC, *Hom.* ii. 60, 26.

"hafa ðé mínne stæf on handa" (take my staff into thy hand).—*Ibid.* ii. 416, 35.

"þá cnitton hí rápas hire tó handum and fótum" (they put ropes on her feet and hands).—*Ibid.* i. 488, 35; *Lives of Saints,* ix. 100; *Beówulf,* 2405.

The Demonstrative Pronoun.

§ 314. The syntactic use of the demonstrative pronoun has undergone but slight alterations from Old English down to modern times.

"An" (one) used as a Demonstrative.

§ 315. It is a noteworthy point that the numeral *án* (one) was, in Old English, used as a demonstrative = this or that.

"Swá þá driht-guman dreámum lifdon eádiglíce, óð þæt *án* ongan fyrene fremman, feónd on helle" (thus the warriors lived in joy happily, till that one began to work crimes, the fiend of hell).—*Beówulf*, 99—101.

án, sc. Grendel, mentioned above in 86.

The same use prevails in Middle High German.

Cf. Paul und Braune, *Beiträge,* xi. 518-527; xii. 371, 393.

§ 316. "*Sum*," *too, was used in a Demonstrative Sense.*

"Næfre ic máran geseah eorla ofer eorðan, þonne is eówer sum, secg on searwum" (never saw I a greater earl on earth than is some one [that one] of you, the man in arms).—*Beówulf,* 248.

"gúð-beorna sum wicg gewende, word æfter cwæð" (the one of the warriors (= the warrior, who in this case is a solitary one, not one of a troop, as the phrase might lead one to imagine) turned his horse, said a word after).—*Ibid.* 314.

In both passages the person referred to was mentioned before.

"*These Seven Years.*"

§ 317. *Se, seo þæt* having lost their inflexions, and being turned into the monotonous article *the*, their demonstrative function was taken up by *this*.

Expressions like the following are scarcely to be traced back to the oldest periods of English.

Middle English.—"I have served thy brother *this sixtene yeer*."— *Tale of Gamelyn*, 400. *Cf.* 354.
"Here wille I lig *this fourty dayes.*"—*Town. Myst.* p. 16.

"*Ere this.*"

§ 318. *This* used as a local or temporal adverb as in *ere this, by this, between this and the Pyramids* (Bulwer, *Money*, 2, 5), is found as early as Old English.

Old English.—"Swá swá heo stent óþ þis."—BASILIUS, *Hexameron*, 6. [Quoted by Mätzner, iii. 244.]
"Nú ðonne óð þis wé reahton hwele se hierde bion sceal" (hitherto we have said what the pastor is to be).—*Cura Pastoralis*, 172, 14, A.D. 890.
Middle English.—"þer nas bituene þis and Spayne no prince withoute al þis."—ROBERT OF GLOUCESTER, 3915.

"*This*" and "*Thai.*"

§ 319. *This* as denoting what is nearer, contrasting with *that* as denoting what is farther off, is of a recent date.

Cf. "þatt an wass o ȝonnd hallf þe flumm,
      And o þis hallf þatt oþerr."—*Orm.* 10588.

Cf. *ibid.* 10611.

"God shal destroye and this and that."—1 *Cor.* vi. 13.

"For that, and this, that lyys here,
Have cost me fulle dere."
Town. Myst. p. 13.

"*That*" = "*The.*"

§ 320. *That* is, as late as the end of the fifteenth century, used without any demonstrative force.

"Germania þat contray."—TREVISA, i. 171.
"Beaneus Apollo that man."—*Ibid.* i. 221.
"þat man Paris."—*Ibid.* 225.
"Parthia þat kyngdom."—*Ibid.* i. 85.
"Hibernia þat lond."—*Ibid.* 143.
"Cappadocia þat londe."—*Ibid.* 147.

Cf. "that one, that other" = "each other."

"*That one* looked upon *that other* for to see who wolde sette fyrst honde upon hym."—CAXTON, *Charles the Grete*, 44, 26.
"*that one* was named babtysme, and *that other* grabam."—*Ibid.* 59, 17, 18.

Cf. *ibid.* 59, 24-25 ; 62, 19 ; 70, 21.

The following passage shows the transition from *that* to *the* :—

"For other (= either) he shall hate the one and love the other ; or els he shall lene to the one, and despise *that other*."—TYNDALE, *Matth.* vi. 24.

"*That*" *in connection with the Genitive.*

§ 321. *That* + genitive used with reference to a preceding noun in order to avoid repetition is scarcely to be traced back to Old English, where the single genitive was considered sufficient, as in *Latin*.

"Eówer rihtwísnys máre is, þonne þǽra wrítera" (your righteousness is greater than that of the scribes).—*Matth.* v. 20.

But there are Middle English instances of this use.

"ȝe schulle undirstonde that it (this crounc) was of jonkes of the see . . . for I have seen and beholden many tymes *that of Paris* and *that of Constantynoble.*"—MAUNDEVILLE, p. 13.

"The emperour of Constantynoble seythe that he hathe the spere heed : and I have often tyme seen it ; but it is grettere than *that at Parys.*"—*Ibid.* p. 14.

§ 322. "*Such*" as a Demonstrative Pronoun

has, on the whole, undergone no syntactical change ; there is, however, a marked difference between the old and modern use of *such and such ;* while nowadays its function is that of an indefinite pronoun, its meaning, in older periods, was merely demonstrative, always pointing to a preceding noun.

Instances are not frequent.

Old English.—" Be swilcum and be swilcum þú miht ongitan þæt se cræft þæs lichoman bið on þam móde " (by such and such [things] thou mayest understand that the power of the body is in the mind).—BOETH. 58, 1.

Middle English.—" All þeȝȝre lac wass *swille annd swille* " (all their offerings were such and such).—*Orm.* 1006.

" And seggesst *swille and swille* wass þu."—*Ibid.* 1512.

" All *swille annd swille* comm Sannt Johan to shæwenn."—*Ibid.* 9381.

" For *swille annd swille* wass Drihhtin laþ Saducewisshe leode."—*Ibid.* 9749.

While in all these instances *such and such* serves to avoid repetition, the following passage shows it in another shade of meaning.

"Joseph soght on me in bour
þat suikeful fals, þat fole lichour,
Al *suilk and suilk*, sir, was þe scam
þat he can seke on mi licam"

(Joseph called on me in [my] chamber, that deceitful false [one], that foul fornicator, *such and such* was the shame that he did seek on my body).—*Cursor Mundi,* 4413.

Potiphar's wife feigns to be ashamed of mentioning the proper word for Joseph's shameful offer, and substitutes *such and such*.

Note.—For *swilc* as a relative pronoun see below, § 334.

"*The same*" *instead of the Personal Pronoun.*

§ 323. *The same* is often used as a personal pronoun without any demonstrative force.

"He had of me a chain: at five o'clock I shall receive the money for the same (= it)."—SHAKSPERE, *Comedy of Errors*, iv. 1, 11.

"Give me the paper, let me read the same."—*Ibid. Love's Labour Lost*, i. 1, 116.

Cf. German, *derselbe*, *dieselbe*, *dasselbe* = he, she, it.

The Interrogative Pronoun.

There are but a few noteworthy points in the development of this pronoun.

"*What*" *used Substantively.*

§ 324. *What* is originally, as in the other Teutonic languages, used only as a substantive, and, as such, governs the genitive case. But after the decay of the inflexion, what was originally a genitive, was looked upon as a nominative, so that *what* became an adjective.

Old English.—"þá geseah selfa sigora waldend *hwæt* wæs monna *mánes* on eorðan" (there saw himself, the ruler of victories what crime of men was on earth).—CÆDMON, *Genesis*, 1271.

Perhaps the phrase "What news?" is a remnant of this old use.

Cf. the following instances :—

"Ne secʒe we nán þing *niwes* on þissere gesetnisse" (we say nothing new in this book).—ÆLFRIC, *Lives of Saints*, p. 4, l. 46.

"*What nwes* so þay nome, at naȝt quen þay metten
þay acorded of þe covenauntes byfore þe courte alle"
(what news so [ever] they took [heard?], when they met at night, they
accorded of the covenants before the whole court).—*Sir Gawayne and
the Greene Knight*, 1407.

"*What*" *referring to Persons.*

§ 325. In Old and Middle English *what* refers predicatively to *persons* as well as to things; it is not before the fourteenth century that we note the tendency to put *who* for *what*.

Old English.—"*Hwæt syndon* ge" (who are you?)—*Beowulf*, 479.

"Sege ús, Crist, *hwæt is* se þe þe slóh?" (say unto us, who is he that struck thee?)—*Matth.* xxvi. 68.

"*Hwæt synd* þás?" (who are these?)—*Gen.* xxxiii. 5.

Middle English.—"*What* beoð þeos ut-laȝen?" (who are these outlaws?).—LAYAM. iii. 91.

"And wiste wele, *what* he wes."—*Sir Tristrem*, 598.

"*quat* art thou?"—*Cursor Mundi*, 3725.

Thus the Cotton, Göttingen and Trinity MSS.; Fairfax has "*qua* art þou."

"*Quat* art þou, he said, lemman?"—*Ibid.* 38, 39.

Thus the Cotton, Fairfax, Göttingen and Trinity MSS.

"And *quat* art þou me beddes sua?"—*Ibid.* 5202.

Thus the Cotton, Göttingen and Trinity MSS.; Fairfax has "*qua* art þou."

Cf. *ibid.* 7370, 7887.

"She loked backward for to see *what* he was that so hastely rode after her."—CAXTON, *Blanch.* 41, 30.

"Moche grete desyre I haue to wyte and knowe *what* he may be."—*Ibid.* 64, 1.

"(He) asked of him *what* he was, of what lande and of what lynage."—*Ibid.* 99, 35.

Tudor English.—"(Huon demaundyd) *what* he was, and who was hys father."—LORD BERNERS, *Huon,* 17, 22.

"He demaundyd *what* we were."—*Ibid.* 29, 11.

Cf. *ibid.* 30, 3; 30, 13, &c.

§ 326. "*What*" *used Adjectively,*

= *qualis* is of a recent date. In Old English and the first periods of Middle English this function was performed by *hwylc,* in later Middle English by *whatkyn* ("kynnes"), *what maner.*

Old English.—"Mé com on gemynd *hwelce* wutan gio wǣron geond Angelkynn" (it occurred to my mind what wise men were once in England).—*Cura Pastor.* 2, 2.

"geðenc *hwelc* witu ús þa becómon" (consider what punishments came on us).—*Ibid.* 4, 4.

Very frequent.

Middle English.—"þu nast, of whulche londe heo com hider liðen, ne whulc king is hire fader, ne whulc quen hire moder."—LAYAMON, i. 98.

"þench, mid wulche deden þu miht werien þine leoden."—*Ibid.* i. 365.

"Her mann unnderstanndenn maȝȝ, whilc mann iss drihhtnenn cweme" (here man may understand what man is agreeable to the lord).—*Orm.* 3965.

For the other constructions with *kynn, maner,* see *Genitive Case,* § 167-172.

§ 327. "*What*"

as an exclamation is very old.

Old English.—"*Hwæt!* þá Job árás" (Lo! then Job rose).—*Job,* 2, 2.

Middle English.—"What! be ye wood?"—1 *Cor.* xiv. 23.

Modern English.—"What! must our mouths be cold?"—*Tempest,* 1, 1, 56.

§ 328. "*Who is who.*"

For this expression see Morris, *Accidence, Indefinite Pronoun.*

The Relative Pronoun. Origin.

§ 329. Comparative syntax teaches us that the relative sentence was primarily expressed by being immediately subordinated to the principal clause without the addition of any explanatory word : "This is the man I saw." For the sake of clearness and emphasis, however, the object of the antecedent clause was repeated in the consequent by some demonstrative term signifying locality, and the attention was thus drawn to the idea intended to be signalised. But after a time, this pronoun, this representative of the object denoted, came to be used in all cases, and not merely where peculiar stress was wished to be laid upon it; and when analogy had thus uniformly extended this particular employment of the word, it ceased to convey any longer a purely demonstrative sense, and assumed a relative signification, which was then applied by the further operation of analogy to instances in which the demonstrative could hardly have been employed.[1]

In Old English as well as in the other Teutonic languages the primary way of joining together sentences and adjectival clauses without any outward mark of their relation to each other survived. See above, § 109. But as a rule, the relative sentence was introduced by a demonstrative pronoun, or a particle of probably demonstrative character. The development of the English relatives is shown in the following sections.

[1] Sayce, *l.c.* p. 370; cf. Jolly: "Ueber die einfachste form der Hypotaxis im Indogermanischen;" and Windisch, "Untersuchungen über den Ursprung des Relativpronomens," in Curtius' *Studien*, vi. 1, and ii. 2.

§ 330. *The Demonstrative Pronoun.*

Old English.—*Se, seó, þæt* were used as relatives, either by themselves or in connection with the indeclinable particle *þe*.

"móste wesan on worulde, se þæs wæstmes onbát" (he was to live eternally, who ate of this fruit).—CÆDMON, *Gen.* 470.

"þæt wæs deáðes beám, se bær bitres fela" (that was the tree of death, that bare much bitterness).—*Ibid.* 479.

"gé tó déaþe þone déman ongunnon, sé ðe of ðéaðe sylf worn áwehte" (you began to deem to death him that awaked many from death).—*Elene*, 303.

"weras, þá þe eówre ǽ on ferhðsefan fyrmest hæbben" (men who have your law foremost in their mind).—*Ibid.* 315.

§ 331.
As early as the time of Alfred the Great, the neuter *þæt* seems to become indifferent to gender and number, as may be inferred from the following instances.

"Aefter þæm Romane curon III hund cempena and siex, *þæt* sceolde to ánwige gangan" (after that the Romans chose three hundred and six warriors that should go to single combat).—*Orosius*, 72, 15.

"He hæfde eahta and eahtatig coortona, *þæt* we nu truman hátað" (he had eighty-eight cohorts that we call now 'truman').—*Ibid.* 240, 32.

"and hie benóman heora heofodstedes *þæt* hie Capitoliam héton" (they invaded the chief place, which they called Capitolium).—*Ibid.* 86, 30.

"ðone Nazareniscan Hǽlend *ðæt* wæs afanden wer, etc." (the Saviour of Nazareth, a man approved, etc.).—*Cura Pastor.* 443, 5.

"ðæt hie magon eac be ðisse bisene ongietan *ðæt* him is to gecueden" (which they can also understand from this example, which is addressed to them).—*Ibid.* 189, 21.

§ 332.
In *Middle English* the other forms of the demonstrative *se, seo', þæt* disappear at a very early period, and *þæt* takes their place. The use of Old English *þe* as a relative died out in Early Middle English. The two texts of Layamon's *Brut* are very instructive in this respect.

Text A. (the older) exhibits several remnants of the old demonstrative, while B. levels all to the uniform *that*.

	A.	*B.*
13827.	An alle mine liue þe ich iluued habbe.	In al mine lifue þat ich ileued habbe.
13851.	of þat ilke ænde þe Angles is ihaten.	of þan ilk hende þat Englis his ihote.
13897.	We habbeð godes gode þe we luuieð an ure mode.	We habbeþ godes gode þat we louieð in mode.

Cf. *ibid.* 14127, 14211, 14255.

For the history of *that* in Modern English see Morris, *Accidence*.

§ 333. "*Swá.*"

Old English.—So far as I can see only after *swá hwá* and *swá hwilc* = *whosoever*.

Middle English.—*So* is scarcely to be met with in Middle English.

> "He was holden most of myghte
> Off all next the whyte knyght,
> *So* did hym mekill dere."
> *Ipomadon*, 3272.

This, however, admits of another explanation. *Cf.* Tobler, *Germania*, xvii.

But *so* certainly survived as a relative in the compound *as* (*alswa*), used not only after *such*, but also after other correlatives.

Middle English.—"The first Soudan was Zarocon ... as was fadre to Sahaladyn."—MAUNDEV. v. 36.

"Tho *as* were present."—*Book of Noblesse*, 32.

Modern English.—"The ymages *as* they used in olde tyme to erecte in worshyp."—LORD BERNERS, *Froissart*, ii. Preface.

"That kind of fruite
   As maids call medlars."
                SHAK. *Romeo*, ii. 1, 36.

"To those *as* have no children."—HOLLAND, Plutarch's *Morals*, 222.

"It's he *as* lives in the great stone house."—*Lamplighter*, 91.

New English Dictionary, s.v.

§ 334. *"Swilc"* = such.

Swilc was used in Old English as a proper relative.

"eall *swylc* him god sealde" (all that God gave him).—*Beówulf*, 72.

"ne aron nu cyningas ne câscras *swilce* iu wǽron" (there are not now the kings and emperors that were once).—*Seafarer*, 83.

There are instances of this use in Early Middle English.

§ 335. *Interrogative Pronouns used as Relatives.*

The transition from the Old English relatives to those used in Middle and Modern English was effected by the *indefinite* or *general relatives*. It is in these that the interrogatives *who* and *what* were first used in the relative sense.

Old English.—"Swá *hwá* swá" = whosoever, "swá hwæt swá" = whatsoever, "swá hwilc swá" = whosoever, "*swá hwá swá* þæt secgan cymeð," whosoever comes to say that.—CÆDMON, *Gen.* 438.

"*swá hwá swá* gebyrgde, þæs on þam beáme geweóx" (whosoever tasted of that which grew on that tree).—*Ibid.* 483.

"Eac is to geðencenne þæt on ðá tíd þe se biscephád swæ gehered wæs, *swæ hwelc swæ* hiene underféng, he underféng martyrdóm" (we must also reflect that at the tyme when the office of bishop was in such high estimation, he who accepted it accepted martyrdom).—*Cura Pastor.* 52.

"*Swæ hwelc* ðonne *swæ* ðissa uncysta hwelcre underðieded bið, him bið forboden ðæt he offrige Gode hláf" (whoever, then, is subject to one of these vices is forbidden to offer bread to God).—*Ibid.* 72.

Middle English.—"*Wha swa* wulle libba, halde þas sibba" (whosoever will live, hold peace).—LAYAM. i. 155.

"*Wha swa* in þeu stræten breken grið, þe king him wolde binimen his lif; ah *wha sa* oðerne imette þer, fæire hine igrætte" (whosoever break the peace in the street, the king will take his life; whosoever meet another there, may fairly greet him).—*Ibid.* 206.

"*Whase* is þatt briddgumess frend, he stannd wiþþ himm" (whosoever is the bridegroom's friend stands with him).—*Orm.* 18375.

§ 336. From indefinite relatives, *who* and *which* become proper ones, though after a long struggle, *who* in the nominative scarcely being generally accepted before the sixteenth century (Lord Berners's *Arthur of Little Britaine*, A.D. 1532). There are, however, instances as early as the tenth and twelfth centuries.

"þæt deofol openlice þone sandige, *hwa* him fulfylligean wille" (the devil tempts him *who* will follow him).—WULFSTAN, ed. Napier, 95, 19.

"A hwam mai he luue treweliche *hwa* ne luues his brother" (Ah! whom may he love truly who does not love his brother).—*Old English Hom.* i. 274.

For other relatives and their functions see Morris, *Accidence*, § 188–210.

For omission of the relative, see *Adjective Clauses*, § 109.

THE VERB.

Impersonal Verbs.

"I'll dispose them as *it likes* me best."—MARLOWE.

§ 337. THE impersonal verbs denoting natural or else external events, as raining, thunder, freezing, &c., have remained the same with regard to their syntactical use, from Old English down to modern times. We still say: "it rains" (Old English *hit rinð*), "it thunders" (Old English *hit þunrað*), "it freezes" (Old English *hit freóseð*), "it happens that" (Old English *hit gelimpeð*), &c.

§ 338. But those verbs which express states or actions of he human mind have undergone an important change. As stated above (see *Nominative Case*), many once impersonal verbs became personal,[1] and we have now scarcely any instances of such verbs, as "it likes me." This tendency to replace impersonal verbs by personal expressions may be seen at work in Middle English, but even as late as the Elizabethan times the process is not yet quite completed. A few instances may suffice to show the development from Old English down to Middle English times.

Ail, Old English *eglan*, Middle English *eilen*, originally only impersonal; but there is a trace of personal use as early as 1250.

"ʒet he aʒlen on here red" (yet they ail [become weak] in their counsel).—*Story of Gen. and Exod.* 3809.

"For who loueth God can *ayle* nothynge but good."—SKELTON, *Magnyfyc.* 2393.

"Thou ask'st the Conscience what she *ails*."—QUARLES, *Emblems* ii. 5, 82.

"I knew not what I *ayled*, but I knew I *ayled* something more than ordinary: and my heart was very heavy."—ELLWOOD, *Autobiog.* 20.

"What can the fool mean?" said old Richard; "what can he *ail* at the dogs?"—HOGG, *Tales and Sketches*, iii. 191.

New English Dictionary, s.v.

Forthynke = repent. In Middle English only impersonal. This was replaced in Modern English by repent, used personally.

Like continued to be used impersonally until the sixteenth century.

[1] The slow development of verbs expressing subjective states is also noticed by Max Müller, though not with regard to impersonal verbs. "It is more difficult to understand how roots, if originally expressive of acts only, could be made to express mere subjective states. It may be true that the necessity of expressing subjective states arose at a much later time, and was not called forth by any such pressing wants as, for instance, the necessity for ordering people to dig or to strike or to pull. Nor must we suppose that the growth of language was ever determined by the clear consciousness of a want, and by a deliberate consideration of the best means of meeting it."—MAX MÜLLER, *l.c.* p. 321.

"Therefore 'tis best, if so *it like* you all,
To send my thousand horse incontinent."
MARLOWE, *Tamburlaine*, i. 51.

Cf. Schmidt, *Shakspere Lexicon, s.v.*

For a fuller account of this development, see my Introduction to Caxton's *Blanchardyn*, p. xlvii.

Intransitive, Transitive, and Reflexive Verbs.

§ 339. It has generally been supposed that originally all roots expressive of act, were what we call intransitive, and expressed merely the act without any reference to the result produced by an act. Such suppositions are difficult to prove or to disprove. Each root, if it expresses an act, implies no doubt a subject and an object, whether they are expressed or not, and though it may be argued that nouns which express the object must be later than the verbs expressing the subject, every root, as root, would seem to possess potentially a transitive as well as an intransitive character.[1]

Hence, even in Old English many verbs were used both as transitives and intransitives, *e.g.* :

"swógað windas, *bláwað* brecende" (winds roar, they blow breaking); "háteð hie béman *bláwan*" (he bids them blow horns).—GREIN, *s.v.*

But apart from these words, the double character of which is due to the very nature of the verb, there were several phonetic and syntactic factors at work which brought about the unparalleled freedom of the English language to use the same verb in an intransitive, transitive, or causative and reflexive sense, *e.g.* change, mend.[2]

[1] Max Müller, *l.c.* p. 319.
[2] *Cf.* the cobbler's inscription : "Never too late to mend."

Transitive and Intransitive Verbs Interchanged.
" The ship will not sink in the water."
" Kate sank her head upon his shoulder."

§ 340. In Old English, as well as in the other Teutonic languages, intransitives became transitives, or rather causatives, by adding the suffix *-ja* to that form of the verb-stem which appears in the singular of the preterite, or, in other words, by becoming weak verbs from strong ones. The suffix *-ja* further effects a mutation of the root-vowel, which thus comes to be a characteristic of causative verbs in English—*sit, sat, sat-jan, settan, sinc, sanc, sanc-jan, sencan.* Thus *búgan* (Gothic *biugan*) means to bow to somebody, but *býgan* (from *bedgjan*, Gothic *baugjan*) means to bow something, to bend; *sincan* means to sink (intransitive), *sencan*, to make something sink; *sittan*, to sit, *settan*, to set; *licȝean*, to lie, *lecȝan*, to lay; *fallan*, to fall, *fellan*, to fell.

§ 341. If a verb was derived from an adjective, it split at once into forms of different meaning. If formed by means of *-ja* (first conjugation) it had a causative meaning, if by *ó* (second conjugation) an intransitive one. Hence the following double forms from the same root:

Stem.	First Conjugation. Causative.	Second Conjugation. Intransitive.
bald.	byldan (to make strong).	bealdian (to be strong).
blác.	blácan (to bleach).	blácian (to grow pale).
cól.	ácélan (to cool).	cólian (to become cool).
ful.	fyllan (to fill).	fullian (to become full).
hard.	á-hyrdan (to harden).	heardian (to become hard).
long.	lengan (to make long).	longian (to be long, weary)
naru (w).	genyrwan (to make narrow).	nearwian (to be narrow).
wac.	weccan (to wake).	wacian (to be awake).
warm.	wyrman (to warm).	wearmian (to grow warm)

§ 342. Now, even in Old English we see that this distinction is no longer strictly observed.

Thus *fleón*, which is a strong verb, and originally means to flee, is found with the meaning of the causative *to put to flight.*

"Hundteóntig eówer *fleóþ* hira tyn þúsendu" (your hundred shall put to flight their ten thousands).—*Lev.* xxvi. 8.

"Ure hǽlend *áhangen* wæs on róde" (our Saviour was hanged on the cross).—*Legends of the Holy Rood*, 7.

On the other hand, we find intransitive forms of verbs when we are authorised to expect transitive ones, *e.g. nearwian* instead of *nyrwan.*

"Féleð sóna mines gemótes, seó þe mec *nearwað*" (she soon feels my resistance that makes me narrow).—*Riddles*, xxvi. (GREIN).

Perhaps verbs like *meltan* (to melt and to make melt) and *belgan* (to be angry and to anger), in which there was an accidental likeness of the intransitive and the causative forms in some of the moods and tenses, contributed to break down the line of meaning which originally existed between the two classes of verbs, just as *schmelzen* in Modern German is used in both its strong and weak forms, as intransitive and causative.

§ 343. In *Middle English* the confusion went on increasing from century to century.

"Swo doð þe fule man þe folegeð his wombes wil, and of unrihte bigete ofte *filleð*" (so doth the foul man who follows the will of his belly and often fills [himself] with unlawful gains).—*Old English Homilies*, ii. 37—A.D. 1200.

"þe storm *bisinkeð* þe ship gif he mai" (the storm sinks the ship, if it can).—*Ibid.* 177.

"Nu wot Adam sum del of wo
Her-after sal he *leren* mo" (leren = learn).
Story of Genesis and Exodus, 354—A.D. 1250.

"Ai was borgen Bala-segor
ðor quile ðat loth dwellede ðor;
Oc siðen loth went ut of hine
Brende it ðunder, *sanc* it erðc-dine" (ever was safe Bala-segor, as long as Lot dwelt there, but when he left it, thunder burnt it, earthquake sank it).—*Ibid.* 1108.

"Heore liʒt *queincte* over-al" (their light went out everywhere).— *Legendary* (ed. Horstmann), 19, 6.—A.D. 1280-90.

"'This worlde,' he seide, 'more than an hour
Schal ben i-dreynt, so hideous is the schour:
Thus schal mankynde *drench*, and leese his lyf.'"
CHAUCER, *The Miller's Tale*, 335.

The following list, taken from Caxton, will show the progress in that development in the second half of the fifteenth century.

Cease, causative = stop.

"Soo pray I you that ye wyl *cesse* your grete sorowe."—CAXTON, *Blanch.* 44, 2.

Cf. *ibid.* 53, 27.

Learn = teach.

"She was not *lernyd* to receyue suche geestes."—*Blanch.* 67, 29.

Cf. 141, 4.

Lose = ruin.

"But through fortune chaungeable, my lande hath be wasted and *lost* by Darius."—*Blanch.* 146, 5.

Possess = put in possession.

"When he had gyuen to me my lande, and *possessed* me in my countrey, I wold not accepte it."—*Charles the Grete*, 147, 16.

Succumb = subject.

"In their folysshe pryde I shal *succombe* and brynge a lowe their corage" (original: Et de la foll entreprinse quilz out faicte pour l'orgueil et oultrage qui les ensuient contre vous vouldroy *abaissier* leur couraige follastre).—*Blanch.* 104, 30.

Sit = set.

"And he *sat* al his folk in a bushment within a grete wode."— *Aymon*, 136, 18.

"(they) *sate* themself at dyner."—*Melusine*, p. 157.

Tarry = delay.

"Other infynyte thynges that are wont to *tarye* the corages of some enterpryses."—*Blanch.* 17, 11.

"here we shall *tarye* styll oure penne."—*Ibid.* 182, 11.

Walop = gallop.

"But Blanchardyne wyth a glad chere *waloped* his courser as bruyauntly as he coude" (= made to gallop).—*Blanch.* 42, 5.

§ 344. *Modern English.*—This most valuable freedom develops into full bloom in the sixteenth century, and the popular language of our own days goes even beyond the licence of Elizabethan authors.

Cease, causative = stop.

"Here *cease* more questions."—*Tempest*, i. 2, 184.

Decrease = lessen.

"Left solely heir to all his lands and goods,
Which I have rather bettered than *decreased*."
Taming of the Shrew, ii. 119.

Fall = let fall.

"Mine eyes, even sociable to the show of thine,
Fall fellowly drops."
Tempest, v. 64.

Fear = frighten.

"Of such a thing as thou, to *fear*, not to delight."—*Othello*, i. 2, 71.

Fly = cause (falcons) to fly.

"Believe me, lords, for *flying* at the brook
I saw not better sport these seven years' day."
2 *Henry VI.* ii. 1, 1.

Increase = extend.

"And your affections are
A sick man's appetite, who desires most that
Which would *increase* his evil."
Coriolanus, i. 1, 183.

Cf. Spenser, *Faerie Queene*, i. 4, 15.

Issue = send forth.

"The paper as the body of my friend,
And every word in it a gaping wound,
Issuing life-blood."
Merchant, iii. 2, 269.

Learn = teach.

> "To you I am bound for life and education:
> My life and education both do *learn* me
> How to respect you."
>
> *Othello*, i. 3, 183.

Cf. French *apprendre quelqu'un* = *enseigner*.

Lose = ruin.

"Her eyes had *lost* her tongue."—*Twelfth Night*, ii. 2, 21.

Perish = kill, slay.

> "Because thy flinty heart, more hard than they,
> Might in the palace *perish* Margaret."
>
> 2 *Henry VI.* iii. 2, 100.

Possess = put in possession of.

"I will *possess* you of that ship and treasure."—*Antony*, iii. 11, 21.

Remember = remind.

> "Let me *remember* thee what thou hast promised,
> What not yet is performed."
>
> *Tempest*, i. 2, 243.

Run = cause to run.

"If you *run* the nuthooks humours on me."—*Merry Wives*, i. 1, 171.

"My father went down to *run* his last horse at Newmarket."—BULWER, *Pelham*, 1.

Sink = submerge.

"I would have *sunk* the sea within the earth."—*Tempest*, i. 2, 111.

"*Sinking* his voice almost to a whisper."—DICKENS, *Sketches*, p. 363.

Sit = seat.

"Then she *sat* herself down."—TROLLOPE, *American Scenes*, i. 140.

"Whatever he did, he was constantly *sitting* himself down in his chair, and never stopping in it."—DICKENS, *Chimes*, 86.

"*Sitting* himself down on the very edge of the chair."—DICKENS, *Pickw.* ii. 356.

Stand = set, put.

"The pretty housemaid had *stood* the candle on the floor."—DICKENS, *Pickw.* ii. 377.

Sup = feed.

"If a' have no more man's blood in his belly than will *sup* a flea."—*Love's Labour Lost*, v. 2, 698.

Transitive Verbs used in a Reflexive and Passive Sense.

"I pray, now, keep below."—*Tempest*.
"Prepare for dinner."—*Lear*.

§ 345. The other peculiarity of Modern English to use a transitive where the older periods and other modern languages require the reflexive, was probably brought about by the *tendency to drop the reflexive pronoun*.

Thus, for instance, the older expression, "make *yourself* ready for dinner," became the modern one by dropping "yourself." This use, too, can be traced back to the oldest periods of English.

Old English:

Baðian, bathe.

"Seldon heó *baðian* wolde" (she would seldom bathe).—BEDA, 4, 19.

Dǽlan, divide.

"þonne on þreó *dǽleð* . . . folc" (they are divided into three parts). —*Elene*, 1286.

Middle English:

Beten, originally transitive, to mend.

"þenne wulle ic birewsien and *beten*" (then will I repent and mend). —*Old Eng. Hom.* i. 23.

Make merry.

"þay *maden* as *mery* as any men moȝten."—*Sir Gawayne and the Green Knight*, 1953.

Shed.

"Balearis, þe firste greet hauen and passage of þat see, *schedeþ* into Spayne."—TREVISA, *Polychr.* i. 55.

Turn.

"he forlet þat god him het don, and dide þat god him forbet ; and on þese wise *turnde* fro him" (he omitted to do what God bade him do, and did that which God forbade him ; and in this way turned from him). *Old Eng. Hom.* ii. 59.

Cf. "Turneð *giu* to me" (turn yourself to me), *ibid.*

In *Modern English* instances abound.

§ 346. As a consequence of this use of transitive verbs in a reflexive sense, many transitive verbs came to be used also as passives, e.g., *the book never sold*, the function of the passive being very near that of the reflexive, and both being often interchanged.

Breed.
"Fair encounter
Of two most rare affections ! Heaven rain grace
On that which *breeds* between them."
Tempest, iii. 1, 76.

Cure.
"One desperate grief *cures* with another's anguish."
Romeo, i. 2, 49.

Fill.
"Now quick desire has caught the yielding prey,
And glutton-like she feeds, yet never *filleth*."
Venus, 548.

Miscarry.
"There *miscarried*
A vessel of our country richly fraught."
Merchant, ii. 8, 29.

Quench.
"Weeps she still? Dost thou think
She will not *quench* and let instructions enter?"
Cymbeline, i. 5, 47.

Read.
"Vows, love, promises . . . how queerly they *read* after a while."— THACKERAY, *Vanity Fair*, i. 1.

Sell.
"But as they (the treatises) never sold."—GOLDSMITH, *Vicar of Wakefield*, 1.

Shape.

> "Their dear loss
> The more of you 'twas felt, the more it *shaped*
> Unto my end of stealing them."
> *Cymbeline*, v. 5, 346.

Stain.

> "If virtue's gloss will *stain* with any soil,
> Is a sharp wit matched with too blunt a will."
> *Love's Labour Lost*, ii. 48.

Yoke.

> 'Twere pity
> To sunder them that *yoke* so well together."
> 3 *Henry* vi. iv. 1, 23.

AUXILIARY VERBS.

Functions of the Auxiliary Verbs.

§ 347. The loss of verbal forms expressing tense and mood has given rise to the extended use and greater importance of auxiliary verbs in English. While, for instance, in Greek there exists a special ending to express action belonging to the past (*perfectum*), and another to express repeated action (*aoristus gnomicus*), Modern English must recur to the auxiliaries *have* and *will:* "I *have* done," "he *would* say"=he used to say. Instead of the short expressive *optativus* we must make use of the periphrasis with *may:* νῦν γάρ κεν ἕλοι πόλιν, "now he *may* take the town"; instead of the polite so-called Attic optative we use *shall:* "I *should* think so," &c. The most important auxiliary verbs, which make up for the loss of verbal inflections, are: *be, have, may, let, shall, will.*

"*Be.*"

§ 348. Generally speaking, the functions of "be" are the same now as in Old English, only it has been considerably encroached upon by *have.*

SYNTAX OF THE PARTS OF SPEECH

Formerly *be* was used to form the perfect tenses of intransitive verbs, and *have* those of transitives. Now *have* is used for intransitives too.

Old English.—Mostly "be." *Cf.* however Beda 1, 23 :—

"(heo) sumne dǽl þæs weges gefaren *hæfdon*" (they had journeyed part of their way).

Middle English.—"Brennes *wes* awæi aflogen."—LAYAMON, i. 203.

"A traitor...*yflou was* out of Engelond."—ROBERT OF GLOUCESTER, 5609 (B).

Modern English.—"This gentleman *is* happily arrived, my mind presumes, for his own good and ours."—*Taming* i. 2, 213.

"Miracles *are* ceased."—*Henry V.* i. 1, 67.

"My Lord Chesterfield had killed another gentleman, and *was* fled."—PEPYS, *Diary* 1659.

On the other hand *be* is now invariably used in all passives, while in older periods it shared this function with the verb *weorðan* (German *werden*).

"Have."

"*Have* at thee with a downright blow."—2 *Henry VI.* ii. 3, 92.

"He that will caper with me for a thousand marks, let him lend me the money, and *have* at him."—2 *Henry IV.* i. 2, 213.

§ 349. This peculiar use of "have," which occurs very frequently in Elizabethan authors, is hard to account for; but it may be traced back to the fourteenth century.

"Haue at !" seyd Douwal, "now is leyser !"—ROBERT DE BRUNNE, *Story of England*, 2753. A.D. 1336.

"'*Haf* at þe þenne,' quod þat oþer, & heueʒ hit" (*sc.* the ax) alofte, & wayteʒ as wroþely, as he wode were."—*Sir Gawayne and the Gr. Knight*, 2288. A.D. 1360.

"*Have* at thee !"—*Townley Myst.* 26. A.D. 1440.

"Will."

§ 350. "Will" as an auxiliary expressing *customary* action is met with at an early date.

"So *wole* ech man þat oþer louie can" (so does every man that loves another).—LAYAMON, ii 541.

"She was so pitous, she *wolde* wepe if that she saw a mouse."—CHAUCER, *Canterb. Tales Prol.* 143.

In this function *will* shares with *shall*.

"Ful redily with hem the fyr they hadde,
Thencens, the clothes, and the remenant al
That to the sacrifice longen *schal*."
CHAUCER, *The Knightes Tale*, 1420.

"For ofte *shall* a woman have
Thing, whiche a man may nought areche."
GOWER, i. 150.

"Let."

"Let us go for a walk."

§ 351. This auxiliary came in as a compensation for the decay of modal inflection, *e.g.*, in "let us go," "let him do his worst"; in the older periods the verb alone in the subjunctive mood was used, or *uton* + infinitive, *uton* being an old verb employed specially for this function = "let us."

Old English.—"*Upp-áhebben* we his naman" (let us exalt his name). *Ps.* xxxiii. 2.

"*Uton* faran" (let us go).—*Luke*, ii. 15.

Middle English.—"*Ga* we nu."—*Orm.* 3390.

"*Sende* we to Rome."—LAYAM. ii. 59.

Modern English.

The simple subjunctive is still common in poetry.

"Come! *be* we bold and make despatch."—COLERIDGE, *Piccolomini*, 2, 1.

"*Part* we in friendship from your land."—SCOTT, *Marmion*, 6, 13.

"*Do.*"

"How *do* you?" = How do you do?—BEAUMONT AND FLETCHER, *The Scornful Lady*, iv. 1.

§ 352. There is a great difference between the Middle and Modern English use of *do*. From the beginning of the thirteenth century to the end of the fifteenth, *do* means "to cause," thus *making up for the loss of causative verbs* (*cf.* above, § 340–342).

"*Min engel* sal ic *don* ðe biforen gon" (I shall make my angel to go before thee).—*Story of Gen. and Exod.* 3607.

"I shal *doo* folow hym" (= I shall cause him to be followed: original: Ie le ferai Sieuir).—CAXTON, *Blanch.* 44, 10.

§ 353. But as early as the time of Robert of Gloucester "do" occurs redundantly along with *can* or *gan*.

"Fos me clupeþ þilke wei, þat bi mani a god toun *deþ* wende" (foes call me that way that does go by many a good town).—ROBERT OF GLOUCESTER, 179.

"I vuele tyme . . . reste thou *dust* chese" (in evil time didst thou choose rest).—*Id.* 8809.

Cf. "Sone o morwen he *gan* him garen" (early in the morning he made himself ready).—*Story of Gen. and Ex.* 1417.

Quite common in Middle English.

The same use of *do* is common in German, and occurs also here and there in Old French.

"Adont *font* un sentier maintenant *traverser*" (then they cross a foot-path).

"Couvoitise *fait* son arc tendre" (Covetise bends its bow).

"*Faites* moi escouter" (listen to me).—TOBLER, *Beiträge*, p. 19.

§ 354. *Do* = to be in the phrase "how do you do?" is scarcely met with in older periods.

Dr. Furnivall thinks this phrase has been borrowed from the French.

"Que fait mes sires?" (how does my lord?).—*Roncevaux*, 159.

Cf. Caxton's *Eneydos*, p. 21.
This use is common in the time of Caxton.
Cf. my Introduction to Caxton's *Blanchardyn*.

"*Stand.*"

§ 355. *Stand* as an auxiliary = "to be" is common in Elizabethan writers and modern times.

"The truest issue of thy throne by his own interdiction *stands* accursed."—*Macbeth*, iv. 3, 107.

"How *stand* you affected to his wish?"—*Gentlemen of Verona*, i. 3, 60.

"*Shall*" and "*will*" used Elliptically.

"I *shall* no more to sea."—*Tempest*, ii. 2, 44.
"I *will* to my honest knight."—*Merry Wives*, iii. 2, 88.

§ 356. This use is very common in Old and Middle English, and has not disappeared even in modern times.

Old English.—"Ic him æfter sceal" (I shall go after him).—*Beówulf*, 2817.

"Ic to sǽ wille" (I will go to the sea).—*Ibid.* 318.

Middle English.—"Bot I *wyl* to þe chapel, for chaunce þat may falle."—*Sir Gawayne and the G. K.* 2132.

"I *wylle* to morowe to the courte of kyng Arthur."—Malory, *Morte d'Arthur*, 446, 1.

Cf. *Greek*: ἐκέλευσαν ἐπὶ τὰ ὅπλα (Xenophon); φανηρὸς ἦν οἴκαδε παρασκευαζόμενος (*ibid.*).

Latin: "Quando cogitas Romam?" (Cicero); "ipsest quem volui obviam" (whom I wished that he should meet me)—(Terence).

§ 357. "*Shall*" and "*will*" forming the Future Tense.

Old English.—"(Ic) nú wið Grendel *sceal* . . . ána gehegan þing wið þyrse" (I alone shall now defy Grendel).—*Beówulf*, 424.

"Ic *cume* eft tó þé on þisne tíman, and þin wíf Sarra *sceal* habban sunu" (I shall come again to thee at that time, and thy wife Sarah shall have a son; Vulgate: et habebit filium Sara).—ÆLFRIC, *Genesis* 18, 10.

"Wé willað wunian on ðǽre strǽte (Vulgate: in platea manebimus)." —*Ibid.* 19, 2.

The Modern English restriction of "shall" to the first person, and of "will" to the second and third, is of recent date.

"Should" with Infinitive instead of the Subjunctive Preterite.

§ 358. This use, too, may be traced back to Old English, where it is found side by side with the subjunctive.

"And hi þa eft sendon ǽrendracan tó Róme and wǽpendre stefne him fultumes bǽdon, þæt þæt earme eðel mid ealle ne fordiligad ne *wǽre*, ne se nama ðǽre Romaniscan þeode, se ðe mid him swá lange sceán and bryhte, fram fremdra ðeoda ungeðwǽrnesse fornumen and fordilgad *beon sceolde*" (and they again sent messengers to Rome and with weeping voice asked for aid, that the poor country were not utterly destroyed, and that the name of the Roman people, which was so long bright and shining among them, should not be overcast and obscured by the violence of foreign nations).—BEDA, i. 12.

Cf. *ibid.* 14, 23.

Sceolde is also used in reported (indirect) speech; generally when the reporter does not wish to commit himself or wishes to imply that the statement which he quotes is not trustworthy or not true.

"Dá sǽdon hi þæt ðæs harperes wíf *sceolde* acwelan" (they said that the harper's wife *died*).—ALFRED, *Boethius*, cxxxv.

"To the second (imputation) therefore, that they (poets) *should be* the principall lyars; I aunswere paradoxically, but, truely, I thinke truely; that of all Writers under the sunne, the Poet is the least lier."— SIDNEY, *Apologie for Poetrie*.

§ 359. *"May"*

as a modal verb is met with in the oldest periods.

"(híe) georne sóhton
þá wísestan wordgerýno,"

"þæt hío þǽre cwéne oncweðan *meahton*" (anxiously they sought the wisest word secrets, that they might tell the queen).—*Elene*, 324.

"óþþæt hé þa menigu forlǽtan *mihte*" (Latin: donec demitteret turbas).—ÆLFRIC, *Homilies*, ii. 384.

VOICE.

Relation between Reflexive and Passive.

"O that even I had squared me
  To thy counsel."
      Winter's Tale.

§ 360. 1. It is a matter of fact that illiterate people very rarely use the passive voice, simply because they do not want it. Psychologically the passive voice may be traced back to three sources, neither of which is to be found in the language of children and common people. In the first place, the passive appears when the subject of a verb is either unknown, or, at least, not present in the mind of the speaker, *e.g.*, in the phrase "*it is said* that there will be a war before long." The passive in this case is not of a very old date, nor is it very familiar to simple people. Either the third person plural is employed as in *Greek* and *Latin* (λέγουσιν, *dicunt*), or the indefinite "man," "men" = one (*German* "man," *French* "on"—*homo*).

§ 361. 2. The subject may be known, but the object of the verb is much more prominent in the mind of the speaker: then the passive is a very convenient form, *e.g.*, such books are written by him.

§ 362. 3. The passive alternates with the active to give change and colour to the speech. It is evident that the two last cases are not of a compulsory nature, and but for the first cause, the passive would never have come into use.

Now the science of language teaches that the want of the first kind was in the oldest periods, and is still in our days supplied not by the passive, but by the *reflexive*, this practically being the oldest form of the passive voice. If, for instance, the door is opened from without, and nobody is seen doing it, people said: "The door opens itself." Thus in *French:* "La porte s'ouvre"; in *German:* "Die Thüre öffnet sich." Thus the middle or reflexive voice was used as passive in *Sanscrit, Greek, Latin*, and in the *Norse* languages.

This close relation between the reflexive and passive is still seen in *Elizabethan English* when both may be interchanged.

"I did *collect myself.*"—*Winter's Tale*, iii. 3, 38.

Cf. *Be collected!*—*Tempest*, i. 2, 13.

"Therefore, good Brutus, *be prepared* to hear" (= prepare yourself). —*Julius Cæsar*, i. 2, 66.

Passive of Verbs with a Double Object.

§ 363. The peculiarity of forming the passive voice also from verbs with a double object, which is peculiar to English among the modern languages, is originally a conversion of what is, logically speaking, the object of a verb into the subject: he was given a book = a book was given to him. This was brought about by two facts. First, the dative and accusative were confounded, so that objects governed by verbs like "answer," "help," "thank," were consequently looked upon as accusatives, and were treated accordingly; secondly, what was originally a dative was mistaken for a nominative, as in the following instances:

"Ure Lauerd beo iþonked" (Our Lord be thanked).—*Ancren Riwle*, p. 8.

"nes among al moncun oni holi dole ifunden þet muhte beon ileten blod." (There was not found among all mankind any holy portion that might be let blood.)—*Ibid.* 112.

Hence already in Middle English the passive of intransitive verbs.

"þat we beon iquemed" (that we be pleased).—LAYAMON, I, 40.

"He þat was mast for-given till
Mast aght to luue him wit skill" (he to whom most was forgiven ought reasonably to love him most).—*Cursor Mundi*, 14048. A.D. 1300.

"Louerd, iþanked be þou ay
þat i have beden þat ilke day."
ALEXIUS, ed. Schipper, *Version* I, 157. A.D. 1350.

"I fand Jesus bowndene, scourgede, gyffene galle to drynke."—HAMPOLE, *Prose Treatises*, p. 5. A.D. 1370.

"He schal be sclaundrid for a cursed man and forboden to teche."—WYCLIF, *English Works* (Early English Text Soc.), p. 74. A.D. 1370.

"I am commandid."—CHAUCER, *Clerkes Tale*, iii. 85.

"ye schal be payd."—*Id. Frankeleynes Tale*, 495.

"Thembassatours ben answerde for fynal."—*Id. Troylus and Cryseyde*, iv. 117.

Passive of the Infinitive.

"Yet, if men moved him, was he such a storm
As oft 'twixt May and April is *to see*."
Lover's Complaint, 102.

"What 's *to do*?"—*Twelfth Night*, iii. 3, 38.

House *to let*.

§ 364. There are verbal forms which, in Old English, were indifferent with regard to voice. These were the infinitive, the verbal *noun* (*-ung*, *-ing*), and sometimes the participle past, when used adjectively.

Whenever there is an action without a subject to do it, we find the passive construction in Latin, *infinitivus passivi* (or rather *gerundium*), *e.g.*, "militem occidi iussit; credendum est." So far as I am aware, both these constructions are translated in Old English, as well as in Middle English of the first centuries, by the simple infinitive.

"þa hi þæt ne geþafodan, þa hét he hi *behedfdian*" (when they did not suffer that, he gave orders to behead them).—SWEET, *Oldest English Texts*, p. 177.

"hit is lang to *arrecene*" (it is long to be recounted).—WULFSTAN, 7, 12.

Cf. Introduction to Caxton's *Blanch.* § 25.

The few Old English instances are probably due to the Latin original:

"he wolde hine *genemnedne beon*" (he would have him called).— *Luke*, i. 62. Vulgate: quem vellet *eum vocari*.

Middle English.—"heo wes wurse to þolien þenne efreni of alle þa oþre pine" (it was worse to endure than any of the other torments).— *Old Eng. Hom.* i. 43.

"hwet is us to *donne?*" (quid nobis faciendum est).—*Ibid.* i. 91.

"Foul artow to *embrace*,"—CHAUCER, *Pardoneres Tale*, 90.

" But ay thay wondren what sche mighte be,
That in so poure array was for *to se.*"
Id. Clerkes Tale, vi. 82.

§ 365. In Middle English there is a faint beginning of creating new passive constructions of the infinitive after the Latin type; but before the Elizabethan age the modern construction is not completed.

"þair siluer he tok and gaue þam corn
And to þair inne did it *be born.*"
Cursor Mundi (Cot. Gött. and Trin. MSS.), 4856.

Cf. 5004, 5080, 9098.

"worthy to *be* . . . *i-preysed*" (= praeconiis attollendi).—TREVISA, i. 3.

"suche serueþ and is good *to be knowe* of Christen men."—*Ibid.* 1, 17.

"that made hem gentil men *y-callid* be."—CHAUCER, *Wyf of Bathes Tale*, 267.

"And suffrith us . . . .
Ful ofte *to be bete* in sondry wise."
Clerkes Tale, vi. 220.

(Petrarch's Original, p. 170: "et saepe nos multis ac gravibus flagellis *exerceri* sinit ").

The tendency to discard the old use is of an early date; as we may gather from the various readings of the following passage of the *Cursor Mundi*.

"Many oþer maiden þat þar were
For to foster and to lere."
　　　　　　　　Cotton MS. 10608.

Fairfax, Göttingen, and Trinity have "to fosteryng and to lare."

Modern English instances of the active construction :—

"We have debts of our own *to forgive.*"—THACKERAY, *The Newcomes.*

"He was furnished with a variety of other necessaries too numerous *to recapitulate.*"—DICKENS, *Pickwick* I. Chapter xiii.

"Their tea had not grown cool enough to swallow."—CONWAY, *Called Back.*

"That would be a very strong measure *to take.*"—NORRIS, *Mrs. Fenton.*

TENSE.

The Present Tense.

§ 366. Originally the present and preterite tenses were made to express all the time-relations of the verb, the present being also used for the future, and the preterite for all the past tenses. But already in Old English the auxiliary verbs *to have* and *to be* came in to form the other periphrastic tenses.

§ 367. But there are remnants of the old use in Middle and even in Modern English.

"Goð in þane castel þet is onȝein cou, and ȝe *findeð* redliche þar ane asse" (go unto the city that is against you, and ye shall straightway find there an ass).—*Old Engish Homiies*, I. p. 3.　A.D. 1200.　Cf. *ibid.* p. 16.

"Wanne Hengist is aslawe, Aureli *worþ* king.
Apoysened he worþ atte laste, and after him *worþ* ido
His brother in þe kinedom þat apoysend *worþ* also"
(when Hengist is slain, Aurelius *will become* king; at last he *will be* poysoned, and after him his brother will be placed on the throne, and he, too, will be poysoned).—ROBERT OF GLOUCESTER, 2839–2842. A.D. 1290.

One MS. has "*schal be.*"

"For-þi me for to fynde if þou fraystes, *fayles* þou neuer (me to find wilt thou not fail, if thou askest).—*Sir Gawayne and the Greene Knight*, 455. A.D. 1360.

"This nine monthis thou *seyst* me nowth" (thou wilt not see me these nine months).—*Coventry Mysteries*, 104. A.D. 1440.

In *Modern English* the old use occurs in the idiom "I *tell* you what."

§ 368. *The Historical Present*

is scarcely to be met with in Old English; but there are numerous instances of it from the thirteenth century down to our times.

"Quilum er Pharao hire toc
Nu takeð Abimelech hire oc"

(Once before Pharao had taken her, now Abimelech takes her also).— *Story of Genesis and Exodus*, 1172. A.D. 1250.

"þir kinges *rides* forth þair rade
þe stern alwais þam forwit glade"

(these kings ride forth [on] their road, the star always glided before them).—*Cursor Mundi*, 11427. A.D. 1300.

Frequent in Chaucer and Elizabethan writers.

§ 369. *Note.*

It is worth remarking that Modern English has produced a sort of Preteritive Verb (Preterite in form, but Present in meaning) similar to Greek οἶδα, Latin *novi*, Old English *wát* etc., namely the idiom "have got" = have.

"Well, Ma'am *have you got* anything to say?"
DICKENS, *David Copperfield*, i. 276.

Very frequent in familiar speech.

The Preterite and the Perfect Tenses.

§ 370. The distinction between the preterite and the perfect tense as defined in our grammars and observed in good prose is of quite a modern date.

This is best proved by the fact that both tenses are interchanged.

Middle English.
"Wiþ wines drinc he wenten is ðhogt,
So ðat he *haueð* ðe dede *wroght*."
Story of Gen. and Exod. 1149, 50.

"Symeon and leui it bi-speken,
And *hauen* here sister ðor i-wreken."
Ibid. 1855, 56.

Cf. *ibid.* 2043, 2101, 2312, 2609, 2622, &c.

Modern English.
D. *Pedro.* "Runs not this speech like iron through your blood?
Claud. I *have drunk* poison whiles he utter'd it."
Much Ado. v. 1, 253.

§ 371. *Sequence of the Tenses* ("consecutio temporum").

"*Principal tenses depend on principal tenses; historical on historical.*"

On the whole, this rule of the Latin Grammar holds good in all the periods of English; only there are exceptions.

The Present instead of the Preterite Tense.

"Therefore they *thought* it good you *hear* a play."—*Taming of the Shrew*, Induction, 2, 136.

§ 372. This is due to a sort of anacoluthon. The speaker begins to give an objective account of something that happened in the past; but his imagination being enlivened by his own account, he sees, as it were, what he relates happening in the present, under his eyes.[1] This change of the tense has some resemblance to the sudden transition from indirect to direct speech, which is, indeed, very common in the older stages of the language.

Old English.—"Ða unrihte men þa códan þæt hie þa men útgelǽddon, and hie to mete gedón" (then went out those wicked people that they might bring forth the men, and eat them).—*Blick. Hom.* 232.

"A morwe, when it was day,
þe leuedy of heiȝe priis
Com þer Tristrem lay,
And asked, what he *is*."
          Sir Tristrem, 1214.

Cf. *ibid.* 1541, 2752.

"He toke and tolde him his corage,
That he *purposeth* a viage."
          GOWER, i. 244.

"(Blanchardyn) prayed hym that he *vousshesauff* to helpe hym tha he were doubed knyght" (original: quil le aidast a adouher de ses armes).—CAXTON, *Blanchardyn,* 24, 2.

Modern English.—"Thus he besought god of perdon and to gyue hym grace to dystroy his enemy, who *is* orryble to beholde" (edition of 1605: who was so . . .).—LORD BERNERS, *Huon,* 146, 3.

"For he knew wel that Raoull, if he coude fynde the meanes, he *wyll* haue from hym his wyfe" (edition of 1605: he would . . .).—*Ibid.* 216, 17.

"The people, therefore, of the fair, made a great gazing upon them: some said they were fools, some they were bedlams, and some they *are* outlandish men."—BUNYAN, *Pilgrim's Progress,* 89.

"He was come on purpose to talk with me about a piece of home-news that everybody in town *will* be full of two hours hence."—ADDISON, *Essays,* ed. R. A. Green ('Humours of the Town'), 121.

The Preterite instead of the Past Perfect Tense.

§ 373. The relative time-relation of two events which take place in the past or in the future remains in many cases

---

[1] It is possible to explain this in a different way—namely, that to the speaker in this case, *their thinking* is really past, *your hearing* is not:—not yet realised.

undefined. It is well known that in Greek the aorist stands in by-sentences instead of the Latin *plusquam perfectum*, in Latin the perfect even after *postquam ;* in the old Teutonic languages the simple preterite is quite common, where we now employ the periphrasis, which has to take the place of the past perfect tense. This inaccurate employment of the tenses is the more primitive. The past perfect tense is merely a secondary formation.

Old English.—" þa wæs syxte geár Constantínes cáserdómes, þæt hé Rómwara in rice wearð áhæfen to heretéman " (it was the sixth year of Constantine's reign, after he *had been* elected chief of the Romans).—*Elene*, 7.

Middle English.—" Efter alle þe schendfulle pinen þet he þolede oðe longe uriniht, me ledde him amorwen vorte hongen o waritreo " (after all the disgraceful torments that he *had suffered* in the Friday eve, they led him in the morning to be hanged).—*Ancren Riwle*, 122.

"he sawe the serpent which that he *helpe* against the toode."—*Gesta Rom.* 6.

Modern English.—"Huon shewyd hym all the adventure that he *had* syns he cam fro bourdeux."—LORD BERNERS, *Huon*, 54, 18.

" Huon thus beyng in dyspleasure wyth hymselfe for the lye that he *made*, went forth tyll he came to the palays."—*Ibid.* 116, 20. (The edition of 1605 alters into "had made.")

" He, back returning by the ivory door,
Remounted up as light as cheerful lark,
And on his little winges the dream he bore
In haste unto his lord, where he him *left* afore."
SPENSER, *Faërie Queene*, i. 1, 44.

" I discovered one of the inhabitants advancing towards the stile, of the same size with him whom I *saw* in the sea pursuing our boat."—SWIFT, *Gulliver*, ii. 1.

Past instead of the Present Tense.

§ 374. These instances illustrate a very old and interesting syntactic fact, viz., the relation existing between *mood and tense*. The use of putting the future instead of the imperative ("you will do it at once!") is well known; but it is a less familiar fact that the functions of the subjunctive mood are in a manner connected with the past. If what a person thinks, hopes, or tries, does not agree with the facts, the verb containing the object of the verbs *think, believe, trow, fear, hope, try,* &c., appears, as a rule, in a tense anterior to that of those verbs. This may be pyschologically accounted for by the desire of the speaker to remove the action which he considers to be at variance with reality out of the present, this being psychologically the tense of visible certainty and truth.

This use being only a substitute for the subjunctive mood, it does not occur before the formal endings of the verbs are in decay.

"He *trowed* that sche *hadde ben* a comoun woman that dwelled there."—MAUNDEVILLE, p. 24.

"Sche *wende* that he *had ben* a gardener."—*Ibid.* p. 79.

"The prouost and the other of the towne entred ayen in to the cyte, wenyng to them that Blanchardyn had be wyth them, but he was not." CAXTON, *Blanchardyn,* 88, 8.

"for well he wend that he sholde neuyr haue seen ayen her."—*Ibid.* 95, 30.

"I expected that he *would have praised* me for my prudence; but on the contrary, he blamed me."—EDGEWORTH, *Popular Tales,* ii. 13.

§ 375. There is scarcely any parallel of this use to be found in inflectional languages endowed with the subjunctive mood, so far as the finite verb is concerned; but the infinitive being incapable of expressing mood is met with exhibiting the same use in Latin as in the English of the older periods.

"ne quis Bacchis initiatus esset, *coisse* out *convenisse* causa sacrorum velit."—LIV. 39, 14, 8.

"ne quis quid fugae causa *vendidisse* neve *emisse* vellet."—*Ibid.* 39, 17, 3.

"dum se . . . *refugisse* volunt longe longeque *recesse.*"—LUCR. 38.

"Immanis in antro
Bacchatur vates, magnum si pectore possit
Excussisse deum."
                                    VERG. A. 6, 78.

"sunt, qui nolint *tetigisse*," &c.—HOR. S. 1, 2, 28; "ne quis *humasse* velit Ajacem, Atrida, vetas cur?"—*Ibid.* 2, 3, 187.

"But faire and wel sche creep in to the clerk,
And lith ful stille, and *wolde han caught* a sleep."
                                    CHAUCER, *Reeve's Tale*, 306.

"He wende *to haue tourned* the brydell of his horse."—CAXTON, *Blanchardyn*, 140, 32.

This use was continued in the sixteenth century.

"He fell to the erthe, wenyng he *had been slayne*."—LORD BERNERS, *Huon*, 29, 25.

"he was about in such familiar sort *to have spoken* to her."—SIDNEY, *Arcadia*, p. 27.

"I was about *to have told* you my reason thereof."—SPENSER, *Ireland*, p. 613.

"I hope *to have kept*."—*Ibid.* p. 620.

Mood.

§ 376. The characteristic features in the development of the English moods are:

(*a*) The subjunctive *preterite* instead of the Old English subjunctive *present* in such clauses as are dependent on sentences with the present tense;

(*b*) The use of auxiliaries as modal verbs to make up for the loss of perceptible forms of the subjunctive mood;

(*c*) The tendency of the language to restrict the *subjunctive* to the most necessary functions, or to get rid of it altogether.

The Preterite instead of the Present.

§ 377. 1. *Clauses implying Unreality.*

Old English.—"Him sculon eglan óðerra monna bróca, swelce he efnswiðe him ðrówige" (he must grieve for the troubles of others, as if he suffer equally with them).—*Cura Pastoralis*, 74, 10.

"Đonne he underféhð þæt fenn ðara ðweandra, him ðyncð swelce he *forleóse* þá smyltnesse his clǽnnesse" (when he receives the dirt of the washers, it seems to him as if he loose the splendour of his purity).— *Cura Pastoralis*, 104, 24.

Middle English.—"Wateres he [Engelond] haþ ek inouȝ, ac at uore alle oþere þre
Out of þe lond in to þe se, armes as þei it *be*" (rivers it has also enough, but especially three, out of the land into the sea as though it *be* [*were*] arms).—ROBERT OF GLOUCESTER, 20, A.D. 1290.

Later on we find ' as it *were.*"

The same development is met with in German.

§ 378. 2. *Noun Clauses dependent on Impersonal Verbs.*

"'Twere better she *were* kissed in general."—SHAKESPEARE, *Troilus and Cressida*, iv. 5.

Old English.
"Sélre bið æ̆ȝhwǽm
þæt he his freónd *wrece,* þonne he fela murne."
(It is better for everybody that he revenge his friend than that he mourn much).—*Beówulf,* 1386.

The Preterite in these clauses seems to be of recent date.

§ 379. 3. *Noun Clauses after Verbs expressing Wish.*

" I wish, grave governors, '*twere* in my power
To favour you, but 'tis my father's cause."
MARLOWE, *Jew of Malta,* i. 2.

Middle English instances are frequently met with.

"Thus my wille is that it *were.*"—*Townley Mysteries,* p. 167.

Auxiliaries as Modal Verbs.

See Auxiliaries, § 347 *seq.*

§ 380. *The Decay of the Subjunctive Mood.*

The following synoptic table will serve both to show the use of the Subjunctive in older periods and its gradual decay in later centuries.

§ 381. The Subjunctive in Principal Sentences.

(Chiefly expressing wish).

OLD ENGLISH.	MIDDLE ENGLISH.	MODERN ENGLISH.
Si Gode lof (Praise be to God). —*Chronicle*, 1009.	"I-blessed *be* God that I have weddyd fyve."—CHAUCER, *Prologue of the Wyf of Bath*, 44.	"*Please* you, sir Do not omit the heavy offer of it." SHAKESPEARE, *Tempest*, ii. 1, 193.

Instances with Indicative.	*Instances with Indicative.*	*Instances with Indicative.*
None.	"Bot on I wolde you pray, displeses you never."—*Sir Gawayn and the Greene Knight*, 2439, A.D. 1360. "Suffice*th* this ensample oon or tuo, And though I couthe reken a thousand mo." CHAUCER, *Knightes Tale*, 1095. "Suffice*th* the, but if that thy wites madde, To have as gret a grace as Noe hadde." CHAUCER, *Miller's Tale*, 373.	"Please*th* it you therefore to sit down to supper." LYLY, *Euphues*, p. 28, A.D. 1579. "Please*th* you ponder your suppliant's plaint," SPENSER, *Shepherd's Calendar*, February. A.D. 1579. Cf. SHAKESPEARE, *Comedy of Errors*, iv. i. 12.

§ 382. The Subjunctive in Noun Clauses (especially Indirect Assertion, Oratio Obliqua).

OLD ENGLISH.	MIDDLE ENGLISH.	MODERN ENGLISH.
"þa indleiscan axodon Crist hwæt he *wære*" (the Jews asked Christ who he was).—AELFRIC, *Lives of Saints*, i.	"esca hine hwet he habbe biȝeten mid his woke domas" (ask him what he has gained by his unrighteous dooms).—*Old English Homilies.* i. 3, A.D. 1200.	Rare. "Hieronimo, it greatly pleaseth us That in our victory thou *have* a share." KYD, *Spanish Tragedy*, p. 16.
"Titus sǽde þæt he þone dæȝ *forlure* ðe he naht to góde on ne gedyde" (Titus said that he lost that day on which he did nothing good).—*Chronicle*, 51.	"for he dredde him to lete is lif if he wisten ȝhe *wore* his wif." (he was afraid of losing his life if they knew she *was* his wife.) *Story of Genesis and Exodus*, 768, A.D. 1250.	

Instances with Indicative.	*Instances with Indicative.*	*Indicative the Rule.*
"Ne mihte him bedyrned wyrðan þæt his engel *ongan* ofermód wesan" (it could not be concealed to him that his angel began to be arrogant).—CÆDMON, *Genesis*, 262.	"And wiste wele what he *wes*."— *Sir Tristrem*, 598.	"I asked him whether it *was* difficult to learn." MARRYAT, *Peter Simple.*
"Hæfde þa gefrunen hwanon sió fǽhð *árás*" (he had learned whence the strife had begun).—*Beowulf*, 2404.	"But she her wolde not confesse Whan they her axen, what she was." GOWER, *Confessio Amantis*, i. 184.	

§ 383. The Subjunctive in Clauses expressing Wish or Command.

OLD ENGLISH.

"Ic *wille* þæt he *wunige*" (I will that he wait).—John xxi. 22.

"*Biddaþ* dryhten þæt his þunorráda *geswícen*" (entreat the Lord that His thunder cease).—*Exodus* ix. 28.

Subjunctive the rule.

Instances with Indicative.
Rare.

"*Wyltu* we *secgaþ* þæt fýr cume of heofene?" (wilt thou that we say that fire come from heaven?)—*Luke* ix. 54. Quoted by MÄTZNER, ii. p. 124.

MIDDLE ENGLISH.

"Eure heo *bad* for Horn child þat Jesu Crist him *beo* myld."
    King Horn, 79, A.D. 1260.

Subjunctive the rule.

Instances with Indicative.

"I *wille* that she disposyth as she and her frendes thinke beste."—*Bury Wills*, 48, A.D. 1400.

"I beseke and *praye* þe, in the worship of the goddes, that at tyme of nede thou *wylt* uttir and shewe that which I see appiere wit-in þe."—CAXTON, *Blanchardyn*, 104, 22, A.D. 1485.

MODERN ENGLISH.

"Law *will* that each particular be known."—MARLOWE, *Jew of Malta*, iv. 3.

"I charge thee
    That thou attend me."
SHAKSPERE, *Tempest*, I, ii. 453.

Instances with Indicative.

"For I *wylle* thou knowyst she is the fairest maide that is now lyuynge."—LORD BERNERS, *Huon*, 50, 14. Cf. *ibid.* 51, 9 ; 87/28. *Bad*

"I wish the scoundrel hanged. I wish he *was* shot."—STERNE, *Tristram Shandy*, p. 88. *Bad*

"If it was summer-time, which I wish it *was* on your account."—DICKENS, *Little Dorrit*.

"I only wish I *was* a solicitor."—R. L. STEVENSON, *The Wrong Box*. *Bad*

§ 384. The Subjunctive in (Indefinite) Adjective Clauses.

OLD ENGLISH.	MIDDLE ENGLISH.	MODERN ENGLISH.
"Nú gé raðe gangað and findað gén, þá þe fyrngewritu þurh snyttorcræft sélest cunnen" (now, go ye quickly, and find those that know best old writings through discretion).—*Elene*, 374.	"Nolde he cunnen god ðonc anne monne þet wurpe up on him a bigurdel ful of þonewes vorte acwiten him mid?" (would he not thank any man who threw up to him a girdle full of pennies?) —*Ancren Riwle*, p. 124, A.D. 1200. Cf. *ibid.* p. 8.	Scarcely any instances to be met with.
Instances with Indicative (indicative clause subordinate to subjunctive : indicative containing matter of fact).	*Instances with Indicative.* Quite common.	*Indicative the Rule.*
"þone ienne genam Júdas tó gísle and þá georne bæd þæt hé þe þære róde riht getǽhte þe sió in legere wæs lange bedyrned" (Judas alone she took for hostage and requested him zealously, that he might teach her right [truth] about the rood, that had been lying so long concealed).—*Ibid.* 602.	"What is þat me fliteð wið?" LAYAMON, iii. 35.	"He never does anything that *is* silly." — BULWER, *Money*, i. 2.

240   ENGLISH SYNTAX

THE SUBJUNCTIVE IN ADVERBIAL CLAUSES.

§ 385. *Clauses of Place.*

OLD ENGLISH.	MIDDLE ENGLISH.	MODERN ENGLISH.
"Hafa blessunge ofer middangeard mine, þǽr þú fére" (have a blessing all over my earth wherever thou goest).—*Andreas*, 224. Instances rare.	Scarcely ever met with.	No instance.
Indicative the Rule.	*Indicative the Rule.*	*Indicative the Rule.*
"Hwearf þa hrædlice þǽr Hróðgár sæt" (he walked to where Hrothgar sat).—*Beowulf*, 365.	"Ech man mot wende woder his louerd *hoteþ*" (every man must turn where his lord bids).—LAYAMON, ii. 622.	"The star... stood over where the young child *was*."—*Matthew*, ii. 9.

§ 386. Clauses of Time especially in a Future and Indefinite Sense.

OLD ENGLISH.

"Gif þé þæt gelimpe on lif dagum . . . þone þu snide gecyð, min swæs sunu, ǽr þec swylt nime" (if that happens in thy life . . . . then tell [it] quickly, before death takes the away).—*Elene*, 447.

Cf. *ibid.* 673, 863, 1082.

MIDDLE ENGLISH.

"Gudemen, wite ge hwet þes sinagoge [wes] on þam alde lage ere crist were iboren" (good men, learn what this synagogue was in the old law, ere Christ was born).—*Old English Homilies*, I. 9.

Cf. TREVISA, I. 27; 237. *Early English Wills* (Furnivall), pp. 82, 123.

MODERN ENGLISH.

"Stay, monster, ere thou *sink*."
BEN JONSON, *Poetaster*, Prologue.
"The tree will wither long before he *fall*."
BYRON, *Childe Harold*, 3, 32.

Instances with Indicative.

"Nihtes nearwe nysse ic gearwe be þǽre róde riht, ǽr me rúmran geþeaht þurh þā mǽran miht on módes þeaht wisdom *onwráh*" (in the narrow of night I knew not exactly the truth about the road, before wisdom manifested to me wider knowledge through the glorious might in the mind).—*Elene*, 1243.

Instances with Indicative.

"Biforr þatt ȝho wiþþ childe *wass*."—ORM, 6484.

"Seynt Poul him self was there a phisicien before he *was* converted."
—MAUNDEVILLE, p. 123.

Indicative the Rule.

"Pause, ere thou *rejectest*."
BYRON, *Manfred*, ii. 1.

§ 387. Clauses of Manner (with a sense of Reality).

Old English.	Middle English.	Modern English.
"Dó swá þé þynce" (do as thou thinkst fit).—*Elene*, 541. "Þone sceolan þa biscopas and þa maessepreostas gehwylces hádes men georne þreatigean, and him bebeódan, þæt hi Godes domas on riht healdan, þa Godes þeowas heora tidsangas and heora cyricean mid rihte healdan, and þa lǽwedan *swá* him mid rihte *tóbelimpe*" (then shall the bishops and priests diligently urge men of all ranks and bid them rightly to observe God's decrees; the servants of God to keep their divine services and their churches rightly, and the laity *as* it properly behoves them).—*Blickling Homilies*, 49.	Instances are scarcely met with.	No instances.
Indicative the Rule.	*Indicative the Rule.*	*Indicative the Rule.*

§ 388. Clauses of Manner (*with a sense of Unreality*).

OLD ENGLISH.	MIDDLE ENGLISH.	MODERN ENGLISH.
"Sumre tide mid þý þe wé wǽron mid úrum drihtne, we astigon mid him on scip, and he ateowde us swá he slépende *wǽre* to costianne" (once upon a time when we were with our Lord, we ascended with him on board a ship, and he appeared to us as if he were asleep, to prove us).—*Blickling Homilies*, 235.	"The statue of Mars upon a carte stod, Armed, and lokede grim as he *were* wood." CHAUCER, *Knightes Tale*, 1184.	"I hope our credit in the custom-house Will serve as well as I *were* present there" (as=as if). MARLOWE, *Jew of Malta*, I. 1.
Instances with Indicative.	*Instances with Indicative.*	*Instances with Indicative.*
None.	None.	"That Illo fought as he *was* frantic" (as=as if).—COLERIDGE, *Wallenstein*, v. 4. "He has lost that stoop which used to make him look as if he *was* always working out a difficult problem."—BESANT AND RICE, *The Monks of Thelema*, I. 81.

§ 389. Clauses of Condition (supposed as Unreal).

OLD ENGLISH.	MIDDLE ENGLISH.	MODERN ENGLISH.
"Weorþan we forþon Drihtnes godcundnesse; gif he nǽre sóþ God, ná him englas ne þegnodon" (let us worship the Lord's divinity; if he were not true God, angels would not have ministered unto him).—*Blickling Homilies*, 35.	"Þe wind þere iwis Up of þe erþe oft comþ, of holes þei it were, . . . so þat it wolde arere and bere up grete clopes ȝif hii were þer nei."—*Robert of Gloucester*, 167.	"If it *were* so, it was a grievous fault."—SHAKSPERE, *Jul. Cæsar*, iii. 2, 84.
Instances with Indicative. None.	*Instances with Indicative.* None.	*Instances with Indicative.* "If his mind *was* changed, he would be otherwise."—BUNYAN, *Pilgrim's Progress*, 87. "If I *was* a lord or a bishop, I would not put a fellow in my livery that had not a wooden leg."—ADDISON, *Essays* (ed. R. A. Green, Sir Roger de Coverley) p. 46. "*Was* I an absolute prince, I would appoint able judges . . ."—STERNE, *Tristram Shandy*, p. 28. Cf. *ibid.* 31, 39, 41, 59, etc. "If I *was* not a farmer, there would be some hopes for me."—EDGEWORTH, *Popular Tales*, I. 98. Cf. *ibid.* 33. "When she *was* told that it was for her sake, she would come, I think."—TROLLOPE, *The Duke's Children*, I. 17.

§ 390. Concessive Clauses (supposed as Real).

OLD ENGLISH.	MIDDLE ENGLISH.	MODERN ENGLISH.
"And (se lichoma) bið ðonne undeaðlic þeáh he ǽr deáðlic *wǽre*", (and the body shall then be immortal, though it was previously mortal).— *Blickling Homilies*, 21. Cf. *ibid.* 33, 12; *Elene*, 509; *Beówulf*, 590.	"And þe edmeda riche þar he ehte *habbe*, mei beon godes wrecche" (and the humble rich, though he has wealth, may be amongst God's poor).—*Old English Homilies*, I. 115.	"No marvel though thou *scorn* thy noble peers, When I, thy brother, am rejected thus." MARLOWE, *Edward II.* 2. "And oft though Wisdom wake, Suspicion sleeps At Wisdom's gate." MILTON, *Paradise Lost*, iii. 686.

Instances with Indicative.

"Ne nom he in þǽm wícum Weder-Géata leód, Máðm-ǣhta má, þéh he þǽr moniᵹe ᵹesēðh, Búton þone hafelan and þá hilt samod", (he, the prince of the Weder-Geátas, took in that place no more of things of price, though many he saw, than the head and the hilt).—*Beówulf*, 1613-14.

Instances with Indicative.

"Thow that Mary Magdalyn in Cryst dede sone beleve, And I *was* longe dowteful, ȝitt putt me in no blame." *Coventry Mysteries*, p. 376.

Indicative the Rule.

"My woes are tedious, *though* my words *are* brief." SHAKSP. *Lucrece*, 1309.

§ 391. *Final Clauses.*

Old English.	Middle English.	Modern English.
"He bið geseald haþnum mannum þæt hie hine bysmrian" (he shall be given into the hands of heathen men, that they may mock him).—*Blickling Homilies*, 15.	"ȝe iherden er on þe godspel hu ure drihten sende his II. apostles onȝein þene castel þet heo *unbunden* þat assa" (ye heard erewhile in the gospel, how our Lord sent two apostles towards the city that they should unbind the ass).—*Old English Hom.*, l. 5.	Then give me leave that I may turn the key, That no man *enter* till my tale be done. SHAKSPERE, *Richard II.* v. iii. 37.

Subjunctive the Rule.

Instances with Indicative.	*Instances with Indicative.*	*Instances with Indicative.*
"Æfter þon ic sende to þé Andreas þinne bróðor, þæt he þé útálǽdeþ of þyssum carcerne" (after that I will send to thee Andrew thy brother, that he may bring thee out of this prison). —*Blickling Homilies*, 231. Cf. *ibid.* 293.	"At the table men shall them assure That there escape*th* them no such langage As myght turne other folke to disparage." *Book of Curtesye*, 160 (Oriel Text). "Wacchemen shulde go about the cete, and visit eche house, þat þere *was* no mysgouernayle."— *Gesta Romanorum*, p. 93.	"He bid him call a hackney coach, and take care it *was* an elderly man that drove it."—ADDISON, *Essays* (Sir Roger), p. 36. "I am bound in honour to see that your father knows a thing which is of such vital importance." —TROLLOPE, *The Duke's Children*, I. 30.

The Simple and Gerundial Infinitive.

§ 392. The infinitive in the older periods of the language was still felt as a noun in every respect, and as such it was used in all the functions belonging to a noun, without the help of *to*. The so-called gerundial infinitive, however, came in very early, went on gaining ground from century to century, until it succeeded in restricting the simple infinitive to the few cases in which it occurs nowadays, viz., after the auxiliaries: *may, do, can, must, shall,* and *will;* and after the following principal verbs: *dare, let, bid, see, hear, feel, need, make, have.*

§ 393. The struggle between the two infinitives may be seen in all the Old and Middle English texts, and even in the sixteenth century the simple infinitive tries still to retain part of its old dominion.

A few striking instances will show the development from the old to the modern use.

Old English.—Very frequent after impersonal verbs, *e.g.*

"*me geþuhte* writan þe" (it seemed good to me to write unto thee).—*Luke*, i. 3.

Middle English.—"*Rihten* hire and *smeðen* hire is of euch religioun and of euerich ordre þe god, & al þe strengðe" (to correct it and smooth it [*sc.* the heart] is the good and strength of every religion and every order).—*Ancren Riwle*, 4.

"Gon iseon swuch & elnen ham & helpen . . . . þis is riht religioun" (to go and visit such, and to comfort and assist them . . . this is right religion).—*Ibid.* 10.

Modern English.—"You ought not *walk*."—SHAK. *Julius Cæsar*, i. 1, 3.

"You were wont *be* civil."—*Othello*, ii. 3, 190.

"I list not *prophesy*."—*Wint. Tale*, iv. 1, 26.

"He thought *have* slain her."—SPENSER, *Faerie Queene*, 1, 1, 50.

"To" after Auxiliaries.

"I would no more
Endure this wooden slavery than *to* suffer
The flesh-fly blow my mouth."
Tempest, iii. 1, 62.

"Who would be so mock'd with glory, or *to* live
But in a dream of friendship?"
Timon of Athens, iv. 2, 33.

§ 394. When in the long struggle between the two infinitives the old demarcation was removed, the gerundial infinitive succeeded for a time even in getting into use after auxiliary verbs; sometimes we see it along with the simple infinitive in the same sentence.

"To do youre biding ay we wille."—*Townley Mys.* p. 38.

"To say the best for sothe I shalle."—*Ibid.* 266.

" that I myȝt the rather *to* haue grace."—*Early Eng. Wills*, 129, 9.

Elizabethan English.

"She tells me she'll wed the stranger knight,
Or never more *to* view nor day nor night."
Pericles, ii. 5, 17.

"Some pagan shore,
Where these two Christian armies might combine
The blood of malice in a vein of league,
And not *to* spend it so unneighbourly."
King John, v. 2, 39.

For to.

§ 395. The preposition *for* prefixed to the gerundial infinitive appears very early, implying the idea of aim and purpose.

"*forr* swa to winnenn blisse."—*Orm.* 896.

"*forr* uss to clennsenn."—*Ibid.* 1384.

"*forr* þe to ȝifenn bisne."—*Ibid.* 1239.

Later on, the original meaning was forgotten, and *for to* was used along with *to* in the same sentence without any real distinction.

"They alle sholde mounte on horsbacke *for* tenquyre and seke after his most dere and welbeloued sone, and *to* brynge hym ayen vnto hym." CAXTON, *Blanchardyn*, 20, 21.

"ye myght well kepe your selfe that ye com not so often *to* see vs and *for to* doo vs harm."—CAXTON, *Aymon*, 83, 9.

In the time of Queen Elizabeth "*for to*" is going out of fashion; for while it occurs very often as a metrical stop-gap in minor poets, and (probably as a conscious) archaism in Spenser, Marlowe and Shakspere seem to have shunned it. In all the works of Marlowe I have counted but seven "for to," while, in Greene's *Alphonsus, King of Arragon*, there are fifty-three "for to" against fifty-two "to," and in Peele's (?) *Sir Clyomon and Sir Clamydes* the number of both is the same, namely fifty.

Functions of the Infinitive.

§ 396. Though the infinitive ranges over a very wide area in Modern English, its functions were more numerous still in earlier periods. There are several interesting remnants in the literature of the Elizabethan age, and even in the popular language of our own times.

§ 397. *Infinitive instead of the (modern) Gerund.*

"Wythout aduenture *to fynde*."—CAXTON, *Blanch.* 31, 18.

"Wythout *to make* any noyse."—CAXTON, *Aymon*, 78, 24.[1]

"he salued hym prayng that for *to paye* well and largely content hym, he wold vouchsauf to take hym for his hoste."—*Blanch.* 46, 9.

"but none myght compare wyth Reynawde for *to do* well."—*Aymon*, 82, 3.

Elizabethan English.—"*To* fright you thus methinks I am too savage."—*Macbeth*, iv. 2, 70.

Not "too savage *to* fright you," but "*in* or *for* frighting you."

---

[1] This construction is due to the French original: *sans trouver, sans aire.*

"Too proud to be (of being) so valiant."—*Coriolanus*, i. 1, 263.

"I will not shame myself *to* give you (by giving you) this."—*Merchant of Ven.* iv. 1, 431.

"Make moan *to* be abridged."—*Ibid.* i. 1, 126.

Not "*in order to be*," but "*about being* abridged."

Cf. Abbott, *Shakspearian Grammar*, § 356.

§ 398. *The Infinitive used instead of a whole Clause* (as a many-worded adverb).

"*To sue* to live, I find I seek to die,
And seeking death find life."
Measure for Measure, iii. 1, 43.

"He lefte not *for to be* forthwith quartered . . . . but that he toke that same sarasyn by the heyre."—*Charles the Grete*, 132, 18.

"and soo he lete conduyte the harper out of the countrey but *to say* that kyng Mark was wonderly wrothe he was" (conditional clause).—*Morte d'Arthur*, 465, 12.

"Syr, quod they, *to dye* in the quarell we shall ayde and socoure you" (edition of 1601 "were we sure to dye").—LORD BERNERS, *Huon*, 22, 2.

"I thanke the of thy grace *to haue* gyuen me the puyssaunce to sle such a creature" (edition of 1601 "that thou hast gyuen me," &c.).—*Ibid.* 109, 21.

Cf. Abbott, *Shakspearian Grammar*, § 357.

The Absolute Infinitive.

"Moste sencelesse man he, that himselfe doth hate,
To love another. Lo! then, for thine ayd,
Here take thy lovers token on thy pate
So they to fight."
SPENSER, *Faerie Queene* i. 6, 47, 8.

§ 399. There is a peculiar use of the infinitive which is found first in the second half of the fourteenth century.

"I say this, be ye redy with good herte
To al my lust, and that I frely may
As me best liste do yow laughe or smerte,
And never ye to gruch it."
CHAUCER, *Clerkes Tales*, 158.

> "Let hym fynde a sarasyn
> *And y to fynde* a knyght of myn."
> *Guy of Warwick*, 3531, 2

I have tried in vain to find any trace of this use in earlier days, and can only account for it in the following way. There is a distinct tendency in the English of the fourteenth century to supplant adverbial clauses of time, and express a condition by absolute constructions.

"þe *same* Plato *lyvyng*, hys maistre socrates deservede victorie of unriȝtful deeþ in my presence."—CHAUCER'S *Boece*, 184.

(Original: eodemque superstite præceptor ejus Socrates injustæ victoriam mortis me adstante promeruit).

"but I withstod þat ordinaunce and overcom it, *knowyng al þis þe kyng hymself.*"—*Ibid.* 308.

"*The service doon*, they soupen al by day."—CHAUCER, *Squyeres Tale*, 289.

> " *The cause iknowe, and of his harm the roote,*
> Anon he yaf the syke man his boote."
> *Ibid. Canterbury Tales, Prologue,* 423.

§ 400. As appears by the preceding examples, both participles serve to represent clauses in the present and past tense. But how about the future? Why should there be no absolute construction for a clause with a future tense? The want of a proper participle did not prevent the language from completing the use of absolute constructions. *It resorted to the infinitive.* Some writers tried to introduce a future participle.

"For mysbyleued men in tyme *to comynge* schulde þorwȝ hem be conuerted and i-torned to good byleue."—TREVISA, *Polychr.* i. 267.

Cf. Skeat, *Notes to Piers Plowman*, p. 371.

"He was *to dyinge.*"—WYCLIFF, *Luke*, i. 2 (*erat moriturus*).

"*to doynge.*"—*Ibid.* xxii. 23 (*facturus*).

But this innovation was not accepted. There is, however, a similar formation in Caxton.

"Guy, hir loue and *tocoming* husband."—*Charles the Grete*, 134, 27.

i.e. "that was to be."

"Our *tocomyng* souerayne lorde."—*Blades, Caxton*, 139, 40.

This probably gave birth to that peculiar use which, in the course of its development, became more and more free, so that in the fourteenth century the absolute infinitive often serves to alternate with any principal sentence and clause.

> "I dar the better ask of you a space
> Of audience, to schewen oure request
> *And ye, my lord, to doon right as yow lest.*"
>   CHAUCER, *Clerkes Tale*, 49.

> "Men schold him brenne in a fuyr so reed,
> If he were founde, or if men might him spye,
> *And we also to bere him companye.*"
>   CHAUCER, *Second Nonnes Tale*, 315.

"Yf it fortunyd that the vanquisser sle his enemye in the feld, or he confesse the treason for the deth of his sonne, that than *the vanquyssher to lese* all his londys."—LORD BERNERS, *Huon*, 40, 26.

For other instances see Introduction to *Blanchardyn*, § 29.

There are several passages in Elizabethan literature which exhibit the same use.

> "Heaven would that she these gifts should have,
> *And I to live and die her slave.*"
>   *As You like It*, iii. 2, 162.

Cf. *Sonnets*, 58.

"But on this condition, that she should follow him, and he not to follow her."—BACON, *Advancement of Learning*, 284.

Dr. Abbott explains these constructions as a change for clearness' sake; but the historical development does not confirm this explanation. Cf. *A Shakspearian Grammar*, § 416.

Modern English.—"Only once, in place of a neat drawing of mine, in China-ink, representing Miles asleep after dinner, and which my friend Bunbury would not disown, I found a rude picture of myself going over my mare Sultana's head, and entitled 'The Squire on Horseback, or fish out of water.' And the fellow to roar with laughter, and all the girls to titter, when I came upon the page!"—THACKERAY, *The Virginians IV.* 3.[1]

"The caul was put up in a raffle down in our part of the country, to fifty members at half-a-crown a head, the winner to spend five shillings."—DICKENS, *David Copperfield, I.* 2.

"It seems a poor return for all these years, and me to have gone about in the woods with him when we were both boys and all."—BESANT AND RICE, *The Monk of Thelema II.* 285.

The Accusative with the Infinitive.

"*I judged him to be a foreigner.*"—BULWER.

"He frankly *avowed himself to be Wilfred of Ivanhoe.*"—WALTER SCOTT.

§ 401. The accusative + infin. as object of verbs like *biddan* (ask), *hátan* (bid), *seón* (see), *gehýran* (hear), *findan* (find), is quite common in Old English.

" (he) bæd him *engla ward.*
 geopenigean, uncúðe wyrd" (he asked the lord of the angels to open the unknown destiny.)—*Elene,* 1101.

" Swylce ic *magu-þegnas* mine *háte*
 wið feónda gehwone flotan eówerne
 árum *healdan*" (I also bid my men to keep well your vessel against any foe).—*Beówulf,* 293.

" þær meahte *gesion,* se þone sið beheóld
 brecan ofer bæðweg *brimwudu*" (there might see who looked on the road, a vessel break over the bath-way [sea]).—*Elene,* 243.

"þú sæt þær sum blind þearfa beðon wege, and *gehýrde miccle menigo* him beforan *féran*" (there sat by the way a blind beggar, and heard a great multitude go before him).—*Blickling Homilies,* 15.

§ 402. This usage was later on developed in a double way.

First, it was extended from the above-mentioned verbs to others, like *know, think, declare, wish, suffer,* until, in the

---

[1] But this is an intentional imitation of the French idiom: Et nous de répondre, etc.

sixteenth century, the construction of the accusative + infinitive had almost as wide a range in English as in Latin ;

Secondly, there came in the *gerundial infinitive*, while in Old English the *simple* one is the rule.

Modern English.

§ 403. (*a*) Instances with the simple infinitive.

"And ne þole me neuer nan oðer þing aȝain þi wille *luuie*" (and suffer me never to love anything against thy will).—*Old English Homilies I.* 285, A.D. 1200.

"And ȝhe it clepit Moysen
ȝhe *wiste* of water *it* boren *ben*" (she called it Moses, she knew it to be born of water).—*Story of Genesis and Exodus*, 2632, A.D. 1250.

"*Wilde bullokes* heo *wuste* fale ope ane heiȝe hulle *go*" (wild bullocks she knew to go on a high hill).—*Lives of Saints* (HORSTMANN), 38, 67. A.D. 1290.

"Man schal not *suffre his wyf go* roule about."—CHAUCER, *Wyf of Bathe*, Prologue, 453.

"þerfore þey suffreþ no man be a knyght þat will be her lorde."—TREVISA, *Higden's Polychronicon I.* 263, A.D. 1387.

"No woman ought to chide nor to strive with a fole *that* she *supposithe have* a malicious hert."—*Knight of La Tour Landry*, p. 21, A.D. 1440.

Tudor English.—"How is it that thou art so unkynd and outtragyous to me, for so lyttel offence to *suffer me endure* this greate misery?"—LORD BERNERS, *Huon* 124, 31. A.D. 1534.

§ 404. (*b*) Instances with the gerundial infinitive.

"*þole us to bi-wepen* ure sunne" (suffer us to bewail our sins).—*Old English Homilies, I.* 71, A.D. 1200.

"ne nalde he nawt *þolien þe þeof forte breoken* hire" (nor would he suffer the thief to break into it, sc. the house).—*ibid.* 245.

"*Trawes* thou *this lady* bryght of ble
Here loue on thee *to lay*?"—*Ypomadon*, 846-7. A.D. 1340.

"But *suffre me* my mischief *to bywaylle*."—CHAUCER, *Troylus and Cryseyde, I.* 755.

"I shal leue to telle yow of the kynge and the quene, *suffryng theym to demayne* (utter) theire complayntes."—CAXTON, *Blanchardyn*, 21, 6. A.D. 1489.

In the sixteenth century *to* becomes the rule.

Modern English.—Instances abound.

§ 405. *Note.*—While the accusative with the infinitive as object became more and more frequent in modern times, the same construction as subject did not outlive the sixteenth century.

"No wondur is *a lewid man to ruste.*"—CHAUCER, *Cant. Tales, Prologue,* 502.

"now were it tyme *a lady to gette henne.*"—*Ibid. Knightes Tale,* 1430.

"but it is good *a man be* at his large."—*Ibid. Troylus III.* 581.

"(his folke) putte hem self vpon their enmyes, so that it was force *the polonyens to recule* abak."—CAXTON, *Blanch.* 107, 18.

"It may fortune a man to be sorry for his synne."—FISHER, *English Works,* 32, 11.

"Hyt is not sufficient a man to get knowledge and virtue." STARKEY, *England in the time of Henry VIII.* p. 6.

The Nominative with the Infinitive.

"*I to bear* this . . . is some burden."—SHAKSPERE.

§ 406. In the fifteenth century, and even in Shakspere, we sometimes find the infinitive in connection with the nominative case instead of the expected accusative, after substantives, adjectives, and impersonal verbs.

"*Thow to lye* by our moder is to muche shame for vs to suffre."—*Morte d'Arthur,* 453, 4.

"hit was neuer the custome of no place of worship that euer I came in, whan a knyghte and a lady asked her berough, and *they to receyue* hem, and after to destroye them."—*Ibid.* 301, 23.

"A heavier task could not haue ben imposed
Than *I to speak* my griefs unspeakable."
SHAK. *Com. of Errors,* i. 1, 33.

"What he is, indeed,
More suits you to conceive *than I to speak* of."
As You Like It, i. 2, 279.

> "*Thou* this *to hazard*, needs must intimate
> Skill infinite or monstrous desperate."
> *All's Well*, ii. 1, 186.

For the Modern English construction with "for" see *Subject*, § 71.

THE PARTICIPLES.

Voice of the Participles.

> "Let me now conjure my kind, my condescending angel to fix the time when I may rescue her from *undeserving* persecution."—SHERIDAN.

> "In faith he is exceeding well read."—1 *Henry IV.* iii. 1, 166.

§ 407. The present participle seems to be sometimes used in a passive sense. This may be accounted for partly by the want of a passive participle for the present, partly by the close relation that exists between the participle and the verbal noun. Hence the following expressions:

> "Tell him, from his *all-obeying* breath I have
> The doom of Egypt."
> *Antony and Cleopatra*, iii. 13, 77.

> "That hand shall burn in *never-quenching* fire
> That staggers thus my person."
> *Rich. II.* v. 5, 109.

§ 408. The past participle is often met with in an active sense. This is a remnant of the time when the past participle was indifferent as to voice, and was used as an adjective. Thus we have in *Greek:* στακτός (*liquens*), πλανητός (*errans*), ἐπιρρυτός (*affluens*), χαρτός (*delectans*); in Latin: *potus, pransus, cenatus*, &c.

Old English.—"and his bróðer sunu Irtacus, yfele *geworht* man, féng to his ríce" (and the son of his brother Irtacus, a wicked evil-working man, succeeded to his kingdom).—ÆLFRIC, *Hom.* ii. 476, 17.

"ond hie þa wurdan hraþe *gelyfde*, ond Crist him sealde gesihþe" (and they became quickly *believing*, Christ gave them a sight).—*Blick. Hom.* 155, 5. Cf. *forworht* = wicked.—WULFSTAN, 14, 2.

Middle English.—" nu leofe breðre ȝe habbeð iherd hwa crest biwon reste þam *forgulte* saule" (now, dear brethren, ye have heard who first obtained rest for the souls of the damned).—*Old Eng. Hom.* I. 45.

> " Now hadde Calkas left, in this mischaunce,
> Alle *unwiste* of this fals and wikked dede,
> His doughter."
> CHAUCER, *Troylus and Cryseyde*, I. 93.

Modern English.
> " He was a scholar,
> Exceeding wise, *fair-spoken*, and persuading."
> *Henry VIII.* iv. 2, 52.

Cf. "*better-spoken.*"—*Lear* iv. 6, 10.

"*well-spoken.*"—*Rich. III.* 1, 1, 29; i. 3, 348.

"Like one *well-studied* in a sad ostent."—*Merch. of Venice*, ii. 2, 205.

"We were *read* in the classics."—SMOLLETT, *Roderick Random*, p. 49.

The Absolute Participle.

> "*She being down,*
> I have the placing of the British crown."
> SHAK. *Cymbeline*, 3, 5 167.

§ 409. When to a substantive not the subject of a verb, and dependent upon no other word in the sentence (noun, adjective, verb, or preposition), a participle is joined as its predicate, a clause is formed that modifies the verbal predicate of the sentence, and denotes an accompanying circumstance, as in : " Urbe expugnata imperator rediit."[1] This definition is correct with regard to our present conception of this expression. To us the construction as exhibited in the above instances is really *absolute*, i.e. detached from all the members of the sentence.

§ 410. But originally there was no such a thing as an absolute participle. What we look upon as such was simply a very freely used case implying at first instrumental meaning, then including by degrees also cause and time.

[1] Morgan Callaway, *The Absolute Participle in Anglo-Saxon.*

"Crassus cohortatus suos, *omnibus cupientibus*, ad hostium castra contendit."—CÆSAR, *B. G.* 3, 24, 5.

"*Nullo hoste prohibente* aut iter *demorante* incolumem legionem in Allobroges perduxit."—*Ibid* 3, 6, 5.

"Thrasybulus a barbaris, ex oppido noctu *eruptione facta*, in tabernaculo interfectus est."—Nep. 8, 4, 4.

What gives this construction such a strange appearance to our modern eyes is, first, the extensive meaning of the case, then the concreteness of the conception so entirely different from our own. It is not the action or state as an abstract, but the person or thing acting, which is the subject of perception, feeling, or thought.

"hae *literæ recitatæ* magnum luctum fecerunt" (= the reading of this letter).—LIVIUS, 27, 29.

"pœna *violatæ religionis* iustam recusationem non habet" (= for the violation of religion).—CICERO, *De Leg.* 2, 15.

§ 411. This mode of expression was by no means unfamiliar to the English of the older periods. But when we have emancipated our mind from the fetters of our modern languages, and have once got accustomed to the old expression, we find no difficulty in understanding the so-called absolute construction. What makes this explanation sure almost beyond doubt is the use of *be* in Old Frisian and Old English, and *at* in Gothic and Old Norse.

"se *be Diocletiane lyfgendum* Gallia ríce rehte" (= qui *vivente Diocletiano* Galliam regebat).—BEDA, I. 8.

"ðæt heo forlǽten hæfde *hi ðæm fæder lifiendum*" (= idolatriæ, quam *vivente eo* intermisisse videbantur).—*Ibid.* II. 5.

"Wæs he *be ðæm breðer lifigendum* wrǽcca in Gallia" (= qui *vivente adhuc fratre* cum exularet in Galliam).—*Ibid.* II. 15.

Old Frisian.—"*slêpendere thiade* and bi unwissa wakondon" (hominibus domientibus et incertis vigilantibus).—GRIMM, *Deutsche Grammatik*, iv. 905.

"Jah galaiþ in Jairusaulyma Jesus jah in alh ; jah bisaihvands alla, at andanahtja juþan visandin hveilai usiddja in Beþanian miþ þaim tvalibim" (and Jesus entered into Jerusalem, and into the temple : and when he had looked round about upon all things, and now the eventide was come, he went out unto Bethany with the twelve.)—*Mark*, xi. 11.

"Jah sunsaiv nauhþanuh at imma rodjandin quam Judas" (and immediately, while he yet spake, cometh Judas).—*Ibid.* xiv. 43.

Old Norse.—See Grimm, *Deutsche Grammatik*, iv. 906.[1]

So much for the Old English construction.

§ 412. In *Middle English* the surviving of the absolute participle (with the nominative or accusative, of course) is probably due, at least partly, to the French model of the same construction.

"Eus toz veanz = cunctis videntibus"; "tesmonianz les bons et les feoz hommes = bonis ac fidelibus viris attestantibus."

It is, however, worth noting that, in French, the absolute participle is always connected with the oblique case, while, in English, the nominative replaced the Old English dative case.

Instances abound.

THE VERBAL NOUN.

Functions of the Verbal Noun.

§ 413. The verbal noun with its functions of noun and verb has been for a long time the great puzzle of the grammarians, a real *crux philologorum*. In fact, it has absorbed the functions of:

1. The Old English verbal noun in *-ung* (*ing*), e.g., *sceawung* (showing).
2. The present participle.
3. The Latin gerund.
4. The French participle in *-ant*.

---

[1] A similar construction occurs in Modern English. See above *Nominative*, § 154.

But from an etymological point of view the verbal noun may be traced back to only two sources, viz., the Old English verbal noun and the present participle.

The Verbal Noun used Substantively.

" *Returning* were as tedious as go o'er."—SHAKSPERE.

§ 414. In this function the verbal noun simply derives from the Old English abstract in *-ung*. Instances of it are very common in all the periods of the language.

The Verbal disguised as a Predicate.

"The house is *building.*"

§ 415. This use was brought about by the analogy of intransitive verbs. In Middle English the verbal noun both of transitive and intransitive verbs was preceded by *in* or *on* (later on *a*).

" Vor þine men þat beþ ygo to day *avissinge* " (for thy men that are to-day gone a fishing).—ROBERT OF GLOUCESTER, 5351.

"The church was *in byldynge*."—ROBERT OF BRUNNE'S *Chronicle*. I. cxcvii.

(Quoted by Morris, *Accidence*, p. 179.)

"he founde the chirche of saynte peter *a makynge*."—CAXTON, *Aymon*, 576, 8.

" As he rode *in huntinge.*"—*Gesta Rom.* 136.

" And as he was *in making* of his lamentacion."—*Ibid.* 231.

" She wyst not what she sholde saye or thynke thereof, whether she was *a wakyng* or a slepe."—CAXTON, *Blanch.* 152, 34.

Now, the preposition preceding the verbal noun of intransitive verbs, was quite superfluous, and was dropped accordingly: "he is in hunting" became "he is hunting," but false analogy extended this proceeding also to the transitive verbs: "the house is in building" became "the house is building."

The Verbal Noun preceded by Prepositions.

"I never did repent *for doing good.*"—SHAKSPERE.

§ 416. In this instance the verbal noun borders on the nature of the present participle in so far as it governs an object without the help of the preposition *of*. Considering the substantival nature of the verbal noun we should expect "for the doing of good," a construction which really appears pretty frequently in Middle and Modern English times. But "doing good" without *of* was probably modelled on the older type "good-doing," which was continued to the last of the Middle English period.

"Biscopas mid folcum buton ǽnigre *are sceáwunge* fornumene wǽron" (bishops and people without any *mercy-showing* were destroyed).—BEDA, I. 5.

"bi his *cloðes wrixlunge*" (by changing his clothes).—*Old Eng. Hom.* i. 207.

"by his *side openunge*" (opening his side).—*Ibid.*

"late usage be ȝowre solace of seyntes lyues redynge" (derive comfort from reading lives of Saints).—*Piers Plowman*, Text B, VII. 87.

"without any *money payenge.*"—*Early Eng. Wills*, 170, 20 (A.D 1436).

In Wycliff's writings both constructions are met with: *almes doynge* 116, *doyng almes* 83.

§ 417. *Note.*—We now use '*while*' with the verbal noun, where, in Old English, the simple participle was preferred, *e.g.*:

"ealo drincende oðer sǽdon" (= others said while drinking ale).—*Beow.* 1946.

I suppose that *in*, imitated from the French, was grafted upon the old participle, so that it kept its verbal function. Therefore it was not followed by *of*, even in the earliest periods of its use.

"And thei seye, that we synne dedly, *in schavynge oure Berdes.*"—MAUNDEV. p. 19.

"He was a dedly creature, such as God hadde formed, and duelled in the Desertes, *in purchasynge his Sustynance.*"—*Ibid.* p. 47.

Verbal Noun interchanged with the Present Participle.

§ 418. "What's the use of *me* speaking?" "Do not mind *me* coming so late."

This expression is older and decidedly more concrete than the modern "*my* speaking," "*my* coming." The principle is the same which accounts for the so-called absolute participle. See above, § 411.

"To-janes þo sunne risindde" (= at the time of sunrise).—*Old Eng. Miscellany*, 26.

"Alle waters als þai sall rynne
And þat sal last fra þe son rysyng
Till þe tyme of þe son doungangyng."
HAMPOLE, *Pricke of Conscience*, 4777 f.

"After the sunne goyng down."—WYCLIFF, *Genesis*, xxviii. 11.

In later times this use began to decay, as indeed in every respect abstraction supplanted intuition, and the verbal noun took the place of the old present participle. Thus Purvey alters the instance quoted above to "aftir the goyng down of the sunne." Cf. *Exod.* xxii. 26, *Deuteronomy*, xi. 30. There are parallel constructions in Old French writers, and even in Corneille.

"Li rois les fera pendre *ains le soleil escons*" (the king will have them hanged before sunset: literally, before the sun gone down).—*Renaus de Montauban*, ed. Michelant, 189, 19.

"Ains le soleil colchant" (before the sun going down).—*Ibid.* 387, 34.

"A la lune luisant" (at the moon shining).—*La Chanson des Saxons* (par JEAN BODEL), i. 158.

"*Avant ce jour fini*, ces mains, ces propres mains,
Laveront dans mon sang la honte des Romains."
CORNEILLE, *Les Horaces*, iii. 6.

Cf. TOBLER, *Vermischte Beiträge zur frz. Grammatik* (Leipzig, 1886), p. 94 *ff.*

A few instances which answer exactly to those quoted at the head of this section occur in Caxton.

"Moost humblie besekyng my sayd most drad souerayn & naturel liege lorde the kyng and also the Quene to pardon *me* so presumyng." CAXTON'S *Prologue to Life of Jason* (Blades, p. 140).

"Humbly requyryng and besechyng my sayd lord to take no displaysir on *me* so presumyng."—CAXTON's *Epil. to Dictes and Sayings of the Philosophers* (Blades, p. 148).

"Humbly besechyng his hyenes to take no displesyr at *me* so presumyng."—CAXTON's *Epil. to Godefroy of Bologne* (Blades, 165).

§ 419. *Note.*—The editor of the *Spectator* having condemned this use as ungrammatical, a correspondent replied (May 26th, 1890) in the following way: "It is amusing that we have only to look back to the preceding column in order to find that you yourself, Mr. Editor, must be classed with penny paper writers. . . . Remarking on a previous letter, you say: 'We do not wonder at governments hesitating'; and the context requires 'governments' to be plural, as it is printed, and not a possessive singular 'government's.' Hence hesitating must be a participle, not the participle noun which alone the principal could tolerate in such a connection. Now, present participles signify 'in the act of doing' or 'while doing' this or that; so that 'What is the use of me speaking?' means of what use am I or shall I be while, or if, I speak? 'He heard of us coming,' 'I can prevent him doing it.' What in the world is the matter with these? We can see one coming, and also one doing a thing; why not, then, hear of one coming, and prevent one doing? hear of or prevent the self-same thing that we can see? At any rate, if 'what is the use of me' is not ungrammatical, the addition of 'speaking' as a participle, does not make it so."

In fact, the old expression has been gaining ground for the last decades in a surprising manner.

"We have no right to be hurt at a girl telling me what my faults are" (not "a girl's").—THACKERAY, *The Virginians*, iii. 186.

"There is always danger of this disease appearing in the sound eye." —HUGH CONWAY, *Called Back*, 13.

"There are plenty of instances on record of a key having opened a strange lock."—*Ibid.* 25.

"He was the only son of an only son, which fact accounts for Pauline having no near relatives on her father's side."—*Ibid.* 718.

"I had no patience with Croisette talking such nonsense."—WEYMAN, *House of the Wolf*, 45.

"Don't fear *me* being any hindrance to you, I have no more to say." —DICKENS, *David Copperfield*, ii. 290.

"I ask where possibly at Compton Green there could be pictures without *me* knowing it."—BESANT AND RICE, *Ready Money Mortiboy*, i. 289.

"Would you mind *me* asking a few questions?"—R. L. STEVENSON, *The Wrong Box*, p. 80.

The Verbal Noun in Compounds.

"This is the *wandering wood*, this Error's den."—SPENSER, *Faerie Queene*, I, I, 13.

§ 420. The extremely free use of the verbal noun as an adjective to substantives, which is the characteristic of Elizabethan English ("undeserving praise," "unrecalling crime," in Shakspere) is not met with in older periods.

It is simply a shift to make up for two wants.

1. The passive participle present.
2. Composition of nouns with verbal roots, as it was common in the old languages, and is still kept in Modern German to such a great and advantageous extent, e.g., *Fahrweg, Singhalle, Tanzsaal.*

In the French both wants were made up for awkwardly enough by the present participle.

"Séance tenante ; argent comptant ; école payante ; ville passante ; noble parure pas trop voyante ; chemin bien roulant, bien tirant ; café chantant ; morceau chantant ; soirée dansante ; salle dansante."

In English the much more appropriate verbal noun was introduced. Hence the following expressions.

Middle English.
"And siþen þai sal you cast in brine
As men do wit *salting swine*."—
Cursor Mundi, 26775 (Cotton MS.)

i.e. swine destined to be salted.

"Anon go gete us fast into this in
A *knedyng trowh* or else a kemelyn."—
CHAUCER, *Miller's Tale*, 362, cf. *ibid.* 378, 408.

Elizabethan English.
"Tell him, from his *all-obeying-breath* I have
The doom of Egypt."
Antony, iii. 13, 77.

i.e. obeyed by all.

"My lady to the manner of the days
In courtesy gives *undeserving praise.*"
Love's L. L. v. 2, 366.

i.e. undeserved.

Cf. Sheridan, *The Rivals*, iii. 3.

"Let me now conjure my kind, my condescending angel to fix the time when I may rescue her from *undeserving persecution.*"

"And ever let his *unrecalling crime*
Have time to wail th' abusing of the time."
Lucrece, 993.

"I am no *breeching scholar* in the schools."—*Taming of the Shrew*, iii. 1, 18.

"Which raised in me an *undergoing stomach.*"—*Tempest*, i. 2, 158.

THE ADVERB.

Relation between Adjective and Adverb.

§ 421. THE adverb stands in the closest relationship to the adjective. Logically speaking, the department of the former is accurately separated from that of the latter, but just as the line of demarcation between noun and verb is often scarcely recognizable (*cf.* verbal noun, infinitive, participle), so the adverb often borders on the adjective and *vice versâ*. In the phrase "an early riser," 'early' is from the grammatical point of view an adjective; but psychologically and logically speaking it is an adverb, and the uncertainty is due to the fact that "riser" too ranges between a noun and a verb. In consequence of this close relationship between the two parts of speech there are several cases in which both are interchanged.

Adverbs used in the form of Adjectives.

"Some will *dear* abide it."—SHAKSPERE.

§ 422. The adverb occurring in this instance, ended in older periods in the adverbial suffix *-e* (*deóre*); later on, the *e* was dropped, but the adverbial use was kept. Next, analogy introduced adjectives of romance origin in an adverbial use.

This accounts for the form; but as for the syntactic use, the language would certainly have made up for the loss of *e* by some suffix, *e.g.*, by *-ly* (as it did, in fact), if the distinction between the two parts of speech had not been partly dimmed.

Middle English.—"& he *siker* slepte."—LAYAMON, i. 171.

"þa þis child was *feir* muche."—*Ibid.* i. 12.

"So vuel bi-ʒete."—*Ibid.* ii. 506.

"Sanct Andrew wass *Richht god* and haʒherr hunnte" (St. Andrew was a right good and dexterous hunter).—*Orm,* 13470.

"This hille is not *right* gret, ne full highe."—MAUNDEVILLE, p. 31.

Modern English.—"Which the false man does *easy.*"—*Merchant of Venice,* ii. 3, 143.

"Thou didst it *excellent.*"—*Taming of the Shrew,* i. 1, 89.

"Which else should *free* have wrought."—*Macbeth,* ii. 1, 19.

"Raged more *fierce.*"—*Rich. II.* ii. 1, 173.

The sun shines bright.

Instances abound.

Adjectives used instead of Adverbs.

"And *slow* and *sure* comes up the golden year."—TENNYSON.

§ 423. This use is due to the same principle which we saw at work increasing the so-called absolute participle and the gerund with personal pronouns. *Cf.* above, § 411 and § 418.

Here again the sensuous imagination sees the quality rather in the concrete person or thing than in the abstract action or state. Thus, instead of the moon shining *brightly* it sees a *bright* moon shining. The same use is frequent in other languages. *Greek:* "εὗδον παννύχιοι" (Homer); "κρήνη ἄφθονος ῥέουσα" (Xenophon); "Κλέων πολὺς ἐνέκειτο λέγων" (Thucydides). Latin: "*domesticus* otior;" "*vespertinus* pete tectum" (Horace); "altero *duce nocturno* Syracusas introitum erat" (Virgil); "Aeneas se *matutinus* agebat" (*ibid.*).

Middle English.—
"And *lefli*ȝ ȝho him fedde" (and lovingly she fed him).—*Orm*, 3181.
"If ye listen *lefful* to me
Ic wile min folc owen be."—
Story of Genesis and Exodus, 3447.

Modern English.—"(She) lept *fierce* upon his shield."—SPENSER, *Faërie Queene*, I. 1, 18.

"*Clear* shone the skies."—THOMSON, *Spring*.

"While the billow *mournful* rolls."—TH. CAMPBELL, *Battle of the Baltic*.

"My wedding-bell rings *merry* in my ear."—SHERIDAN KNOWLES, *Hunchb.* I, 1.

Adverbs used as Adjectives.

"Thy *sometime* brother's wife."—SHAKSPERE.

§ 424. On the other hand, adverbs are used predicatively as adjectives, *e.g.*, "he is down in the world," the construction being felt by the instinct of the language as identical with the corresponding adjective.

From its predicative position the adverb next proceeds to be used even as an attribute preceding the substantive, *e.g.*, the above instance = the instance above (sc. quoted above). Thus in *Greek:* "τὴν ἐκεῖ παίδευσιν, τὴν πλησίον τύχην, τῷ νῦν γένει." *Latin:* "nunc hominum mores vides?" (Plautus); "ignari sumus ante malorum" (Virgil); "discessu tum meo" (Cicero).

Middle English.—
"My saulle lufes my lord *abuf*."—*Townley Myst.* p. 82.
"For *hys er dedes* wys and wyght."—*Octouian*, 1807.
    "Thou woldest undoing
    Of *thi to-nightes meting*."
            Seuyn Sages, 2405.
Modern English.
    "Say first, of God *above*, or Man *below*,
    What can we reason, but from what we know."
            POPE, *Essay on Man*, I, 17.
"The seed of *the then world*."—BYRON, *Cain*, I, I.
"In the *then* condition of my mind, his former protection of me appeared so deserving of my gratitude."—DICKENS, *David Copperfield*, *II.* 52.

THE PREPOSITIONS.

Close relation between Prepositions and Conjunctions.

"All were gone *save him*, who now kept guard."—ROGERS.
    "None, *save thou and thine*, I've sworn,
    Shall be left upon the morn."
            BYRON.

§ 425. BOTH the prepositions and conjunctions are connective elements, the former being used only in connection with nouns (or other parts of speech in the same function), the latter serving to link together not only single nouns, but also sentences and clauses. This distinction, however, is not essential; hence we see many particles used in the functions both of preposition and conjunction. "He has been about me *since* my arrival" = "he has been about me *since* I arrived." In a few cases it is even difficult to decide whether the particle is to be considered a preposition or a conjunction, and, in fact, we see the use vacillating between both. Thus the particles *but* and *save* are sometimes used governing an oblique case, and sometimes with the nominative.

"Ond eallum dagum bútan sunnan dag*um*" (all days save Sunday). —BEDA, 3, 23.

"Næfð he nán þing þe ne sí on minum anwealde *búton* þú" (he hath nothing that is not in my power *but* thou). —*Genesis* xxxix. 3.

"None but I have seen it."—CAXTON, *Blanch.* 43, 32.

Cf. above, *Interchange of Cases*, § 207.
Cf. *German.*

"Niemand kommt mir entgegen ausser *ein* Unverschämter" (Nobody comes to meet me but an insolent man).—LESSING.

"Dass ich nicht nachdenken kann *ohne* mit der Feder in der Hand" (I cannot think *but with* pen in hand).—*Id.*

"Kein Gott ist *ohne ich*" (there is no God but I).—LUTHER.

Development from Local to Temporal and Modal Meaning.

§ 426. Most of the prepositions serve originally to denote local relation; from this function they pass by degrees also to that of expressing relation of time, cause, and modality. A few instances will suffice to illustrate this development.

At denotes proximity of space.

"Peter stood *at* the door without."—*John*, xviii. 16.

It next refers to objects of all kinds with which a subject is thought to be implicated and engaged: "We were *at* the meeting." "We are hard *at* work."

The notion of proximity of space is then applied to proximity of time: "They returned *at* sunrise." "I saw him *at* our last meeting."

At last *at* is employed to express also modal relation.

"My life is yours, I humbly set it *at* your will."—*Cymbeline*, 4, 3, 13.

From means at first, with regard to space, movement from an object : "I came *from* town." "He is *from* home."

Transferred to time, *from* denotes an activity extending from a starting-point in time to another.

"*From* morn to noon he fell."—MILTON.

The next step is to denote origin.

"This offer comes *from* mercy, not *from* fear."—SHAKSPERE.

At last it comes to denote cause.

"*From* my respect for his father, I'll be calm."—GOLDSMITH, *She Stoops to Conquer*, 4.

The Prepositions make up for the Case-endings.

"Gilpes þu girnest" (= *for* fame thou yearnest).—BOETHIUS, 32.
"Siðes wérig" (= weary *of* the journey).—*Beowulf*, 579.

§ 427. A particular interest attaches to those prepositions which in Middle and Modern English serve to express all those relations which in Old English were denoted by the case-endings. The most important prepositions are in this respect *by, for, of, to, with.*

Of replacing the Genitive.

§ 428. As early as the tenth century there are instances of this preposition, where we should expect the Genitive.

" Ac god hie atredde fram þam réðum wítum and sume eác ablende *of* þam bysmor-fullum þénum " (but God delivered them from the cruel torments, and even blinded some of the blasphemous servants).— ÆLFRIC, *Lives of Saints*, 397-8.

We should expect either '*þára*' instead of '*of þam*,' or of '*sume þá ;*'

Cf. § 175.

Other instances : *án of þǽm* (one of them), *Lindisfarne Gospels* (quoted by Kington Oliphant, *Old and Middle*

English, p. 87); *ʒief of his gáste* (gift of his spirit), *Chronicle*, 1095 (*ibid.* p. 136); *eie of him* (awe of him), *ibid.* p. 141; *saule of him*, *ibid.* 150.

For other instances, see above *Genitive*, passim.

§ 429. *To* replacing the Objective Genitive.

"(He) forgiaf hire hire sinnen for two þinge, an is muchel leðð̄e *to* hire sunne, oðer muchel luue *to* him" (he forgave her her sins for two reasons; the first is her great hatred to her sins, the second is her great love to him).—*Old English Homilies, II.* 141.

Cf. *ibid.* I. 107, II. 159.

To replacing the Dative.

§ 430. There are faint beginnings of this use in Old English.

"(Hagar) þolian ne wolde
yfel and ondleán, þæs þe ǽr dyde
tó Sarran"

(Hagar would not suffer the evil and recompense for what she had done to Sarah).—CÆDMON, *Genesis*, 2265.

Later on, instances become more frequent.

þa þinges þe birisseþ *to* selche kinge (the things that befit every king).—LAYAMON, i. 418; Orm has '*herrsumm till*' (obedient to) (quoted by Mr. Oliphant, *l.c.* p. 199); *Ancren Riwle* '*lufsum to ein*' (lovely to the eyes), *ibid.* p. 239.

But still, throughout the thirteenth century, '*to*' replacing the dative is far from being generally accepted. Cf. the following instance:

"For no man ne mai synnes beten er þanne he hem forlete and shewe(h)em *his prest*" (for no man may repent of his sins, before he has forsaken them, and shown them to his priest).—*Old English Homilies, II.* 57.

"And þeh ure drihten be mild-heorted þo þe him biddeð, he is noðeles rihtwis togenes þo þe his milce bisecheð" (though our Lord be merciful to those who pray to Him, yet He is just to those who beseech His mercy).—*Ibid.* 59.

Cf. *ibid.* 97, 99, 125, 127, 135, 183, 219.

I do not remember any such '*to*' in the *Story of Genesis and Exodus* (A.D. 1250), nor is it frequent in ROBERT OF GLOUCESTER, (A.D. 1290).

In Chaucer '*to*' is common.

With replacing the Instrumental Case.

§ 431. The use of the preposition instead of the instrumental case is met with also in Old English, only here it is always *mid*, while later comes *with*.

Old English.—" hé *mid* handum befíng wuldres wynbeám " (he with his hands seized the glorious tree).—*Elene* 843.

" þa geseah he Crist sylfne *mid* þy ilcan hrægle gegyredne, þe he ǽr þǽm þearfan sealde " (he saw Christ himself clad in the same garment which before he had given to the poor man).—*Blickling Homilies*, 215.

Middle English.
" *Mid* sweord and *mid* spere
Al he todrof þes Ringes here."—LAYAMON, I. 24.

"Thesu, *mit* ti swete blod þu bohtest ful me deore " (Jesus, with thy sweet blood thou boughtest me full dear).—*Old English Miscellany*, 196, 32.

"fram Affric hü wende varþ *mid* þe wind þat was so god."—ROBERT OF GLOUCESTER, 345.

" *Mid* him he hadde an strong axe, þat maniman broȝte to deþe.
Corineus þar*mide* harde smot."—*ibid.* 390.

Thus MS. *a*; others have ' her *wiþ*.'

With = *mid* is found as early as the beginning of the thirteenth century.

"To wurþen god *wiþ* bedes and *wiþ* lakes " (to worship God with prayers and offerings).—*Orm.* 905.

It becomes frequent in the second half of the thirteenth century.
" Al was ðat firme ðrosing in nigt,
Til he wit hise word made light "
(all that first chaos was in night till he with his wand made light).—*Story of Genesis and Exodus*, 44, A.D. 1250.

"He was so faste *wit* yuel fest
þat he ne mouthe hauen no rest."
                    Havelock, 144, A.D. 1280.

"But on þat he nouth *wit* his hend
Ne dreþe him nouth, þat fule fend."
(but with his hands he killed him not, that foul fiend).—*ibid.* 505.

In Robert of Gloucester, A.D. 1290, the MSS. vary between *mid* and *wiþ*.

§ 432. Quite exceptionally we find *to* and *at* used in the same way as Old English *mid*.

"[þei] serveden me *to* fote and honde."—*Alexius* (ed. Schipper) I. 161.

"I shal amende aftere thys
Ryght as thin owyn wyl is
To serve the *at* foot and honde."
                    Coventry Mysteries, 123.

Note.—The old instrumental case survived throughout the Middle English period in the idiom 'his own hand (hondes)' = with his hand.

"þe pope bitok him armes, and *his owe honde* made him kniȝht."—
ROBERT OF GLOUCESTER, 3776.

  . . . "he hath with a dedly wounde
Fightend *his owne hondes* slain
Branchus."
                    GOWER, *Confessio Amantis*, 90.

Cf. § 194.

Prepositions introducing the Agent (in Passive Constructions).

§ 433. In *Old English* this function is limited to '*fram*' (from).

       . . . "swá *fram* Silvestre
         lǽrde wǽron"
(As they were taught by Silvester).—*Elene*, 190.

"Her sagaþ Matheus se godspellere þætte Hǽlend wǽre lǽded on Eesten, and þæt he wǽre costod *from* deofle" (here says Matthew the wvangelist, that the Saviour was led into the wilderness, and that he was tempted by the devil).—*Blickling Homilies*, 27.

§ 434. But there are a few instances with '*of*' instead of '*fram.*'

"Aeþelstán wæs *of* Myrcum gecoren tó cinge" (Athelstan was chosen king by the Mercians).—*Chronicle*, 925.

"He wearþ þǽr ofslagen *of* his ágenum folce" (he was killed there by his own people).—*Ibid.* 1030. Quoted by Mätzner, II. 252.

§ 435. In *Middle English* there are three prepositions to introduce the agent, namely, *of, with*, and *by*. Of these '*of*' is the rule, especially in early Middle English, *with* (mid) is not unfrequent, while '*by*' is the exception.[1]

... "þæt be þǽre cennendra gefyrhtum þæs bearnes weorþe ongyten wǽre *be* þysum eallum oþrum mannum" (that by the doubts of the parents the child's dignity should be understood by all these other men).—*Blickling Homilies*, 163.

(a) *Of.*

"Ne hit nes nefere ifuled *of* nanre oðre assa" (nor had it ever been defiled by any other ass).—*Old English Homilies*, *I.* 5, A.D. 1200.

"Abel an hundred ger was old
ðan he was *of* is broðer wold."
(Abel was a hundred years old when he was killed by his brother).—*Story of Genesis and Exodus*, 420, A.D. 1250.

"Suþþe has Engelond ibe iwerred ilome
Of þe folc of Denemarch"
(Since England has been often invaded by the people of Denmark).—ROBERT OF GLOUCESTER, 52, A.D. 1290.

"Galle hit was cald þat tyme *of* alle."—ROBERT DE BRUNNE, *Story of England*, 1600. A.D. 1338.

"þese novelries maad *of* ydiotis and synful wracchis."—WYCLIFF, *Unprinted English Works*, p. 3, A.D. 1380.

"His sowle in helle ful peynfully
Of develis is al to-torn."
Coventry Mysteries, 187, A.D. 1440.

(b) With (mid).

"Heo is dust and unstable þing þet *mid* a lutel wind of a word is anon toblowen."—*Ancren Riwle*, 122, A.D. 1220.

---

[1] There are a few instances of this last in Old English.

" If erf or man ðor-one take,
It deað ðolen, wið stones slagen,
Or to deað wið gores dragen"

(If cattle or man touch it [the mountain], they shall suffer death, slain with stones, or drawn to death by darts).—*Story of Genesis and Exodus*, 3458, A.D. 1250.

"Now sith that maydens hadde such despit
To ben defouled *with* mannes foul delit,
Wel aught a wyf rather hir-self to sle,
Than be defouled, as it thenketh me."
    CHAUCER, *The Frankeleynes Tale*, 660.

"I trow your prison shuld not be so harde to me as it shulde be, and I were take *with* Englisshe men."—*Knight of La Tour-Landry*, 18, A.D. 1440.

(*c*) *By*.

"Þes psalm is iwriten *bi* Davide."—EADWINE'S *Canterbury Psalter*, p. 268, A.D. 1150.

Quoted by Mr. Kington Oliphant, *Old and Middle English*, p. 160.

. . . "and it may be prouyd *be* men of þe self gyld, he shal payyn di. li. (½ lb.) wax."—*English Gilds*, 63 A.D. 1329.

"Yet eft, *be* huam þet angel is ymad, *be* him is ymad þe smale werm."—*Ayenbite of Inwyt*, 270, A.D. 1340.

"This child Maurice was siththen emperour
I-maad *by* the pope."
    CHAUCER, *Man of Lawes Tale*, 1024.

In Caxton's time '*of*' still prevails. The proportion of the three prepositions in Caxton's '*Blanchardyn and Eglantine*' is as follows :—

  of : by : with = 20 : 3 : 2.

In the sixteenth century '*by*' rapidly comes to the fore.

In Hugh Latimer's *Sermons on the Card*, A.D. 1529, '*by* is the rule, and in Shakspere it is extremely common, although '*of*' in the same function is frequent.

'*For*' + *Accusative* + *Infinitive*.

§ 436.

"*For* Coriolanus neither to care whether they love or hate him, manifests the true knowledge he has."—SHAKSPERE, *Coriolanus*, II. 2, 13.

For this use, see § 71.

' With' in connection with Participles.

§ 437.

" *With* the enemy invading our country, it was my duty to go on the campaign."—THACKERAY, *The Virginians*.

For this use, see § 154.

Prepositions Omitted.

§ 438. In many idioms of Elizabethan and modern times, there is a striking want of prepositions, which was somewhat rashly termed 'ellipsis of preposition.' Thus Dr. Abbott devotes several sections of his *Shakspearian Grammar* to that point. But in examining closely the instances quoted by Dr. Abbott, we find that they do not justify such an appellation. 'Ellipsis' of a preposition implies that a preposition was generally used for a time, but was dropped in a following period, or that is was generally used, but was omitted by Shakspere or other poets; but the history of English shows that, in most of the quoted instances, this is not the case.

§ 439. After '*worth*' and '*worthy*.'

"Some precepts *worthy* the note."—*All's Well that Ends Well, III.* 5, 104.

Worthy like *worth* governs here the *accusative of measure*, originally genitive. Instances of *worth* + *accusative* are met with in the first period of Middle English.

" þu art best *wurð* my luue þat for my luue deidest " (thou art most worthy of my love, thou that didst die for the love of me).—*Old English Homilies, I.* 285, A.D. 1200.

" þis liues blisse nis *wurð* a sloe."—*Old English Miscellany*, 160, 28, A.D. 1220.

" We shalle see if he is *worthi* mede " (reward).—*Gesta Romanorum*, 248, A.D. 1440.

§ 440. After '*listen*' and '*hearken*.'

"To *listen* our purpose."—*Much Ado About Nothing, III.* 1, 12.

In *Middle English* this construction is the rule.

"He þe luueliche ˑhlisteð godes lore, he shal hauen eche lif on blisse" (he who joyfully listens to God's lore, shall have everlasting life on bliss).—*Old English Homilies, II.* 155.

"Jacob listenede ðo frendes red" (Jacob listened to a friend's advice).—*Story of Genesis and Exodus,* 1597.

Cf. *ibid.* 2222, 3403.

Hearken exhibits the same construction.

"Heȝly he þonkes
Jesus and Saint Gilian, þat . . . his cry *herkened*."—
Sir Gawayne and the Greene Knight, 775.

"The pepul [should] wyth more dylygence *kerken* the storys of the Bibul."—STARKEY, *England in the Time of Henry VIII.* 212, 568.

The editor unnecessarily inserts [to].

Cf. *Hearken* the end.—2 Henry IV. ii. 4, 305.

§ 441. After '*swear*.'

"Thou *swearest thy gods* in vain."—*Lear,* i. 1, 193.

This too is very frequent in Middle English.

"þe mariner swore his faye (faith)."—*Sir Tristrem,* 318.

"Huo þet *zuerþ* wiþ-oute skele *þane name* of oure lhorde, he him forzuerþ" (who swears without motive by the name of our Lord, he forswears himself).—*Ayenbite of Inwyt,* p. 6.

"I *swere* to the my troth."—CAXTON, *Charles the Grete,* 50, 29.

"The *swore God*."—CAXTON, *Aymon,* 38, 4; 73, 14.

Cf. Thackeray, *The Virginians, II.* 197; 'he *swore his great gods* that henceforth he would be Harry's truest, humblest friend.'

442. But there seems to be 'omission' in the following idioms.

(a) "*Spite* of thy hap, hap hath well hapt."—WYATT, *Poems,* 38.

Cf. French : en dépit.

(b) "þey haue a vestment, a chalys, and a massebok, *pris* of x. marks."—*English Gilds*, p. 8.

(c) "*What occupation* are you?"—*Mucedorus*, 213, A.D. 1590(?).

"*What trade* art thou?"—2 *Henry IV.* iii. 2, 160.

(d) "She was *his own age.*"—WALTER BESANT, *Such a Good Man*, 20.

"I had fought a dozen times, when I was *your age.*"—WEYMAN, *House of the Wolf*, 35.

(e) "We three sat down, *Turkish fashion.*"—*Ibid.* 12.

"She lifted her head, *Pythoness fashion.*"—MRS. EDWARDS, *Pearl-Powder*, 241.

§ 443. *Dependent Prepositions.*

"He lent me his horse *to escape upon.*"
SCOTT, *Lay of the Last Minstrel*, 4, 11.

This use of the prepositions may be traced back to the oldest periods of English.

Old English.—"He bebeád ðæt menn námen hiora sweord Godes andan *mid to wreccanne*" (he bade men take their swords to avenge God's anger *with*).—*Cura Pastoralis*, 381.

"Donne bringe he of hriðerum án unwemme oxan cealf tó þære hálgan stówe dura Drihten *mid to gladienne*" (then let him bring of cattle a male calf without blemish to the door of the holy place *to please* the Lord *with*).—*Leviticus*, i. 3.

Middle English.

"Swylke an hors . . .
I wolde have *to ryde upon.*"—*Richard Cœur de Lion*, 5470.

"Thei han a spere in here hond *to fighte with.*"—MAUNDEVILLE, p. 197.

NOTE.—In Middle English *with* is always near its verb:

"Such weddynges to worche, to wratthe with treuthe" (i.e. *to anger Truth with*).—*Piers Plowman*, ii. 116.

Modern English.

Instances abound.

The Conjunctions.

Development from the Concrete to the Abstract.

§ 444. What we have stated with regard to prepositions holds good with regard to conjunctions—both start from a concrete, demonstrative meaning, afterwards denote abstracts (time, manner), and at last become purely formal, that is, mere symbols of connection between notions and thoughts.

The conjunctions *when*, *then*, Old English þá (German *da*) are good illustrations of that development.

Relation between Prepositions and Conjunctions.

§ 445. Even in Modern English there are particles which serve both as prepositions and conjunctions, *e.g. after, before, ere, till.* But they are more numerous in the older periods.

Again = about the time that.

> "Bot Leyl *ageyn* þat he schold deye,
> Preyed faste in his elde."
> ROBERT DE BRUNNE, *Story of England*, 2216.

fro = from the time that, since.

> "for *fra* þis lagh was þar bigunnen
> Son oueral þan was it runnen"

(since this law was introduced there, it soon was accepted everywhere). —*Cursor Mundi*, 2299.

> "*fro* she come to here above,
> Her thought no prynce her pere."—*Ipomadon*, 103.

Bituix and is often used with the meaning of 'until.'

> "*Bituix and* þou again be gan
> Unto þat erth þou was of tan"

(until thou art gone again to the earth thou wert taken from).—*Cursor Mundi*, 297.

Thus Cotton MS. ; Trinity MS. has '*til* þou turne,' &c.

Mid (with) is often used for 'and.'

Old English.—" Biscopas *mid* folcum buton ǣnigre ȧre sceȧwunge ætgædere mid iserne and lige fornumene wǣron " (bishops and people, without regard for mercy, were destroyed together by fire and sword).— BEDA, I. 15.

Middle English.—
  " Hwer beað þine dihsches
    Mid þine swete sonde ? "
(Where are thy dishes and thy sweet messes ?).—*Old English Miscellany*, 174, 106.

forto, to, unto = until.

  " þerçuore leoue lefdi long hit þuncheð us wrecchen,
   Vort þu of þisse erme liue toðe suluen us fecche "
  (Therefore, dear lady, long will it appear to us wretches
  Until thou from this poor life to thyself us fetch).
            Old English Homilies. I. 195.

  " þare stoden þis ȝeordene grene : more þane a þousend ȝer,
   forto seint Daui þe Kyng cam : þat was of so gret power "
(There stood these green yards more than a thousand years until the holy King David came who was of such a great power).—*Legendary*, (HORSTMANN), I, 8, 243-4.

" And there the spottis is, *to* the body that hathe done the synne be confessed."—*Knight of La Tour-Landry*, 11.

  " He slepeth, and he fareth in his gyse
   All nyght, *unto* the sonne gan arise."
        CHAUCER, *The Man of Lawes Tale*, 693.

§ 446. *And*, used redundantly is often met with in older periods.

  " Sufficeth this example oon or tuo,
   And though I couthe reken a thousend mo."
        CHAUCER, *Knightes Tale*, 1096.

" The vertu of the broche is this, that who so ever ber hit upon his brest, late him thinke what he wolle, *and* he shalle mete perewith at his likinge."—*Gesta Romanorum*, p. 181.

" O brother Reynawd, *and* what doo you here ?"—CAXTON, *Agmon*, 235, 11.

" Warre would he haue ? *and* he shall haue it so."—*Gorboduc*, 689.

Cf. Abbott, *A Shaksperian Grammar*, § 97.

§ 447. *That* used redundantly before the direct speech (oratio recta).

"I said *that* 'all the years invent;
. . . .
Were this not well to bide mine hour?'"
TENNYSON, *The Two Voices.*

For this use see § 107.

§ 448. *That* as a substitute for other Conjunctions.

Like '*que*' in French '*that*' often serves to supply the place of other conjunctions in the second part of a clause.

"*When* they of the cyte had seen the manere and the rewle of their enmyes, and *that* all wyth leyser they had seen their puyssaunce and their manere of doynge, the captayne and the prouoste of the towne dyde ordeyne a stronge and a bygge worde."—CAXTON, *Blanchardyn and Eglantine*, 58-17.

"And *after* that the worke was ended, and *that* all their enmyes were taken or slayn, they brought hym and entred wythin the cyte."— *Ibid.* 195-26.

"thother laborers had so grete enoy *by* cause he dide better his devour than thei, and *that* he was better loved than thei."—CAXTON, *Aymon*, 575-16.

"And *that* no lawful means can carry me
Out of his envy's reach, I do oppose
My patience to his fury."
SHAKESPERE, *Merchant of Venice, IV.* 1, 9.

"*If* he think it fit to share them again and *that* the complaint they have to the king concerns him nothing, let him call me rogue for being so far officious."—*Ibid. Winter's Tale, IV.* 4, 869.

"You see, Sir, by the long letter I have transmitted to you, that, *though* I do most heartily wish that France may be animated by a spirit of rational liberty, and *that* (= though) I think you bound, in all honest policy, to provide a permanent body in which that spirit may reside, and an effectual organ, by which it may act, it is my misfortune to entertain great doubts concerning several material points in your late transactions."—BURKE, *Reflexions*, Second Paragraph.

PART III.
ORDER OF WORDS.

PART III.

ORDER OF WORDS.

General Remarks.

§ 449. THERE is a great difference between the natural and artificial arrangement of words. The former is uttered unconsciously, and is, generally speaking, a true image of the psychical process in the speaker's mind, the latter is more or less consciously altered. If we uttered the words in the order in which they come into our mind, we should hear the strangest sentences. Thus, for instance, instead of "May I trouble you for the butter?" we should most probably hear, "The butter, trouble you may I?" this order answering to that in which the ideas come into our mind. We do not, however, speak ingenuously on the spur of the moment, but either our mode of speaking (and thinking) is modelled on old patterns (analogy), or we arrange our words with constant regard to our interlocutor, sometimes speculating on his feelings, sometimes on his mind.

In tracing, therefore, historically, and explaining psychologically the arrangement of words, we must keep in mind three principles.

1. Analogy (the most usual type of arrangement).
2. The psychical order of words.
3. Conscious arrangement with regard to the recipient.

Of course, all the three principles may give in certain cases the same result, but this is not the rule. Generally, there is some discrepancy between the psychical order of words and the two other principles, and the shape of the sentence in good prose and poetry is the result of a compromise between all the three.

Subject and Predicate.

§ 450. As the psychological subject is that idea or group of ideas which first comes to the speaker's mind, and as there is no predicate without an underlying subject, the natural order of words in the simple sentence is : first subject, then predicate. In fact, the oldest Teutonic dialects exhibit, as a rule, this arrangement.

Inversion.

" *Pass'd he* who bore the lions and the cross."—BULWER.

" He *is* a good man, *is* Mr. Brown."

§ 451. But the inverted order is by no means rarely to be met with. From the oldest times down to Modern English the predicate may under certain circumstances precede the subject. This inversion of the regular order is brought about in several ways.

§ 452. 1. The subject is present before the eyes of the speaker, as in the imperative. Then there is either no need of mentioning the subject at all, or, if mentioned, it occupies the second place. Hence : *go ! stay !* or *go thou !*

There are, however, many exceptions to this rule.

Old High German.—"*thû*, druhtîn, *rihti* wort mîn" (thou, O Lord, arrange my words).—OTFRID, i. 2, 32.

Old English.—" þú tó heofenum *beseoh* " (look thou to the heavens).—*Elene*, 83.

" nú *gé* raþe gangaþ " (go ye now quickly).—*Ibid.* 372.

Middle English.—

This order of words is very frequent in poetry, and is found here and there also in prose.

"Almigtin louerd, hegest kinge,
ðu giue me seli teminge"
(almighty Lord, highest king, give thou me propitious opportunity).—*Story of Gen. and Exod.* 31.

"Adam, ðhu knowe eue ðin wif" (Adam, know thou Eve, thy wife).—*Ibid.* 397.

Cf. *ibid.* 737, 1492, 2072.

"þu teche him of alle þe liste
þat þu euere of wiste."
King Horn, 235.

Cf. *ibid.* 207, 322.

"A schip þou bring me tille,
Mine harp to play me þare."
Sir Tristrem, 1147.

Very frequent *ibid.* and in the *Cursor Mundi.*

"But wel *ye knowe* that he was not hadde sore ferre from the kynge his fadre" (original: *sachiez*).—CAXTON, *Blanchardyn*, 13, 1.

"A, fayr damoysels, said Amand, *ye recommaunde* me unto la Beale Isoude."—MALORY, *Morte d'Arthur*, 436, 16.

Perhaps the modern colloquial English order has kept this use: "*You do* what I tell you."

§ 453. 2. For the same reason the subject is either omitted altogether, or inverted in interrogative sentences, "Are you ready?"

Cf. omission of the personal pronoun.

§ 454. 3. The object placed at the head of the sentence draws the verb immediately after it, both being intimately connected.

Old English.—"Feala worda gespræc se engel" (many words spoke the angel).—*Genesis*, 271.

Middle English.—"Weorre makede Turnus."—LAYAMON, i. 8.

Modern English.—"Friends have I none."—WARREN, *Diary*, i. 4.

"Much hast thou learnt, my son, in this short journey."—COLERIDGE, *Piccolomini*, i. 4.

§ 455. 4. A verb in the negative has, as a rule, more weight than the subject; this accounts for the tendency to use negative predicates in the inverted position.

In Old English, as in the other Teutonic languages, the inverted position is the rule.

Middle English.—"Ne maȝȝ nan man her wurrþi ben."—*Orm*, 17158.

"Næs næuere king nan."—LAYAMON, ii. 563.

Very frequent.

Modern English.—"*Never* was there a mind keener or more critical than that of Middleton."—MACAULAY, *Essays*, iii. 4.

"*Never* were such thrice magnificent carnival amusements."— CARLYLE, *Frederick the Great*, 6, 3.

§ 456. 5. The principal sentence following the clause sometimes shows inverted order. This use may be traced back to the oldest periods, but while German has developed it into a rule, English has more and more replaced it by the usual arrangement.

Old English.—"Syððan he com ofer Wætlinge-stræte, *worhton hi þæt mæste yfel*" (since he came over W. they did the most evil).— *Chronicle*, 1013.

Middle English.—"Forr well biforr þatt Sannt Johann wass borenn of his moderr, Cnew he full well þe Laferrd Crist I Sannte Marȝess wambe."—*Orm.* 10382.

Modern English.—"Wherever flagged his own, or failed the opposing force, *glittered his white robe*, and *rose his bloody battle-axe*."— BULWER, *Rienzi*, 5, 3.

"While the government of the Tudors was in its highest vigour, *took place an event* which."—MACAULAY, *History of England*, i.

Two other cases of inversion are worth mentioning, though they belong almost entirely to the past.

§ 457. 6. In epic poetry the second of two co-ordinate sentences is often inverted. For the most part, the inverted position serves to replace a conjunctive, or adversative particle, answering to Latin *enim, autem, tamen,* &c. A few instances from the *Tale of Gamelyn,* wrongly attributed to Chaucer, will illustrate this use.

"Tho made they Gamelyn to sitte, might he nat stonde."—*The Cokes Tale of G.* 381.

"They hyeden faste, wold they nought bylynne."—*Ibid.* 557.

"He was wonder sory, was he nothing light."—*Ibid.* 732.

"And sithen was Gamelyn graven under molde,
And so schal we alle, may there no man flee."
Ibid. 900.

This use may be traced back also to the oldest periods.

Old Saxon.—"Johannes was êr themu hêrôston kûð, be thiu môsta he an thena hof innan thringan mid theru thiod : *stôd* allaro thegno betsto Petrus thâr ûte" (John was known of old to the captain, therefore could get in with the multitude : stood the best of men, Peter, outside).—*Heliand,* 4950.

"Than ligid eft ôðar engira mikilu weg an thesro weroldi, ferid ina werodes lut" (there is another much narrower path in this world : *walk it few*).—*Ibid.* 1782.

Old English.—"Swá þá drihtguman dreámum lifdon eádiglíce, óð þæt an ongan fyrene fremman, feónd on helle : *wæs se grimma gæst* Grendel háten" (thus the valiant men lived in joy happily, until the fiend of hell began to work mischief : was the grim ghost called Grendel). —*Beowulf,* 102.

Cf. 271, 349, 1699.

§ 458. 7. Co-ordinate sentences introduced by *and* are often inverted. This use may be traced to the pre-historic time of the English language. It appears in the oldest Teutonic dialects, and is still kept in Modern German, though learned grammarians are untiring in ridiculing this time-honoured use.

Old English.—"Her Aeþelheard cyning forþférde and *féng Cuþræd* to Westseaxna rice" (then Ethelheard died, and Cuþræd succeeded to the kingdom).—*Chronicle,* 741.

Middle English.—"Syon was sum hwile iclepet þe hehe tur of Jerusalem. And *scið syon* ase muchel on englishe leodene ase heh sihðe, and *bitacneð* þis tur þe hehschipe of meidenhad" (S. was once called the high tower of Jerusalem, and says S. as much in English as high sight and betokens this tower the elevated state of maidenhead).—*Hali Meidenhad*, p. 5.

> "And tanne comm he siþen ut
> All dumb and butenn spæche,
> And toc to beenenn till þe follc,
> *And space he* nohht wiþþ tunge"

(and then came he out all dumb and without speech, and began to beckon to the folk, and spoke not with tongue).—*Orm.* 224.

> "For moche he langed that he myght there be arryued for to shew hym all the tydynges. *And dured* not long *the scarmoush*."—*Melusine*, 127, 4.

Elizabethan English.—We meet with traces of this use in the literature of the sixteenth century.

> "The day is spent, *and cometh* drowsy *night*."—SPENSER, *Faerie Queene*, i. 3, 15.

> "High Amurack is lulled fast asleep,
> *And doubt I* not but, ere he wakes again,
> You shall perceive Medea did not gibe."
>
> GREENE, *Alphonsus*, 235, a.

For the arrangement of words in a sentence with a double subject or predicate, see *Contraction*, § 471.

Place of the Verb in Clauses.

> "As much as in them lay."—*Huon*, 25.

§ 459. In dependent sentences inversion is still rare; in older periods not only the regular position was the rule, but the verb, especially the auxiliary verb *to be*, used to be placed at the end of the clause.

This means of expressing subordination was probably common to all the Teutonic languages, as it occurs frequently in Old High German, Old Saxon, and Old English. But there must have been a sudden stop in the development of this use in English; the *Chronicle*, for instance, is rather inconsistent in this respect.

Old English.—"þæt wæs ymb twá ger þæs þi hie hider ofer sǽ cómon" (that was about two years since they had come over sea).—*Chronicle*, 895.

"and þa ieldestan men ealle mǽste. ðe to Bedan forda hierdon. and eac monige þara þe to Hamtúne hierdon" (and the oldest men who bylonged to Bedford, and also some of those who belonged to Hampton).—*Ibid.* 918.

But there are instances in the *Chronicle* of modern arrangement.

"Da mynte Laurentius þe ða wæs ercebiscop on Cant. he wolde súð ofer sǽ" (there intended Laurentius, who was archbisbop in Canterbury, to go southward over sea).—*Ibid.* 616

Middle English.—"þes we ahte to beon þe edmoddre . . . and þonkien hit ure drihten þe hit us lende" (the meeker ought we to be . . . and thank our Lord for it who hath given it).—*Old Eng. Hom.* i. 5.

"forðon heo ne mei abeoren alla þa sunne þe þe mon uppon hire deð" (because she may not endure all the sins that man putteth upon her).—*Ibid.*

"Nu ye habbet i-herd þo signefiance of þo offringes þet maden þo prie kinges" (now you have heard the signification of the offerings which the three kinges made).—*Old. Eng. Misc.* 28.

"Swa summ itt wollde Godd" (as God would it).—*Orm.* 749.

In *Modern English* the old use has scarcely survived; *cf.* however, the expression, "as much as in me lies."[1]

Position of the Object.

"I thee anointed king in Israel."—PEELE.

§ 460. We must distinguish between the object when a noun and when a personal pronoun.

When the object is a noun in an independent sentence, its place is, as a rule, behind the verb: "Thou gavest me my being." But there are exceptions.

---

[1] "By Richard that dead is."—1 *Henry IV.* I. 3, 146.

(*a*) The object is emphatically placed at the head of the sentence.

"*One thing* thou lackest."—*Mark*, x. 21.

(*b*) In poetry it is placed between subject and verb, especially before infinitives.

"Draw me your sword, if he *your way* withstand."—GREENE, *James II*. 210, *a*.

"I mean the wounds, which do *the heart* subdue."—*Ibid*. 212, *a*.

"*Your presence* to behold."—PEELE, *Arraignment of Paris*, 354, *a*.

§ 461. The personal pronoun as an object is not bound by this rule. In Old English its place was generally before the finite verb, as may be seen from the *Blickling Homilies* and the *Chronicle*, where more than eighty per cent. of the pronouns in the oblique case precede the verb. In Middle English prose the modern arrangement carries the day; in Modern English it is only in poetry that we meet with the old tradition.

A few instances will illustrate this use.

Middle English.—"Dere frende, god *the* yelde for the gentilnesse that thow seist to me."—*Gesta Rom.* 199.

"Holi Scripture *it* not dooth only or al oon."—PECOCK, *Repressor*, 11.

"and therfore as in that he not *hem* groundith."—*Ibid.*

"I *me* recommende ryght humbly vnto your good grace."—CAXTON, *Blanch.* 133, 18.

"I *you* supplye wyth all myn herte."—*Charles the Grete*, 49, 28.

"I *you* commande that ye cesse of this heuynes."—*Melusine*, 155, 8.

Modern English.—"The whiche syngularly not [only] *themselfe* applyed dayly to pronounce the wordes of our blyssed sauyour . . . but also the sayd doctours them endeuoyred wyth dylygent labour."—JOHN FISHER, *Eng. Works*, 1.

". . . . since that I *me* repent
Of my lost years."
                       WYATT, *Poems*, p. 2.

" or youth led me, and falsehood *me* misguided."—*Ibid.* p. 3.

PLACE OF THE ATTRIBUTIVE DETERMINANT.

Place of the Article.

"If you should need a pin,
You could not with more tame *a* tongue desire it."
Meas. for Meas. ii. 2, 46.

§ 462. The place of the indefinite article in connection with an adjective qualified by *so* was fixed at a very early date. In analogy of this use we sometimes find the indefinite article between the adjective and substantive, even when the former is qualified by other adverbs than *so*.

"It nedith not to be doubted that he is come . . . wythout that amours hathe be the cause in the persone of some hyghe *a* pryncesse."—CAXTON, *Blanchardyn*, 72, 20.

"which is the most fayr, and the most noble, and the most complete *a* lady."—*Ibid.* 156, 13.

"I would have been much more *a* fresher man."—SHAK. *Troilus and Cr.* v. 6. 20.

"What poor *an* instrument."—*Antony*, v. 2, 236.

In connection with *all, both, half*, &c., the article is placed between the adjective and the substantive from the oldest periods. Cf. *Gothic:* "Alla sa hairda" (all the troop); besides *Greek:* πᾶσαν τὴν ἀλήθειαν ἐρῶ (I shall tell the whole truth); *French:* "tout le troupeau."

Place of the Numerals.

"They pass the planets *seven*."—MILTON.

§ 463. The place of the numerals is commonly before the substantive; but the poetry of old and modern times often deviates from this rule.

Old English.—"Æþelwulfes suna *tuegen*" (Æthelwulf's two sons).—*Chronicle*, 855.

"Cómon þær scipu *six* tó Wiht" (there came six ships to Wight).—*Ibid.* 897.

"Oone God in persons *thre.*"—*Town. Myst.* p. 1.

Modern English.—"And thank the gracious ladies *three.*"—PEELE, *Arr. of Paris,* 353 b.

"Myself and children *three.*"—COWPER, *John Gilpin.*

Place of the Adjective.

"There was no reason why Lady Mabel Grex should not be *good enough* wife for the son of the Duke of Omnium."—TROLLOPE.

§ 464. From Old English down to modern times the adjective, as a rule, is placed before the noun, exceptions being only poetical licences, remnants of French phrases, &c., *e.g.,* "The Lords *spiritual,*" "The Lords *temporal,*" and adjectives preceded by adverbs, *e.g.,* "A liberty of discussion and of individual action *never before known*" (Macaulay).

§ 465. The arrangement exhibited in the last instance is being replaced, it seems, by the regular position, viz., the adjective preceding the substantive. This Modern English way of overcharging the adjectival phrases, by putting too many qualifying words between the article (or pronoun) and the substantive is frequent in Carlyle and Dickens.

"Under the to me unmeaning title."—*Sartor Resartus,* 173.

"He also informed me that our principal associate would be another boy whom he introduced by the to me extraordinary name of Mealy Potatoes."—*David Copperfield,* i. 202.

"I had still no other clothes than the anything but ornamental garments."—*Ibid.* i. 269.

"That never enough to be celebrated capture."—*Life of Frederick the Great,* 8, 7.

"It was the great, the precious, the never-to-be-sufficiently-impressed-upon-a-child Duty of Discontent."—*Such a Good Man.*

The last two instances are an imitation of "the-never-enough-to-be-celebrated knight" (Don Quixote).

There are a few instances of the same use in Pecock's *Repressor:*

"summe of the *bifore seid* men " . . . 5.
"thilk *now seid schort compendiose* logik were ful preciose."—9.
" which is the *bifore set* first principal conclusioun."—12.
"of alle these, and *alle to hem lyk* mannis witt can teche."—13.
"thouȝ ech of hem hath his *propre to him limytid* boundis."—33.

If more than two adjectives qualify the substantive, their usual place is before the substantive. But the older periods exhibit another arrangement; *cf.* "This is a *foul* custom and a *shameful.*" This occurs sometimes also in modern writers. See *Contraction*, § 472.

§ 466. *Adjectives separated from their Adverbial Determinants.*

"Bring me a constant woman to her husband."—SHAKSPERE.

This bold construction, which is well known from Shakspere, is scarcely to be found in the older periods. There are, however, a few examples in *Middle English.*

"ful fain war þai, þai sua had spedd,
þaa Kinges thre are broght to bedd,
Thre *weri* Kinges *o* þair *wai*"
= thre Kinges weary of their way.—*Cursor Mundi*, 11521.

" A louly lady on leor" (a lady lovely of face).—*Piers Plowman*, c. ii. 3.

"*holy* prestis *of lif*" = priests holy of life.—WYCLIF, *English Works*, 78.

Tudor and Elizabethan English.—"That mynyng fraude shale find no way to crepe into their *fensed* ears *with grave advise*" = ears fensed with grave advise.—*Gorboduc*, 433.

"Their *tempered* youth with *aged father's awe.*"—*Ibid.* 200.

" And *worthie* work *of infinite reward.*"—SPENSER, *F. Qu.* III. ii. 2.

" Thou *little better* thing *than earth.*"—*Rich. II.* III. iv. 77.

" As a *long-parted* mother *with her child.*"—SHAKSPERE, *Ibid.* III. ii. 8.

§ 467. *Place of the Possessive Pronoun.*

"How saidst thou, good *my* friend?"—BEAUMONT AND FLETCHER.

While in common prose the place of the possessive pronoun is after the substantive, it often occurs before in poetry and elevated style.

Old English.—"þonne bróðor þín onféng . . . fulwihtes bæð" (when thy brother received the bath of baptizement).—*Elene,* 489.

Middle English.—"Lording *myne.*"—*Gesta Rom.* 23.

"frende *myn.*"—*Ibid.* 140.

Modern English.—"Nay, sweet lady *mine.*"—BULWER, *Rienzi,* 3, 2.

The position of the possessive pronoun between the adjective and substantive, which is so frequent in Elizabethan writers, does not, it seems, outlive the eighteenth century. But it is still frequent in Richardson.

"Good *your* honour, said the well-meaning gentlewoman."—*Pamela,* 28 a.

"Good *your* ladyship."—*Ibid.* 180 b.

Cf. *ibid.* 37, *b*; 183, *a*; 183, *b*.

The following passage from Beaumont and Fletcher seems to ridicule this use.

"Good *my* lady's gentlewoman, or my good lady's gentlewoman this trope is lost to you now), leave your prating."—*The Scornful Lady,* iv. 1.

Place of the Preposition.

"The corn-sheaves whisper *the grave around.*"—HEMANS.

§ 468. As a rule, the preposition precedes the noun or pronoun to which it belongs:—round the grave, notwithstanding his faults, above us. But the exceptional arrangement of noun (pronoun) + preposition is met with in all the periods of English.

(a) The preposition is placed immediately behind the noun or pronoun.

Old English.—"Dær mon Hygelác slóh . . . *Freslondum on*" (when Hygelac was slain in Friesland).—*Beówulf*, 2358.

"Ne gefeáh he þære fǽhðe, ac he hine feor forwræc metod for þý máne *man-cynne fram*" (he did not enjoy the enmity, but the Lord removed him, for his crime, from mankind).—*Ibid.* 110.

"Júdas *hire ongen* þingode" (Judas spoke against her).—*Elene*, 667.

Middle English.—"Forði, leofe breoðre, haldeð broðerreddene *cow bitwenen*" (therefore, dear brethren, hold brotherly love among you).—*Old English Homilies*, i. 41.

"God sette ðis dai *folk bitwen*
Dai of blisse and of reste ben"
(God set this day among people to be day of bliss and rest).—*Story of Genesis and Exodus*, 251.

"He ȝaf it all for Cristes sake
þat sitteþ *us alle aboue*."—*Alexius* (ed. Schipper) i. 120.

Tudor English.—"Have they not gotten into theyre hondes more londes sins then eny duke in ynglond hath, *the statue notwithstonding?*"—SIMON FISH, *A Supplication for the Beggars*, p. 9.

"Ye know right well the greate tyme and space that I haue bene kyng of Fraunce and emperour of Rome, *the whiche tyme durynge* I have bene seruyd and obeyed of you."—LORD BERNERS, *Huon*, 3.

Modern English.
"She must lay her conscious head
A husband's trusting *heart beside*."—BYRON, *Parisina*, 5.

"She has a generous feeling towards you, your *faults notwithstanding*."—MRS. EDWARDS, *Pearl-Powder*, 94.

(b) The predicate is inserted between the noun (pronoun) and preposition.

Old English.—"Se here *him* fleáh *beforan*" (the army fled before him).—*Chronicle*, 1016.

"Drihten *him* cwæð *tó*" (the Lord said to him).—*Job*, v. 10.

Middle English.—"*Two thefys* hang thei me *bitwene*."—*Townley Myst.* p. 260.

Modern English.
"*Who* join'st thou *with* but with a lordly nation
That will not trust thee but for profit's sake."
  SHAK. *I. Henry VI.* iii. 3, 62.
"*Logic* I made no account *of.*"—SMOLLETT, *Roderick Random*, 6.

(c) *Place of the Preposition in Adjective Clauses.*

In Old English adjective clauses the place of the preposition was invariably after the indeclinable þe. This probably accounts for the Middle and Modern English use of placing the preposition after the relative pronoun, or, when this is omitted, after the substantive to which it belongs.

Old English.—"Sig se man ofslagen beforan ús eallum þe þú þine hæðenan godas *mid* finde" (the man be slain before us all with whom thou find'st thy heathen gods [idols]).—*Genesis*, xxxi. 32.

Cf. *Chronicle*, 885, 893, 904, 1070.

Middle English.—"þat Ilde þou hast *of* herd,
  Wiþ se on alle halue is sperd"
(the island which thou hast heard of is on all sides surrounded by the sea).—ROBERT DE BRUNNE, *The Story of England*, 1399.

"They that be crokyd, he xal cause hem to goo
  In the *wey* that John Baptyst *of* prophecyed."
  Coventry Mysteries, 254.

Modern English.—"To him will I give the land *that* he has trodden *upon.*"—*Deuteronomy*, i. 36.

"He ended, or I heard no more; for now
My earthly, by his heavenly overpowered,
Which it had long stood *under*, strained to the highth
In that celestial colloquy sublime."
  MILTON, *Paradise Lost*, viii. 554.

Apposition.

"Gweneuer, *the Kynges douhter Lodegrean.*"—MALORY.

§ 469. A word in apposition to a possessive genitive is, in Middle English, put after the noun governing the genitive, *e.g.*, "The kynges douhter Lodegrean" = "The kyng Lodegrean's douhter"; "For *the kynges loue of heuen*" = "The kyng of heuen's love."

This arrangement is very old, though the modern one may be found exceptionally as early as the *Chronicle* (A.D. 890).

Old English.—"for his wed bróðeres luuen Oswi" (for the love of his Christian brother Oswin).—*Chronicle*, 656.

"for Saxulfes luuen þes abbodes" (for the love of the abbot Saxulf).—*Ibid.*

Middle English.—"þur daviðes muð þe prophete" (through David's the prophet's mouth.).—*Old E. Hom.* i. 139.

"my lords sone þe emperowere."—*Guy of Warwick*, 2827.

"he saw his broders sheld syr Lyonel."—MALORY, *Morte D'Arthur*, 185, 6.

Place of the Adverbial Determinants.

"I was by Him eased of my burden."—BUNYAN.

§ 470. The place of the simple adverb has undergone no essential change; its position was perhaps more free in older periods, but on the whole it has remained the same. It is different with the adverbial phrases, as, for instance, in passive construction. A construction like that exhibited in the above-quoted instance is scarcely found in Modern English prose; in the older periods as late as the seventeenth century, this arrangement is frequently met with.

Old English.—"hér Paulinus fram Justo þam ercebisc. wæs gehádod Norþhymbrum to biscepe" (in this year Paulinus was by the archbishop Justus installed bishop to the Northumbrians).—*Chronicle*, 625.

Middle English.—"This is not sufficient cause forto *therbi thus seie* and holde."—PECOCKE, *Repressor*, 24.

"tho branchis grewen out of the bowis upon whiche they *in Bischopis wode* stoden."—*Ibid.* 28.

"So was he *by the two doughters* brought into a chambre."—CAXTON, *Blanchardyn*, 50, 21.

Tudor English.—"Water whiche of his nature is very colde is not sodeynly *by the fyre* made hote to the vttermost."—FISHER, *English Works*, 46, 35.

"he shewyd and declaryd ... the great damage that *by Huon* he had sufferyd."—LORD BERNERS, *Huon*, 388, 12.

"hyt hath plesyd me well to here you, with such phylosophycal resonys *out of nature* drawne, confyrme the same."—STARKEY, *England in the Reign of K. Henry VIII.* 21, 714.

> "Ourself, by monthly course,
> With reservation of an hundred knights
> *By you to be sustained*, shall our abode
> Make with you by due turns."—*Lear* i. 1, 132.

Arrangement of Words in Contracted Sentences.

"They were young men and strong."—BUNYAN.

"There is his country before him and its welfare."—TROLLOPE.

§ 471. Instead of saying, "the father came, and the son came," as primitive tribes still do, we use the contraction, "the father and the son came." The older periods exhibit several interesting traces of that state of the language, which takes the middle course between the primitive repetition (*anaphora*) and the modern contraction.

§ 472. 1. *Two Adjectives and one Noun.*

Old English.—"Gif ænig man hæbbe *módigne sunu and rancne*" (if a man have a refractory and rebellious son).—*Deuter.* xxi. 18. The Vulgate has: "filium contumacem et protervum."

"he gefór ... gód man and clǽne and swiðe æðele" (he died ... a good man and a pure and a very noble).—*Chronicle*, 1056.

Middle English.—"heo wulle under fon *swa heʒ þing and swa hali* swa is cristes licome" (he will receive so high and so holy a thing as is Christ's body).—*Old Engl. Hom.* i. 25.

"*Rihhtwise men and gode.*"—*Orm.* 116.

"*A young wif and a fair.*"—CHAUCER, *Marchaundes Tale*, 313.

Tudor English.—"Some *grete mater and weyghty.*"—STARKEY, *England in the Reign of King Henry VIII.*, 19.

"*A plain truth and manifest.*"—*Ibid.* 132.

"Why, sir, *an ancient lineage and a princely.*"—BEN JONSON, *Every Man in his Humour*, 5 a, (i. 4).

Modern English.—"A long road and a strange."—CARLYLE, *Frederick the Great,* iv. 426.

"A strenuous march and a well-schemed."—*Ibid.* viii. 172.

"She is a good girl, God help me, and a beautiful."—THACKERAY, *The Virginians,* iv. 8.

§ 473. 2. *Two Subjects and one Predicate.*

Old English.—"ond æfter þam Hengest féng to rice, ond Aesc his sunu" (after that Hengest succeeded to the kingdom, and Aesc his son)."—*Chronicle,* 455.

"her Aldferþ... forþferde, ond Seaxulf biscep" (in this year Aldferþ died and the bishop S.)—*Ibid.* 705.

Middle English.—"*He* suanc and swet, *and cue* his wif" (he worked and sweat, and Eve his wife).—*Cursor Mundi,* 1047.

"*Abram* went ham, *and his wijf* sare."—*Ibid.* 2437.

"Thar *loverd* liggeth, *and lavedi*" (there the lord lies and the lady).—*Owl and Nightingale,* 957.

"(He answered) that he sholde putte peyne that *his honoure* sholde be kepte, *and his body* agenst hym."—CAXTON, *Blanchardyn,* 48, 19.

Modern English instances are rare.

"*My mother* I trust be a lyue, and *a brother* of myn whom I haue left with her."—LORD BERNERS, *Huon,* 61/30.

Modern English.—"*The curate* of the parish is a gentleman, *and the medical man* who comes here from Bradstock."—TROLLOPE, *Duke's Children,* i. 95.

§ 474. 3. *One Verb and two Objects.*

Old English.—"And hie þa ymb þa gatu feohtende wǽron oþþæt hie þær inne fulgon, and *þone eþeling* ofslógon *and þa men* þe him mid wǽrun" (and they were fighting at the gates, until they got in, and slew the etheling and the men that were with him).—*Chronicle,* 755.

Middle English.—"þat bihald as of heh *alle widewen* under hire *and weddede* baðe" (that beholds as from on high all widows under her, and wedded ones too).—*Hali Meidenhad,* 5.

"*Salues* haþ he soft *and drinkes.*"—*Sir Tristrem,* 1244.

"he toke *his sone* with him, *and a sworde.*"—*Gesta Rom.* 225.

Tudor English.—"When the goode Abbot saw *hys nephew* depart, *and hys companye,* he had grete petye."—LORD BERNERS, *Huon,* 22, 9.

§ 475. 4. *One Object governed by two Verbs.*

"Her for se here of Cirenceastre on East Engle, and *gesæt* þæt lond, and *gedǽlde*" (in this year the army marched from C. to E. and invaded the country and divided [it].—*Chronicle*, 880.

Middle English.—"To *lufen* Godd and *dredenn*."—*Orm.* 852.

"To *gladenn* hire and *frofrenn*" (to gladden and support her.)—*Ibid.* 2180.

"To froffrenn himm und wissen."—*Ibid.* 10823.

"Als ye haue *sene* inogh and *herd*."—*Curs. M.* 92; cf. *ibid.* 13015, 20103.

"But yit will *I cry* for mercy and *calle*."—TOWNL. *Myst.* 21.

§ 476. *Chiastic (crosswise) Arrangement of Words.*

"for why he is god and lorde of our helth, gyuynge temporall *helth to our bodyes, and to our soules the helth* of grace in this lyfe."—JOHN FISHER, 90, 92.

This position appears not only in poetry and modern rhetorical prose, but seems to have been relished in English from the oldest times, so that the ordinary arrangement of words was often altered in favour of it even in prose.

Old English.—"Se þe God ne ongit, ne ongit God hine" (he that cares not for God, God cares not for him).—*Cura Pastoralis*, 28.

"þæt we lufien geswinc, and orsorgnesse we us ondræden" (that we love hard work, and be afraid of ease).—*Ibid.* 34.

Middle English.—"ant te þridde is meað. rightwisnesse þe feorðe" (and the third is moderation. Righteousness is the fourth).—*Old Engl. Hom.* i. 247.

"Whille lac wass offredd forr þe preost, whille forr þe biscopp offredd" (which sacrifice was offered for the priest, and which for the bishop).—*Orm.* 1132/3.

"Biforr þatt ȝho wiþþ child wass, and whil ȝho wass wiþþ childe" (before she was with child, and while she was with child).—*Ibid.* 2087, 8.

"Wisdome also hit haþ in wille
þe good to do and leue þe ille."
Cursor Mundi, 568.

"(they) spenden liȝt and oþere costis maken."—WYCLIF, *English Works*, 133.

SUMMARY AND CONCLUSION

Periods of English Syntax.

§ 477. *Internal Development of Syntax.*

The development of English syntax is, like that of English sounds, inflexions, and words, in the main due to internal causes; it is spontaneous. The reduction of Old English final *a, o, u* to the uniform *e*;—the raising of Old and Middle English long *e* to *ee*;—the decay of case-endings;—the bringing down of the two different vowels in the preterite singular and plural of strong verbs to one;—*with* supplanting *mid*, *take* coming in for *niman*—all these changes would, in all probability, have taken place, even if English had been left to itself, and had not been subject to the influence of Latin and French. The English sentence would have become what it now is, even if the Latin had not, in the sixteenth century, served to hasten its development, for the natural progress from the concrete to the abstract took place in spite of Latin and French. The Old English idiom 'before the sun going down' changed into the more abstract one 'before the going down of the sun, before sunset, although the French with its 'avant le soleil couchant' tended to preserve the old expression.—Prepositions became more and more important as case-endings tended to decay, and the Nominative supplanted the Dative in consequence of the same process. When the genitive ending began to disappear, *of* stepped in to fulfil its functions; when in the idiom "the King is woe" *the King* was no longer recognisable as a dative, a new idiom was coined "he is woe." *Cf.* § 210.—The use of *auxiliaries* to denote *tenses* and *moods* also developed spontaneously, and the gradual disappearance of the *subjunctive* took place in spite of Latin and French. *Cf.* §§ 347—359.

§ 478. *External Influences.*

Besides this principal organic development there is another of less importance, but which has given to English syntax some of its most characteristic peculiarities—I mean the external influence of foreign languages, chiefly of Latin and French. It is by no means an easy matter to say, such and such a construction is due to such and such influence, and dates from such and such a time. First, the Old English texts have not yet been sufficiently investigated; and secondly, what we find in literary language is generally only the result of a long development which has been going on for some time in the spoken language, and thus naturally escapes our observation and research. The *Objective Absolute* (§ 206), which is very frequent in the fourteenth century, is generally attributed to the influence of the French :—aloit en pelerinaige à Mahomet, *sa teste descouverte* (he went on pilgrimage to Mahomet, his head bare). Now it is true that this construction is extremely rare in Old English, but there *are* some instances, and we are not justified in saying that this idiom was forgotten and borrowed anew from the French, simply because we do not see the development in the literary language of Early Middle

English. *Cf.* § 206. We should be inclined to attribute the later and Modern English development of the *Order of Words* to French influence, and in fact there is good ground for this assumption. The Old English order of words in a sentence corresponded generally to that of German, as in the following instance from King Alfred's *Orosius*—

"ðonne þý ilcan dæge hi hine tó þæm áde beran willað, ðonne tódǽlað hi his feoh, þæt þær tó láfe bið æfter þæm gedrynce and þæm plegan, on fíf oððe syx, hwílum on má, swá swá þæs feos andefn is (then the same day [that] they him to the pile bear will, then deivid they his property that there to remainder is, after the drinking and the sports, into five or six, at times into more, according as of the property the value is)—

quoted by Dr. J. A. H. Murray in the *Encyclopaedia Britannica*, s.v. English Language, p. 392.—But long before the Norman invasion, this order of words ceased to be the rule; and in the Parker MS. of the *Chronicle* there are nearly as many instances of the French as of what we are inclined to call the German order of words. *Cf.* § 459.

Another instance. When we find "I me repent" (Caxton) we put it down as a Gallicism (*je me repens*), but the history of English syntax shows that this order of words, namely, the personal or reflexive pronoun before the verb, is the rule in the Old English, and that this rule survived as late as the sixteenth century. The development from the Old English rule to the modern usage again took place in spite of French. *Cf.* § 461.

I also object to an eminent scholar's attempt at deriving the *Omission of the Relative Pronoun* from the French. There are instances of this usage in Old English, and it is frequent in the thirteenth century; as for the gap which lies between the two periods, it is sufficiently explained by the scarcity of colloquial texts in the time of the first Norman Kings. *Cf.* § 111.

Statements with regard to *foreign idioms* are therefore more or less probable, never certain.

§ 479. *Latin Influence.*

Latin influence seems to have prevailed to a certain extent in Old English Prose. The so called *Absolute Participle* is generally assumed to be imitated from Latin. *Cf.* § 56. The Accusative with the Passive Infinitive—which is rare in other Old English writings but occurs several times in the Old English version of Bede's *Ecclesiastical History*—is probably due to Latin influence.

In Middle English, scarcely any idioms were borrowed from Latin; but in the first period of Modern English, and even in the time of Milton, Latin idioms abound in poetry and prose, and some of these have been preserved to this day.

The *Accusative with the Infinitive*, which, in Old and Middle English, was restricted to a certain number of verbs, was extended so as to have the same range as in Latin. Moreover, the Passive Infinitive became quite common. *Cf.* § 401—404.

The use of the Relative pronoun instead of the demonstrative is not found in older periods, but occurs in Elizabethan writers. *Cf.* § 122.

The plural of abstracts is often obviously an imitation of Latin models : *loves* = amores, *terror* = metus. *Cf.* § 144.

The Elizabethan peculiarity of using adjectives with both an active and passive, intransitive and causative, meaning is, in all probability, due to Latin models; *hateful*, (1) full of hate, (2) hated. *Cf.* § 251, 252.

The absolute use of the comparative in Spenser and other writers of the same period is also a Latinism : Entire affection hateth *nicer* hands = too nice. *Cf.* § 255.

In the eighteenth century Latin influence is chiefly represented in Dr. Johnson's writings, and Mr. Earle gives instances of it in prose writers of our own time. *Cf. English Prose*, p. 285.

§ 480. *French Influence.*

The most characteristic feature of English syntax after the Conquest is regularity, and even stiffness to a certain degree. Unfortunately we have little or no original prose dating from the twelfth century; but when we compare Orm's or even Layamon's verse (Layamon is certainly more faithful to the national tradition than Orm) with that of Cynewulf or Ælfric, the contrast, also from a syntactical point of view, is striking. The order of words, in the old national poetry, is nearly as free as that of Virgil or Horace; in Orm and Robert of Gloucester strict order of a nearly modern character is observed. Read the first ten lines of Cynewulf's *Elene:*

"ðá wæs ágangen, ʒeára hwyrflum
tú hund and þreó geteled rímes
swylce xxx eác þingʒemearces
wintra for worulde, þæs þe wealdend god
ácenned wearð cyninga wuldor
in middanʒeard þurh mennisc heó,
sóðfæstra leóht, þá wæs syxte ʒeár
Constantínes cáserdómes
þæt he Rómwara in ríce wearð
áhafen hildfruma tó heretéman."

(There was gone in the years' course two hundred and three, told by number, also thirty, in order, of winters for the world, since ruling God born was, the Kings' splendour, into the earth in human shape, of the faithful the light, there was the sixth year of Constantine's reign, that he of the Romans in the empire [in the empire of the Romans] was raised, the warrior, to general). [1]

---

[1] Literal translation.

Compare with this Orm, in his first Homily (lines 109—118):—

> " An preost was onn Herodess da₃₃
> Amang Judisskenn þeode,
> & he wass, wiss to fulle soþ,
> ȝehatenn Zacariȝe,
> & haffde an duhhtiȝ wif, þatt wass
> off Aaroness dohhtress ;
> & ȝho wass, wiss to fulle soþ,
> Elysabæþ ȝehatenn.
> & teȝȝ wæren biforenn Godd
> Rihhtwise menn & gode."

(A priest was in Herod's day among the Jewish people, and he was, certainly in full truth, called Zacharias, and had a good wife, that was of Aaron's daughters ; and she was, certainly in full truth, called Elizabeth. And they were before God righteous men and good.)

The "innate love of order and regularity, sobriety and economy," which was peculiar to the Conquerors (Thomas Duffus Hardy, *Descriptive Catalogue of Materials relating to the History of Great Britain and Ireland*, Vol. II., from A.D. 1066 to A.D. 1200, p. xvii.) seems to have communicated itself to the English writers of the thirteenth century,

Besides the new order of words, French influence introduced a great number of new phrases and idioms, such as "he came to the above of his enemies" = he got the better of his enemies (French: venir au-dessus de quelqu'un); "as who would say" (French : comme qui dirait) etc.

But the influence of French on *Syntax Proper* has been over-rated. English syntax, in the main, is still Germanic, just as English sounds, inflexions, and word-formation are.

In the following details French influence may be assumed with much probability.

The so-called *Absolute Constructions* are due, to a certain extent, to French.

The Nominative Absolute.

"They failing I must die your debtor."

Cf. § 153.

The Infinitive Absolute.

"I am content that any man amend it, or, if I have said too little, *any man that will, to add* what him pleaseth to it."—ASCHAM, *Toxophilus*, p. 17.

The Adjective Clause used as a conditional one was hardly known in Old English.

"Who touches pitch, will be defiled."

Cf. § 133.

The Possessive Pronoun has, in some cases, supplanted the personal one. We say in Modern English (as in French) "he had in *his* hand fire and sword"; in Old English it was put differently:—"he hæfde him on handa fýr and swurd." *Cf.* § 313.

The use of the Possessive Pronoun in "My Lord," "My Lady" is probably also due to French. *Cf.* § 306.

Verbs used both as intransitives and causatives can be explained without any external influence, cf. § 339 *seq.*; yet the same use, which was frequent in Old French, may have favoured the development of the English verb in that direction. The following verbs were, and are still, used both as intransitives and transitives: abîmer (to sink), amender (to mend), approcher (to approach), arrêter (to stay, to stop), assembler (to gather), augmenter (to increase), briser (to break), changer (to change), clore (to close, to shut), dériver (to derive), descendre (to go down, to put down), diminuer (to decrease), épandre (to spread), étouffer (to choke) fléchir (to bow), fondre (to melt), guérir (to cure, to recover), hausser (to raise, to rise), joindre (to join), monter (to mount), pousser (to push, to sprout), etc.

The development of the Gerund shows marked traces of French influence. There are Middle English instances which show that, in certain cases, people did not know whether they ought to translate French idioms by a verbal noun or a participle present. *Cf.* the following instances from Dan Michel's *Ayenbite :*—Guo into helle ine þine *libbinde,* þet þou ne guo ine þine *steruinge,* p. 73. French : en ton vivant, en ton morant. Bearing in mind the Old English construction "be him lifiendum " = in his life-time, § 411, we cannot but assume that the Possessive Pronoun with the Verbal Noun is due to the French. *Cf.* § 309 and my *Introduction to Caxton's Blanchardyn and Eglantine,* § 8, c.

In some points in which Middle English favoured the French, Modern English has returned to the old Germanic construction.

In the fifteenth century we find " he toke *the his*" (French : le sien). *Cf.* § 222.

The which was quite common even in the first period of Modern English (French : lequel).

The idiom " hwat he is good " = how good he is (French : qu'il est bon), was frequent in the fourteenth century, but was scarcely ever used in the spoken language.

Without as a conjunction occurs in Middle English, and did not die out before the end of the sixteenth century.

"Takith ensaumple...that ye turne not youre hede hedirward and thedirward, *withoute ye turne* the body with."—*Knight of La Tour-Landry,* p. 17.

"*Without* you were so simple, none else would."—SHAKSPERE, *The Two Gentlemen of Verona,* II. 1, 38.

Bishop Fisher, *English Works,* p. 89 ; Berners, *Huon de Burdeux,* p. 37.

For other points, see § 224, 254, 309.

PERIODS OF ENGLISH SYNTAX.

§ 481. The results at which we have arrived in dealing historically with English Syntax enable us to draw marked lines between the three great periods of English, and to give, from the point of syntax, the chief characteristics of Old, Middle, and Modern English.

§ 482. I. OLD ENGLISH (A.D. 500—1200).

(1) Old English syntax is, on the whole, genuinely Germanic, and not yet influenced by any other language. There were, however, attempts at introducing Latin constructions, made chiefly by prose-writers, or rather translators (see § 479), and further investigation will perhaps trace back certain idioms to Danish sources.

(2) The order of words is, in poetry, very free, and, in prose, nearly the same as in Modern German. In clauses the verb is often placed at the end, and dependent sentences are often marked by the inverted order of words (see §457, and 459). The Pronoun-Object is placed before the verb (§ 461).

(3) Concrete constructions are frequent (see § 12, 13, 20—24).

(4) The structure of sentences is in its infancy; co-ordination is frequent, conjunctions are not always made use of in connecting sentences and clauses (§ 96—103).

(5) The noun-clauses are still redundant, as in the phrase "he saw the light that it was good" (§ 104—106).

(6) The adjective-clause is (from a modern point of view) wanting in unity and apt to be tautological (§ 109—113).

(7) The *cases* are strictly synthetic: their functions are expressed by the case-endings.

(8) The genitive has a very wide application (§ 158).

(9) The indefinite article is hardly beginning to develop out of the numeral (§ 225).

(10) Any adjective can be used substantively (§ 237—248).

(11) The personal pronoun as subject is frequently omitted (§ 268—273).

(12) *Thou* is the only pronoun used from one person to another, no matter whether from superiors to inferiors, or the reverse (§ 277).

(13) *Self* is used adjectively and appositively only:—ic self (I myself), we seolfe (we ourselves) (§ 291).

(14) Intransitive and transitive verbs are strictly kept apart with regard to meaning :—*sincan* (to sink) is clearly distinguished from, and never interchanged with, *sencan* (to cause to sink) (§ 340—342).

(15) The use of the auxiliary *to be* is restricted to intransitive verbs, as in Modern German (§ 348).

(16) The present tense is also used for the future (§ 367), and the preterite for the pluperfect.

(17) The subjunctive mood has about the same range as in Latin (§ 380—391).

(18) The simple infinitive prevails. (§ 392—393, 401).

(19) The preposition of the agent in passive constructions is *fram* (from), exceptionally *of* (§ 433—434).

§ 483. II. MIDDLE ENGLISH (A.D. 1200—1500).

The inflexions (noun and verbal endings) tending to decay, language introduces new means to supply the old functions.

This is the chief characteristic of Middle English syntax.

The following changes are due to this principle.

(1) When the dative-ending was dropped, the nominative and dative became alike; hence substantives which were objects were mistaken for subjects. In the phrase "Wo wes Brutus þer fore," Brutus was originally a dative-object; but there being no dative-ending to mark it as such, it was

looked upon as a nominative-subject. This accounts for the gradual decrease in the number of *Impersonal Verbs* (§ 151, 337).

(2) The passive of intransitive verbs is due to the same cause:—"*Our Lord be thanked*" was quite correct, *our Lord* being a dative; but in analogy to this seeming nominative was formed "we are thanked," "we are answered" (§ 152, 363).

(3) In such instances as "Good is therefore a man to hide his pride" (Gower, *Confessio Amantis*, I., 131), we look upon *a man* as an accusative or nominative; but in Old English it was the dative

See § 70, 405.

(4) The nominative in absolute construction ("*he* being there, I retired") was also originally an oblique case.

(5) Such constructions as "*he was bound, hand and foot*" come under this head. In Matthew (Old English) xxii. 13 we read: *gebindað him fét and honda*, where *him* is of course a dative, *fét and honda* accusatives. In Middle English, when *him* had absorbed the function of the accusative *hine*, the word *him*, in the instance quoted was mistaken for an accusative; hence we have: *he wolde me binden, hond and fet.—Havelok*, 1916; (*he* was) al to-brised, bac and þe (he was bruised, back and thigh).—Ibid. 1950. *I am heavy, heed and foote.—Coventry Mysteries*, 170.

(6) As soon as the case-endings began to decay, prepositions came in to take their place:—*of* (like French *de*) stands for the genitive, *to* for the dative, *with* for the instrumental (§ 427–432).

(7) Juxtaposition instead of the partitive genitive is, to a certain extent, due to the decay of the genitive-endings (§ 174).

(8) The strictly observed order of words (subject + predi-

cate + object) is partly due to the desire of making up for the want of visible marks of subject and object.

(9) The gradual weakening of verbal endings is followed by the gradual decay of the subjunctive mood (§ 380—391), and

(10) The importance of auxiliaries increases (§ 347).

(11) The dropping of the final *e* in adverbs pulls down to a great extent the old boundary line between adjectives and adverbs (§ 422—423).

Other characteristics of Middle English syntax are :—

(12) " It is I " instead of the older expression " it *am* I." (§ 79).

(13) Substantives used adjectively :—

"I have a *pris* presant, to plese wiþ þi hert" (I have a valuable present to please thy heart with).
WILLIAM OF PALERNE, 411.

Cf. þat *choys* child. *Ibid.* 399, 400 (§ 135).

(14) The pseudo-partitive genitive : "*a friend of his*" (§ 180).

(15) The objective absolute :

"Hii come barefoot, hor heued bar þerto" (they come barefoot, their heds, moreover, uncovered).
ROBERT OF GLOUCESTER, 10827.

(§ 206).

(16) Comparison of the adjective by means of *more* and *most;* double comparison (§ 254).

(17) Substantives followed by *one* (§ 256).

(18) "*Him one*" = he alone, "*his one*" (same meaning) are peculiar to Middle English.

(19) The plural of courtesy *ye*, later *you*, instead of Old English *thou*, is met with in the thirteenth century (§ 277).

(20) *Myself, thyself*, instead of Old English *ic self, þu self*,

or *me self*, *þe self*, appear in the first half of the thirteenth century (§ 290—298).

(21) Omission of the relative pronoun, which occurs rarely in Old English, becomes quite a feature of English at the end of the thirteenth century (§ 109).

(22) Verbs are used indiscriminately as intransitives, reflexives, and causatives (§ 340—346).

(23) The auxiliaries *can* (*gan*), and *do* are used redundantly (§ 353).

(24) The passive use of the infinitive comes in (§ 365).

(25) The gerundial infinitive tends to restrict the simple one (§ 392); *for*, and *for to* with the infinitive (§ 395).

(26) The absolute infinitive is introduced (§ 396—400).

(27) The gerund absorbs the functions of the verbal noun and the present participle (§ 416—417).

28) Adjectives are used instead of adverbs (§ 423).

§ 484. III. *Modern English* (A.D. 1500—Present).

The most characteristic feature of Modern English syntax is *perfection in the structure of sentences*.

Both Old and Middle English sentences are wanting in unity and proportion; in Modern English both are attained, favoured, in all probability, by the models of Greek and Latin prose-works (§ 8, 97).

This perfection of structure appears in several details.

(1) Anacoluthic sentences disappear (§ 8).

(2) Direct and indirect speech are strictly kept apart (§ 108).

(3) In adjective clauses, the redundunt personal pronoun, which was frequent, not to say the rule, in Old and Middle English, is dropped (§ 112—119). Such sentences as "The land *that* they hold, give *it* to Charles" (§ 117) got out of use.

(4) The double negative which was common in Old and Middle English, and still frequent in Elizabethan writers, was given up in the seventeenth century, and is now considered vulgar.

(5) The concord between subject and predicate is strictly observed (§ 84—89).

(6) The sequence of tenses is regulated by the Latin rule. Principal tenses depend on principal tenses; historical on historical (§ 371—375).

(7) The well-constructed period is of comparatively recent date.

Other characteristics of Modern English syntax are :—

(8) The accusative with the infinitive preceded by *for* :— "*It is better for a sinner to suffer tribulation*" (§ 71).

(9) *With* preceding the (once absolute) participle : "*With the enemy invading our country, it was my duty to go on the campaign*" (§ 154). The beginning of this innovation reaches back to the end of the fourteenth century. "Alle þe prisoneres schulde folwe þe chaar *wiþ hire hondes i-bounde* byhynde her bakkes" (Latin original : ligatis post terga manibus).—Trevisa, *Higden's Polychronicon*, I. 239.

(10) Such constructions as "*What occupation are you?*" are scarcely to be met with before the sixteenth century (§ 136—442).

(11) The oblique case supplanting the nominative may be traced back to the last period of Middle English, but it does not become common before the sixteenth century.

(*a*) *You* instead of *ye* (§ 212).

(*b*) It is *me* (§ 214).

(12) Adjectives used indiscriminately with active and passive, transitive and intransitive meaning (§ 249—251).

(13) *One* used after adjectives which refer to preceding

nouns occurs here and there in Middle English, but it is not established before the seventeenth century (§ 256).

(14) *Themselves* comes in in the first half of the sixteenth century (§ 300).

(15) *What* used adjectively = *qualis* is of recent date (§ 326).

(16) *Who* as a relative, although there are instances as early as the tenth and twelfth centuries, does not become general before the sixteenth century (§ 336).

(17) The auxiliary *do* is restricted to emphatic interrogative and negative phrases (§ 352).

(18) The idiom "*I am going, writing,*" etc. comes to be generally used in Modern English.

(19) The tendency to restrict the subjunctive, which appears already in Middle English, goes so far as nearly to get rid of it altogether (§ 376, 380—391).

(20) The accusative with the infinitive (as object) develops rapidly in the time of Queen Elizabeth (§ 402—404).

(21) "*The house is building*" is a sixteenth century growth, and "The house is being built" of a still more recent date (§ 415).

(22) "*Would you mind* me *asking a few questions?*" "*We have no right* to be hurt *at a* girl *telling me what my faults are.*"

These idioms, although very old, had become obsolete and were introduced again into literary language about the middle of our century (§ 419).

(23) Such idioms as "*rambling passion,*" "*undergoing stomach*" were developed in Shakspere's time (§ 420).

(24) The tendency to be terse and curt is characteristic of the English prose of our own time. This tendency appears in several sorts of omission.

(*a*) The copula *to be* is, as a rule, omitted in such expressions as "*no matter,*" "*no doubt,*" etc.

(*b*) "It was *no use* trying" is now very common; in older authors we always find "It was *of no use*."

(*c*) "*She sat down*, Turkish fashion" (§ 442).

(*d*) "*He will go, though I advise him not* to." This ellipsis is of a very recent date, and is getting fast into literary language.

LIST OF ENGLISH TEXTS QUOTED IN THIS BOOK.

I. Old English.

Ælfred, King—
    (1) The oldest English version of Bede's Ecclesiastical History, Ed. Dr. T. Miller. Early English Text Society, 1890, 1891. (Attributed, probably falsely, to Alfred.)
    (2) King Alfred's Anglo-Saxon version of Boethius, de Consolatione Philosophiæ, with an English Translation and Notes. Ed. Fox (Bohn's Library). London, 1864. A.D. ab. 888.
    (3) King Alfred's Orosius. Ed. H. Sweet. Early English Text Society, 1884. A.D. ab. 893.
    (4) West-Saxon version of Gregory's Pastoral Care. Ed. H. Sweet. E.E.T.S., 1872. A.D. ab. 897.

Ælfric, Abbot—
    (1) Genesis. Ed. Grein (Bibliothek der angelsächsischen Prosa. Erster Band, 1872). A.D. ab. 1000.
    (2) Exodus. *Ibid.*
    (3) The Homilies of Ælfric, with an English Translation. Ed. Benj. Thorpe. Ælfric Society, 1843, 1845. A.D. ab. 1000.
    (4) Ælfric's Metrical Lives of Saints. Ed. Rev. Prof. Skeat. E.E.T.S., 1881, 1886, 1890. A.D. ab. 1000.

Andreas, Ed. Grein (Bibliothek der angelsächsischen Poesie). A.D. ab. 1000.

Apollonius of Tyre. Ed. Benj. Thorpe, London, 1834. A.D. ab. 1000.

Basil, Hexameron. Ed. Norman. A.D. ab. 1000.
Beda, see Ælfred.
Beowulf. Ed. M. Heyne. Paderborn, 1879. A.D. ab. 1000.
Blickling Homilies. Ed. Rev. Dr. R. Morris. E. E. T. S., 1874, 1876, 1880. A.D. 971.
Boethius, see Ælfred.
Byrhtnoth. Ed. Grein. Bibl. der ags. Poesie. A.D. 991.

Cædmon (?), Genesis, Exodus. Ed. Grein, *Ibid.* A.D. ab. 1000.
Chronicle. Two of the Saxon Chronicles parallel. Ed. with Introduction, Notes, and a Glossarial Index. T. Earle, 1865. Parker M.S. A.D. 905.

Cura Pastoralis, see Ælfred.
Cynewulf—
    (1) Crist. Ed. Grein, Bibl. der ags. Poesie. A.D. 730-750.
    (2) Juliana. *Ibid.* A.D. 730-750.
    (3) Elene. Ed. Zupitza. A.D. ab. 750.

Lindisfarne Gospels. Ed. Skeat (The Holy Gospels in Anglo-Saxon, Northumbrian, and Old Mercian Versions synoptically arranged) Cambridge, 1871-1887. A.D. ab. 1000.

Orosius, see Ælfred.

Salomon and Saturn. Ed. Grein, Bibl. der ags. Poesie. A.D. ab. 1000.

Wulfstan, Homilies. Ed. A. Napier. Berlin, 1883.

II. Middle English.

Alexius. Alexiuslegende, herausgegeben von J. Schipper (Quellen und Forschungen). A.D. ab. 1340.
Alisaunder. King Alisaunder. Ed. Weber (Metrical Romances, I.). A.D. ab. 1300.
Amadas. Ed. Weber (*Ibid.* III.). A.D. ab. 1440.
Ancren Riwle. Ed. T. Morton. Camden Society. A.D. ab. 1225.
Ayenbite. Dan Michel's Ayenbite of Inwyt. Ed. R. Morris E.E.T.S., 1866. A.D. 1340.
Aymon, see Caxton.

Beves of Hampton. Ed. E. Kölbing, E.E.T.S. 1885-6. A.D. 1350.
Blanchardyn, see Caxton.
Boece, see Chaucer.

Caxton, William—
    (1) The Foure Sonnes of Aymon. Ed. Octavia Richardson. E.E.T.S., 1884, 1885. A.D. ab. 1489.
    (2) Blanchardyn and Eglantine. Ed. L. Kellner. E.E.T.S., 1890. A.D. ab. 1489.
    (3) Book of Curtesye. Ed. F. J. Furnivall, E.E.T.S., 1868. A.D. ab. 1478.
    (4) Charles the Grete. Ed. S. J. Herrtage, E.E.T.S., 1880, 1881. A.D. ab. 1485.
    (5) Alain Chartier's Curial. Ed. F. J. Furnivall, and Paul Meyer. E.E.T.S., 1888. A.D. ab. 1484.
    (6) Eneydos. Ed. M. T. Culley and F. J. Furnivall. E.E.T.S., 1890. A.D. ab. 1490.
    (7) Prologues and Epilogues. Ed. Blades in "The Life and Typography of William Caxton." London, 1861, 1863.

LIST OF ENGLISH TEXTS QUOTED

Chaucer, Geoffrey, Poetical Works. Ed. R. Morris, 1866.
   (1) Boke of the Duchesse. A.D. ab. 1369.
   (2) Canterbury Tales. A.D. ab. 1386.
   (3) House of Fame. A.D. ab. 1384.
   (4) Legend of Good Women. A.D. ab. 1385.
   (5) Troylus and Cryseide. A.D. ab. 1374.
Chaucer, Boece. Ed R. Morris, E.E.T.S. and Chaucer Society, 1866. A.D. ab. 1374.
Coventry Mysteries. Ed. J. O. Halliwell, 1844. A.D. ab. 1468.
Cursor Mundi. Ed. R. Morris, E.E.T.S., 1874-1878. A.D. ab. 1300.

Ferumbras, Sir. Ed. S. J. Herrtage, E.E.T.S., 1879. A.D. ab. 1380.

Gamelyn. The Coke's Tale of Gamelyn (Chaucer's Works, Canterbury Tales). A.D. ab. 1400.
Gawayne, Sir, and the Green Knight. Ed. R. Morris, E.E.T.S., 1864. A.D. ab. 1360.
Gesta Romanorum. Ed. S. J. Herrtage, E.E.T.S., 1879. A.D. ab. 1440.
Gilds. English Gilds, their Statutes and Customs, 1389, A.D. Ed. Toulmin Smith, and Miss L. T. Smith. E.E.T.S. 1870.
Gower's Confessio Amantis. Ed. R. Pauli, 1860. A.D. ab. 1393.
Guy of Warwick, 15th century Version. Ed. J. Zupitza, E.E.T.S. 1873, 1876. A.D. ab. 1440.

Hali Meidenhad. Ed. O. Cockayne, E.E.T.S., 1866. A.D. ab. 1230.
Hampole, Richard Rolle de Hampole—
   (1) Prick of Conscience. Ed. R. Morris, Philological Soc. 1863. A.D. ab. 1340.
   (2) Prose Treatises. Ed. G. G. Perry, E.E.T.S., 1866. A.D. ab. 1350.
Havelok the Dane. Ed. W. Skeat, E.E.T.S., 1868. A.D. 1280 (or 1300).
Horn, King. Ed. J. R. Lumby. E.E.T.S., 1868. A.D. 1250.

Ipomadon. Ed. E. Kölbing. Breslau, 1889. A.D. 1340.

Knight of La Tour Landry. Ed. T. Wright, E.E.T.S., 1868. A.D. 1440.

Layamon. Ed. Madden, 1847. Text A ab. 1205. Text B. ab. 1275.
Legendary. Early English Verse Lives of Saints (earliest version) Ed. C. Horstmann. E.E.T.S. 1887. A.D. 1290.

Malory, Morte Darthur. Ed. O. H. Sommer. London, 1889, A.D.
Manning, see Robert de Brunne.

Y

Marherete, Seinte. Ed. O. Cockayne. E.E.T.S., 1866. A.D. 1220.
Maundeville. The Voiage and Travaile of Sir John Maundeville. Ed. T. O. Halliwell, 1839. A.D. 1400.
Melusine, the prose Romance. Ed. A. K. Donald, E.E.T.S. A.D. 1500.

Old English Homilies and Homiletic Treatises of the 12th and 13th centuries. Ed. R. Morris, E.E.T.S., I. 1867. II. 1868. Second Series 1873. A.D. 1150–1230.
Old English Miscellany, containing a Bestiary, Kentish Sermons, Proverbs of Alfred, and Religious Poems of the 13th century. Ed. R. Morris, E.E.T.S., 1872. A.D. 1200–1270.
Orm. The Ormulum by Ormin. Ed. White-Holt, 1878. A.D. 1200.
Owl and Nightingale. An Old English Poem of the Owl and Nightingale. Ed. F. H. Stratmann, 1868. A.D. ab. 1225.

Pecock, Reginald, The Repressor of Over Much Blaming the Clergy. Ed. Churchill Babington, 1860 (Rerum Britannicarum Medii Aevi Scriptores). A.D. 1449.
Piers, Plowman. The Vision of William (Langland) concerning Piers the Plowman. Ed. W. W. Skeat, E.E.T.S., 1867–85. A-Text ab. 1362, B-Text 1377, and C-Text 1393.
Poema Morale (contained in Old English Homilies, Old English Miscellany, Zupitza's Lesebuch, and lastly ed. by Levin). A.D. 1200.

Richard Cœur de Lion. Ed. Weber, Metrical Romances, II. A.D. ab. 1330.
Robert de Brunne—
   (1) Peter Langtoft's Chronicle, as illustrated and improved by Robert of Brunne. Ed. Th. Hearne, Oxford, 1725. A.D. 1330.
   (2) The Story of England by Robert Manning of Brunne. Ed. F. J. Furnivall, 1887. (Rerum Brit. Medii Aevi Scriptores.) A.D. 1338.
Robert of Gloucester, The Metrical Chronicle of. Ed. William Aldis Wright, 1887. (*Ibid.*). A.D. 1297.
Romaunt of the Rose (falsely attributed to Chaucer, and therefore printed in Chaucer's Poetical Works. Ed. Morris). A.D. ab. 1408.

Sawles Warde (in Old English Homilies, II.). A.D. ab. 1235.
Seuyn Sages. Ed. Weber, Metr. Romances, III. A.D. ab. 1320.

Townley Mysteries. Ed. Surtees Society, 1836. A.D. ab. 1450.
Trevisa. Polychronicon Ranulphi Higden, together with the English Translation of John Trevisa. Ed. Churchill Babington and R. Lumby, 1865–86. (Rer. Brit. Medii Aevi Scriptores.) A.D. ab. 1387.

Tristram. Die Nordische und Englische Version der Tristansage, herausgegeben von E. Kölbing. Heilbronn, 1883. A.D. ab. 1320.

William of Palerne. Ed. Skeat, E.E.T.S., 1867. A.D. ab. 1340.
Wills—
   (1) Wills and Inventories from the Register of the Commissary of Bury St. Edmunds. Ed. S. Tymms, 1850. Camden Society. A.D. 1380-1450.
   (2) The 50 Earliest English Wills in the Court of Probate. Ed. Furnivall, E.E.T.S., 1882. A.D. 1387-1439.
Wohunge of Ure Lauerd (in Old English Homilies, II.). A.D. ab. 1240.
Wyclif—
   (1) The English Works of John Wyclif, hitherto unprinted. Ed. F. D Mathew, E.E.T.S., 1880. A.D. ab. 1380.
   (2) The Holy Bible in the earliest English versions made from the Latin Vulgate by John Wycliffe and his followers. Ed. Forshall and Madden, 1850. A.D. ab. 1380.

York Plays. Ed. Miss L. T. Smith, 1885. A.D. ab. 1430.

III. MODERN ENGLISH.

Addison—
   (1) Cato. A.D. 1713.
   (2) Essays. Ed. J. R. Green. London, 1880. A.D. ab. 1711.
Arcadia, see Sidney.
Ascham, Roger—
   (1) Toxophilus. Ed. Arber. A.D. 1545.
   (2) The Schoolmaster. Ed. Arber. A.D.
Austen, Jane. Pride and Prejudice. A.D. 1813.

Bacon, Advancement of Learning. Ed. Skeat. A.D. 1605.
Beaumont and Fletcher, Works. Ed. George Darley. London, 1839.
   (1) The Scornful Lady. A.D. 1609.
   (2) The Faithful Shepherdess (by Fletcher). A D. 1610.
Ben Jonson, Works. Ed. W. Gifford. London, 1838.
   (1) Every Man in his Humour. A.D. 1598.
   (2) Cynthia's Revels. A.D. 1600.
   (3) The Poetaster. A.D. 1601.
Berners, Lord—
   (1) Froissart's Chronicles. A.D. 1523, 1525.
   (2) The History of the moost noble and valyaunt Knight, Arthur of Lyttil Brytaine. A.D. 1533.
   (3) Huon of Bordeaux Ed. S. L. Lee, E.E.T.S., 1882-1887. A.D. 1534.

Besant and Rice –
    (1) Ready Money Mortiboy.
    (2) The Monks of Thelema.
    (3) Such a Good Man.
Boorde, Andrew—
    (1) Dyatary of Health. Ed. Furnivall, E.E.T.S., 1869. A.D. 1542.
    (2) Introduction of Knowledge. *Ibid.* A.D. 1547.
Braddon, Miss. Ishmael. A.D. 1885.
Bulwer—
    (1) Pelham. A.D. 1828.
    (2) Rienzi. A.D. 1835.
    (3) Money. A.D. 1840.
Bunyan, John, The Pilgrim's Progress. London, Nimmo, 8vo. A.D. 1684.
Butler, Samuel, Hudibras. Ed. H. Morley. A.D. 1678.
Byron, Lord—
    (1) English Bards and Scotch Reviewers. A.D. 1809.
    (2) Bride of Abydos. A.D. 1813.
    (3) Childe Harold (IV.). A.D. 1818.
    (4) Cain. A.D. 1817.

Carlyle, Thomas—
    (1) Sartor Resartus. A.D. 1831.
    (2) French Revolution. A.D. 1837.
    (3) Heroes and Hero-Worship. A.D. 1841.
    (4) Frederick the Great. A.D. 1865.
Clyomon, Sir, and Sir Clamydes (attributed to Peele). Ed. Al. Dyce in Peele's Works. A.D. 1599(?).
Coleridge, S. T. Wallenstein. A.D. 1800.
Cowper, Works. Globe Edition.

Defoe, Daniel, Robinson Crusoe. A.D. 1719.
Dickens, Charles—
    (1) Chimes. A.D. 1844.
    (2) Christmas Carol. A.D. 1843.
    (3) Cricket on the Hearth. A.D. 1845.
    (4) David Copperfield. A.D. 1849–1850.
    (5) Pickwick Papers. A.D. 1836.
    (6) Sketches. A.D. 1836.

Drayton, Michael, Polyolbion. A.D. 1613.
Dryden, John, Poetical Works. London, Macmillan.

Edgeworth, Maria, Popular Tales. A.D. 1832.
Eliot, George, Silas Marner. A.D. 1861.

Fielding, Henry, Joseph Andrews. A.D. 1742.

Fisher. Bishop Fisher's English Works. Ed. J. E. B. Mayor. E.E.T.S. 1876. A.D. 1509.
Fletcher, see Beaumont and Fletcher.

Gammer Gurton's Needle. Ed. Dodsley-Hazlitt. A.D. 1575.
Gay, John, Beggar's Opera. A.D. 1727.
Gascoigne, George, The Steel-Glasse. Ed. Arber. A.D. 1576.
Goldsmith, Oliver—
    (1) She Stoops to Conquer. A.D. 1773.
    (2) The Vicar of Wakefield. A.D. 1766.
Greene, Robert. Ed. Al. Dyce (The Dramatic and Poetical Works of Robert Greene and George Peele), London, 1861.
    (1) Alphonsus, King of Arragon. A.D. ab. 1599.
    (2) Friar Bacon and Friar Bungay. A.D. ab. 1592.
    (3) George-a-Greene, the Pinner of Wakefield. A.D. ab. 1593.
    (4) James the Fourth. A.D. 1592.
    (5) A Looking-Glass for London and England. A.D. ab. 1593.
    (6) Orlando Furioso. A.D. 1591.

Irving, Washington—
    (1) Bracebridge Hall; or, the Humourists. A.D. 1822.
    (2) The Life and Voyages of Christopher Columbus. A.D. 1828.

John Halifax, Gentleman. A.D. 1857.

Knowles, Sheridan, The Hunchback. A.D. 1834.

Latimer, Hugh, Sermons on the Card. Ed. H. Morley. A.D. 1555.
Lewes, George Henry, Life and Works of Goethe. A.D. 1855.
Lodge, Thomas, The Wounds of Civil War. Ed. Dodsley-Hazlitt. A.D. ab. 1590.
Lyly, John. Euphues, Ed. Landmann (Englische Neudrucke, Heilbronn). A.D. 1580.

Macaulay, Lord. History of England. A.D. 1848.
Marlowe, Christopher. Ed. Al. Dyce. London, 1858.
    (1) The Tragedy of Dido, Queen of Carthage. A.D. ab. 1586(?)
    (2) Edward II. A.D. ab. 1592.
    (3) The Tragical History of Dr. Faustus. Ed. Breymann, (Englische Neudrucke). A.D. 1590.
    (4) The Jew of Malta. Ed. Alb. Wagner (Engl. Neudrucke). A.D. 1592.
    (5) Tamburlaine the Great. Ed. Alb. Wagner (*Ibid.*) First Part A.D. 1587. Second Part 1590.
Massinger, Philip. A New Way to Pay old Debts. Ed. Hartley Coleridge (The Dramatic Works of Massinger and Ford), London, 1839. A.D. ab. 1633.
Milton, John, Paradise Lost. A.D. 1667.
Mucedorus. Ed. Dodsley-Hazlitt. A.D. ab. 1598.

Payn, James, Found Dead.
Peele, George. Ed. Al. Dyce. See Greene.
    (1) The Arraignment of Paris. A.D. ab. 1584.
    (2) The Battle of Alcazar. A.D. ab. 1591.
    (3) The Old Wives' Tale. A.D. ab. 1594.
Pepys's Diary. Ed. Lord Braybrooke. A.D. 1659-62.
Pope, Alexander. Ed. William Roscoe, London, 1824.
    (1) Essay on Man. A.D. 1732.
    (2) Universal Prayer.
Puttenham, George, The Arte of English Poesie. Ed. Arber. A.D. 1589.

Ralph Royster Doyster. Ed. Dodsley-Hazlitt. A.D. 1553.
Reade, Charles. A Terrible Temptation.
Richardson, Samuel, Pamela; or, Virtue Rewarded. Ed. Ballantyne's Novelist's Library. Vol. VI. A.D. 1741.

Scott, Sir Walter.
    (1) Guy Mannering. A.D. 1815.
    (2) The Lady of the Lake. A.D. 1810.
    (3) The Lay of the Last Minstrel. A.D. 1805.
    (4) Marmion. A.D. 1808.
    (5) Rob Roy. A.D. 1818.
Shakespeare, William Globe Edition—
    (1) Antony and Cleopatra. A.D. 1606.
    (2) As You Like It. A.D. 1600.
    (3) All's Well that Ends Well. A.D. 1601.
    (4) Comedy of Errors. A.D. 1590.
    (5) Hamlet. A.D. 1602.
    (6) King Henry VI. First Part. A.D. 1590(?)
    (7) King Henry VI. Second Part. A.D. 1591
    (8) King Henry VI. Third Part. A.D. 1593.
    (9) King Henry IV. First Part. A.D. 1596.
    (10) King Henry IV. Second Part. A.D. 1597.
    (11) King Henry V. A.D. 1599.
    (12) King Henry VIII. A.D. 1613.
    (13) King John. A.D. 1595.
    (14) Julius Caesar. A.D. 1601.
    (15) King Lear. A.D. 1605.
    (16) Love's Labour's Lost. A.D. 1588.
    (17) Lucrece. A.D. 1593.
    (18) Macbeth. A.D. 1605.
    (19) Measure for Measure. A.D. 1604 (?).
    (20) Merchant of Venice. A.D. 1596.
    (21) Merry Wives of Windsor. A.D. 1598.
    (22) A Midsummer Night's Dream. A.D. 1590.
    (23) Much Ado about Nothing. A.D. 1599.
    (24) Othello. A.D. 1604.
    (25) Pericles. A.D. 1608.

(26) King Richard II. A.D. 1593.
   (27) King Richard III. A.D. 1594.
   (28) Romeo and Juliet. A.D. 1592.
   (29) Sonnets. A.D. 1598—1601.
   (30) The Taming of the Shrew. A.D. 1596.
   (31) Tempest. A.D. 1610.
   (32) Timon of Athens. A.D. 1607.
   (33) Titus Andronicus. A.D. 1589.
   (34) Troilus and Cressida. A.D. 1606.
   (35) The Two Gentlemen of Verona. A.D. 1588.
   (36) The Winter's Tale. A.D. 1611.
Sheridan, Richard Brinsley. Ed. H. Morley.
   (1) The Rivals. A.D. 1775.
   (2) The School for Scandal. A.D. 1777.
   (3) A Trip to Scarborough. A.D. 1777.
Sidney, Sir Philip, Arcadia. London, 1623. fol. A.D. 1580.
Smollett, Tobias, Roderick Random. A.D. 1748.
Spenser, Edmund. Ed. R. Morris (Globe Edition).
   (1) The Faërie Queene. A.D. 1590-96.
   (2) The Shepherd's Calendar. A.D. 1579.
   (3) A View of the Present State of Ireland. A.D. 1596.
Starkey's England in Henry VIII's Time. Ed. J. M. Cowper, E.E.T.S. 1879. A.D. 1538.
Sterne, Lawrence, Tristram Shandy. Ed. H. Morley. A.D. 1759.
Steele, Sir Richard, The Funeral (The Modern British Drama, Vol. IV.). A.D. 1702.
Swift, Jonathan, Gulliver's Travels. A.D. 1726.

Tancred and Gismunda. Ed. Dodsley-Hazlitt. A.D. 1590.
Tennyson, Lord, Works. London, Macmillan.
Thackeray, W. M.—
   (1) The Newcomes. A.D. 1853-55.
   (2) Vanity Fair. A.D. 1847-48.
   (3) The Virginians. A.D. 1857-59.
Trollope, Anthony—
   (1) American Scenes.
   (2) The Duke's Children.

Ward, Mrs. Humphry—
   (1) Robert Elsmere. A.D. 1888.
   (2) The History of David Grieve. A.D. 1891.
Weyman, Stanley, The House of the Wolf. A.D. 1889.
Wyatt, Sir Thomas, Poems. Aldine Edition. A.D. 1541.

Young, Night Thoughts. A.D. 1742

INDEX

(*The numbers refer to the sections*)

A.

'A' = about, 226
  before numerals, 226
absent hours = hours of absence or separation, 252
absolute dative, 196, 409-412
  objective (accusative), 206
  participle, 22, 56, 57, 409-412
  pronoun in the oblique case, 211
  infinitive, 155, 399-403
abstract, development from the concrete to the, 9, 20-24, 410
abstracts and concretes interchanged, 137
abstract neuters, 245
  nouns used in a concrete sense, 138
  substantive instead of an adjective, 162
accidence, relations between accidence and syntax, 2, 19
accusative instead of an object in the genitive, 183
  signification of the, 197
  as the object of transitive verbs, 198
  governed by intransitive verbs, 199
  cognate ("we dreamt a dream"), 200
  as adverb denoting place, 203
                time, 204
                manner, 205
  with the infinitive, as subject, 70, 405
  as object, 401-404
adjectives used attributively, 36
  used substantively, 64
  converted into substantives, 134
  used as substantives, 236
  denoting nations and tribes, 243
  with active and passive meaning, 250
  with passive and active meaning, 250
  with transitive and causative meaning, 251

adjectives instead of substantives in the genitive case, 252
  comparison of the, 254
  followed by "one," 256
  used instead of adverbs, 423
  place of the, 464, 466, 472
  clause, 47, 109-119
    oldest shape of the, 109
    development of the, 112-119
adverb instead of an adjective, 45
adverbs used in the form of adjectives, 422
  used as adjectives, 424
adverbial clauses relating to place, 124
  time, 125-126
  manner and degree, 127-128
  cause, 129
  purpose and consequence, 130
  development of, 130
  relating to condition, 131
    replaced by the infinitive with *for*, 132
  determinants, place of the, 470
again = about the time that, 445
aged contusions, = contusions of age, 252
Alfred's English, 6, 7, 9
án emphasizing the possessive pronoun, 310
  used demonstratively, 315
anacoluthic sentences, 73
  expressions, 25, 112-119, 209
analogy, 15-18, 241
and, used redundantly, 446
  inverted order of words after, 458
ánra gehwylc = each alone, 260
ἀπὸ κοινοῦ, 111, 274
apposition, development of the, 37
  supplanting the partitive genitive, 39
  place of the apposition in Old and Middle English, 42, 469
article, absence of the, 38

article, definite, 217-224
    before possessive pronouns used substantively, 222
    indefinite, 224-227
    omission of the, 228-235
        before the second object, 230
        before a substantive used predicatively, 231
        before a substantive in apposition, 232
        after, "*never*" and "*ever*," 233
        after "*as*" in comparisons, 234
        before nouns beginning with *s* or *th*, 235
    place of the, 462
"*as I please*," 19, 151
as before the gerundial infinitive, 130
    (alswa), used after correlatives, 333
    used as a relative (to those *as* have no children), 333
asyndetic co-ordination, 100
at in conection with participles, 411
    denoting proximity of space, of time, and modal relation, 426
    = *with*, 432
attributive relation, 36 *seq*.
auxiliary verb, 347 *seq*.
    function of the, 347

B.

Baðian, bathe, in a reflexive sense, 345
"*be*" (auxiliary verb), used to form the perfect tense, 348
be (= by), in connection with participles, 141
belgan = "to be angry," and "to anger," 342
beten, originally transitive, = to amend, 345
"*betters, you are my*," 147, 241, 304
bituix and = until, 445
both their hopes = the hopes of both of them, 303
breeching scholar, 420
breed = to be bred, 346
breast used in the plural, 147
broun = deer, 244
but, used as a preposition and conjunction, 425
by, in passive constructions, 435
    omitted (?), 141

C.

Cardinals used substantively, 257-259
    instead of ordinals, 264
    instead of multiplicatives, 265

careless (passive) = not cared for, 250
careless day = day spent in carelessness, 252
cases interchange of, 207 *seq*.
case-endings made up for by prepositions, 19, 148, 427
cease = stop, 343, 344
certeyn = quantity, 244
clauses, order of words in, 456, 459
cognate accusative, 54, 200
cold = chilling, 251
collective nouns with predicates in the plural, 85
    used as class nouns, 140
comparative used absolutely, 255
comparison, double, 254-255
complement of a predicate, 78
complex predicate, 77
    sentences, 58, 96-133
    sentence in shape of two co-ordinate sentences, 97-100
concord not always observed, 17
    want of concord between a noun and its apposition, 40, 156, 209
    84-92
    of the predicate with several subjects, 90
    of the copula, 91-92
concrete, development from the concrete to the abstract, 9, 20-24, 410
    nouns used in an abstract sense, 139
conjunctions, relation between conjunctions, and prepositions, 445
contracted sentences, order of words in, 471-475
contraction of two sentences, 67
co-ordinate sentences, order of words in, 457, 458
co-ordination (parataxis), 98
copula, 91-92
    omitted, 81
crosswise arrangement of words, 476
cunnes, alles cunnes þing, 168
cure = to be cured, 346
cyning cyning (king of kings), 164
cynnes, 168

D.

Dǽlan = divide, in a reflective sense, 345
dative, functions of the, 187
    becomes the subject in passive constructions, 188
    represents the instrumental case, 193
dative instead of the genitive, 195
    absolute, 196
dativus commodi et incommodi, 190
deadly meed = reward of death, 252
decrease = lessen, 344

definite article, names of persons with the, 218
    before names of persons preceded by attributes, 219
    before nouns with possessive pronouns, 220
    preceding the possessive pronoun, 221
    before nouns in the vocative case instead of "*Oh*," 223
    before numerals, 224
demonstrative pronoun, use of the, 314
dependent sentence introduced by the particle, 103
direct and indirect speech, 107
    change of, 108
discrepancy between grammatical and psychological predicate, 80
disdainful (passive) = despicable, 250
do = to be, 354
double genitive, 33
    subject, 72-74
    object, 201, 202
    comparison, 254
drench = to be drowned, 343

E.

Economy or ellipsis, 26-29
ellipsis, 26-29
    of the copula "to be," 81
    of the noun, 238, 244
    of prepositions, 438
elliptic expressions, 26-29, 207
    genitive, 29, 177
emphatic pronoun, 290
"*ere this*," 318
ethic dative, 191-192

F.

Fair = beauty, 248
    -spoken, 408
fall = let fall, 344
fear = frighten, 344
    -ful = dreadful, 249
fill = to become full, 343
    = to be filled, 346
fléon (to flee) = to put to flight, 342
fly = cause (falcons) to fly, 344
"*for*" preceding the substantive, 71
    in connection with the accusative and infinitive, 130, 436
"*for to*," 395
formal endings, decay of, a factor of weight in the department of syntax, 19

forthynke = repent, 337
forto = until, 445
fro = from the time that, 445
friends, I am friends with him, 17, 147
fruitful prognostication = a prognostication of fruitfulness, 252

G.

Gallicisms, 133, 153, 222, 224, 254, 309, 313, 399-400, 411, 480
Genitive attributive, 158
    denoting birth and relation, 159
    rule or power, 160
    possession, 161
    quality, treated like an adjective, 166
    double, 33
    superlative, 163
    represented by the prepositions *over, towards, against,* etc., 165
    of '*cyn*" (cun) used as an adjective, 168
    pseudo-partitive (a knight of King Arthur's), 178-180
    instead of apposition ("*vice of a king*"), 181
    expressing the functions of origin, cause and reference, 183
    governed by verbs and adjectives, 182
    replaced by the accusative or the object preceded by prepositions, 183
    used adverbially, 184-186
    denoting space (genitivus loci), 184
    denoting time, 185
    denoting manner, 186
    case, signification of the, 158
greedy (passive) = greedily desired, 250
Greek and Latin models studied in the 16th century, 8

H.

Hang, transitive and intransitive, 342
hateful = hated, 249
    (act.) = full of hate, 250
"*have at thee*," 349
    got = have, 369
heart, his heart of hearts, 17
helpless (passive) = irremediable, incurable, 250
heofon (heaven) used in the plural 147
"*himself*" as subject, 295
"*his*" instead of the genitive case, 308
his own hand = with his hand, 432

hisself, 17, 300
how do you do? 352
hungri here = years of famine, 252
hypotactic adjective clause, 112
    construction, 99-100

I.

I am woe, 19, 131
I am thanked, 210, 363
Imperative (with and without a pronoun), 269
    sentences used in a conditional sense, 132
    order of words in imperative sentences, 452
impersonal verbs, 337 *seq.*
increase = extend, 344
indefinite article, functions of the, 225
    used pleonastically, 227
indefinites followed by adjectives in the superlative degree as *pear* as attributes, 115
infinitive gerundial instead of an adverbial clause, 130
    with "for" instead of an adverbial clause, 130
    with the nominative, 156,
    passive of the, 364
    past instead of present, 375
    simple, 392, 393
    gerundial, 392, 393
    instead of the gerund, 397
    instead of a whole clause, 398
    absolute, 399
instrumental case represented by the dative, 193
    represented by prepositions (by, with), 194
interchange of cases, 210
interrogative sentences, 213
    pronouns used as relatives, 335
    sentences, order of words in, 453
intransitive and transitive verbs interchanged, 340
    forms of verbs instead of transitive ones, 342
inversion of subject and predicate, 451-458
joyous = joy-producing, 251
issue = send forth, 344
"*it*" used as a predicate of any gender or person with the verb '*to be*,' 280
    instead of "*there*," 281
    used redundantly, 283
    omitted, 279
    he made it strange, 283.
"*it is*" emphasizing nouns and sentences, 282
it am I, 281

it is I, 280
it is me, 79, 214
it likes me, 337

K.

"*Kind*," all kind *of condiciouns* 169
    condiciouns of all kind, 169
    these kind of knaves, 172
knedyng trowh, 420
kynnes, "*what kynnes treason is þis?*" 171

L.

Latinisms, 56, 122, 144, 248, 251, 252, 255, 401-404, 479
learn = teach, 343, 344
leren = learn, 347
let us go, 351
like used impersonally, 334
liues creature = living creature, 158, 166
lively = enlivening, 251
lose = ruin, 343, 344
luckless = fatal, 251

M.

Make it strange, 283
make merry, 345
maner followed by "of," 170
    not followed by "of," 171
manner, what manner *musick*, 171
may as a modal verb, 359
me instead of *my* in such phrases as "don't mind *me* leaving so soon," 13
    "*it is me*," 79
    for "I," 214
meltan = to melt; to make melt, 342
merry = producing merriment, 251
mid = and, 445
miscarry = to be miscarried, 346
mister, "*what mister wight*," 171
mixed construction, 18, 176
modal clauses become causal ones, 127
    used in a concessive sense, 128
mortal = deadly, 251
my betters, elders, equals, 241, 304
    lord, 306
    used as a term of courtesy, 306.
myself, 296

N.

"*Nearwian*" instead of "*nyrwan*," 342
negative sentences, order of words in 455
never his life, 204

never too late to mend, 339
noun. See also substantive noun in apposition, 37
noun clause and adjective clause intermixed, 120
    replaced by the interpolated principal sentence, 120
noun clauses dependent on impersonal verbs, 378
    after verbs expressing wish, 379
nouns, classes of nouns interchanged, 137-141
nominative instead of the dative, 19, 41, 151, 152, 210
  functions of the, 149-150
  instead of the accusative after "hatan," 150, 202, 208
  instead of the oblique case in old impersonal verbs, 151
  absolute, 153, 154
  with the infinitive, 155, 405
  in apposition, 156
  supplanted by the oblique case, 157, 211
  instead of the oblique case, 207
  after "but" and "save," 207
  anacoluthic, 209
  with verbs once impersonal, 210
  with verbs in passive constructions, 210
number, subjective character of the, 142
number of abstracts, 143
  of common nouns, 147
numerals, fractional, 266
  place of the, 463

O.

Object of impersonal and transitive verbs turned into subject, 59
  double, 201, 202
  placed at the head of the sentence, 454, 460
  placed before the verb, 461
  order of words in sentences with two objects, 474
  order of words with one object and two verbs, 475
  pronoun omitted, 275
objective relation, 48
  genitive, 164
  absolute, 206
oblique case supplanting the nominative, 157, 211
  the absolute pronoun in the, 211
  instead of the nominative, in connection with "all" and numerals, and after "than" "as," 215
"*of mine*," 311

of after the verbal noun, 416, 417
  replacing the genitive, 482
  instead of "from," 434
  in passive constructions, 435
  omitted (?), 439
old wrinkles = wrinkles of age, 252
omission of the personal pronoun, 62, 75, 268-274
  of the name of God, 63
  of a substantive subject, 75
  of the predicate, 82-83
  of the relative pronoun. 109-111, 335
"*one of the best knight*, 18
the best knight," 176
  = alone, 260
  the personal pronoun with, 261
  following substantives and adjectives, 262
  = a certain, 263
ordinals followed by "some," 267
"*other his prisoners*," 176

P.

Parataxis or co-ordination, 98
participle absolute, 409-412
  present used as a substantive, 242
  present in a passive sense, 407
  present with "*be*" and "*at*," 411
  past in an active sense, 408
participles, voice of, 407
partitive genitive, 173
  juxtaposition instead of the, 174
passive of intransitive verbs, 19, 152, 363
past instead of present tense, 374
perfect and preterite tenses interchanged, 370
periphrastic expression with "*it is*," 80
perish = kill, slay, 344
personal pronoun, 268 *seq.*
  pleonastic use of the, 284-286
  used redundantly in complex sentences, 287-289
  emphasized by "*self*," 299
piteous = pity-producing, 251
"*please, as I*," 19, 151
pleonastic use of the personal pronoun, 74, 114-119, 284-286
plural of abstract nouns, 21
  of proper names, 145
  of material names, 146
  nouns with a singular predicate, 86-89
pluralis majestaticus, imitation of the, 144
popular talk a help in the study of syntax, 10
possess = put in possession, 343, 344

possessive pronoun replaced by "*of*" + pronoun, 301
    relative referring to a, 302
        equivalent to a personal pronoun, 303
        before substantival adjectives, 304-306
        followed by the adjective used substantively, 304
        preceded by a demonstrative pronoun, 305
        used indefinitely, 307
        occurs sometimes in connection with the gerund, where we should expect the oblique case of the personal pronoun, 309
        emphasized, 310
        used substantively, 312
        the dative of the personal pronoun instead of the, 313
        place of the, 457
"(*I*) *pray to God to gyf my body care*," 274
predicate simple, 76
    complex, 77
    omitted, 82-83
        substantive predicate after *weorðan* is put in the dative, 189
        place of the predicate in the sentences, 450
        preceding the subject (inversion), 451-458
predicative relation, 76-90
"*prepare for dinner*," 345
prepositions, close relation between prepositions and conjunctions, 425
    making up for the case-endings, 427
    introducing the agent, 433
    omitted, 438-442
    dependent, 443
    place of the, 468
present, the historical, 368
    instead of preterite tense, 372
preterite and perfect tenses interchanged, 370
    instead of the past perfect tense, 373
    subjunctive instead of present subjunctive, 377
prolepsis or redundant object, 24, 94
pronoun, see personal, demonstrative, relative, &c.
proper names used as common names, 141
pseudo-partitive genitive, 178-180
psychology must be consulted in the study of syntax, 9

Q.

Qualifying genitive (genitivus qualitatis), 166
    some peculiarity of the, 167-172
quench = to be quenched, 343, 346

R.

Read = to be read, 346
    past participle in an active sense, 408
reflexive pronoun dropped, 345
    verbs, 339
relation of words, 34 *seq.*
    constructions, three types of, 114-119
    subordination instead of demonstrative co-ordination, 122
    clauses, 217 *seq.*
    clauses used for conditional ones, 133
    pronoun, omission of the, 109-111
        origin of the, 329
        demonstrative pronoun used as a, 33
remember = remind, 344
run = cause to run, 344
ruthful (passive) = piteous, 250

S

Salting swine, 420
same, the, instead of the personal pronouns, 323
save used as a preposition and conjunction, 424
se preceding names of persons, 218
self, 17, 290, 298
    used appositively, 291
    in connection with the dative, 292
    as subject, 293
    in connection with a pronoun as subject, 297, 298
sell = to be sold ("*this book never sold*,") 346
sentences, structure of sentences in Old English, 6
"*serves him right*," 279
"*shall*," used elliptically 356
    forming the future tense, 357
shape = to be shaped, 346
shed in a reflexive sense, 345
"*should*" in reported speech, 358
    with the infinitive instead of the subjunctive preterite, 358
sink = to make sink, 343
    = submerge, 344

sit = set, 343
 = seat, 344
skynnes, "*no skynes labour*" 168
"*some*" after ordinals, 267
sort, "*these sort of people*," 172
stain = to be stained, 346
stand = set, put, 344
 = to be, 35
sterile course = course of sterility, 252
stony = benumbing, 241
subject and predicate, 59 *seq.*
subject, 59 *seq.*
  of a finite verb, 59
  of a sentence is simple, 61-66
  of a sentence an infinite mood or gerund, 65
  complex, 68-74
  reduplication of the, 71, 74
  reduplication of the subject by one and the same word, 72
  reduplication of the subject by means of a personal pronoun, 73
  repetition of the subject after an extensive member of a sentence, 74
  omitted, 75-81
  place of the subject in the sentence, 450
  following the predicate (inversion), 451
  words in sentences with two subjects, 473
  substantive omitted, 63
subjunctive in final clauses, giving way to the indicative, 130
  mood, decay of the, 380-391
substantive or pronoun with the Infinitive, 70
  accompanied by an infinitive (accusativus cum infinitivo), 95
  transformation of substantive into an adjective, 134
  double function of the, 136
  used attributively, 36 *seq.*
  used as adjective metaphorically, 136
  singular and plural of, 142-147
  named after quality, 237
  clause with "that," 69
  predicate after the verb "*weorðan*" is generally put in the dative, 189
succumb = subject, 343
"*such*" as a demonstrative pronoun, 322
"*sum*" used in a demonstrative sense, 316
sup = feed, 344
superlative used absolutely, 255
"*swá*," 33
  hwá = whosoever, 333
  hwile = whosoever, 333
syntax, object of, 1 *seq.*
  study of, 5 *seq.*
  some principles of, 14 *seq.*

T.

Tarry = delay, 343
tautology, 30-33
temporal clauses denoting causal, conditional, and adversative relations, 126
tenses, sequence of, 371
term of his life, 204
terrible (passive) = awe-struck, affrighted, 251
"*that*" in introducing the noun clause dropped, 121
 = the, 320
 in connection with the genitive, 321
 used as a relative, 331
 used redundantly, 447
 as a substitute for other conjunctions, 448
the king = oh king ! 223
theirself, 300
"*then*" used adjectively (the then world) 424
"*these seven years*," 317
"*this*" and "*that*," 319
"*thou*" and "*you*," 277
"*thou*" and "*ye*" used indiscriminately, 278
though, use of, 101
"*thy*" and "*your*," 278
time enough. 204
"*to*" instead of "*of*," 165
  after auxiliaries, 394
  replacing the objective genitive, 429
  replacing the dative, 430
  = mid, 432
  omitted (?), 440
  = until, 445
transitive verbs, 339
  and intransitive verbs interchanged, 340 *seq.*
  verbs used in a reflexive and passive sense, 345
  verbs used as passives, 346
"*þe*" supplanted by "*that*," 332

U.

Undergoing stomach, 420
undeserving praise, 420
unhappy = mischievous ; fatal, 251
unrecalling crime, 420
unto = until, 445
unwiste (unconscious), 408

V.

Verbal noun, 413-420
verbs of movement omitted after auxiliary verbs, 83
  used both as transitives and intransitives, 339

336 INDEX

verbs with causative and intransitive meaning, 341
    reflexive and passive, closely related, 360
    passive of, with a double object, 363

W.

Wandering wood, 420
"*we*" instead of "*I*," 276
weak = weakness, 248
weary = wearying, becoming weary, 251
well-spoken, 408
weorðan (to become) with the dative of the substantive predicate, 189
"*what*" used substantively, 324
"*what news*," 324
"*what*" referring to persons, 325
    who instead of, 325
    used adjectively, 326
    as an exclamation, 327
    used in the relative sense, 335
"*which*," the indefinite relative *which* becomes a proper one, 336

"*who is who*," 328
"*who*" used in the relative sense, 335
    the indefinite relative *who* becomes a proper one, 336
"*will*" expressing customary action, 350
    used elliptically, 558
    forming the future tense, 357
"*with*" in the absolute construction, 154
    replacing the instrumental case, 431
    in passive constructions, 435
    in connection with participles, 437
wo "*I am ful wo*," 151
worldes thing = worldly thinges, 166
wylde = wild beasts, 244

Y.

Yoke = to be yoked, 346
"*you*" supplants "*ye*," 212
"*your fat king*," 307
youthful suit = suit of a youth, 252
    travel = travel made in youth, 25

THE END.

RICHARD CLAY AND SONS, LIMITED, LONDON AND BUNGAY.

www.ingramcontent.com/pod-product-compliance
Lightning Source LLC
Chambersburg PA
CBHW020241240426
43672CB00006B/597